Humanities Computing

Humanities Computing

Willard McCarty

Department of Digital Humanities, King's College London, UK; Research Group in Digital Humanities, University of Western Sydney, Australia

palgrave
macmillan

First published 2005 in hardback
First published in paperback 2014 by
PALGRAVE MACMILLAN

Palgrave Macmillan in the UK is an imprint of Macmillan Publishers Limited, registered in England, company number 785998, of Houndmills, Basingstoke, Hampshire RG21 6XS.

Palgrave Macmillan in the US is a division of St Martin's Press LLC, 175 Fifth Avenue, New York, NY 10010.

Palgrave Macmillan is the global academic imprint of the above companies and has companies and representatives throughout the world.

Palgrave® and Macmillan® are registered trademarks in the United States, the United Kingdom, Europe and other countries

ISBN: 978–1–4039–3504–5 hardback
ISBN: 978–1–137–44042–6 paperback

A catalogue record for this book is available from the British Library.

Library of Congress Cataloging-in-Publication Data
McCarty, Willard, 1945–
 Humanities computing / Willard McCarty.
  p. cm.
 Includes bibliographical references (p.) and index.
 ISBN 978-1-4039-3504-5 (cloth) 978-1-137-44042-6 (pbk)
  1. Humanities–Data processing. 2. Humanities–Research–Data processing. 3. Information storage and retrieval systems–Humanities.
I. Title.

AZ105.M245 2005
001.3'0285–dc22   2005043356

Transferred to Digital Printing in 2014

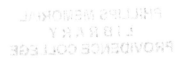

To Harold Short, *nisi tu* ...

Contents

List of Figures

Preface to the Paperback Edition

In the Acknowledgements to the original edition I quoted Jacques Derrida to express my ambivalence and melancholy at finishing a book I had been mulling over and working on for many years. Then, in hope of a resurrection, I added John Milton's soaring declaration from the *Areopagitica* that 'books are not absolutely dead things'. But, I realize now, to have the 'potency of life' Milton ascribed to books, 'to be as active as that soul whose progeny they are', means that they change with us, their readers, and with the world we inhabit. Some bits of a book retain their truth-value or relevance, other bits become quaint, musty and then in time interesting for what they tell us about how people once thought and wrote. Insufficient time has passed for much of historical interest to have surfaced from this book but enough for a paperback edition to require comment and invite reflection on the bits which I think remain true to the field and those that have been superseded.

This would not be happening if our tendency to professional amnesia and naïve belief in technologically deterministic progress were winning. (They aren't, but the battle continues. Vigilance is still called for!) There are now signs that we may one day have a genuine history of digital humanities and with this history a perspective from which a trajectory for the discipline can at last be glimpsed. A few who suffer from lack of history assert that 'humanities computing' denotes an irrelevant set of concerns quite distinct from those of 'digital humanities'. It's true that the former was a child of a different time, one ruled by the defining grip of the Cold War. It is abundantly clear that the onset of the Web in the mid to late 1990s brought about a diluvian change in the discipline and became part of if not directly energized a slower change in scholarship. But to sever the discipline so rudely from its past and so heedlessly deprive it of continuity with its previous half-century of work is to render it directionless, hence vulnerable to whatever forces might wish to co-opt it. *Mirabile dictu* – and it does seem a miracle to someone who cut his rhetorical teeth on colleagues' dismissal of and contempt for computing – digital humanities has become an object of desire and so worth stealing. For this reason, were I to rewrite the book's last chapter I would move the seventh item on my proposed agenda, 'Writing history', to first place, which it must inhabit. But more about the agenda later.

Humanities Computing was written in direct response to personal experience with my own and others' research and to the many claims made in preceding years for the value of subjecting the interpretative disciplines to the rigour of algorithmic methods. Intense struggle over a decade and a half to render Ovid's imaginative language computationally tractable (pp. 55–71, below) led me to the idea of modelling that is this book's central concern and the subject of its first chapter. It seemed to me then, and seems to me now, that the stark oxymoron which became the book's title captures what modelling is all about: collision of two forms of reasoning, or to paraphrase Jerome McGann and Philip Davis together, crafting of a gap between representation and what it stands for, not to eliminate difference but to open up a cornucopia of difference for us all to feed off and develop (pp. 1, 4, below).

There's truth in Brian Cantwell Smith's argument, also from 2005, that the genius of the digital computer is to make digital representation irrelevant. Belief in that irrelevance puts the machine's reasoning processes in a black box and turns our attention to their effects on people and cultures. This book holds to the opposite belief in the microcode of the discipline. It struggles to pop open that black box and, as Ian Hacking recommends, 'take a look' – by which he means much more than just looking, or thinking or discussing in isolation from one another. He means a kind of reasoning that puts them all together with making and from them crafts means for intervening in the world. But as a result of fascination with those inner workings through years of interventionist analytical modelling, I gave short shrift in the book to simulation and the question of complexity (pp. 34–5, below), which now seem to me a large part of the future for digital humanities. Were I writing this book now I would devote an additional chapter to simulation of complex systems (such as we and our cultural expressions are), say what I think we can learn from its enormous importance in the physical and social sciences and give a far better account of it in digital humanities, especially in relation to gaming and the arts.

The chapter on modelling would doubtless change as a result: I would put at its centre historian David Gooding's crucial work on construal (e.g. 1990), which I had not yet encountered when I wrote the book. I would also devote much attention to the statistical modelling of patterns in textual data on both small and large scales, e.g. in studies of authorship and of literary history. I would argue that modelling is what they are doing. I would find a much more perspicuous example of modelling than my own work toward an *Analytical Onomasticon* (pp. 53–71, below). Although labouring over the *Onomasticon* taught me most of what I know about the subject, including the great value of failure, the problem it attempted to address was too far beyond the state of the art then *or now*. Embarrassingly I did not take David Hilbert's wise advice, that a problem 'should be difficult in order to entice us, yet not completely inaccessible, lest it mock at our efforts' (1902: 438). Those pages on the *Onomasticon* mock me.

To my knowledge the strongest criticism of the book was provoked by its emphasis on the sciences. I reasoned along with those who argue for 'thing knowledge', distributed cognition and material culture that an originally techno-scientific instrument embodies cognitive tendencies from the sciences which must not be ignored and cannot be understood without bringing their originating contexts into view. Putting so much emphasis on the sciences was in fact implicit in the book's oxymoronic title: I wanted to invoke the very sense of the alien that upset those critics. It was an integral part of my programme to focus sharply on both components in the transformative collision of reasoning styles denoted by Natalia Cecire's formula, 'digital + humanities' (2012: 55). For this I remain not merely unrepentant but insistent. (In my current research I am using the anxiety techno-science has always provoked as an essential clue to the intellectual common ground of computing and the humanities.) In his keynote address to the Toronto digital humanities conference in 1989 Northrop Frye recollected similar hostility for his use of the word 'scientific' in the introduction to *Anatomy of Criticism* (1957). He noted that software programming and computer modelling, unknown to the humanities when he wrote, were closer to what he intended (1991). But they too are scientific – if also responsible for changing our idea of the meaning and scope of science. For the humanities, and for digital humanities especially, there is no avoiding the great engine of 20th- and 21st-century change, of which computing is its most potent expression. The annoying distinction of separate cultures, used so often to rule the sciences out of bounds, is an increasingly obvious illusion: 'How does one distinguish between nature and artifact when we rely on artifacts to produce or afford access to natural phenomena...?' (Mahoney 2011: 159).

The sequence of the book, 'from the microscopic and private to the macroscopic and social' (p. 7, below), still seems right to me for a digital humanist's training as well as a rough description of the discipline's history. The great rush into online and inevitably social media, taking hold as the book was being written, has unfortunately deprived many eager participants of the grounding in computational nitty-gritty to which the following pages are dedicated. Last year in a moving and humorous tribute Marco Passarotti quoted Fr Roberto Busa's assertion that such close work as I explore in this book is *sine qua non*, training us, Busa said, 'for an exploration of our own inner logic, which is the spiritual centre of the personal dignity and consistency of each of us'. This, Passarotti comments, 'is a continuous "know thyself" activity' (2013: 21). It is the implicit aim of all that *humanities* computing/digital *humanities* entails.

The question of genre addressed in Chapter 2 is still hanging, still being addressed and experimented with at all levels across several disciplines. It remains vexed by the separation of human and machine, which are kept apart as much or more by fear of techno-science as by technological insufficiencies. Terry Winograd's suggestion that we think in terms of habitat or 'interspace' rather than interface and Jerome McGann's insistence on resonance beyond interaction remain as cogent (pp. 74f, below). Winograd's 'new ways for people to communicate with other people' online have developed beyond anything I anticipated in 2005 – but, I fear, to the neglect of new ways for people to communicate with themselves, with artificially intelligent approximations and, for editors and readers of texts, with authors. We are as far as I know still lacking detailed comparisons of printed books in their expressive range and power to digital productions, as I attempted briefly to explore in Chapter 2 with Dodds' *Bacchae*. We still use the problematic term 'digital library' mostly letting pass without comment the challenging operational differences which it could reveal if pressed. How do we in fact and in detail use our own and others' digital collections?

My recommendation of ethnography and its explication in Chapter 3 as meta-discipline for exploring disciplines seems now as solid an idea as ever. But now I would say more about how interdisciplinary research can be undertaken, with what kind of expectations and perils, as counterbalance to the dominant focus on what interdisciplinarity (a reifying abstraction) might be in relation to other kinds. (See my chapter, 'Becoming interdisciplinary' in the forthcoming *New Companion to Digital Humanities*, ed. Schreibman, Siemens and Unsworth.) The focus of Chapter 3 on how in any particular case 'we may get to the disciplinary conditions from which specific methods arise as desire or need direct' seems right as well – with one serious qualification, however: the tendency in the very idea of method to confuse roles with rules. I find the same problem in that 'intellectual and disciplinary map of humanities computing' (p. 119, below), which in the manner of a cosmological diagram implicitly asserts definition of our disciplinary world as a 'Methodological Commons' with 'formal methods' at its core. What that map mapped was the institutional environment in which the mapping was done. But digital humanists are still in the process of figuring out what kind or kinds of environment might be most conducive to that which the discipline is becoming. The big problem with this map is that presenting it as 'a model *for* the field's extensions of itself into the humanities' is prescriptive – a political act. Oddly I argued against precisely that at some length in Chapter 1 (pp. 32–4, below) but did not, as I would now, carry over the lesson into Chapter 3. But an even more serious problem is the implicit suggestion in 'formal methods' of a finite set of methodological primitives, i.e. an operational axiomatic bedrock for the discipline based, as Hilbert's formalist ambitions were, on pure manipulation free of significance (see pp. 81–2, 167–8, 217–20, below). To leave meaning to the other disciplines would be fatal. I suspect that the anxiety of the time, over whether the discipline had anything to say for itself, made the chimera irresistible – though the question of autonomy remains. But that is a subject for another book.

The power of examining a discipline's 'tropes and imageries of explanation' (Geertz's phrase) remains, I think, primary to explorations of disciplines other than one's own, and then perhaps one's own. This power has been demonstrated many times over by another scholar of whose work I would, if rewriting this book, take much more account: Evelyn Fox Keller. Among many other things I commend to your attention 'Language and Ideology in Evolutionary Theory' (1991) and *Making Sense of Life* (2002).

Chapter 4, Computer Science, was intended insofar as possible to provide as simple an account as I could manage of the discipline's mathematical and logical aspects in their historical origins. Again in the spirit of oxymoronic collision my aim was to confront head-on what digital humanists were at the time and perhaps still are mostly avoiding. Had I known Hugh Kenner's *The Counterfeiters: An Historical Comedy* (2005/1968) this chapter would have grown. But I also wanted to get close enough to a recognizable description of computer science to provoke computer scientists, other than those two who helped me with it, to offer commentary and corrections (which, alas, has not happened). Since then I have not seen much evidence of systematic, institutionalized cross-talk between digital humanities and computer science apart from the Chicago Colloquium, though steps are being taken at the University of Western Sydney. The creative arts (which take what works and use it) have been ahead of the humanities in this respect since the post-war beginnings of digital computing. See, for example, the journal *Leonardo* and its several spin-offs, especially its book series; see Hannah B. Higgins and Douglas Kahn's *Mainframe Experimentalism* (2012). A rewritten *Humanities Computing* would pay very close attention to the arts.

For a long time it has been broadly obvious through the channels of science fiction and other forms of popular culture that robotics would one day put before us a device that requires no hype to be considered a 'life's companion'. Only a matter of time, I say. The desire for such an entity is clear, as we have seen recently through such films as the Bollywood *Enthiran* (2010), Spanish *Eva* (2011), the Swedish *Äkta Människor* ('Real Humans', 2012) or 'Be Right Back' from the British *Black Mirror* (2013). In 2013 the Science Forum of the IEEE International Conference on Robotics and Automation, at the instigation of roboticists, hosted a session entitled, 'Robotics Meets the Humanities'. An additional chapter? The hypothetical rewritten book grows again.

I have already taken Chapter 5, Agenda, to task by moving to top place the writing of a genuine history, from whose perspective the facts we have in abundance become questions toward a realization of how we got here. My comments on the *Analytical Onomasticon* will have suggested why analysis cannot come first. With one exception (computational stylistics) we not only do not know how to advance beyond basic corpus techniques to a genuinely *close*, i.e. intimate co-reading but have no language in which to theorize the problem. Theories from elsewhere are on offer, as McGann has demonstrated (2004b), but which of these fits digital humanities well enough not to pull it disastrously off course? This, again, is the question of which course we are on. The move that Franco Moretti has championed (but Mark Olsen advocated a decade earlier, at the MLA in 1991; see Olsen 1993) ironically requires us to trade close reading of individual texts for close reading of experimental results (Sculley and Pasanek 2008: 417). This may suit the literary historian who has already done his or her close reading, as Moretti has, and so should be welcomed, but as is so often the case many seem to have taken it as a replacement for a practice away from which literary theory has turned. The same bandwagon-effect with the same deleterious effects is well known in digital humanities.

The discussion of 'Disciplinary relations and kinships' as an agenda item seems now to me both naïve and excessively tentative. For reasons Frye understood well, autonomy is basic to a discipline's integrity and survival. Underscoring the importance of Alan Liu's question long before he asked it (2012), Frye observed of his own discipline exactly what we can see in ours now: that 'the absence of systematic criticism has created a power vacuum, and all the neighboring disciplines have moved in' (1957: 12). Where indeed is the criticism in digital humanities? Like literary studies in the mid 1950s we are now 'in the cultural situation of savages who have words for ash and willow and no word for tree' (13). Digital humanities still cannot adequately theorize what it is about because 'the terms in which such formulations can be cast are, if not wholly nonexistent, very nearly so. We are reduced to insinuating theories because we lack the power to state them' (Geertz 1993/1973: 24; p. 150, below). And that is not a problem which can be solved by being useful to others. The knowledge and wisdom gained from the work in crafting useful products does, however, offer raw material for a language that would allow us to make sense of ourselves and so make sense of ourselves to others. The resources digital humanists have built are not in themselves the discipline's achievements but materially uttered questions tending to one big question that will be a great achievement once addressed: what are the organizing or containing forms of digital humanities' conceptual framework? (Frye 1957: 16)

To me the most interesting problem regarding forms of publication and conversational activity, only touched on in Chapter 5, is extending the 'mantle of recognizable scholarship to cover ... the software arising from this work' in digital humanities, which as noted depends on the ability 'to *read our machines*' (p. 210, below). The literature on 'thing knowledge' (Davis Baird's phrase), 'epistemic things' (Hans-Jörg Rheinberger's) or 'things that talk' (Lorraine Daston's) has grown enormously since the turn of the century and demands complementary work from software studies and from digital humanities especially. The unique nature of computer software, as Mahoney's editor Thomas Haigh put it, 'a self-executing text bridging ... mathematics and machinery' (Mahoney 2011: 7), immaterial yet materially effective, brings us by a different route back to the collision that I celebrate in the title of this book, the crash-site that needs interpretation. Much more in the rewritten book would now have to be said about the hermeneutic puzzle of software in light of this literature. Hackers will know well their online equivalent (in blogs with bits of code, breadboard wiring diagrams, videos and photos) of Renaissance engineers' communication through diagrams and drawings (Ferguson 1994). A start has already been made but needs sustained critical attention.

The bibliographic problem, or 'Doing the homework' (pp. 215–17, below), looks considerably different now, again because of the extent to which the Web has grown and become part of ordinary research life. As I found out in working on *The Humanities Computing Yearbook* in the late 1980s, digital humanities had already put comprehensiveness beyond reach or sense. Now it is hard to imagine that anyone would try. It is not just or even primarily a matter of the shift from difficulty of accessing to difficulty of coping with secondary literature. The bibliographic problem has become the problem interdisciplinary research, since research now, only with the greatest (and I think doomed) effort, can remain within well travelled and well structured disciplinary ruts. In other words, the whole style of doing one's homework has changed, even what it means to get that homework right.

Evidence of an early stage in that shift is among the first things one is likely to notice about *Humanities Computing*. Even for an obsessively referential author, it seems odd now to plow into such a thicket of quotations as meet the reader of this book – evidence, I have just suggested, not simply of diluvian change in access but of early days in digesting the riches. Consider the prefatory and often verbose gestures of obeisance, gratitude and respect in early printed books, which today may seem barriers between reader and text. This book was in its way similarly beholden to an older, far more accomplished and powerful establishment. Roaming far and wide through its disciplines collecting what one can is more than ever imperative to connect digital humanities with them, to grow and strengthen it. Obvious referentiality beyond digital humanities helps make that point. But we grope for fit styles of expression. None of what we find will in fact do. Other signs of reaching out are the length of the bibliography, density of internal quotations and a rather formidable index, analytical to an extreme, with its own way of denoting the levels. But my point in putting this book's attempt under a microscope is not to identify changes I would make (of which there are many) but to suggest how questions of style and design are informed by the discipline's history, by its (if I may) trajectory. Form and content are, we know, inseparable.

That is enough, I think, to indicate both this author's delight in finding so much he can stand by and so much he would change better to be true to the maturing of digital humanities over the last dozen years. My thanks to Benjamin Doyle, Senior Editor at Palgrave, for the chance to propel *Humanities Computing* into an extended life in paperback and for the suggestion that the contents might need comment.

Willard McCarty
February 2014

Acknowledgements

Many years ago, as a budding literary critic, I made an attempt to identify *all* allusions in about twenty lines of John Milton's *Paradise Lost*. The project began with the sleuth's mundane pleasures, soon plunged me into utter frustration as the allusions multiplied out of all control, then, suddenly, ended in the realization that the project had been wrongheaded from the start: clearly Milton's verse was resonant rather than only referential. Now, attempting to acknowledge the intellectual and personal debts accrued in the writing of this book, I come to a similar realization: that, as Milton's German Pietist contemporaries said, *Denken ist Danken*, 'to think is to thank' (Steiner 1978: 21).

Help has been everywhere at hand during this project: directly from friends, teachers, students, colleagues and institutions, indirectly through the wealth of literature in the numerous disciplines to which humanities computing is related. (Yes, the impediments were there too, some of them quite serious, but these no longer matter, except as fuel to the fire.) Before turning to those who helped directly, allow me to register my gratitude to significant others whom I have not met – disciplinary masters, such as Clifford Geertz, Peter Winch and Solomon Feferman, who have written for the intelligent non-specialist, or simply written so well that the likes of me can follow. In doing so (may their tribes increase) they have opened up many avenues of research I otherwise would not have been able to follow. In this book I struggle to be like them.

Contemplating the end of a project that began decades ago, these acknowledgements are bound to seem, as Jacques Derrida said in his *Work of Mourning*, words spoken at a death, to put the seal on the entombment of ideas and feelings, inevitably before their time, within the covers of a book. There would be much less here that is worthy of such an expensive burial if it were not for the help I have received. But even so, the burial would be hopeless were it not for the truth that 'books are not absolutely dead things, but do contain a potency of life in them to be as active as that soul whose progeny they are' (Milton, *Areopagitica*). Hence helpers and helped alike must turn to the future, giving so that others may give. That is *why* this book has been written. I invest all my hope in those who read it and by their questioning show that questioning is not just the piety of thought but its fertilizing power as well.

The book was written, start to finish, during my 2003–4 sabbatical year, with a generous grant from the Arts and Humanities Research Board and the strong support of the Centre for Computing in the Humanities (CCH) and the School of Humanities at King's College London. To the Director of the CCH, Harold Short, and the then Head of School, David Ricks, I express my thanks. The valiant efforts of those who took up my various duties were also key. Ray Siemens and Laszlo Hunyadi, both on leave from their own universities and in London, taught my classes. John Lavagnino did various other things on my behalf. My time off coincided with rapid growth of my department and its physical relocation, yet I was able to work undisturbed. My colleagues in the CCH have professed that during this time of enormously increased workload they did not miss me. I choose to think otherwise and here record my profound gratitude. Together they have made the best sort of working environment this man could imagine.

Years ago, when we were both in Toronto, Jed Buchwald was the first to tell me that I had to write what has turned out to be this book. Some time later I found myself sitting at a table, in a hotel not all that far from London, listening to people who should have known better declare that humanities computing did not exist. Actually the experience has been repeated numerous times in various venues, physical and virtual, but this one sticks in mind because I was then moved to write the first paragraph towards the manifesto Jed had told me I had to publish. Some years later he generously invited me to give a paper at the Dibner Institute (MIT) that became a piece of it. About that time, back in London, John Lavagnino wisely advised me over coffee that I should allow the one paper that I kept rewriting and publishing under different titles to become the book it was trying to be. So, at last, I did. He has been generous with his great learning throughout its composition.

Several friends and colleagues gave their time to reading and commenting on portions in draft. Brad Inwood, a good mate from graduate student days at Toronto, commented in detail on Chapter 1; so did Jan Christoph Meister, some of whose comments became parts of my text. So also with Wendell Piez's comments on Chapter 2. Peter Shillingsburg and Ray Siemens looked over both chapters. Peter Galison read what became a significant portion of Chapter 1, assuring me it was not utter tripe. Meurig Beynon and Steve Russ magnanimously arranged for me to spend a weekend in Warwick with them, during which Chapters 1 and 4 were greatly improved. Michael Mahoney (who as reader of the Dibner paper on its way into publication had previously helped me to clarify my ideas on the historiography of computing) most generously read through and gave detailed comment on these chapters as well. Harold Short, dear friend as well as boss, contributed substantially to Chapter 3 in several ways. These include an interview with him one evening in which, on the basis of many years' experience watching the encounter of the humanities with computing, and being collaborator in its outcomes, he sketched its anatomy. The previous year he and I had developed the disciplinary map from which Chaper 3 sprang. The remainder of my indebtedness to him, requiring a different mode of expression, is reserved for the dedication.

Out of the goodness of her heart, Jane McGary, friend from undergraduate days, read through and corrected the entire book amidst other editorial tasks, demands of the garden, threat from a nearby volcano (which remains dormant) and a distracting election with depressing results. She also commented on it from the perspective of a nonspecialist, thus helping me to reach an audience I hope for. The book owes much to her skill and patience. Palgrave editors Emily Rosser, then Paula Kennedy, ably saw the book through its initial stages. Jo North came in at the end, copy-edited the final draft, proofread the typeset copy and did much else skillfully, and with considerable good will, to bring it into the light of day.

Many members of *Humanist* wittingly and unwittingly contributed during the writing of it by responding to my numerous queries and to the ideas I tried out on them. I heartily recommend such debate with one's peers as a compositional method.

Now that the book exists, it has a formative prehistory. Thanks thus go to Ian Lancashire, who in the mid 1980s invited me to help him build the Centre for Computing in the Humanities at Toronto and who supported my first activities in the field, including organization of the software fairs at two major conferences, involvement with the first *Humanities Computing Yearbook* and two extensive lecture-tours of Europe. It was then that I first met Antonio Zampolli (whose tragic death we all mourn), Tito Orlandi, Wilhelm Ott and Manfred Thaller, all of whom have influenced the ideas developed here. The strong sense of a world-wide community that I gained on those tours has stayed with me as the face-to-face counterpart of *Humanist*.

My *animi hortator* at Toronto, Russon Wooldridge, encouraged me to apply for the grant that funded the *Analytical Onomasticon* project, described in Chapter 1, from which I learned so much. My first research assistant on that project, Burton Wright, taught me by his stubborn other-mindedness the powerful virtues of collaboration.

In 1991 Susan Hockey, then Director of the Center for Electronic Texts in the Humanities, invited me to join her in the Summer Seminar at Princeton University, where during five wonderful summers I had the chance to teach and learn from an international group of senior colleagues and graduate students. Michael Sperberg-McQueen, fellow teacher in the Seminar, had some years earlier inspired the first thoughts towards what became *Humanist*; my other debts to him are innumerable. Through conversations dating from this time but thankfully extending into the present, John Bradley has been the sort of intellectual friend one most hopes for.

Great and good friends have shaped my thinking about the humanities and computing, among them Stanley Katz, John Burrows and Jerome McGann. I owe to Katz a great deal, including all that he did to make the American Council of Learned Societies the noble institution that it is, with a wonderful publication series. Perhaps the best he has done for me directly was to insist that I meet Greg Dening, which I did, at the Australian National University in Canberra, in July 2001. Dening changed my understanding of history by teaching me to think with the present participle. Burrows, Hugh Craig and Wayne McKenna generously arranged for the event that in turn made this meeting possible, and three years later for the return engagement that allowed me to try out, before an audience of Australians, what I had learned from Dening and his countrymen David Malouf and Tim Winton about the special qualities of their sea-dreaming and land-dreaming imaginations. Burrows has in addition shown me by example how experiment works in the humanities as well as reminded me how crucial a deeply informed love of literature is to the success of computer-based experiment in literary studies. McGann's influence goes beyond what the several references in this book indicate, to an attitude towards scholarship that has given me the courage to venture the book. He has opened many doors that I did not even know were there to be opened.

The writings of Ian Hacking, Michael Mahoney, Thomas Kuhn, Peter Galison, Greg Dening, Clifford Geertz and Terry Winograd are fundamental to the book, as should be obvious throughout. So are the effects of studying with Northrop Frye – being 'deep-fried', as it was popularly called at Toronto. In my case this meant not learning how to think, rather how well I could think when I got out of the way. In 1988, at Lancashire's suggestion, I approached and somehow persuaded Frye to give the opening plenary lecture at the 1989 Toronto conference, the first to bring together the Association for Computers and the Humanities and the Association for Literary and Linguistic Computing (where I first met Short). Frye began his lecture by declaring his qualifications for speaking at it to be 'as close to absolute zero as it is possible to get' (1991: 3), then went on to indicate, in terms it would take me several years to understand, what computing principally has to do for the humanities.

Further back in time and perhaps deeper still are the lessons in craftsmanship from Lloyd Reynolds, at Reed. He also taught me how to get out of my own way, but in order to 'stain the water clear' and make letters with a pen. The road from then to now plots a story so long and so full of changes that its continuity may be difficult for any but me to discern. Nevertheless Reynolds' passionate sense of craftsmanship is still with me, and here.

Thanks are due to all the students who have sat through my struggles to articulate the new subject matter of humanities computing and to all those colleagues whom I have advised about their research. In the early days, at Toronto, the students persuaded me by their persistent attendance at non-credit evening classes, through the depths of icy Canadian winters, that the subject had to exist. By describing their research problems, colleagues across the disciplines have given me the particulars from which to abstract common patterns. To paraphrase Hacking, disciplined experience has an intellectual life of its own: supplemented by my own experiments in computing, it has provided the research imperative that here struggles towards a theory.

Help has come from so many, in disproportionally influential amounts, that it seems likely I have overlooked important contributions. (I might, for example, simply have absorbed Morgan Tamplin's unassuming but eye-opening phrase, 'to see an artifact *as data*', without remembering who said it. I am certain that bits of conversations and correspondence with Charles Ess and James O'Donnell have informed my thinking deeply, though I cannot say exactly how.) We are all indebted to Roberto Busa and Joseph Raben. To those whose memes I transmit here unconsciously and unacknowledged, my apologies.

In earlier states of development, Chapter 1 appeared as McCarty 2004b and Chapter 2 as McCarty 2002; the latter includes the entirety of the note on ll. 661–2 from Dodds 1960/1944: 159f. My thanks to Blackwell Publishing, Brill Academic Publishers and Oxford University Press, respectively, for permission to republish. My thanks also to the

Musées royaux des Beaux-Arts de Belgique for permission to reproduce Pieter Bruegel's *La chute d'Icare*.

It is both conventional to say and true that whatever errors, infelicities and muddle-headedness remain, depite all the help, are mine.

Your move.

Willard McCarty
London
January 2005

Im folgenden *fragen* wir nach der Technik. Das Fragen baut an einem Weg. Darum ist es ratsam, vor allem auf den Weg zu achten und nicht an einzelnen Sätzen und Titeln hängenzubleiben. Der Weg ist ein Weg des Denkens. Alle Denkewege führen, mehr oder weniger vernehmbar, auf eine ungewöhnliche Weise durch die Sprache ... Denn das Fragen ist die Frömmigkeit des Denkens.

In what follows we *question* concerning technology. Questioning builds a way. Therefore it is advisable above all to pay heed to the way, and not to fix our attention on particular sentences and topics. The way is a way of thinking. All ways of thought lead through language, more or less perceptibly, in a manner that is extraordinary ... For questioning is the piety of thought.

Martin Heidegger, 'Die Frage nach der Technik' (1977/1955)

Some men went fishing in the sea with a net, and upon examining what they caught they concluded that there was a minimum size to the fish in the sea.

R. W. Hamming, 'The Unreasonable Effectiveness
of Mathematics' (1980: 89)

Let us get nearer to the fire, so that we can see what we are saying.

The Bubis of Fernando Po, quoted by C. K. Ogden and
I. A. Richards, *The Meaning of Meaning* (1949/1923: 1)

Introduction

The end ... is that of delineating, or, as it were, painting what the mind sees and feels: now let us consider what it is to portray duly in form and colour things material, and we shall surely understand the difficulty, or rather the impossibility, of representing the outline and character, the hues and shades, in which any intellectual view really exists in the mind ... Is it not hopeless, then, to expect that the most diligent and anxious investigation can end in more than in giving some very rude description of the living mind, and its feelings, thoughts, and reasonings?

John Henry Newman, *University Sermons*, 13

Taking a chance rather than being parasitic upon modish doubt, having the bravery that comes from a risky faith: these are what Newman uses a sense of limitation none the less to stand for ... [A]rt begins to go wrong ... when it pretends that it is not so much a language of thought to be read and interpreted but a God-like power that can simply reproduce the world ... The gap between the representation and what it stands for itself constitutes part of the communicative power of art; the gap holds within it a silent and implicit call, which the work incorporates within its very means and limitations, a call for a bridging imaginative vision between the work and the life it recalls.

Philip Davis, 'Keeping faith with real reality', *Times Literary Supplement* 4806 (12 May 1995): 13f.

1 Words

The title of this book, *Humanities Computing*, names a field of study and practice found both inside and beyond the academy in several parts of the world.[1] This name for it is now quite common among anglophone practitioners, but it and near equivalents in other languages do not exhaust the possibilities, among them combinations of 'humanities', 'arts', 'philology' and the like with variants of 'computing', 'informatics', 'technology', 'data processing', 'digital', 'multimedia' and so forth. In choosing a particular name for the field I have no wish to restrict these possibilities, since they express differences of emphasis that are most welcome in a time of disciplinary experimentation. I have adopted 'humanities computing' in particular for certain suggestive qualities in the name: a potential still to be taken as an oxymoron, thus raising the question of what the two activities it identifies have to do with each other; the primacy it gives to the 'humanities', preserved as a noun in first position while functioning as an adjective, hence subordinated; and its terse, Anglo-Saxon yoking of Latinate words. I read it first as a challenge to what we think we are doing, then as its name.

I bother to draw out my choice of a title for two reasons: to defamiliarize the juxtaposition and to alert the reader to a philological turn of mind that will dominate throughout. Words can be *very* rich in possibilities of meaning. I take them when the need arises almost as if they were verbal equivalents of the aleph in Jorge Luis Borges' story. There are times and contexts, such as now with computing, when meaning needs to be excavated and brought to bear on a situation we do not understand. On what they argued was another such occasion, C. K. Ogden and I. A. Richards wrote:

> There are some who find difficulty in considering any matter unless they can recognize it as belonging to what is called 'a subject' ... These need only be reminded that at one time there were no subjects ... But the discomfort experienced in entering the less familiar fields of inquiry is genuine. In more frequented topics the main roads, whether in the right places or not, are well marked, the mental traveller is fairly well assured of arriving at some well-known spot, whether worth visiting or not, and will usually find himself in respectable and accredited company. But with a new or border-line subject he is required to be more self-dependent; to decide for himself where the greater interest and importance lies and as to the

results to be expected. He is in the position of a prospector. (1949/1923: vii)

So are we, with few or no such assurances.

2 History

Although better historical knowledge may enlighten us otherwise, I like the notion that what once was 'computers and the humanities' (when the relationship was desired but largely unrealized), and then 'computing in the humanities' (once entry had been gained) is now being resolved into the confident but enigmatic 'humanities computing'. Although this confidence is strengthening and most welcome, the enigma bears the meaning that animates this book. If at the end of it you have the enigma firmly in mind and are engaged in the questioning which it provokes, then the book has done its essential job.

We are nagged, as I say at the end, by the persistent if largely tacit sense of witnessing an enormously important cultural change. Many claims concerning this change have been made. In the following I attempt to articulate what I think it means for research in the humanities. My argument is the result of many years' effort to make sense of my own experience with computing both as a scholar and as an adviser to others, from whom I learned more than I can tally.

During most of that time, my thinking was driven by impatience with the discrepancy between the potential of computing for scholarship, emerging clearly in the work of many individuals across the humanities,[2] and various misconstructions or attempts to turn it aside. The latter I have come to characterize by two related strategies: either *dismissal* of any basis for humanities computing, on the grounds either of the irrelevance, imprecision or triviality of its problems or of its lack of identifiable turf; or *deferral* of promised solutions to these problems, for which the sarcastic phrase 'Real Soon Now' has become proverbial.[3] Impatience is hardly a virtue, but in my case it had the virtue of stirring me to probe these strategies for what they might teach us, other than never to underestimate human perversity. As a traditionally trained scholar (a Miltonist, with strong research interests in Greco-Roman literature) I already took seriously the grounds for seeking out and holding to the most difficult intellectual problems one can find: how, for example, reliably to identify instances of a literary-critical idea, such as personification. But the trickier rhetoric of deferral led me to the root lesson. The central error of these strategies, I concluded, is not the demand for relevance, for which some kind of response is reasonable. Nor is it the demand for patience: meaningful results take time. Rather the error lies in the concealed assumption that solving a problem is the end of the matter that generated it. As someone with an earlier background in programming and the arts and crafts, I was prepared to admit that problem-solving skills are required, for example to debug a program or sharpen a chisel. But both the arts and scholarship had taught me that when knowledge is the goal of work, the purpose of solving problems is to get to harder, worthier ones. Hence the fundamental question to which my experience led me. What precisely does computing itself have to do with rendering knowledge problematic? If it is to serve the humanities as they deserve, it must do that.

In the mid to late 1980s, when impatience began driving me to ask this question, I also started teaching the subject. My students, from across the humanities and social sciences, taught me in turn that there was in fact a subject, and that it had to be about *method* – the only scholarly concern all of us shared. So I asked: what is it about computational method that problematizes? The answer had to be what those two strategies of avoidance, with their focus on solutions, were trying to avoid: precisely the systemic failure of computing reliably to solve problems requiring even a minimal degree of intelligence. So what if, I thought, we were to put aside the distracting promise and embrace rather than try to avoid the self-evident crudity of computing, treating the machine exactly as the scholar finds it – 'a stone adze in the hands of a cabinetmaker', as Vannevar Bush said about searching, famously in 1945 and again, 'in spite of great progress', in 1965.[4] What if we were to ask what we can do, not just within the limits its propensity to failure imposes, but also *with* these limits? 'What if the point were not trying to bridge [the] gap but to feed off and develop it?' (McGann 2001: 103) What do the failures tell us? What epistemological value do they have?

My evolving question had thus succeeded in becoming a very simple one with a very simple answer. It amounted merely to this: first to observe that people learn through an iterative trial-and-error process, then to ask what form this process takes for computing. We know that this process governs the mastery of skills such as riding a bicycle or soldering pipe-joints.[5] If we look at scholarship as what scholars actually do, we can find trial-and-error in it as well, though without the sense of closure that mastery and performance of a practical skill entail. With intelligence, skill and practice, one gets good at interpreting poetry, but interpreting it is not a job that can be completed in the sense that soldering a pipe-joint can be (one hopes). My questioning had thus brought me to conclude first that computing fits into scholarship as a rigorously disciplined means of implementing trial-and-error, second that its purpose is to help the scholar refine an inevitable mismatch between a representation and reality (as he or she conceives it) to the point at which the epistemological yield of the representation has been realized.

The nature of this mismatch became clear in my first postdoctoral research project, which applied text-analysis to a long, complex poem. (An example from this project is discussed in Chapter 1.) Such analysis, I discovered, exacts two requirements: first, that all textual entities in question be explicitly, algorithmically identifiable; second, that any two which the scholar regards as identical be rendered identically. Nothing, and so everything, is left to the imagination. Satisfying these requirements in software was forbiddingly difficult, as is normally true for such research, so I turned to metalinguistic encoding. This had the advantage not only of practicality but also of heuristic encounter on a case-by-case basis with the unsayable subtlety and stubborn particularity of poetic language. The conflict between the entities of this language and the twin computational requirements of complete explicitness and absolute consistency then opened up to me the *via negativa* or 'negative way' to knowledge for which I argue here. Because of their particularizing focus on transcendent objects of study, the humanities have always had to deal with what the net does not catch, but the point I make is not confined to them. Sir Arthur Eddington (whom Richard Hamming paraphrases in the second epigraph to this book) describes just such a role for the philosopher in the natural sciences, whose contribution is to examine 'the sensory and intellectual equipment used in observation'.[6] Humanities computing, being incorrigibly dual, must play both physicist and philosopher.

Another way of approaching the same point opened up for us all as soon as significant quantities of source material became available in digital form, principally with the Web. The importance of accessing this material is no surprise. What can now be done because of the abundance online – despite its sometimes dubious quality and nature – should not be underestimated, though it often is by those committed to doing better. But the torrent rushing out of computers into the various disciplinary heartlands pulled attention away from the difference between cultural artifacts and the data derived from them – away from the analytic concerns of earlier work, as several people have remarked, to a great stocking of the shelves. Revealing much, it simultaneously obscured the quantum leap from seeing such artifacts to seeing them *as data*. Hence the distinction I make in Chapter 1 between the use of a computing system to deliver results for analysis elsewhere – what I call there a 'knowledge jukebox' – and the heuristic use of computing. My argument is essentially that as far as the humanities are concerned, all meaningful uses of computing are heuristic, and therefore that mere 'delivery' is dangerously misleading.

Allow me to pick at words for a moment. The problem is not with 'delivery' as a synonym for publication (or, more broadly, communication). Rather it is with the metaphorical freight of this particular word, which harkens to the commodification of knowledge as something that can be packaged in units, stored somewhere and delivered to a consumer or dispensed from a machine on demand. This is a different, infrastructurally more sophisticated metaphor than Mr Gradgrind's empty vessel, but it is an equally inadequate if not pernicious basis on which to found one's ideas of learning and teaching. Its rapid spread strongly reinforced my conviction that unless practitioners such as myself could show ourselves to be more than mere assistants or delivery-boys to scholarship happening elsewhere, academic credibility would not be forthcoming to our practice. Its lack, inhibiting the creation of dedicated jobs in the field and investment in the research, is a serious matter not only because humanities computing has so much more to offer than convenient vending machines for knowledge. It is also serious because without this research the humanities have difficulty addressing a society (and the students it sends to universities) whose idea of knowledge is defined by such a metaphor. Attending to the problem is not, as I argue in Chapter 4, evidently the concern of mainline computer science. It is the concern of the humanities.

3 Purpose and method

The aim of this book, then, is to open up what has been cast as the new jukebox of knowledge and to demonstrate persuasively not only that *constructing* indefinitely many such machines is the way forward, but also that doing so is a new form of traditional scholarly practice. This dynamic form of practice holds a far greater potential for scholarship than any number of well-crafted products, although crafting them well is essential to that practice.

In this book I anatomize the method of humanities computing into four perspectives: analysis, synthesis, context and profession. The first, second and fourth of these get one chapter each. The third, context, requires two chapters: one devoted to the disciplinary environment within which humanities computing does its work, and the other to a single discipline, computer science, with which its relationship is rich, poorly understood, problematic and always uneasy. Roughly speaking, the sequence of the book defines a moving focus from the microscopic and private to the macroscopic and social. It also defines a movement of thought-style that has been influenced in turn chiefly by philosophy, history and ethnography. Some sequence or other is inescapable: the linear flow of time and language require it, especially in an expository work of academic prose. The sequence I have chosen reflects a way of prioritizing attention. It begins with the intellectual nub, which remains invariant whatever the job-titles may be, wherever the activity is being practised, whether it is solitary or collaborative and whatever importance it may be given by those who do it.

Other sequences are possible. The most significant alternative would put context first, based on the argument that humanities computing is whatever it is because of the disciplinary and institutional setting in which it arose. The main benefit of this arrangement would be the crucial reminder that its daily work is precisely in that context, that it continues to draw institutional breath because of the good it does for the disciplines it serves. I chose my sequence because I believe that within institutions of higher learning the intellectual case is primary, but I try never to forget the constant work that allows it to be made and heard.

4 Audience

By now I trust that the intended audience of this book will have recognized themselves in my appeal to the traditional focus of the humanities and nearby social sciences, which extends beyond their own specializations to possibilities for a thoughtful, culturally informed and intellectually rich life. Several of these specializations and practitioners are invoked here for the help they offer and for the precedent that connecting with them offers to other possible connections. But in doing so I am not *restricting* the book to these or other specialists, though I hope for their attention. I look to John Dewey's attempt to bring ordinary experience and specialized work into an active relation. I ask his question, drawing it from Thomas Bender's recent essay in *The Transformation of the Humanities in the Twenty-First Century* (1997: 4):

Does the scholar's special knowledge, when 'referred back to ordinary life-experiences ... render them more significant, more luminous to us, and make our dealings with them more fruitful? Or does it terminate in rendering the things of ordinary experience more opaque?'

I am only too keenly aware that much of the following is likely to seem far more a 'dark night of the soul' than the promised luminosity, but at least my intention should be clear. Dewey was not proposing a simplistic reduction of subtle ideas, reverse-engineering a cartoon from the fresco, rather he suggested that we actually communicate the results of our work, not obfuscate the urgent problems with which it is concerned. But in the struggle to do so, now after Babel, the present-day audience is no passive judge. It must participate in the profoundly challenging effort to be clear. Of you I therefore make two non-trivial demands: one for curiosity, the other for magnanimity.

Curiosity is the passion for 'taking a look',[7] following clues, digging into things as our ancestors dug into the innards of the earth for food, treasure, knowledge. Its primary instrument is questioning, which I take to be – in the epigraphic words of Martin Heidegger – *die Frömmigkeit des Denkens*, 'the piety of thought'. To paraphrase my late, greatly missed friend Don Fowler at his playful best, the primary function of the humanities is to do just this: not to solve problems but to make them worse by the risk-taking exercise of that piety (1999: 442). Both piety and play join hands in the task of keeping the light of knowledge burning brightly. This book is meant to burn in that sense and in T. S. Eliot's, 'a lifetime burning in every moment'. No corner of the academy or of society at large goes unaffected by the snuffing, darkening opposite: the promoter's aggressive pitch, the consumer's passive hunger and the anxiety that drives them both towards an end of thinking. With its promise of solutions, computing is at the crossroads where they meet. So there we must be. And relentless curiosity is our brightest torch.

The magnanimity or 'generosity of mind' that my book requires of you is just the kind called upon by my former teacher Northrop Frye about fifty years ago in his great project, *Anatomy of Criticism*. This book, he wrote, 'can only be offered to a reader who has enough sympathy with its aims to overlook, in the sense not of ignoring but of seeing past, whatever strikes him as inadequate or simply wrong. I am convinced that if we wait for a fully qualified critic to tackle the subjects of these essays, we shall wait a long time' (1957: 29). Often sitting on limbs much thinner than the thinnest of his, I too hope for my subject to be more competently addressed. I also am convinced that mere waiting is unwise, despite the peril of what may seem a premature venture, despite the half-century since humanities computing began. I take the English folk injunction, 'Be bold, but not too bold', as a call to action strong enough to provoke improving conversation but not to derail it. The chief threat of derailment that I see for this book is its potential misconstruction as a 'god-damned jail' where, as Frye said of a hostile reviewer's misunderstanding of the *Anatomy* (1991: 6), practitioners 'would do nothing but clean out its cells'.

Boldness is required because, as the poet confesses in 'East Coker', '... each venture / Is a new beginning, a raid on the inarticulate / With shabby equipment always deteriorating ...' The comparison may seem a bit much, but it is only by bringing together such unlikely bedfellows in just such a love-making struggle that a humanities computing worth the candle may be made – and remade, and made again. Of course, the thought of incompetence is not a happy one. But part of my argument in Chapter 5 is that we need to respond to the dilemma that the demand for competence forces on us – the mandate to know everything about something drives us to an epistemological vanishing point – by enlarging the domain of competence from the individual to the scholarly community. The project that this book describes, implicitly and explicitly, might be possible for an individual with the capacities of a Leibniz, but to be sustainable it requires a rather fundamental change in how work is done and judged. Here lie the roots of a genuine collaborative ideal rather than merely one of a set of 'transcendental virtues' that pepper the nervous discourse of so many twenty-first-century academics (Galison 2004: 380).

5 Weed control

In scholarly writing, acknowledgements, references and bibliographies recognize indebtedness to the past. Indebtedness to the future is expressed in the ancient formula of reprocity, *do ut des*, 'I give that you may give'. Gathered together in the present, past and future indebtedness form the basis for the ideal to which I refer. But how practitioners work together is something each discipline must evolve for itself. In the specific sense, collaboration is only one expression of the social contract binding practitioners together. When we take the term as denoting a transcendental virtue, to be applied regardless of context, we act as if different styles of work had no organic relation to the intellectual cultures within which we find them. Abundant research as well as common sense tells us, however, that a work-style expresses in its 'epistemic culture' and its modes of communication the fundamental goals of that culture.[8] This is not to deny that such a community of practice, for example as we find in the humanities, can be reformed from the outside, nor that a change from the inside expresses the need for reformation supplied from without. My point is that the issues involved are too important not to take care in promoting such a reformation. Hence the need for what Clifford Geertz has called 'intellectual weed control' (1993/1973: 27), to extract the ideal from its entanglements so that we may understand when and how collaboration suits the humanities. All too often we speak instead of how the humanities may be reconfigured to suit collaboration.

There are, however, two closely interrelated thought-weeds to be dealt with here, both varieties of a single kind. The other, which I discuss below, is the common notion that *the* computer has a single nature we should regard as its essence and emergent evolutionary form, whether this be modelling machine, interactive environment, appliance or whatever. There are very strong reasons for believing this not to be true; I will draw these out later. For now the important matter is the implication, that having discovered what the single nature of computing is, we must either take it or leave it. There is then no point in asking how the computer might be adapted to suit the humanities. The question is then how to adapt the humanities to suit computing.

Both thought-weeds, in other words, interfere with the attempt to set forth what a computing *of* as well as *in* the humanities might be by misdirecting us to begin the wrong way around, with some ghostly construction of *the* machine and *the* work-habits it defines. As a result, scholarly practice is reconceived as a passive response to extrinsic forces and scholars at best as the welcoming conquered. I urge instead that we begin with as clear a vision of the humanities as we can manage, privileging that vision so that we may then ask what the device can do that we want done. The device, being ours, will of course help us to imagine what we want to do, but the effort begins at home.

5.1 Collaboration

Studies of collaboration (as opposed to invocations of it) converge on the serious question of authorship: in the sciences, 'the intricacies of credit and demonstration', i.e. who gets the credit, how significant contribution is demonstrated;[9] in the humanities, what it means to be an author.[10] On the one hand, the cultural authority of the sciences has made it easy to form an idealized image of productive teams from which the complex and problematic realities of the struggle for recognition are missing. On the other hand, 'the romantic myth of the author as solitary genius',[11] deconstructed by studies of authorial indebtedness and of actual but poorly recognized collaborations, has made the solitary worker an easy target. The result is confusion.

Out of this confusion arises the caricature popularly known as the 'lone scholar', whose physically solitary work now appears an indulgence that we can no longer afford – and from which the computer offers us the welcome escape-route. Let me be quite clear on this point. I am not denying that collaboration can be good for research, nor that scholarly practice is changing, nor that it should. Quite the contrary: computing brings people together and offers opportunities for practice to change; not only can these effects be very good, but in particular cases they have proven beneficial, as I detail in Chapter 3. But there are questions: What *is* collaboration, exactly?[12] Where in the spectrum from broad, indirect and tacit indebtedness to explicitly joint work do we locate research in the humanities, especially in light of computing? What conclusion do we draw from the attested benefits of collaboration? Evidence of change is not proof of a systemic change.

The myth of the lone scholar is strongly reminiscent of the situation depicted by C. P. Snow in his 1959 Rede Lecture at Cambridge, 'The Two Cultures', in which he compared 'literary intellectuals' with scientists. His portrait of self-indulgent privilege versus upstart vigour would seem to be fulfilled by the popular scenario of the lone scholar, artifact of a bygone age, tiredly shuffling off while sociable collaborators stride confidently onto the academic stage.[13] Computing allows us to update the picture by supposing that as a result, humanists can behave like scientists and so enjoy renewed vigour as well as social approval. In the decades since Snow's lecture, scientists' behaviour has come to be defined popularly if not always in practice by 'big science' projects, which are massively collaborative. As one prominent scholar in the humanities recently declared, 'specialists should now be able to join together to generate *larger and more meaningful projects*'.[14] (Stop for a moment to weigh the implications of that easy blurring of *large* into *meaningful*.) These projects are not just large, however. They are also extensively managerial. Hence 'large' also implies work that is observed and thus is in current administrative jargon 'transparent', accountable to those who pay for it, who themselves must be accountable for what they do. The outsider's suspicion, driven by enormous, seemingly intractable difficulties between the academy and society, is certainly a problem but not, I think, the root problem. Rather, at root is the insider's suspicion of his or her own irrelevance – we do not work in a social vacuum – and hence the appeal of the putative salvation-through-collaboration, which the realities of funding seem to confirm. The romantic myth of the solitary genius no longer offers secure protection against self-doubt.

Since computing became a possibility for the humanities, scholars have suffered from a misapprehension that the computer is an alien entity, posing a threat or offering salvation. The threat was once foremost. Now the promise of salvation predominates. Both dissolve away, however, when we realize that, like fictional aliens, the computer is a cultural self-expression to be understood and assimilated – a 'monster' in the etymological sense of an omen or portent of change. Similarly with regard to work-style, the collaborative opportunities brought by computing (which is, many argue, primarily a communications device) need to be understood in the historical context of how humanist scholars have in fact done their work. We need to ask how these opportunities fit into and help us to develop particular disciplinary practices in the ways in which we wish to develop them.

The essence of the traditional humanist's work-style is illuminated by comparing the pace and character of research publication across the disciplines, as Thomas Kuhn suggested years ago from his own experience (1977: 8–10). It varies widely, from the rapid exchange of *results* in the sciences to the slower pace of *argument* in the humanities. To varying degrees within the humanities themselves, this argument is the locus of action: the research itself (e.g. in philosophy) or its synthesis into a disciplinary contribution (e.g. in history) takes place *during* the writing, *in* the essay or monograph, rather than in a non-verbal medium, such as a particle accelerator. Contrast, as Kuhn did, the traditional research publication in experimental physics, which reports on results obtained elsewhere. In the natural sciences, as that 'elsewhere' has shifted from the solitary researcher's laboratory bench to shared, sometimes massive equipment or through a division of labour to the benches of many researchers, collaboration has become a necessity. In the humanities, scholars have tended to be physically alone when at work because their primary epistemic activity *is* the writing, which by nature tends to be a solitary activity.[15] Humanists have thus been intellectually sociable in a different mode from their laboratory-bound colleagues in the sciences.

If we look closely at this solitary work, we have no trouble seeing that the normal environment has always been and is *virtually commu-*

nal, formerly in the traditional sense of 'virtually' – 'in essence or effect' – and now, increasingly, in the digital sense as well. However far back in time one looks, scholarly correspondence attests to the communal sense of work.[16] So do the conventions of acknowledgement, reference and bibliography; the crucial importance of audience; the centrality of the library; the physical design of the book; the meaning of publication, literally to 'make public'; the dominant ideal of the so-called 'plain style', *non sibi sed omnibus*, 'not for oneself but for all';[17] and of course language itself, which, as Wittgenstein argued in *Philosophical Investigations*, cannot be private. Writing only looks like a lonely act. Greg Dening quotes Raymond Williams' *Writings in Society* (1983):

> Whenever I write, I am aware of a society and of a language which I know are vastly larger than myself: not simply 'out there', in the world of others, but here, in what I am engaged in doing: composing and relating.

'I think that this is', Dening comments, 'because writing is theatre and the writer a performer. The writer's goal, in the words of the theatre, is to "produce effects". Make someone laugh, make someone cry, make someone angry' (1998: xix–xx). Make someone talk back, provoking further argument.

Recognizing the social qualities of traditional work in the humanities, John Unsworth recommends that we conceptualize the difference computing seems likely to make as a transition 'from a cooperative to a collaborative model', in which 'one works in conjunction with others, jointly producing scholarship that cannot be attributed to a single author' (2003a). The latter model is, he notes, already attested in computer-related work, especially in face-to-face projects such as those I examine in Chapter 3. The question is, however, whether this work indicates a convergent trend – *the* new way of working, or simply another way. Enthusiasm for it is powered, Unsworth notes, by the possibility of escape from our physically enforced provincialism, 'a way to overcome geographical dispersion, the difference in time zones, and the limitations of our own knowledge'. Citing a pronounced trend in the biological sciences towards simulation, Timothy Lenoir predicts a similar transcendence of space and time in 'the fusion of the communication and experimentation functions – the merging of the journal and the lab – in the post-modern academy' (2002: 115). In the early twentieth century the advent of the telephone stirred similar visions of radical, compelling change (Pool *et al.* 1977). Visions of this kind omit tacit physical and social factors crucial to many kinds of work. But the larger problem is the tendency to be swept up in a singular, unifying imperative to become as envisioned, irrespective of circumstances, aims and epistemic culture.

Ursula Franklin, in her Massey Lectures, *The Real World of Technology*, distinguishes between 'holistic' and 'prescriptive' technologies, which she defines as practices of specialization by product and by process, respectively (1990: 18–20). The first comes out of the tradition of the crafts, in which artisans 'control the process of their own work from beginning to finish'. The second is characteristic of industrialized work, in which manufacture is broken down into steps, each carried out by a separate worker. Franklin points out that although we tend to think of collaboration as belonging to the latter sort of practice, we should really be considering two models for it. 'Using holistic technologies does not mean that people do not work together,' she writes, 'but the way in which they work together leaves the individual worker in control of a particular process of creating and doing something.' The idea of holistic collaboration, then, dissolves away what is in fact a false distinction, or at least a very fuzzy one, between styles of socially interactive work.

5.2 The nature of computing

Computing appears to us in a myriad of forms, changing and proliferating as it progresses. What is its essential nature, we ask, so that we may understand what we are witnessing and make best use of the possibilities? But the question turns out to be based on a false assumption: as Michael Mahoney has persuasively argued, there is not one but many computings. He reasons, as I do in Chapter 4, that the computer, unlike other machines we have known, does not have such a nature. Rather, the plural object is indefinitely protean or 'universal', as computer scientists say. Historically, computing is therefore 'what people wanted computers to do and how people designed computers to do it' rather than an essence played out in responses to its impact (2004). The future, this history helps us to see, is up to us.

Hype has hidden this history, as Mahoney says, in predictions of the one future pundits have variously described. By postponing fulfilment of their revolutionary breakthroughs (see my discussion of deferral above), they have fed the illusion that many possibilities of a ragged, diverse, even shapeless present will converge into this future, Real Soon Now. The tendency of chroniclers to write device-histories in which whatever is thought to be the prevailing form of computing is traced back to a particular evolutionary origin, e.g. in Charles Babbage's Analytical Engine, has exacerbated the problem. Thus we find arguments for particular computings (ubiquitous, interactive or whatever) as the essential expression.[18] But the uncertainly bounded set of device-types we might call 'computers' shows no sign of closure. More significantly, the computer is decentred when we turn to the rich contexts of intention, use and creation surrounding the machine – to 'the communities of computing', as Mahoney says (2004). This leads us to a focus on software more than hardware, and thence to the conflict of monothetic enthusiasm with diversifying reality. The compulsive telling of success stories, he argues, has obscured the diversity of attempts to model the world in the machine, and so to create indefinitely many computings answering to indefinitely many ways of construing it.

Mahoney's turning of attention from working out principles to pursuing practice marks a sea-change of mind that I recommend in this book, from the conception of oneself as an 'end-user' to the idea of an experimenting 'end-maker': not as the consumer, who 'comes at the end' of a chain of manufacture, merely using what others have fashioned, but rather as the creator, who begins with his or her own practice, as I do here. This change, I think, answers to a fundamental criticism of current humanities computing practice articulated by Jerome McGann in *Radiant Textuality*. Citing his own *Rossetti Archive* and similar projects, he argues that the user interface we now have fails to implement their decentred theoretical design: 'All are quite "centered" and even quite nondynamical in their presentational structure ... [A] major part of our future work ... will be the search for ways to implement, at the interface level, the full dynamic – and decentering – capabilities of these new tools.'[19] Their centredness, I am suggesting, answers to the understandable but severely limiting focus on the device as a given. Instead we must begin thinking first of our designs as *desiderata* to be realized.

But enthusiasm does meet reality: the machine we have, Mahoney notes, is 'no more personal than a restaurant'. In the following I will repeatedly quote and allude to William Wulf's eloquently brief aphorism that engineering is 'design under constraint' (2000). This is tellingly what we face with the computer. 'It is not bad,' Mahoney remarks,

> but it does have implications for the critical, reflective use of computers, especially in the humanities. It means that the computer as

tool and medium is not neutral, but rather informs (or, as Bolter and Grusin put it, re-mediates) the work that one does with it, if only by setting possibilities and limits on what can be done (or even thought). It calls for critical awareness. (2005)

The universality of computing is thus bounded in principle, however incomplete our knowledge may be of the principles. We can also qualify plurality by discriminating two aspects of the manifold and indefinitely proliferating uses of computing, to which Chapters 1 and 2 are respectively dedicated. In a sense, both Brian Cantwell Smith and Terry Winograd are right: modelling and communicating are both essential, the *yang* and *yin* of the machine, neither meaningful without the other.

6   Style and dependencies

As this book is first of all an act of communication, however, let me end my Introduction by laying the emphasis on conversation, to which this is an invitation in a voice echoing with a multitude of other voices. Here I make every effort to point out the echoes by means of an intensely referential style of writing. Online publication has within the past few years made possible multidisciplinary explorations and massive, digitally searchable collections of writings the like of which would once have been forbiddingly difficult, time-consuming and expensive to locate and very slow to peruse. Online bookshops have simultaneously made conventionally published sources trivial to obtain (though with expensive consequences). This book would have been impossible otherwise. It would have been a different book. I have deliberately kept my stitching together of sources an obvious feature of my style. I have done so not to avoid a charge of plagiarism or to hide uncertainty in a bibliographic flourish, but for two reasons, amplified in Chapter 3: first, to emphasize the historical trajectory of work into collaborative alliances with the disciplines of the humanities; and second, to point emphatically and self-consciously to the origins of a theory of humanities computing in them, and hence to directions for further work.

Many of the stitches will draw attention to my heavy dependence on writings in the history and philosophy of science, especially in Chapter 1. Common sense may no longer hold 'that the scientist's answer is the only ultimately true one' and that in modern civilization science is *'quasi lignum vitae in paradiso Dei, et quasi lucerna fulgoris in domo*

Domini' ('as the tree of life in the paradise of God, and as a lamp of splendour in the house of the Lord'), as Thorstein Veblen wrote in 1906, quoting Pope Alexander IV's words to the University of Paris in 1255.[20] But strong traces of that attitude remain to power an anxious disciplinary reach for authority and so must be taken into account. The English word 'science', John Searle points out, 'has become something of an honorific term'; he would do without it if he could (1991/1984: 11). But we cannot. Better is to confront it historically, to ask what is meant by the claim to be doing science, what sort of a science is in view – there are many, as we will see – and what effects making the claim has on those who are making it. One of course conjures the miasma of scientism with the word, but dispelling it is simply part of the job of nurturing a beneficial relationship between humanists and their equipment. Two related points are to be made about this here.

First, the history and philosophy of science are disciplinary bridges from the humanities to the sciences and back, so it would seem reasonable to look to them for guidance in the not entirely dissimilar operation of connecting the humanities as a whole to computing. We need their help with the shared question of how machines are involved in making knowledge. An immediate fruit of this turn is the suggestion that experiment is the proper context for work in humanities computing. From that suggestion and the wealth of philosophical, historical and sociological insight into experimental knowledge-making, the coherent way of understanding my subject follows. Another, meta-theoretical fruit is the realization that forming disciplinary kinships is not limited to the intellectual bonds a humanities computing practitioner forms with his or her colleagues outside the field. It is an invaluable (and, in fact, a time-honoured) way of building a field of study and integrating it into the company of others. Hence Chapters 3 and 4.

My second point about 'science' is that however two-cultured we make out the sciences and the humanities to be – and that is changing – neither can be properly understood without the other (Collini 1998). Both together comprise our intellectual landscape and horizon. Even if it were true that these two cultures could have been cleanly separated when C. P. Snow delivered his famous lecture, they certainly cannot be now that they share the same basic equipment for much of their essential work, are found with it in physical and virtual laboratories (the sciences normally, the humanities occasionally) and, as I argue in Chapter 1, converge by virtue of it on a sense of experimental knowledge-making. Clearly the sciences and the humanities remain different

in several important ways. But there appears now to be a basis for convergence, so it would be foolish not to make the right kind of reach.
One reaches out for help, to satisfy a need, a hunger, a desire. Thus
the historian of science Lorraine Daston has recently noted that apart
from 'some older work on hermeneutics', such as Gadamer's *Truth and
Method*, and Anthony Grafton's *The Footnote: a Curious History*, we
simply lack 'an epistemology based upon the practices of humanists,
on what they do' (2004: 363). To her list one should add, among
others, Carlo Ginzburg's remarkable essay 'Clues: Roots of an
Evidential Paradigm' (1989/1986), on which I draw heavily in Chapter
3. Still, her point is well taken: the list is quite short. History and philosophy of science, though very helpful in suggesting further directions, will not suffice. But it is worth asking, why *now* do we feel the
need, notice the lack? Ginzburg's argument about the differentiation of
the particularizing humanities from the nomological sciences gives
good reasons for not feeling it earlier. I suspect for reasons given here
that the culture responsible for computing has created the very
methodological need computing promises to satisfy. If so, then in
advancing the cause of humanities computing we are not changing the
humanities but responding to a change that has already happened. It's
like balancing on a ball, perhaps: movement occasions movement.

The question of culture, Clifford Geertz has taught us, leads to 'thick
description', to a hovering barely above the minute particularities of
study. In this book I try to speak about a subject, making an abstraction out of experience, mine and others, in an attempt to render this
experience communicable, arguable, persuasive. But there are large
tracts of this experience from which I cannot generalize because I do
not read well enough, or at all, the many languages other than English
in which work in and thought about humanities computing are done.
So this book must also be a kindly call from anglophone humanities
computing to the others. With it comes a problem, and a request to
consider it: the problem of translation. I invoke here Umberto Eco's
sense of that act, from his *Experiences in Translation* (2001): the interpretation of a text in two different languages, involving the culture of
each. More precisely, the problem is this: to assess in a thick description how the field, as it is developing in its various national and linguistic cultures, is responding to particular features of them. In coming
to a view of what *the* field is or might be, in arguing across these cultures with one another about what needs doing, who has done what,
and so forth, comparative studies are essential. These seem most likely
to be done by non-native speakers of the current *lingua franca*.

I deliberately steer clear of political and professional questions, preferring to put the intellectual case first, and leave necessary attention to the social conditions for enacting it to others. Of course each has much more to do with the other than I am admitting here for discussion. I argue from the primacy of desire – or, if you prefer, the imagination. When in the late 1980s I entered the nascent North American scene, dragging experience with computing from the mid 1960s behind me, conditions for humanities computing as a professionally autonomous field of academic work seemed dismal at best. I do not think what has happened since then has happened all by itself. I think people made it happen, despite the obstacles, because of what they were able to imagine, *because of what they desired.* After you have read this book, I ask you to consider what you want to happen and to push for it with all your strength.

1
Modelling

The more narrowly we examine actual language, the sharper becomes the conflict between it and our requirement. (For the crystalline purity of logic was, of course, not a *result of investigation*: it was a requirement.) The conflict becomes intolerable; the requirement is now in danger of becoming empty. – We have got on to slippery ice where there is no friction and so in a certain sense the conditions are ideal, but also, just because of that, we are unable to walk. We want to walk: so we need *friction*. Back to the rough ground!

Ludwig Wittgenstein, *Philosophical Investigations*, 107[1]

Knowledge requires that there is a means, not that the means is a final truth ... for there is knowledge of the truth even through a belief which is false.

Brahma-siddhi of Mandanamisra 41, 11–15

1 Introduction

In her course of lectures at the Roanne *lycée* in 1933–4, Simone Weil asked how by methodological procedures 'the working of the mind [can] lead the mind itself to problems? ... This happens', she answered, 'whenever a definite method meets its own limit (and this happens, of course, to a certain extent, by chance).'[2] Although computing allows us sometimes to avoid, sometimes to exploit, the element of chance, her answer jumps off the page for its identification of the epistemological power of self-limiting method. Proud as we are of our engineered methods, their indisputable usefulness is only a shadow of their value for scholarly research. This value surfaces, Weil is saying, when useful-

20

ness fails us, when the method we have devised in pursuit of a question runs aground on its own assumptions. There is, of course, nothing new in this. Weil's argument is as old as philosophy. But for reasons that would take me too far afield to explore, we who use computers appear to need reminding that answers are short-term, finite byproducts of the scholarly life, not the focus of its energizing passion. Not then, not now, not ever. 'Is it possible', Alan Perlis asked in one of his delightful epigrams, 'that software is not like anything else, that it is meant to be discarded: that the whole point is to always see it as soap bubble?' (74, 1982: 11) For the analytic aspect of humanities computing, the answer is 'Yes!'

This chapter takes up the fundamental problem of how computing, in its special dependence on 'definite method', responds to the scholar's defining passion. I take a largely philological and philosophical approach to this problem in order to coax out the meaning we require from the relevant words and set it into the most promising context of ideas in the traditions we inherit. The chapter concludes with an extensive example to illustrate the implications of Weil's straightforward response to her deceptively simple question.

The initial difficulty we face is that computing is too recent a phenomenon to have developed its own critical discourse. Philip Agre, for example, has commented, 'Technology at present is covert philosophy; the point is to make it openly philosophical' (1997: 240). One way to do this, and so to generate a critical discourse, is to allow the research programme of theoretical computer science, especially artificial intelligence, implicitly to map out the concealed philosophical terrain, then dig it up (e.g. Colburn 2000). For humanities computing and some forms of computer science, however, the philosophy is more potential than covert – much less a system of ideas, beliefs and positions revealed in the shared assumptions of a research programme than an emergent assembly of conceptual tools brought together to make sense out of practical experience.

My starting point is, again, the fundamental dependence of any computing system on an explicit, delimited conception of the world or 'model' of it – in other words, an implementation of Weil's 'definite method'. Thinking in these terms helps by rooting a nascent critical discourse for humanities computing in a particularly rich way of talking about how we understand the world and by connecting it with an extensive critical literature in the history and philosophy of the sciences, where modelling has been a standard method for a very long time. As I noted in the Introduction, this argument runs into trouble for simulations of complex systems, as we will see, but elsewhere it holds. 'In a real sense', Michael Mahoney comments, 'computers came into existence for the sake of modeling' (2000c).

For historical reasons the literature on modelling in the sciences has until recently concentrated on physics, with particular emphasis on formal scientific theory. But owing to developments in the last few decades – the historicizing of science in the 1960s, the philosophical emancipation of experiment in the 1980s and the spread of computational techniques since then – interest has diversified across the natural and social sciences, and the sciences themselves have moved significantly closer to the humanities. Comparative study of modelling in these disciplines gives us a start at defining the common ground Weil indicated and at understanding how the basic terms change from one discipline to another. The shift in the history and philosophy of science to include laboratory work has meanwhile been complemented by increasing attention to engineering and technology as autonomous fields of knowledge, and by the influence of phenomenology. These changes are reflected in the growth of a philosophy of technology.[3]

Such is in rough and summary form the promising situation we inherit. In this chapter I argue that the fundamental idea denoted by 'model' and other terms in its synonym-set misses the point, however. We require instead the process implied by 'model' and denoted by its corresponding verbal noun, 'modelling'. Implementation in software renders *any* model so conveniently mutable that the essentialist notion of an ideal form recedes into the background, especially where practice is concerned, surviving in the sense of a plan meant to be attempted if not realized. As Marx Wartofsky has said, 'model' becomes a mode of action, a way of constructing the future (1979). Hence in the vocabulary which properly reflects the constructivist leanings of computer-based work, 'modelling' should be regarded as the semantic lemma for 'model'. I argue here that the point of all modelling exercises, as of scholarly research generally, is the process seen in and by means of a developing product, not the definitive achievement. I argue further that in order to understand that process we need to see it within a broad, everyday engagement with implements of all kinds. We need to see it as a form of craftsmanship set into the context of scholarship.

My concern is to draw from studies of prior experimental, technologically mediated practice an idea of 'modelling' from which we may build a disciplined way of thinking and talking about the analytic core of our subject. Such a *philosophy* of modelling, which begins with Weil's answer, would appear to bring together disparate elements of heretofore distinct (but perhaps converging) traditions. I indicate roughly how these might form a coherent account, and then explicate at length a specific example of computational modelling from my own literary-critical research on Ovid's *Metamorphoses*. Since my ideas towards a philosophy of modelling have their origins in this research, it may help to take a preliminary look at the example I have in mind before turning to matters of even pre-theoretical concern. The *Metamorphoses* is a mythological compendium of stories about changing form – a woman into a tree or a man into a stag; a breeze into a woman or a stone into a man.[4] The example I use here is of the latter kind, a non-human entity changed into something like human form. This is known as *personification*, or 'person-making', a common rhetorical device of great importance in the history and theory of literature. I assume that personifications are made by the cumulative effect of identifiable causes in language, are maintained by the presence of these causes and unmade in their absence. For a given candidate I identify these causes (nearby words and other contextual factors), classifying each according to a provisional scheme and assigning to it a numerical 'weight' that expresses the personifying force I provisionally suppose it to have. Summing the weights thus measures the degree to which a candidate is supposedly personified. A discrepancy between the measured degree of personification and my perception from a re-reading of the relevant passage leads to adjustments in the model (or, on occasion, to the reading). Since assignment of weights is applied with rigorous consistency across all candidates, an adjustment to accommodate one affects all others that share the adjusted factor, provoking further adjustments and revisions. Hence by an iterative, perfective process – by *modelling* – an improved and improvingly explicit understanding of the modelled phenomenon arises. Or one arrives at an impasse, forcing rather more drastic revisions, perhaps a rebuilding of the model and many further trials. Deepened understanding is, however, the common goal.

2 Pre-theoretical notions

The key distinction I will develop in this chapter is between *model* and *concept*. Unlike the latter, a model in my sense instantiates an attempt to capture the dynamic, experiential aspects of a phenomenon rather than to freeze it into an ahistorical abstraction. Thus it connects with the sensorial and pragmatic apparatus on which many now argue our cognition relies in the first place,[5] making it a richer, better informed, more powerful heuristic than the abstraction. Details and supporting arguments may seem formidable, opening up here into many pages and numerous references, but these express the richness of the idea rather than its essential difficulty. The basic idea is elegantly simple.

Let me begin with provisional definitions. By 'modelling' I mean *the heuristic process of constructing and manipulating models*; a 'model' I take to be either *a representation of something for purposes of study*, or *a design for realizing something new*. These two senses follow Clifford Geertz's analytic distinction between a denotative 'model *of*', such as a grammar describing the features of a language, and an exemplary 'model *for*', such as an architectural plan.[6] Both kinds are by nature simplified and therefore fictional or idealized representations. In experimental practice, when models are used as pragmatic instruments of investigation, these can take quite a rough-and-ready form: hence the term 'tinker toy' model from physics, accurately suggesting play, relative crudity and heuristic purpose (Cartwright 1983: 158). This is not to suggest a slapdash approach, but rather the crudity of any mechanical approximation to a subtle and complex reality. By nature modelling defines a ternary relationship in which it mediates epistemologically, between modeller and modelled, between researcher and data or between theory and the world.[7] Since modelling is fundamentally relational, the same object may in different contexts play either role: for example, the grammar may function prescriptively, as a model *for* correct usage, or the architectural plan descriptively, as a model *of* an existing style. The distinction also reaches its vanishing point in the convergent purposes of modelling: the model *of* exists to tell us that we do not know, the model *for* to give us what we do not yet have. Models *realize*.

These definitions place 'model' within the broader framework of conceptualization. Thus when Gordon Leff argues that models have always been *implicit* in historical scholarship – he cites the notion of 'epoch' as an example – he marks the relationship of a typically historiographical idea with a related but quite different intellectual form (1972). Leff notes that, as M. I. Finley said in *Ancient History: Evidence and Models*, model-construction is rare among historians (1986: 61), further marking the difference between 'concept' and 'model' as a function of discipline. (Finley preferred Max Weber's concept of 'ideal types', which 'expresses clearly the nature and function of models in an historical inquiry'.) In comparative politics, where the scholar's job is to foreground, analyse and interpret how others conceptualize society and devise schemes for a different world, the foregrounded concepts are models explicitly (Mironesco 2002). Evidently the more schematic the conceptualization in a discipline, the more its practitioners are likely to engage with models rather than concepts.

The disciplinary gulf across which we gaze from the humanities to these schematic disciplines is exemplified by the stylistic alienness of Marvin Minsky's simple, straightforward definition of a computational model: 'To an observer B, an object A* is a model of an object A to the extent that B can use A* to answer questions that interest him about A.'[8] There is much to recommend this definition. Minsky's words are, however, more immediately useful as clues to the historical imagination we require properly to understand the nature of computational modelling from the perspective of a non-technical discipline. My point is that we would be committing a fundamental error (to which our historical moment makes us prone) if we were to dismiss these differences and to accept the reified, explicit 'model' of Minsky's definition as what we *really* have been doing all along. As with the relationship of hypertext to earlier ways of referring (explored in Chapter 2), the new form of expression, with its vocabulary and tools, means an altered way of thinking.

Two effects of computing sharpen the distinction between 'concept' on the one hand and the 'model' on the other: first, the computational demand for tractability, i.e. for complete explicitness and absolute consistency; second, the manipulability that a digital representation provides.

The first effects a sea-change by forcing us to confront the radical difference between what we know and what we can specify computationally, leading to the epistemological question of *how we know what we know*.[9] On the one hand, as Michael Polanyi observed, '*we can know more than we can tell*' (1983/1966: 4). Computational form, which accepts only that which can be told with programmatic explicitness and precision, is thus radically inadequate for representing the full range of knowledge – hence useful for isolating what gets lost when we try to specify the unspecifiable.[10] On the other hand, we need to trust what we somehow know, at least provisionally, in order not to lose all that goes without saying or cannot be said in computational form.

Take, for example, knowledge one might have of a particular thematic concentration in a deeply familiar work of literature. In modelling one begins by privileging this knowledge, however wrong it might later turn out to be, then building a computational representation of it, e.g. by specifying a structured vocabulary of word-forms in a text-analysis tool. In the initial stages of use, this model would be almost certain to reveal trivial errors of omission and commission. Gradually, however, through perfective iteration trivial error is replaced by meaningful surprise. There are in general two ways in which a model may violate expectations and so surprise us: either by a success we cannot explain, e.g. finding an occurrence where it should not be; or by a likewise inexplicable failure, e.g. not finding one where it is clearly present to our own perception. In both cases modelling problematizes. As a tool of research, then, modelling succeeds intellectually when it results in failure, either directly within the model itself or indirectly through ideas it shows to be inadequate. This failure, in the sense of expectations violated, is fundamental to modelling, as we will see.[11]

The second quality of 'model' that distinguishes it from 'concept' is manipulability, i.e. the capability of being handled, managed, worked or treated by manual and, by extension, any mechanical means. Alteration is common to both models and concepts, but at greater or lesser metaphorical distance 'model' denotes a concrete, articulated device inviting manipulation, in the etymological sense of action-by-hand (L. *manus*). Manipulation in turn requires something that can be handled (physical objects, diagrams or symbols of a formal language) – and a time-frame sufficiently brief that the emphasis falls on the process rather than its product. In other words, the modelling system must be interactive. Manipulable objects, from the physical to the metaphorical, have characterized mathematics, engineering, the physical sciences and the arts *ab ovo*, but with exceptions the necessary time-frame, allowing for interactivity, has become possible only with computing. Computers, Minsky has noted, have allowed models to be 'conceived, tested, and discarded in days or weeks instead of years'.[12] Computing met research easily in fields where modelling was already an explicit method because models are fundamental to computing. But – here is the vital matter – models *per se* are not the point. What distinguishes computers from other kinds of machines is that 'they run by *manipulating* representations, and representations are always formulated in terms of models'.[13]

The computational emphasis on process rather than product tends profoundly to affect the ontological status we accord any one construct. The drastically reduced investment in an obviously temporary product, plus the means at hand to alter it immediately, mean that one is much less likely to mistake this product for a true or final representation, indeed unlikely to think that any such product would ever reach perfection. One is much more likely to abandon altogether the idea of closure and to concentrate on exploration, evolutionary development and reuse – and of course also on methodology, since modelling implements method. In the sense of an established or mechanical procedure by which knowledge is generated, method is anathema to intellectual work,[14] but modelling answers the objection by relativizing method. In other words, computational models, however finely perfected, are better understood as *temporary states in a process of coming to know* rather than fixed structures of knowledge. Even if it were true that such structures are emergent in current or foreseeable work,[15] these would not then be *models* and would no longer have reason to exist in software. (Note that the history of computing is the story of ever more complex and extensive software, not less, despite the fact that implementations in hardware are faster and can be cheaper.) I conclude that although efficient access to data is an essential function of computing, the greater potential is for *computers as modelling machines, not knowledge jukeboxes.* To think of them as *only* the latter is profoundly to misunderstand human knowledge.

In analytic terms, as I have suggested, modelling has two phases: first, construction; second, manipulation. Examples come readily to mind from ordinary technical practice, e.g. building a relational database, then querying the data thus shaped to explore emergent patterns. As experience with databases shows, the two phases often blur into each other, especially in the early stages when use uncovers faults or suggests improvements that direct redesign. A model *of* and a model *for* may be regarded as distinct types, but the symbolic formulation fundamental to the idea of 'model' already makes possible their mutual transposability (Geertz 1993/1973: 94). Modelling *of* something readily turns into modelling *for* better or more detailed knowledge of it; similarly, the knowledge gained from realizing a model *for* something feeds or can feed into an improved version. This characteristic blurring of design into use and use into (re)design is what denies modelling *of* any sense of closure. Modelling *for*, utopian by definition, is denied it in any case.

3   Learned complaints and alternatives

'Model' is vexing: it seems hopelessly polysemous but refuses to go away. Nelson Goodman, for example, complains that 'model' is able to denote 'almost anything from a naked blonde to a quadratic equation'; H. J. Groenewold declares we have 'no model of a model'; Peter Achinstein advises against making the attempt; and John Ziman declares that it 'defies formal definition'.[16] Yet, as he notes, despite all the objections 'it is so widely used in scientific practice that it has become almost a synonym for "theory".' A recent book on the topic in the social sciences confirms that 'model' remains indispensable to them as well (Franck 2002: 5). But why?

Other terms overlap 'model' – principally 'analogy', 'representation', 'diagram', 'map', 'simulation' and 'experiment'. (One can of course add to this list, for example 'plan', but the terms chosen for attention should be sufficient.) These are variously used, sometimes as if they were synonymous, sometimes clearly indicating different but related notions. Two of these, 'map' and 'diagram', come strongly recommended for their greater clarity and precision.[17] All are worth considering in some detail because the individual tendencies of mind they signal help to clarify the semantic field and so to sharpen our ability to sketch out a philosophical perspective. Here I propose to examine them, using as my touchstone *the continual process of coming to know by manipulating things*, not an achievement but an approximating convergence.

3.1 Analogy

'Analogy' (Gk. *analogía*, 'equality of ratios, proportion') is, like 'model', a highly polysemous term with a long and complex history.[18] Two definitions quoted in the *Oxford English Dictionary* – Dr Johnson's pithy phrase, 'resemblance of things with regard to some circumstances or effects', and Richard Whately's even pithier one, 'resemblance of relations' – give us an idea of why it is so fruitful.

In its original meaning in Greek mathematics, analogy specifies proportionality as 'a condition that may or may not obtain between four objects', e.g. *a*, *b*, *c* and *d*, asking if these quantities are proportional, or if *a* is to *b* as *c* is to *d*, or asserting that they are (Fowler 1999/1987: 16). Extended since then to more complex, multi-factorial systems, analogy yields a powerful (but still poorly understood) means of inferring from the one system to the other. Like most of the words under consideration here, 'analogy' is proleptic: a means of inference, based on conjecture, to something unknown or uncertain. Examples in the history of science are plentiful, e.g. Kepler's discovery of the *vis motrix*, or cause of planetary motion, by reasoning that as the sun radiated light, so it must also radiate this motive power (Gentner 2002). 'Since the 17th century (and even earlier in astronomy),' Michael Mahoney explains, 'scientists have sought to reduce nature to physical models and the physical models to mathematical relations. They have proceeded on the premiss that the structures of those relations mirrored the structures of the physical models, which in turn mirrored the structures of nature' (2002: 39).

Here I wish to argue two points. The first is that analogy is basic to the entire vocabulary. Although not every model is as strictly based on an analogy as Kepler's, modelling is inherently analogical, with just the features that make the idea attractive for our purposes. Thus we require a relation between model and artifact so that by playing with the one we can infer facts about the other. (For example, by adjusting choice of words and weightings for a distribution-display across a textual corpus, one can investigate the effect of vocabulary on the interplay of meanings in that corpus.) The second point is that 'analogy' is inherently static: it means either a type of relationship or an instance of one, never an object and not, literally or directly, a process. Action is implied in the ratio of quantities – thus Kepler's 'as A *does* B, so C *does* D' – but *acting* is not denoted by the analogy. The word has no commonly used verbal form ('analogize' and 'analogizing' are rare if not strange). Although an analogy may be algebraically or geometrically expressed and may refer to concrete objects, it itself is abstract. At the same time 'analogy' lacks the specifically symbolic formulation that 'model' adds to the relationship (Geertz 1993/1973: 94).

Because analogy works so well as a way of describing how we often think, efforts to understand acquisition of new knowledge tend to engage with theories of analogy and to propose many mechanisms, e.g. in cognitive science, educational theory and artificial intelligence (Hoffmann 1995). Because modelling is analogical, this work is potentially relevant to questions raised in computing the artifacts of the humanities. We need to pay attention here.

3.2 Representation

'Representation' in Nelson Goodman's terms is defined by a symbolic denotative correspondence, not likeness or imitation (1976/1969: 3–43).[19] In a less philosophically precise sense, however, we may say that 'representation' displays strong mimetic tendencies, e.g. in the definition given by the *OED*: 'An image, likeness, or reproduction in some manner of a thing ... A material image or figure; a reproduction in some material or tangible form; in later use esp. a drawing or painting (of a person or thing).' The history of aesthetics from earliest times, in fits and starts of fashion, demonstrates that the copy-theory of representation remains a habit of mind. This is as true of computer science as aesthetics.

A well-attested verbal noun and a full complement of other verbal forms establishes the action of *representing*, but semantically this action is bounded by its relationship to the represented object, whether this be symbolic or imitative. A representation must be *of* something, which thus sets the bounds of representing it.

As with 'analogy', the semantic fields of 'model' and 'representation' clearly overlap, but the situation is more complex because of the mimetic and proleptic kinds of 'model'. Hence we may say that modelling *of* is representational, but not modelling *for*. The crucial difference between model *of* and representation is the quality of the action implied. Unlike representing, modelling *of* is denied closure, as I noted earlier. It has no satisfactory *trompe l'oeil* or symbolizing conclusion. If the researcher calls a halt, then the last state of the system, as it were, is better called a 'representation'.

In the context of computing, the meaning of 'representation' is dominated by the subfield of artificial intelligence known as 'knowledge representation' (KR). Given the scope of this chapter I can do little more than make a few observations, chiefly about the assumptions built into the name and apparently into tendencies in some KR work. In brief, my argument concerning KR is that it needs to be understood as a particularly rigorous control on model-building suitable to that which can be stated in propositional form.[20]

Independently of computing, the term 'knowledge' already has strong association with demarcational issues of the sort that computing forces us to resolve. It is 'an honorific title we confer on our paradigm cognitive achievements', Michael Williams has argued, '... not just a factual state or condition but a particular *normative status*.' As such it involves 'putting some claims or methods before others', and at the extreme, distinguishing between meaningful and meaningless (2001: 11–12). The compound expression 'knowledge representation' pushes sense towards this extreme by losing the hint (that, for example, 'representation *of* knowledge' gives us) of a non-representational or even unrepresented kind. For those who do not look beyond it, computing then seals knowledge up in representation by making the demarcational act absolute. 'Perhaps there are some kinds of knowledge that cannot be expressed in logic', the author of *Knowledge Representation: Logical, Philosophical, and Computational Foundations* declares (Sowa 2000: 12). Perhaps indeed – but we hear no more about them under that roof.

KR is exemplified by the well-known Cyc project, whose objective is an extensive representation of commonsense knowledge for use by other AI systems so that they can interact with the world more robustly.[21] Such projects are based on the long-discredited idea that an accumulation of knowledge in vast quantities will one day, somehow, result in understanding.[22] They clearly assume if not perfect closure then a threshold beyond which its lack ceases to matter. But with respect to whom, and for what purposes? Apart from such questions, and the serious doubts within computer science on the wisdom of building massive knowledge-bases for expert systems[23] – the very serious demarcational issues stubbornly remain.

3.3 Diagram

A diagram (Gk. *diágramma*, 'that which is marked out by lines, a geometrical figure, written list, register, the gamut or scale in music') is an analogical drawing, 'a figure drawn in such a manner that the geometrical relations between the parts of the figure illustrate relations between other objects' (Maxwell 1911: 146). It ranges from the precisely drawn schematic, whose measurements are significant, to the rough sketch intended to express symbolic relations only. But what makes a graphic a diagram, properly so called, is the way in which it is read, not its resemblance to anything (Goodman 1976/1969: 170f.). Reviel Netz argues the point for the lettered diagram in Greek mathematical texts: 'It is only the diagram perceived in a certain way which may function alongside the text' – irrelevant discrepancies are overlooked, the important matters denoted by the lettering: 'All attention is fixed upon the few intersecting points, which alone are named' (1999: 33f.). Even when the diagrammed entity is a physical object, the diagram represents structure and interrelation of essential parts, foregrounding interpretative choice and conscious purpose. The ability to manipulate structures and parts may be implied.

The word 'diagram' doubles as noun and verb and has a full range of verbal inflections. Like 'represent' its action is bounded, but more by ideas than appearance, even when that appearance is precisely delineated. As Maxwell notes for physics, diagrams often represent force or movement, even if only implicitly, though the form is static. As a means of communication, e.g. in a lecture or discussion between collaborators, diagramming is the point, not the static trace left behind. That trace may in fact be unintelligible apart from the discussion of which it was a dynamic part.

The focus on ideas rather than things *per se*, the role of manipulation where diagramming is heuristic, and the kinaesthetics of the action suggest the close relationship between diagramming and modelling for which Goodman argues. Models *of*, he declares, 'are in effect diagrams, often in more than two dimensions and with working parts ... [and]

diagrams are flat and static models' (1976/1969: 172–3). Nevertheless, the two-dimensionally graphic, geometrical and finally static qualities of the diagram define it, not 'model', which has considerably broader applications.

Sun-Joo Shin and Oliver Lemon note that although diagramming is very likely one of the oldest forms of communication, modern logicians and philosophers have tended until recently to regard it as only of marginal importance.[24] That is changing very rapidly now. As a cognitive, reasoning process it is studied in relation to Greek mathematics and geometry in particular (Netz 1999). Modern philosophical attention can be traced from Descartes's 'La Géométrie' (1637) and Kant's *Kritik der reinen Vernunft* II.1.1 (1781) to Peirce's 'existential graphs' in the late nineteenth century, significantly as part of his much broader interest in scientific discovery, to which I will return.

Shin and Lemon delineate three branches of research in the last decade: (1) multi-modal and especially non-linguistic reasoning, in the philosophy of mind and cognitive science; (2) logical equivalence of symbolic and diagrammatic systems, in logic; and (3) heterogeneous systems implementing theories of multi-modal reasoning, in computer science. The close relationship of diagramming and modelling makes this research immediately relevant.

3.4 Map

A map may be defined as a schematic spatial representation, or following James Clerk Maxwell, a diagram of anything we can imagine spatially. The impulse to do so is fundamental: 'Everything is somewhere,' Arthur Robinson and Barbara Petchenik comment, 'and no matter what other characteristics objects do not share, they *always* share relative location, that is, spatiality; hence the desirability of equating knowledge with space, an intellectual space' (1976: 4). In that they express ideas, diagrams are map-like. If not for the geographical focus of mapping, the semantic fields of 'map' and 'diagram' would completely overlap: both have a full complement of verbal forms, their action bounded by a graphical representation that has both strongly mimetic and ideational aspects; both manipulate data for specific purposes and introduce fictional elements to serve these purposes. But the long history of mapping the physical world for exploration and description gives 'map' specific, evidently powerful and strongly limiting connotations. These are brought out in several recent studies that deconstruct our fascination by and complicity with mapping.[25]

Mapping is particularly characteristic of an early, exploratory period, when a territory is unknown to its discoverers (or conquerors). Mapping constructs while it objectifies the world it represents, selectively, therefore shaping thought and guiding action. A map is pragmatic if not programmatic. It orients the newcomer, giving him or her control of the mapped terrain, at the same time expressing, though perhaps covertly, a perspective, a set of interests and a history. Mapping attaches meaning to place – or, as Denis Wood has argued, transforms it into an object of veneration (1992: 66). Like modelling it can be either *of* or *for* a domain, either depicting the present landscape or specifying its future – or altering how we think about it, e.g. by renaming its places. A map is never entirely neutral, politically or otherwise. Indeed, it is a post-heuristic prescript, defining the pathways and the names of things. David Turnbull, quoting Wood, brings together science and cartography as practices of social domination symbolized by the map (2000: 94–7).

John Ziman and Stephen Toulmin before him have argued persuasively as theorists for describing scientific research as mapping – that which follows the pathways already defined by theory. They are joined by Michael Polanyi – 'all theory may be regarded as a kind of map extended over space and time' (1962/1958: 4) – and by Thomas Kuhn (1970/1962: 109). Hence the immediate relevance of the cartographic imagination to my project. Mapping particularly fits a Kuhnian view of research: long periods of stable activity within a settled terrain interspersed by revolutionary, and perhaps incommensurable, reconceptualizations of that terrain. Mapping is for our purposes more to the point than representation, because we always know that there can be many maps for any territory and that all of them have a fictional character – which is why the map is a standard example of an interpretative genre for data.[26] But because its action is bounded and its result defines a world, mapping better suits the theoretician's than the experimenter's view. By evoking the disciplinary politics of conceptual territory (for which see the next chapter), mapping also distracts from the specifically analytical issues I need to isolate here. It is not the term we need.

In computer science, mapping is used in knowledge and argument representation. The term surfaces in 'Topic Maps' and 'Concept Maps' and is implicit in talk about e.g. 'semantic networks'. This interest seems to originate with Toulmin's mapping of argument (1958), which suggests techniques of automated inferencing in AI. (Maps of argument look like flowcharts.) As a form of data-visualization, mapping also connects with a very strong and recent interest in humanities computing (Kirschenbaum 2002), and so connects this interest with modelling.

3.5 Simulation

Simulation is '[t]he technique of imitating the behaviour of some situation or process ... by means of a suitably analogous situation or apparatus ...'. Its mimetic tendencies and so bounded action are perhaps most emphatic among the terms we are considering. Again, total replication is not at issue: a simulation attends to selected details of the world and thus can be exploratory, as when relevant conditions of flight are simulated for purposes of study or training. Simulation also relies on abstraction from the original to the analogue system (Simon 1996/1969: 15–17), which makes it a kind of representation. But in usage, the connotation if not denotation of an *exact* correspondence between simulation and original remains paradoxically alongside knowledge of real difference – hence, perhaps, the implication of intent to deceive often attributed to the word. Knowledge of difference, however uneasily, can be put aside, as in what we now call 'virtual reality' (VR).[27]

In its current form VR is quite a recent phenomenon, but the essential movement of simulation on which it is based, from self-conscious imitation to displacement of reality, is attested from the beginning of applied computing and is present in the history of mechanical automata.[28] In the development of physics immediately following World War Two, computer simulation was adopted as a technique of research because the central problem at issue had become, as Peter Galison says, 'too complex for theory and too remote for experiment' (1997: 690). Physicists turned instead to mimicking the random real events of nuclear interaction by 'using random numbers (chosen *à la roulette)*' in the so-called Monte Carlo simulation.[29] 'Proven on the most complex physical problem that had ever been undertaken in the history of science', Galison continues, simulation came to replace experimental reality, thus blurring multiple boundaries that had previously defined research, redefining it in new terms.[30] Since then the turn away from traditional analytic methods to simulation has spread to several other fields (Burch 2002). As the biologist Glenn W. Rowe points out, with this turn has come the realization that 'a great many systems seem to have an inherent complexity that cannot be simplified ...'[31] – and so must be studied *as simulations*. Thus simulation brings to attention new problems with which it can deal. At the same time, Mahoney notes, the displacement of reality in the simulation of complex systems leads to a more general problem with the notion of modelling under circumstances where no analogical congruence obtains (2000c). What and how do we learn? He quotes the mathematical biologist Robert Rosen on the danger of extrapolating from the model to the modelled system: 'although formal simulators can be of great practical and heuristic value, their theoretical significance is very sharply circumscribed, and they must be used with the greatest caution' (1995/1994: 497).

In the humanities we have known for some years that computer-based simulations can play a role in teaching. An old but very good example is *The Would-Be Gentleman*, a re-creation of economic and social life in seventeenth-century France in which student-players must realize and put aside their modern preconceptions in order to win (Lancashire 1991: 113). In other words he or she must *become* a seventeenth-century Frenchman mentally, i.e. must match the historical type as represented in software. Where much less is or could be known about an historical subject, simulation also offers research possibilities. Several good examples illustrate these.[32] Like game-playing, simulation tends to forgetfulness of the mechanism by which it is created so long as its terms of engagement (expressed in parameters and algorithms) are fixed. Unfix them – e.g., in *The Would-Be Gentleman*, by allowing the player to change the encoded attitude towards marrying above or below one's station – and the simulation becomes a modelling exercise directed to exploring the question of that attitude. Thus simulation crosses over into modelling when the constants of the system become variables. Modelling, one might say, is a *self-conscious* simulation, and simulation an *assimilated* modelling. The difference between the two is, as we will see later, far more significant than these terms indicate.

3.6 Experiment

In common usage 'experiment' (L. *experiri*, to try) is either 'An action or operation undertaken in order to discover something unknown ...' or 'The action of trying anything, or putting it to proof; a test, trial ...' In its broadest sense, the word embraces 'modelling', indeed any heuristic experience of the world, especially that which involves conscious purpose, defined procedure or its material instantiation in equipment. Like 'modelling', 'experiment' refers to a process whose ending is constructed rather than given: as Peter Galison has argued for the physical sciences, the experimenter *decides* if and when the attempt has succeeded or failed, in 'that fascinating moment ... when instrumentation, experience, theory, calculation, and sociology meet' (1987:

1). Modelling and experimenting are by nature open-ended; indeed they are often at the time ill-defined, even quite messy.[33]

The semantic overlap of 'modelling' and 'experiment' is so close that the two can be quite difficult to separate (Guala 2002). Mary S. Morgan, writing about modelling in economics, has argued that they may be discriminated by the degree to which the former involves hypothesis, the latter reality (2002: 49), but as she notes, hybrids provide exceptions and thought experiments – 'devices of the imagination used to investigate nature' (Brown 2002) – a very close analogue to modelling.[34] Perhaps the relationship is most clearly stated by saying, without any great precision, that in the context of research a model is an experimental device, modelling an experimental technique.

The point of considering 'experiment' here is, however, primarily to locate modelling within the context of a particular history of ideas and so to engage with large and important areas of historical and philosophical research. Indeed, as an experimental technique modelling has shared the fate of experiment in the specialist literature, and so also in the popular understanding. This story of modelling is briefly told in Mary Hesse's early and highly influential account, *Models and Analogies in Science* (1963), as the conflict between two philosophical positions, one French, the other English.[35] These represent, respectively, the majority and minority views in the philosophy of science until quite recently. Allow me briefly to summarize the background.[36]

By the mid-nineteenth century, understanding of scientific work had begun to polarize into two epistemological conditions, which physicist and philosopher Hans Reichenbach later famously named 'the context of discovery', performed subjectively, and 'the context of justification', communicated objectively.[37] By the early to mid-twentieth century, discovery had been expelled from mainstream epistemology – a matter perhaps 'of great interest to empirical psychology', as Karl Popper remarked, but 'irrelevant to the logical analysis of scientific knowledge'.[38] Experiment, the means of discovery, was in consequence also demoted and theory, the focus of justification, promoted. 'The asymmetric emphasis on theory in the historical literature', Galison explains, meant that attention was confined 'to the invention and testing of theories' (1987: 8), while the actual conduct and intellectual role of experiments was largely overlooked. In philosophy too 'experiment *for* theory' dominated until (in Ian Hacking's paraphrase of Nietzsche) Thomas Kuhn's *The Structure of Scientific Revolutions* 'unwrapped the mummy of science' by historicizing it (1983: 1f.). What had actually always been happening in experimental work could then become a proper subject of investigation. Furthermore, Kuhn's ample demonstration of 'the essential role theory plays in the conduct of experimentation, the interpretation of data, and in the definition of "relevant" phenomena' depolarized theory and experiment (Galison 1987: 8f.). In other words, from an entirely subordinate and observational role, experiment became visible alongside theory as an interdependent partner.

Subsequently, through the work of Hacking, Feyerabend, Galison and several others, the fiction of a unitary 'scientific method', in which theory cleanly defines the role of experiment, has been dispelled. As Hacking says, calling for a 'Back-to-Bacon' movement, 'Experimentation has a life of its own' (1983: 150), sometimes preceded by theory, sometimes not. But the consequent liberation of experiment from the debilitating pretence of grubby handmaiden to 'pure' theory at the same time directed attention back to the very hard, old problem of discovery: How does this happen? To quote the title of an article by a contemporary of Kuhn's, Norwood Russell Hanson, 'Is There a Logic of Scientific Discovery?'[39] A rationality? A common pattern?

4 Towards a philosophy of modelling

4.1 Preliminaries

My subject is not scientific discovery, but it shares with that topic the question of how, exactly, an inquirer's use of physical equipment advances inquiry – indeed, how in general the user of a tool or implement *knows* what he or she is doing. I enlarge the area of concern almost to the bounds of sentience because half the answer to the narrow question I am pursuing becomes available only if we consider the physicality common to all sentient use of such implements. The other half of the answer is specifically computational. It receives disproportionately small attention here because it is far easier to understand, though its consequences are equally great.

A crude, commonsensical answer to the whole question, posed specifically for computers, is that inquiry is advanced by the useful information that computers provide. Knowledge representation seems to yield a better answer by bringing the mechanism into sharp focus and so detailing how, before a question can be asked with good hope of a helpful answer, complex, ingenious structures of knowledge must be designed and built. But an improved response to my question is not forthcoming, despite the fact that KR results in much interesting research and useful devices. My question requires the opposite approach, as I just suggested: orientation to questioning rather than to answers, and opening up rather than glossing over the inevitable discrepancies between representation and reality on which that questioning focuses. Modelling, I have suggested, provides this orientation and informs (or re-informs) it with the metaphorical sense of a physical *prying into*. Modelling thus defines our instrument as digital in both senses of that term.

At several points in the preceding section clues towards a philosophy have emerged: the manipulatory essence of modelling, with its connotation of embodied action, physically or metaphorically; the mediating role and ternary relationship modelling establishes between knower and known; the directed, vector-like engagement of the inquirer's attention, *through* the model he or she has made *to* the object of study; and the model's consequent function as an artificial agent of perception and instrument of thought. Teodor Shanin, arguing for the role of models in scholarship, concludes that modelling brings the inquirer towards a union of subject and object: '[t]he unbridgeable break between the limited and selective consciousness of the subject and the unlimited complexity and "richness" of the object is negotiated by purposeful simplification and by transformation of the object of study inside consciousness itself' (1972: 10). Shanin thus draws attention to a genuine change in how we work, not simply an annexing of new methods. We know the change is genuine by the fact that it both takes and gives. First it costs us the discards resulting from that 'purposeful simplification' of what is to be studied. Then it gives twice over. The first gift is manipulability, with all the well-heralded benefits, and the one, insufficiently understood benefit on which I will focus: mediated access to the sensorial and pragmatic apparatus on which our cognition relies. The second gift is the ability to focus, by negative means, on the computationally unknown.

Another way of saying the same thing is to note how the new methods of work bear strong relation to the old ones. Both new and old, that is, respond to the transcendence of our cultural artifacts by recognizing that interpretation of them is ongoing and plural. The demand that we pluralize has other origins and expressions, but it becomes especially emphatic with computing because computational form is radically inadequate. My point is that this very inadequacy is a powerful tool and that we come prepared to use it. Facing the prospect of transcendent knowledge with limited equipment is, after all, a very old situation. Michael A. Sells describes three approaches prevalent in medieval Christian, Jewish and Arabic cultures: contemplative silence; analytic distinction of attributes; and specific denial of knowledge (1994: 1–13). Other responses are possible, e.g. the artist's parallel expression or channelling of transcendence into another form, or the exclamatory outburst, as in Emily Dickenson's note to Thomas Wentworth Higginson:

> If I read a book and it makes my whole body so cold I know no fire can ever warm me, I know that is poetry. If I feel physically as if the top of my head were taken off, I know that is poetry. These are the only ways I know it. Is there any other way? (Feinstein 1994/1971: xiii)

The way of humanities computing, with no lesser goal in its sight, I take by analogy with Sells' third approach, which he calls *apophasis* (literally 'un-saying' or 'speaking-away'), a *via negativa* or deliberative method of denial that approaches knowledge of the absolute by detailing specific ignorance of it. Knowledge of a human artifact is not quite knowledge of the divine, but the analogy is very strong. Thus something very much like *apophasis* is central to scholarship as a whole. 'Science in general ...', R. G. Collingwood wrote, 'does not consist in collecting what we already know and arranging it in this or that kind of pattern. It consists in fastening upon something we do not know, and trying to discover it ... That is why *all science begins from the knowledge of our own ignorance*: not our ignorance of everything, but our ignorance of some definite thing ...' (1993/1946: 9, my emphasis).

The question of how we manage the crucial step from ignorance of our own ignorance to knowledge of it – how, to paraphrase Jerome McGann, we *imagine what we do not know*[40] – is Simone Weil's question, with which this chapter began. The answer is hers: by definite, self-limiting method. Thus, again, computing forces the reduction of what we think we know into a more or less adequate account and a more or less irreducible residue of misfits.[41] The moment of revelation comes when we realize that this residue, not always but always possibly, constitutes what McGann has tellingly called 'the hem of a quantum garment' (2004b: 201): seemingly insignificant details that, like the 'splash quite unnoticed' of Icarus drowning in Pieter Bruegel's *Fall of Icarus* (1558),[42] open up one's understanding of the whole.

Any given residue challenges the scheme that produced it and so poses an implicit question from a glimpse of what may turn out to be such a hem. An initial glimpse may be enough – for example, of a crucially significant text not identified by a scheme that should include it – but in general for modelling manipulation is essential. Hence we must face the difficult task of opening manipulation itself up to view and discovering the nature of its epistemic function – without which computing would furnish no more than convenient access to data and communication among colleagues, as 'just a tool'. But such a reduction makes no sense: data mirror the set of possible manipulations that define their difference from real-world objects; communication by any medium requires the modulation of that medium. The fundamental problem here lies in a misunderstanding about tools – not just computer-tools but all instruments we use to act on the world. A tool is more than merely itself: out of hand, an intentional artifact; in hand – that *is* the question.

Unfortunately there is no unified account of epistemic manipulation, and the terms in which we must deal to work on it are confused by their involvement with everyday language. Michel Foucault has observed that 'when it comes to determining the system of discourse on the basis of which we still live, as soon as we are obliged to question the words that still resonate in our ears, that are mingled with those we are trying to speak, then archaeology ... is forced to work with hammer blows' (2000/1967: 293). The blows needed here, to bring to light the foundations we must examine and remake, come from several different angles. I indicate below what I regard as the main ones, drawing on helpful work in recent philosophy of technology.[43] Using primary philosophical sources, I assemble a number of strong, complementary arguments and discuss them. But first, two preliminary impediments.

The first is the discrepancy between current philosophy and the commonsense notions of knowledge, reason and related ideas embedded in computing systems and assumed if not asserted in the surrounding discourse. These notions continue to cause us trouble despite the fact that they are well past their sell-by date. To my philosophically sophisticated readers, their mention may seem curious and argument against them worse than unnecessary. But the need to clear out our shared intellectual pantry is undeniable beyond the immediate circle of professional philosophers, who hardly need to hear what I have to say. I beg their indulgence and hereby invite their help, offering in return the observation that this need sharply demonstrates their discipline's relevance to computing and the culture on which it has massive influence.

The second impediment is the still active divide between analytic and phenomenological traditions in philosophy, largely Anglo-

American and Continental European, respectively. Since I draw freely from both (as others, such as Ihde, have done before me in the context of technology), I run the risk of annoying the practitioners of both. Again I beg their indulgence. As I understand these matters, bringing the traditions together is not a new project.[44] Formulation of a *concordia discors* for technology is still wanting, however. All I can offer here are notes towards a converging of them in a possible philosophy of modelling.

More than fifteen years ago Hilary Putnam identified the old problem we face to this day: 'The question that won't go away is *how much what we call intelligence presupposes the rest of human nature*' (1988: 277).

4.2 Phenomenology

Of all those who have dealt with this question in the context of technology the most important is Martin Heidegger (1889–1976), not so much for his essay 'Die Frage nach der Technik' (1962) as for his much earlier revision of the Western philosophical tradition in *Sein und Zeit* (1927).[45] Many would wish his prominence away, e.g. most recently Paul Edwards, for whom it constitutes a rising 'tide of unreason' that must be stemmed (2004). In his introductory book *Heidegger* (1978) George Steiner faces the stormy collision of learned views: on the one hand, that Heidegger is 'a prolix charlatan and poisoner of good sense'; on the other, that he is 'a master of insight, a philosopher-teacher whose works may renew the inward condition of man' (13). 'The problem is more perplexing and inhibiting' than taking sides, Steiner notes (19): 'To "understand" Heidegger is to accept entry into an alternative order or space of meaning and of being' (18). Steiner compares the process to 'our gradual comprehension or "sufferance" of great poetry'. He concludes with a personal justification for making the attempt: that he has 'found Heidegger to be massively present and in the path of further thinking' (21) – in other words, unavoidable.

Historical reasons for having to deal with Heidegger are to be found in his massive influence on philosophy and criticism, which Steiner catalogues (12–13) – and, more immediately to us, his potent influence on computing since Terry Winograd and Fernando Flores published *Understanding Computing and Cognition* in 1986 and Lucy A. Suchman *Plans and Situated Actions* in 1987.[46] But as both works show, the relevance to computing comes by way of Heidegger's much broader contribution to our understanding of tools in general. That's where the argument lies.

In the pioneering commentary from which both Winograd and Flores and Suchman drew, *Being-in-the-World* (1991),[47] Hubert Dreyfus explains the core of the matter:

> Heidegger not only inverts the traditional interpretation that the disinterested attitude and the entities it reveals are more basic than the interested attitude and the entities it reveals, but he also changes the ontological question itself. It is no longer a question of which sorts of entities can be built up out of which other sorts of entities. This question makes sense only if ontology is a question of reduction, which assumes that entities are reducible to some basic substance or building blocks. (1991: 60)

In other words, Winograd and Flores comment, 'Practical understanding is more fundamental than detached theoretical understanding ... [W]e have primary access to the world through practical involvement with ... the world in which we are always acting unreflectively' (1986: 32). Hence manipulation is not simply another way of knowing objects when tools are involved, it is the primary way.

In their most basic, 'primordial' condition (*ursprünglich*), Heidegger declares, entities are known in the totality of our use or interaction with them. When a tool is in use, in the state Heidegger calls 'ready-to-hand' (*zuhanden*), it disappears or withdraws from us. We deal not with the tool but with the work we accomplish through it (*SZ*: 69/99). In practice, however, this totality of worker and work suffers occasional breakdown, from a failure of the tool, a distraction or other circumstances of use. Breakdown then results in a perceptual shift:[48] holistic 'circumspection' (*Umsicht*) becomes particularizing 'observation' (*Ansicht*), and the tool, no longer ready-to-hand but 'present-at-hand' (*vorhanden*), becomes a separate object with which we can deal analytically, perhaps improvingly, before returning to engaged use. Thus is the genesis of theoretical behaviour out of experiential (*SZ*: 360–1/411–13), when interested engagement *with* gives way to disinterested contemplation *of* the work.

Heidegger's radical inversion of priorities yields what might be termed a craftsman's philosophy, bringing inarticulate skill, exercised in concernful action (*Besorgen*), into the foreground. It repositions theory as an improving response to breakdown by means of which tool and work become once again ready-to-hand and their concernful action re-established. His examples are from the ordinary exercise of skill, but skilled action is no stranger to scientific or scholarly work, for example in the *Fingerspitzengefühl* of the experimenter, whether directly in the adjustment of apparatus or indirectly in the natural physicalism of his or her response, for example to a physically evocative display. Such skill has tended to be undervalued and so overlooked: in the sciences by what Hacking has called a 'theory-dominated philosophy' – and very much so in the humanities by a quieter relegation of method to the scholar's closet. Computing, as a skill-dependent practice, changes all that.

Winograd and Flores construe the progressive cycle of computing systems development in terms of the see-saw defined by experiential engagement and theoretical detachment. Motivated perhaps by the constructivist perspective of the engineer, they give 'the fundamental role of breakdown in creating the space of what can be said' – and so modelled – considerably stronger emphasis than in Heidegger (1986: 78). In other words, their reading yields not an applied philosophy but the beginnings of a philosophical computing, and so access to the centrality of failure and process in the epistemology of modelling.

Other strains of phenomenology contribute to a philosophy of modelling, though less directly. These include most notably the two other great practitioners, Edmund Husserl (1859–1938), Heidegger's teacher, and Maurice Merleau-Ponty (1908–61), who was strongly influenced by Husserl and studied Heidegger closely. I pass over these in silence, except for noting Husserl's significant influence on Kurt Gödel, whose reflections on the foundations of mathematics I consider in Chapter 4, and Merleau-Ponty's strong influence on Michael Polanyi, discussed in the following. I also leave to the reader exploration of the far more extensive importance of Heideggerian philosophy to computing system design, for which Winograd and Flores have provided the still definitive and highly influential sketch.

4.3 Tacit knowing

In *The Structure of Scientific Revolutions*, Thomas Kuhn argues that the paradigms of science 'need not even imply that any full set of rules exists': we may come up with rules, but paradigms work otherwise (1970/1962: 44). For support he points in a footnote to Michael Polanyi's eponymous philosophy of 'tacit knowledge', i.e. knowledge that goes without saying and thus is silent (L. *taceo*).[49]

Polanyi's concern is directly with the positivist's stumbling block, discovery. He argues along with Karl Popper that no rules can account for it; in principle they cannot verify or refute a proposed solution to a problem; and no theory can explicitly account for the guidance it affords to future discoveries. 'It appears then', he concludes, 'that scientific discovery cannot be achieved by explicit inference nor can its true claims be explicitly stated. Discovery must be arrived at by the tacit powers of the mind, and its content, so far as it is indeterminate, can be only tacitly known.' So where to find the elusive logic of discovery? Polanyi, echoing Merleau-Ponty's dictum that 'perception is a nascent *logos*' (1964/1947: 25), gives the phenomenologist's answer: '*We must turn to the example of perception*' (1969: 138).

Polanyi's central and brilliantly simple idea is that engagement with any tool means *attending from* it in an act of tacit knowing so that we may *attend to* the entity it comprehends, to which it makes ontological reference and so literally realizes (1983/1966: 10).[50] Thus the tool becomes transparent as we pass from a *focal* awareness, attending to it, to a *subsidiary* awareness, attending from it to the work (1969: 128). Referring to a common image of perception (to which I will return), he observes that '[t]he impact made by a probe or stick on our fingers is felt at the tip of the probe or stick, where it hits on objects outside, and in this sense the probe or stick is an extension of our fingers that grasp it' (1969: 127). The connection with prosthesis is obvious.[51]

For Polanyi tacit knowing is fundamental: we are always attending from things in order to grasp their participation in a comprehensive whole. Pure focal awareness is inconceivable, but a purely subsidiary awareness is normal in skilled use of tools (when, as Heidegger said, they are ready-to-hand). Once established, the vectored *from-to* relation between tool-in-use and object is durable, but (as in Heidegger) it can be broken, when by some cause we switch 'our attention from the meaning to which it is directed, back to the things that have acquired this meaning' (1969: 146). This 'see-saw of analysis and integration' is, Polanyi argues, the means by which we continually deepen our understanding of an entity, passing from comprehension of the whole to analysis of its parts and back again (1969: 129f.).

Polanyi (1891–1976), originally a physical chemist, differs from Heidegger, originally a student of theology, in his concern with scientific discovery, hence with the theoretical behaviour that in Heidegger is secondary. His focus, like the humanist scholar's, is as a result on understanding pre-existing entities, on *knowing that* as much or more than *knowing how*.[52] I will return to this point below.

Tacit knowing might seem to exclude the verbal arts, such as poetry, and in so doing to render criticism a misfit in the phenomenological model. Were that the case, the role of software as form of criticism would be unclear from the current perspective. Northrop Frye argues, however, that 'there is a most important sense in which poems are as silent as statues. Poetry is a *disinterested* use of words: it does not address a reader directly ... The axiom of criticism must be, not that the poet does not know what he is talking about, but that he cannot talk about what he knows' (1957: 4–5). Poems, like statues, are known tacitly.

4.4 Guesswork reasoning

Charles Sanders Peirce (1839–1914)[53] enters the story of modelling through the concept of *abduction* or *hypothesis*,[54] a form of reasoning by disciplined guesswork which 'proposes a conjecture that explains a puzzling or interesting phenomenon' (Hacking 1990: 207). 'From the time of his Harvard lectures of 1865', Hacking explains, 'Peirce consistently distinguished "three kinds of inference"': *deduction*, from a general law to particular instances of it; *induction*, from instances to such a law; and this third kind, which Gilbert Harman has happily named 'inference to the best explanation'.[55] Several terms for abduction or hypothesis are on offer,[56] but whichever is used the form of reasoning denoted by it is deeply familiar. Sherlock Holmes' detective craft provides a well-studied fictional example, Charles Darwin's principle of natural selection an historical one (he arrived at a very good explanation for the biological evidence that this evidence did not demand).[57] But these are merely two especially prominent cases. Gregory Bateson points out that we simply could not function in our daily lives without such ability to infer likely explanations, to be *good guessers*, though we may not be able to match Holmes' fictional genius. Nor could we function creatively in the arts, letters and sciences without it, as Bateson suggests (2002/1979: 133–5).

At the same time, if as Polanyi argued 'discovery cannot be achieved by explicit inference' (1969: 138), if tacit powers of the mind are required, then we have a further problem. Here modelling supplies one possible approach. The connection between abduction and modelling – between reasoning and manipulating – is hinted in Peirce's writings. But it has been explicitly worked out by Lorenzo Magnani, who argues that modelling is a form of abduction: disciplined inferential guesswork conducted in and through physical and quasi-physical processes of representation, and so a 'thinking *through* doing and not only, in a pragmatic sense, about doing' (2002: 309). Thus modelling amplifies those tacit powers of mind, and we are back with Heidegger's primacy of tools ready-to-hand. Magnani's brilliant term for it, 'manipulative abduction', may be the most compact definition we have. Magnani cites the action of diagramming as an instance. All sorts of semi- and quasi-physical manipulations with computers qualify.

The useful arguments tend to be about the natural sciences, but the disciplined guesswork that provides the broad context for manipulative abduction is just as central to the humanities. Thus the historian Carlo Ginzburg locates it in his essay 'Clues: Roots of an Evidential Paradigm' and explains its centrality:

> The quantitative and antianthropocentric orientation of natural sciences from Galileo on forced an unpleasant dilemma on the humane sciences: either assume a lax scientific system in order to attain noteworthy results, or assume a meticulous, scientific one to achieve results of scant significance ... The question arises, however, whether exactness of this type is attainable or even desirable for forms of knowledge most linked ... to all those situations in which the unique and indispensable nature of the data is decisive to the persons involved ... In such situations the flexible rigor (pardon the oxymoron) of the conjectural paradigm seems impossible to suppress. These are essentially mute forms of knowledge in the sense that their precepts do not lend themselves to being either formalized or spoken. (1989/1986: 124f.)

In Ginzburg's terms, modelling escapes this dilemma by fashioning 'meticulous' formalisms that then may be brought up against these 'mute forms of knowledge', hence severest rigour flexibly applied. 'In knowledge of this type', Ginzburg remarks, 'imponderable elements come into play: instinct, insight, intuition' (1989/1986: 125). The last of these, an 'instrument of conjectural knowledge' and a 'fundamental ability to infer causes from their effects', he identifies with 'the inference which Peirce called presumptive or abductive'.[58] He distinguishes 'a *low* from a *high* form' – the one 'based on the senses (though it skirts them)', the other a 'lightning recapitulation of rational processes'. Magnani's idea of a manipulative abduction allows us to identify modelling with this lower (i.e. embodied) form of intuition – and so, as suggested, to appropriate 'the flexible rigor ... of the conjectural paradigm' to the constrained actions of the modeller.

These actions are constrained because a model is precisely a set of constraints. A software model offers the advantage of constraints that are not only rigorous as logic but also external. Severest rigour is therefore an option. But the specific quality I wish to probe goes further than externality to the *independence* of the model and the modeller *from each other.* The independence of the modeller is a straightforward though crucial affair, as we have seen. It is, crucially, measured by the apophatic difference between what he or she knows, on the one hand, and can implement computationally, on the other. The independence of the model would seem, however, an altogether problematic notion. It claims more than objectivity, i.e. impartiality or detachment. Rather it answers to recent deconstructions of an absolute objectivity, in science, medicine, commerce and other areas,[59] by asking how far we can take the idea of a (semi-)autonomous intentional artifact.[60] The relevant research (to say nothing of the specialized and popular imaginings) is vast. I do not intend even to survey it here. Rather I offer a much more modest probing of what (semi-)independence of artifacts might mean in the humanities.

4.5 Fiction

If by nature a model is a conjectural artifact, then any *independence* it may have beyond mere separateness lies not in its status as an object nor, strictly speaking, as something made-by-art. Rather the place to look is in the conjecture: in its implicit encapsulation of a certain way or template for thinking and acting. In what sense, then, might a conjecture be independent?

What are we trying to do when we make a conjecture? Consider the following contrast, implied by Peirce, between two ways of reasoning from the data of experience: on the one hand, *induction*, a logical inference to a general law, etymologically a leading into (L. *induco*), with no implication of struggle; on the other hand, *conjecture*, an 'opinion offered on insufficient presumptive evidence', etymologically a collecting or throwing together of particulars (L. *coniectura*, fr. *conicio*) in an attempt to make sense of them, with its roots as much or more in divination and hermeneutics than in logic. Though we speak of 'inductive leaps', the point of contrasting induction with conjecture is to identify such events not as aberrations, perhaps inspired though certainly unaccountable in logic, but as indicating their own form of reasoning – presumptive, fictional, 'as if'. To conjecture is to pretend, to tell a story, literally to imagine, i.e. to form images in the mind of that which is not present. A conjecture is thus a kind of *fiction* in the etymological sense of something shaped, moulded, fashioned, made (L. *fictio*). Not all fictions are conjectural. Some are interpretative – equally made by narrative art, bearing family resemblance to less factually constrained fictions, but with different intentionality and trajectory.[61] Here I am interested in the conjectural kind because, as Max Black argues, models are just such fictions.[62] What kind of independence can such a fiction have?

The contribution of Hans Vaihinger's *The Philosophy of 'As If': a System of the Theoretical, Practical and Religious Fictions of Mankind* (1911, translated 1924) is to have sketched out the common ground of imagination shared by all fictive works and so by their corresponding disciplines. The value here is in particular to see the conjectural manipulatory approach we inherit from the natural sciences through modelling as a kind of narration or story-telling, as I have suggested, with the convergence of computing and criticism as one close possibility.[63] Vaihinger's philosophy anticipates what Laurens Laudan has called 'hypotheticalism' in the history of science: the idea, now culturally mainstream, that on the level of explanation 'the scientist must be content with hypothetical principles and conjectures rather than true and valid inductions'.[64] It accords with work in the humanities, in which fictions of one kind comment on fictions of another and are judged by their imaginative fruitfulness or (note the metaphor) their *viability*. They are not established by proof. Here a possibility for the independence of contingent, fictional artifacts arises.

4.6 Story-telling and knowledge-making

Fiction necessarily implies, let us note, a specific kind of impermanence: that of the provisional, since in the apocalyptic language of St Paul, 'when that which is perfect is come, then that which is in part shall be done away' (1 Cor 13:10). My emphasis on the contingent has been quite deliberate and repeatedly made to shift emphasis from the finality of answers to the open-endedness of questioning. But, short of the Apocalypse, this goes too far. Models *for* (or models *of* become models *for*) can in the interim be very robust, like fiction, and prove remarkably long-lasting by what they allow us to do. Note that this 'us' potentially extends far beyond the model-builder and fiction-maker to those who have had no part and may share few to no assumptions with the builders and makers.

Consider, for example, fictions whose duration is measured in decades to millennia, such as fundamental operating system design, the graphical user interface for human-computer interaction, Northrop Frye's archetypes of literature, Galilean science, great literature and the cultural envelopes of mythology.[65] These, in varying ways and to varying degrees, show the independence of the fictional in their ability to create imaginative spaces that become the reality within which people live productively and create other fictions. (The fate of those whose mythology has been destroyed by cultural collision does not undercut this reality, rather redefines what we mean by 'real'.) In the present case, for modelling, my point is that *questioning moves on from the ground solidified in the results provided by models*. This solidified ground is what we call 'real'. The clearest, easiest case to make is for the natural sciences, but other kinds of models solidify (in different senses) other kinds of ground.

In the sciences knowledge grows, as Jacob Bronowski has said, when we push back the boundaries of relevance (1978: 58–60). At least as far as physical entities are concerned, these boundaries appear to stay pushed back however we explain them, however our interests and ideas change. Hacking has suggested that the role of experiment in this pushing back is to transform hypothetical entities into real ones by gaining the ability to manipulate them (1983: 23–5, 262–75). 'Experimenting on an entity does not commit you to believing it exists', he argues. 'Only *manipulating* an entity, in order to experiment on something else, need do that' (1983: 263). Thus a transformation from a conjectured to an established entity through manipulation. One benefit of thinking in this way about the physical world is that we need not suppose either the crude positivist's pre-existing reality 'out there' to be discovered or the relativist's totally invented world, both of which are highly problematic notions.[66] The idea is much closer to Milton's conception of Chaos, part of which God redeemed to create the World. In Hacking's Miltonic view (if I may call it that) the gain is, as far as we can tell, permanent.

If our constructions continue to work no matter how violent the changes in learned opinion – 'once created, there is no reason except human backsliding why they should not continue to persist' (Hacking 1984: 119) – they also bring some part of their original intentionality, some trace of that opinion with them. Peter Galison makes the essential point, that 'there is a partial peeling away, an (incomplete) *disencumberance* of meaning that is associated with the transfer of objects' (1997: 436). Thus, for example, the KWIC (keyword-in-context) layout for concordances has survived its inventor's original purpose, the mechanical analysis of technical documents, and whatever ideas he may have had about language. At the same time it retains in its design the hugely influential notion that what we now call 'span' (the distance measured in words before and after the 'node', or target word) is far more important to meaning than other kinds of context.[67]

Span has more to tell us. In the KWIC design it represents its inventor's conjectural hypothesis or abductive inference that meaning may be determined to a significant degree by looking at the words on either side of a given word. Implemented in software, the KWIC model of meaning is then itself manipulated to investigate other properties of language. Does this hypothetical span thus become real? Certainly not (to use Hacking's example) in the way that the once hypothetical electron is known to be real.[68] But 'span' has proven to be a very fruitful construct, central to corpus linguistics and text-analysis as well as to numerous practical applications. In cognitive psychology the parallel idea that our ability to process information can be measured by the quantifiable bits of it which we are able to keep in mind, i.e. our 'attention span' (Miller 1956), has likewise become a stepping-stone. In both cases manipulating these spans, experimenting not on them but with them, would seem to make the hypothetical notion real *in the sense that knowledge of these kinds is real.*[69] Hence we come at last to an implication I have been pushing forward for the past few pages: that the term 'real' is relative to the discipline or form of life in which the term is used. I have cited Hacking's clear and subtle idea of *scientific* realism in order to give us something to think against (1983: 21–31). I will return to the important question of terminological relativism and to scientific realism in Chapter 3.3.

The question here, however, is: Do our conjectural models solidify, and if so in what sense? For the synthetic phase of scholarly work, they certainly do in the development of new scholarly genres – the meta-fictions with which to make our meta-theoretical statements. I explore this area of research and its working environment in the next chapter. For the analytic phase that has preoccupied us in this chapter, we need not claim to have knowledge as solid as bricks and would be foolish to do so, but there are advantages to being able, for example, to work with the body of literature as a created whole, having autonomy from our contingent views of it. Like Hacking's experimenter we seem clearly to make new knowledge by modelling *for* it from our conjectures.

4.7 Engineering

A complementary approach emerges out of current epistemology of engineering, for example Walter G. Vincenti's historically documented argument for the genesis of new knowledge out of the design and construction of innovative objects.[70] Briefly, his argument is that 'all genuine increases in knowledge ... take place by some form of a process of *blind variation and selective retention*'.[71] By 'blind' he means not random or unintelligent but 'without complete or adequate guidance'. Vincenti offers a common analogy by way of illustration, returning us to the example from Polanyi and to the phenomenological perspective.

An exploratory engineer, he suggests, is like an unaided blind man walking down an unfamiliar street with his cane, probing variously for objects and contours ahead, retaining those features useful to him.[72] Were we to give the man a cane, asking him to describe it, he might tell us, Dreyfus says in his commentary on Heidegger,

> that it is light, smooth, about three feet long, and so on ... But when the man starts to manipulate the cane, he loses his awareness of the cane itself; he is aware only of the curb (or whatever object the cane touches); or, if all is going well, he is not even aware of that, but of his freedom to walk, or perhaps only what he is talking about with a friend.

Dreyfus comes to the now familiar conclusion that 'when it is most genuinely appropriated equipment becomes transparent' (1991: 65), though not uninfluential in its particular characteristics. But the engineer's analogy serves us better if we press it further, beyond the phenomenologist's engaged action with occasional breakdowns and readjustments, to the gradually accumulating knowledge our blind man builds up from his walk – Polanyi's deepened understanding.

In the emerging history of engineering, Vincenti notes, 'technology appears, not as derivative from science, but as an autonomous body of knowledge, identifiably different from the scientific knowledge with which it interacts' (1990: 3–4). This history demonstrates that grasping the intellectual autonomy of engineering allows us to infer its epistemology from its practice and concrete achievements. What in fact happens in that practice is not a mechanical application of scientific laws, as if, impossibly, the blind man were to find his way *solely* on the basis of a pre-existing description. Rather it is a self-directed, non-derivative experimental process based on and developing in part from received knowledge, in part from the constraints of the physical materials in use, in part from experience. What results is not a new law, a confirmation of or failure to falsify an old one but – here the analogy breaks down – a functioning real-world object, to some degree bearing, as noted, the intentionality of its maker. People use it, but at the same time it communicates embodied ideas or ways of forming and entertaining them.

4.8   Review

Heidegger's phenomenological cycle, as I have sketched it, depicts an engagement with tools useful to our understanding of computational modelling in the humanities but incomplete from that perspective in one crucial respect: it has no place for an object of scholarship. It is concerned, as his example of the hammer shows, with making new things rather than investigating old ones. To use Rorty's terms, his is the 'poetic' style of philosophical thought in contrast to Polanyi's Husserlian 'scientistic' style (1991: 9). Polanyi, thinking like a scientist, formulates his philosophy of tacit knowing to admit such an object. His argument that our understanding is deepened by *attending from* it accords well with Hacking's that by learning how to manipulate a hypothetical object we make it real. Vincenti's engineer similarly progresses (in his metaphorical account, feelingly like the blind man) to innovative objects and practical knowledge. This is the path of manipulative abduction.

In comparison to the objects of study in most of the modern sciences, artifacts in the humanities are encountered in a more or less direct way. For practical reasons there are many exceptions (e.g. transcripts or reproductions of manuscripts, digests of widely scattered historical data, lexicon entries), but as Ginzburg notes 'the unique and indispensible nature of the data is decisive to the persons involved', and so as a matter of priority humanists tend strongly to define their scholarship first in relation to the minute particularity of originals.[73] To paraphrase Polanyi, we somehow know more about our artifacts than we can tell in explicit form (1983/1966: 4–5). So we always need that access and begin with whatever it has told us, assuming our initial knowledge, giving it up as experience with the model persuades us otherwise. It can do so, I have noted, in theoretically trivial though consequential ways, e.g. by fetching an overlooked instance or bringing together identical forms. It does so more interestingly by way of the two gifts of computing: apophasis, defining what Collingwood called 'our ignorance of some definite thing', and manipulability, giving us contact with the sensorial and pragmatic apparatus on which cognition relies. So the Heideggerian primacy of concernful engagement can have more to tell us than what we have supposed direct access to entail. I will illustrate the point with my model of personification, discussed below.

The purposeful simplification of modelling implies that models conceal when they reveal. Warnings are common in the literature. 'Among the intellectual sins,' Joseph Gani has said, 'possibly the greatest is an unwarranted reliance on models as a substitute for reality; this often leads to dire practical results.'[74] All devices of thought share this sin in proportion to their intellectual power, but by the phenomeno-logical argument physical models and implements are especially per-ilous. Thus Arno Goudsmit observes that 'it is the usage of a model as a tool for perceiving an essence behind observational data' which renders it invisible, obscuring the fact that 'the model originally was a meaning that [the modeller] assigned to his data. The formal apparatus ... instead of being a mere representation of the natural system, has obtained a status comparable to that of the blind man's stick', by means of which the researcher has contact with the object of study, deals with and relates to it (1998: 93). The primacy of data to the sci-ences and of originals to the humanities answers the danger, though the sciences as a whole are much more dependent on the reliability of instruments – and the made solidity of once conjectural ground.

5 Modelling personification

In the introduction to this chapter I briefly summarized a research project in which I have modelled the literary trope of personification from specific instances of it in Ovid's *Metamorphoses*. The following presents the details of my project in order to illustrate the argument of this chapter.

Some initial qualifications relating to this example will explain the unfinished form in which you find it. Modelling is performative. An example of it, as here, frames an historical sequence of events that in the telling *as a story*, with a plot and outcome already known, loses some to all of its exploratory character and all of its tacit elements. The slow, sometimes erratic, sometimes serendipitous development is streamlined. Steps connected by what for the sake of convenience I will call a 'tacit logic' falsely seem to have an explicit one. Much of what is omitted is, of course, not worth telling (though perhaps well worth having done, perhaps even essential), and is better described in philo-sophical terms, as I have. But the topic demands an example of labora-tory practice. In this one I have tried to preserve the raggedness of the actual work by arresting the process of modelling at a point sufficiently well developed that it can be persuasive yet with enough imperfections to raise a number of unanswered questions for research.

Two brief prefaces are required: one to give the background literary history and theory, the other to introduce the artifact of study, Ovid's classical Latin poem, *Metamorphoses*. Then follows a description of the model.

5.1 Personification[75]

The imaginative act of creating a person by rhetorical means (L. *persona* 'person' + *facio* 'make') is so fundamental to human language that we cannot but do it at some level in all or nearly all speech-acts, whether demotic or literary.[76] Personification, Paul de Man has declared, is 'the master trope of poetic discourse' (Paxson 1994: 1). It has been studied in the Western literary and philosophical tradition since the ancient Greek rhetoricians, for whom it was an essential tool of public speaking. Although its most obvious form, the fully developed, anthropomorphic 'personification character', is now rarely evident in literature or the arts, it was a principal feature in European culture from the time of Prudentius (348–ca.410) until roughly the beginning of the last century and is as fundamental to an understanding of that culture as de Man's sentence would indicate. Although unavoidable in language, it is also common to modern discursive prose in ways that deserve study.

Critical attention to the trope is ancient, but a critical approach amenable to computational modelling was not proposed until 1963, by the medievalist Morton W. Bloomfield, likely because of his deep interest in linguistics and the new methods of the time, such as transformational grammar (Paxson 1994: 31). He suggested that personification should be studied at the microscopic level, 'grammatically', as a phenomenon brought about by discernible operations of language. Despite a flurry of interest in Bloomfield's idea, apparently no attempt (apart from my own) has been made to formulate such a grammar by detailed study of a major literary text.[77]

The key to Bloomfield's approach is his simple but fundamental observation that nothing is personified *independently of its context*, only when an ontologically unusual quality is predicated of it. This emphasis on the act of predication makes ontological change-of-state the defining feature. Two important corollaries follow. The first is uncertainty. Because language is a subtle and variable instrument and 'context' impossible to define precisely – it can mean anything from an adjacent word to the body of literature as a whole – it is seldom if ever possible to agree absolutely on whether a particular entity is personified (Davie 1981: 92). The second corollary is instability. Because predication is central, its loss means the quick if not immediate lapse of the entity back into its original state. (How long the effect lasts and why some appear to last longer than others is a question encountered in the modelling, as we will see.) Personification thus cannot be treated uniformly throughout a poetic text: every instance must be examined on its own merits. But those merits must include how the entity is treated elsewhere, in the same work or in the literature beyond it. If it has a history of personification, then that must be taken into account.

Bloomfield's emphasis on the momentary, ontological dimension of the trope *as a linguistic event* rather than the temporal, narratological one *as a technique of story-telling* leads to a fundamental problem with personifications that endure (Paxson 1994: 30f.). I will return to this problem later.

Two important implications follow from grammaticalization: first that we should be able to resolve the personifying context into discrete contributory factors, second that these should have a uniform syntax. Hence we have the basis for a computational model comprising factors and rules for determining whether any particular combination reaches some arbitrary threshold. This is, in effect, a grammar in Noam Chomsky's early sense.[78] It is not a theory of personification but an emergent opportunity for modelling because of the radical simplifications: context cannot, as far as we know, be thus resolved, and therefore no completely satisfactory syntax can be described. But the reality can be progressively approximated, resulting in better, harder questions as to what exactly we are reacting to.

5.2 The *Metamorphoses*

The *Metamorphoses* of the Roman poet Publius Ovidius Naso (43 BC–13 AD) is a challenging test-bed on which to try out the grammatical hypothesis. Not only does Ovid provide a fecund environment for personification, but he evidently also evokes personifications with great literary skill and subtlety. Indeed, the trope is one of his principal instruments for depicting the world as he imagined it. That depiction has been hugely influential since his own time. Its importance to us is indicated by the fact that, as the poet Ted Hughes recently wrote, 'by now, many of the stories seem inseparable from our unconscious imaginative life' (1997: viii). Puzzled by the power of its influence, Hughes gravitates to its incendiary thematic core, passion. No theme more engages us than that, but as the novelist Toni Morrison observes in a very different context, 'There is really nothing more to say – except why. But since *why* is so difficult to handle, one must take refuge in *how*' (1970: 9).

A partial answer is to be found in the poet's disturbing but irresistible undermining of fixed ontology, which of course befits a work explicitly centred on change of form. Very little if anything is what it seems, and whatever that may seem to be does not persist for long. Personification, which by nature violates ontology, is apt for this undermining. Ovid deploys the trope not so much at the narrative level of personified characters, such as *Invidia* (Envy), rather more at the microscopic level to which Bloomfield drew attention. James J. Paxson explains that all personifications begin and a great majority of them end as 'personification figures' – highly localized, momentary ontological tremors, often lasting no more than a single line of poetry, often subliminal in their effect (1994: 35). Being so brief, they seldom have a chance to acquire human form; thus they are anthropo*centric* but rarely anthropo*morphic*. To do justice to them we are compelled to redefine the trope generally as a shift not merely *to* the human state but also *towards* it, however slight the change. Although arriving at an exact count of them in the *Metamorphoses* is impossible by definition (and may be seriously misleading if we naturalize any criterion), a total number in the range of 500–600 is not unreasonable. In contrast there are only a handful of personified characters in the *Metamorphoses*.

5.3   Modelling the trope

The modelling project described below began as part of a long-term effort to construct an *Analytical Onomasticon to the Metamorphoses of Ovid*, i.e. an extensive set of indexes to all linguistic devices by which persons are named in the poem.[79] In what later turned out to be the first stage in this modelling, I constructed a phenomenology or systematic description of the trope based on minute, recursive examination of a large number of possible instances across the entire poem. Initially I compiled a somewhat educated but unsystematic and doubtless idiosyncratic listing of candidates together with linguistic, literary and broadly contextual elements likely to be responsible.[80] I refined this listing by dint of numerous comparisons and re-examinations. Several passes through the 12,000 lines of hexameter were required even to discover what the causative factors might be and to assess their relative importance. Throughout these passes and several more I strove always to identify *every* factor responsible and to make certain that in *every* case factors and groups of them behaved in as close to a totally consistent way as possible. Hence the need for recursion. The end result is the phenomenology given in Figure 1.1.

As defined in Figure 1.1, a personification is said to happen when an entity is invested with 'a human imaginative component'. The reason for this circumlocution rests with the two groups or kinds identified below: not only those explicitly personified, by specific contextual

I. **Definition**

Any rhetorical act that transgresses normal ontology by investing an entity with a human imaginative component, whether or not the result is anthropomorphic.

II. **Major groups**

  A. **Implicitly** personified (purely fictitious creatures)

  B. **Explicitly** personified (personifications proper)

III. **Contexts**

  A. **Onomastic** : association with an established person (e.g. *sol* with Phoebus); frequent personification elsewhere (*terra, cupido*)

  B. **Narrative** (nature of the individual story and broader narrative context)

  C. **Poetic- mythological** associations (*terra* with earth-goddess; lively movement of water)

  D. **Ontological** (ease of personification inversely related to anthropomorphic distance, e.g. abstractions requiring the least effort)

  E. **Personal** (attributable to the proximity of a person with 'magical' powers, e.g. Orpheus, Medea)

IV. **Local factors**

  A. Strong (capable of personifying alone)

    1. **Apostrophe** (direct address to the entity, response not required)

    2. **Familial relationship**

    3. **Locution** (speech by the entity)

    4. **Mental activity** (emotion, cognition, volition expressed or implied)

  B. Weak (requiring one or more other factors for personification)

    1. **Action**

    2. **Body-part**

    3. **Parallel** (to a person or personified entity)

    4. **Possession**

    5. **Quality/role**

    6. **Self-reference**

Figure 1.1: A phenomenology of personification

factors, but also entities (e.g. Phoebus' flying, fiery horses) that are partially or wholly imaginary. These are taken as personified by their imaginative (hence human-like) nature. Both kinds were included in the modelling exercise.

There were some surprises, for example the relatively weak role played by verbs, on which Bloomfield had laid great stress. Difficult research problems were also uncovered but not pursued, especially by the five denoted 'contexts'. It became apparent, however, that such a descriptive account, though highly suggestive and useful as a guide to encoding entities as personifications for the *Onomasticon*, has very serious limitations. As a statement of results we can place it within the cycle of modelling in a broad sense, as a 'model' *of* the phenomenon and *for* its detailed encoding, but despite both its origins and its purpose, the phenomenology is hardly a computational model. Formally it is reductive and fixed: abstracted, therefore distant from the actual data, not well suited to record qualifying detail and so not manipulable in any meaningful sense. Nor, in fact, is the computationally encoded text a model in my sense. For all practical purposes, given the massive amount and complexity of detail for a microscopic phenomenon across 12 000 lines of text, it is likewise fixed. Furthermore, without software that does not yet exist, mark-up itself provides in general no means of automatically imposing uniform rules on minute local judgements and so no truly systematic way of discovering the limitations of these rules.

I concluded that however well the phenomenology and its corresponding mark-up may be done, these actually represent only a minor step towards the potential that computing holds for Bloomfield's hypothesis, the trope it seeks to explain and the *Metamorphoses*. Indeed, as Jerome McGann has suggested in his criticism of current efforts, the result fails to realize the theoretical potential on which such work is based, and this failure in turn points to the need for a dynamical, decentred approach – that is, for modelling.[81]

The mechanism for modelling that I adopted consists of a relational database, represented by the diagram in Figure 1.2, and a spreadsheet front-end, which generates the graphical display shown in Figure 1.3. Results from the database are generated by a set of queries and automatically imported into the spreadsheet, where a few crucial adjustments are made. The model in its current state is described below and is accessible online.[82]

A wide variety of personification candidates were recorded in the trial dataset: abstractions (e.g. *fortuna* and *fors*, 'fortune, luck'); static natural objects, both living and non-living (*flores* 'flowers', *terra* 'earth',

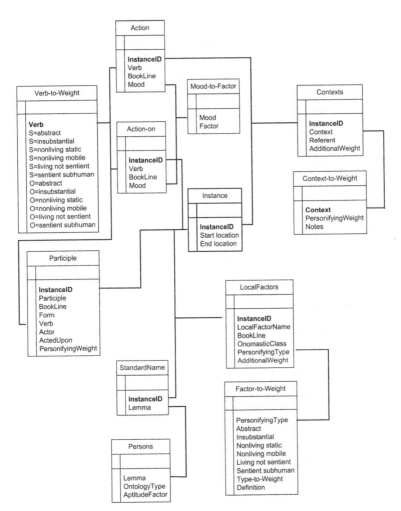

Figure 1.2:   Database structure for modelling personification

arbores 'trees'); moving natural objects (*amnes* 'rivers', *aurae, venti* 'breezes, winds'); animals (*anguae* 'snakes'). Included were a few body-parts, such as Philomela's tongue and Hercules' hands; implements, such as spears and missiles (*hastae, tela*). One personification character (the river-god Inachus) and one instance of supernatural creatures (the fire-breathing horses of Phoebus) were added to test the robustness of the model for lengthy personifications and entities personified by definition.

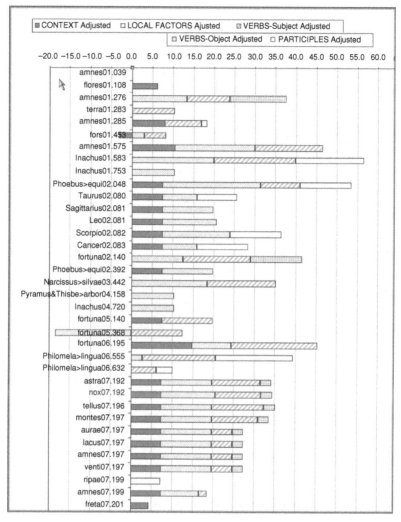

Figure 1.3:   Chart of selected personifications

5.3.1   The database

The database design, with entities, attributes and relationships, is shown in Figure 1.2.[83] The INSTANCE table at the centre assigns a unique identifier to each occurrence of personification – its INSTANCEID, which is used throughout the database. The STANDARDNAME table, below and to the left, correlates this ID to an onomastic lemma, which in the

PERSONS table is given an OntologyType. (More about this in a moment.) The remaining tables in Figure 1.2 form three groups: (a) CONTEXTS and CONTEXT-TO-WEIGHT, above and to the right; (b) LOCALFACTORS and FACTOR-TO-WEIGHT, below and to the right; and (c) ACTION, ACTION-ON, PARTICIPLE, MOOD-TO-FACTOR and VERB-TO-WEIGHT, to the left and above. These groups thus implement the 'contexts' and 'local factors' named in Figure 1.1, separating the verbs for more detailed attention. In each group, the personifying factor is assigned a 'weight', i.e. an arbitrary integer-value from 1 to 10 that denotes the interpreter's provisional sense of how strongly this factor affects the candidate entity. Thus, for example, in book 1, line 578, the rivers (*amnes* or *flumina*) that come to the river-god Peneus, father of Daphne, are said not to know (*nescia*) whether to congratulate or console him. In the LOCALFACTORS table this occurrence of *nescia* for the InstanceID 'amnes01.575' is recorded as the PersonifyingType 'cognition'. Since the personifying force of attributing any such factor depends on the kind of entity in question, the ontology of the entity must be taken into account. Hence the OntologyType for these rivers, 'nonliving mobile', is fetched from the PERSONS table and used to select the appropriate weight out of the the FACTOR-TO-WEIGHT table for the factor 'cognition'. (Clearly saying that a non-living entity does not know whether to do one thing or another is to personify it, so a weight of 10 is assigned.) This weight is then exported to the spreadsheet front-end where it is summed together with all the other weights relevant to the given instance. A graphical display of their total effect is then generated, as in Figure 1.3, to which I will return in detail.

Note that although all weights are arbitrarily assigned, each such assignment of a weight to a factor, such as to 'cognition' for a 'nonliving mobile' entity, applies to all occurrences uniformly. A degree of objectivity is thus achieved by enforcing a total, absolute consistency. How this works should become clear in the following.

The complexity of verbal action is only partially modelled in the current version; grammatical tense, for example, is not – but possibly should be. (Does tense influence the strength of a personification? It seems plausible to suppose that it might, but the consequences of such influence for personification in the *Metamorphoses* remain to be determined by experiment.) The subjects and objects of verbs are distinguished by the tables for ACTION when the entity is subject and ACTION-ON when it is object. Participles have been given their own table to allow for the quite different effect the participial form of a verb can have.[84] Mood-to-Factor records grammatical mood, assigning a modifying integer-value to each mood (indicative, subjunctive, imperative) so that the different effects on a personification may be taken into account. (Consider, for example, the differences between a declaration that a tree moves to hear Orpheus sing, a wish that it might or a command that it do so.) Note that different weights are assigned in Verb-to-Weight according to the effect of the verb on its subject (S=) or its object (O=).

One of the earliest discoveries to come from a breakdown in the preliminary model was the now obvious fact that the effect of all factors is in relation to the initial ontology of the candidate, as I pointed out earlier in my example. (Thus, again, attributing movement to the trees charmed by Orpheus is sufficient to personify them, but attributing it to a river or a breeze is not. Only the tree's ontology is violated.) As shown, the database implements OntologyType partially, only for 'local factors' (immediate attributes of a candidate entity) and for verbs and participles; the broader contexts, recorded in the Contexts table, remain to be brought under the ontological scheme.

Completing the implementation of ontological dependence would address some but not all of the remaining need for special pleading – in the form of additional weights added to achieve a reasonable result from the final calculation. The AdditionalWeight attribute in the Contexts table is such a provision for special pleading that needs to be eliminated to achieve desired consistency. In the current design it is needed, for example, to inflect individual occurrences of the contextual factors I have called 'parallel' and 'group'. Both refer to situations in which the target entity is connected by narrative to one or more persons nearby or to other candidates.[85] Since some of these reinforce while others detract, positive or negative weights specific to each instance are required. The imperative for consistency, however, forces the conclusion that neither 'parallel' nor 'group' should be a factor in the model, at least not as currently conceived. When, for example, *fors ignara* 'blind chance' and *saeva cupidinis ira* 'savage anger of desire' are weighed as causes for Phoebus' love of Daphne (1.452f.), the very weakly personified abstraction *fors* pulls in one direction, the strongly personified *cupido* in the other. Although Cupid is clearly a personification character in the poem at this point, it would certainly not be out of character for the poet to be ever so slightly undermining his status, nor to be undercutting our expectation for the rarely if ever personified *fors*, and so creating an ontological resonance that is itself subversive. As seems true overall, the parallelism, then, is a structural conduit rather than a factor. Development of the model requires a comprehensive look at all such examples.

Such adjustments to accommodate special pleading are in effect concessions to ignorance, but more importantly they are clues: to an as yet undiscovered factor, one in need of refinement, a structural difficulty in the database or simply a misreading. Recording one's impressions case-by-case, if done systematically, has value, but the objective here is to develop a *context-independent* grammar so that in every case the final result is determined solely by factors whose weights remain the same wherever they occur. This not only spurs development of the model as just described and makes the modelling more convenient, it also introduces the tendency for assigned weights increasingly to reflect the poet's usage. In the development of the database a number of revisions were in fact prompted by the ongoing attempt to purge it of special pleadings.

A phenomenon closely related to parallel and group is the stereotype, for example when *fortuna* is said to help Perseus in a fight, *dumque manum fortuna iuvat, Clytiumque Clanique ... diverso vulnere fudit,* 'and while fortune helped his hand, [Perseus] killed Clytius and Clanis with different wounds' (5.140f.). Here the stereotypical help given to an ally in battle obviously strengthens *fortuna*'s case, but the stereotype-form as such is a conduit: different stereotypes will have different effects. Here what would seem to be required is categorization of stereotypes, each member of which is its own contextual factor.

Framing qualifications are unevenly accommodated. The subjunctive mood of verbs, as we have seen, qualifies their weight, but similes, counterfactuals and conjecturals are as yet untouched. Nor is it entirely clear how they should be treated, and if simply by an attenuating factor, by how much. The former question is, of course, the more serious, as once a manner of treatment is implemented, the degree is a matter for experiment to determine by adjusting the assigned value. An example of this kind of problem is the apostrophe or direct address of a person to a candidate entity, as when Narcissus, lamenting his unrequited love for his own reflected image, speaks to the trees: *'equis, io silvae, crudelius' inquit 'amavit? / scitis enim et multis latebra opportuna fuistis ...'* 'Did anyone, o ye woods, ever love more cruelly than I? You know, for you have been the convenient haunt of many lovers ...' (3.142f.).

Personification of the trees *in his mind* might be read as an indication of his loosening mental grip (hence a qualified personification for us) – or a sign of the nature of the world, as it is when the poet is the implicit speaker. If we decide to attenuate such personifications – after all, the presumption or delusion that something hears speech is not quite the same thing as an attested hearing – what do we do about narrative intercalation? Is a personification nested within several levels more or less of a personification? Is a story within a story within a story less credible than a story within a story? Is its credibility affected by the identity of the story-teller?

The six-level ontology currently implemented in the database is also a site for breakdown and hence for more theorizing. As noted earlier, it is applied irrespective of context. How, then, do we treat weapons (*telum, ferum &al.*), for example, as candidates for personification? Are they, in terms of the current model, 'nonliving static' (like a tree) to denote their condition most of the time, and so possibly affected ontologically when in flight or thrust, or are they 'nonliving mobile' (like a river), since following Heidegger we regard them as primordially themselves only when in use? Consider the very specific context in which Cephalus, thinking a noise in fallen leaves is caused by a beast, hurls his *telum* and kills his wife Procris (7.840f.). The situation is quite odd. Earlier, with the help of an oestrous goddess whom he had spurned, he attempted to trick Procris into betraying him by pretending to be someone else and was triumphant when her fidelity faltered for an instant; here he is talking to the (feminine gendered) breeze as if she were a lover. Hence the status of *this* spear, especially given the consequences of its 'concernful use', is of considerable interest of a specific kind. Is a finer set of divisions in the ontology called for, another as yet unidentified factor – or a more radical revision of the entire scheme?

My point, again, is to note the circumstances of modelling under which such questions are asked. In some of these the model can be improved, in others perhaps not, but even catastrophic breakdown does not imply an epistemological waste of time, as long as good questions come of it.

5.3.2 *The spreadsheet front-end*

The function of the spreadsheet is to sum the weights for each instance, make a few global adjustments and display the results graphically, as in Figure 1.3. Changes in the database automatically update the spreadsheet and chart, so that the software comprises an interactive modelling environment.

INSTANCEID is sent to the spreadsheet along with weights for all categories: context, local factors, verbs (subject and object) and participles. The weights for each category are then summed and displayed as distinct data series on a bar-chart. The result is that for each entity, a single bar with segments corresponding to the categories is displayed. Initial experiments demonstrated quickly in the graphical display that modelling personification linearly (i.e. graphing simply the arithmetic sum of the weights) ill accords with a reasonable sense of the phenomenon. Rather, the impression one gets, plausible even in the abstract, is of a rapid increase to the point at which one might recognize the personification as significant, then a gradual levelling off, after which additional weight has a sharply diminishing effect other than to maintain a steady-state.

Since numerical quantities are involved, the question of how to model this impression is a matter initially of finding a mathematical function whose curve has the right characteristics. I began by expressing my kinaesthetic reaction to these ontological shifts as a curve. (Note well the engagement of perceptual memory here, consistent with a phenomenological account of modelling.) Sketches, described to a colleague, elicited his suggestion that I should be modelling a saturation rather than a linear accumulation, i.e. 'the action of charging, or the state of being charged, up to the limit of capacity' (OED 3a).[86]

A common way to proceed at this point is to use one or more plausible analogies to systems for which such functions are known, then apply those functions in modelling the phenomena of interest. Once the right effect is produced, one begins to work with the analogy, testing its strength and seeing what kinds of questions it raises about the target system.

Saturation in fact provides a number of analogies to well-studied physical, chemical, biological, neurological and behavioural systems. These, like personification, not only display a certain capacity or maximum response but also respond in a non-linear, progressively dampening way to an increasing load put on them. (In mathematical terms, that is, they are characterized by a hyperbolic curve.) Figure 1.4 shows the curves generated from the equations for two of these, one electrical and the other biological. As you can see, both of these describe responses apparently similar to what one might imagine (or *feel*) for the accumulation of personifying weight. In both cases the curves can be adjusted dynamically more or less as required. What can we learn from them?

As long as the function produces a curve with the intuitively right shape, it can be used as the basis for testing individual judgements and for experiment with various modifying factors. Two of these factors are currently implemented in the spreadsheet. The first, NARRATIVE FACTOR,

66

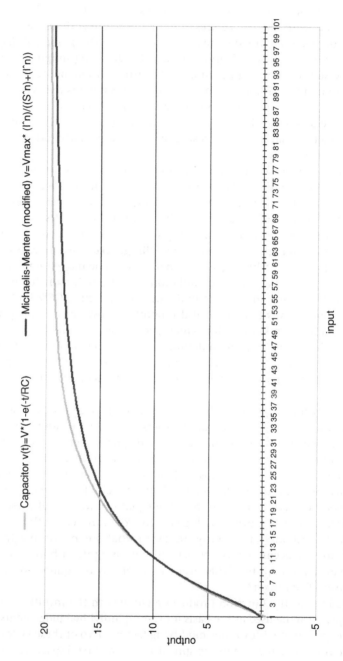

Figure 1.4: Two models of saturation

takes account of whether the candidate occurs as simply factual within the poetic world, is implicitly qualified by occurring within quoted speech, e.g. as what someone says they saw, or even further as part of a clearly unsupported claim. The second, APTITUDE FACTOR, adjusts for the aptitude of the candidate, increasing the overall score if it is especially well attested as a personification in the literature, decreasing the score if it is rarely personified. In the first case it is not at all obvious that quoted speech or unsupported claim should be allowed to make a difference; rather the factor is there to see what happens when one does. The second is supported by the reasonable presumption that frequent personification outside the *Metamorphoses* is significant for the behaviour of an entity within it, but how much of a difference it should make is unknown.

Being so similar the two curves do not give us any basis for choice. Rather we need to look to the analogies on which they are based, *attending to* each so that we may ask how it illuminates the literary-critical phenomenon in question. Thus once again Polanyi's epistemological see-saw: on the one hand, each analogy, through its mathematical function and the display it generates, allows us to attend from the analogical model to the behaviour of personification; on the other, each analogy pushes us to ask whether personification is actually like this or that aspect of the analogical system. Examples follow.

The first of the two analogies I examine here is to the saturation of a capacitor, a device capable of storing electrical energy.[87] Since a capacitor is charged only by a steady flow of current, time is the variable. As the device 'fills up', its resistance to further charge (i.e. 'impedance') increases, with the result that less and less energy is stored, as the chart shows. Eventually it reaches a full charge. As long as the current is maintained, so is the charge, but if the current is switched off, it gradually dissipates – or is suddenly discharged if the circuit is completed, e.g. by crossing the wires.

The hyperbolic response of the capacitor and the flexibility of the modelling function make the analogy quite reliable in its application. But, again, stepping back from it and probing its entailments is how the real power of the analogy is tapped. For capacitance several of these entailments are problematic. (Again, note carefully how working out the entailments of the analogy illuminates or defines what we think about personification.) Thus the analogy stipulates a steady build-up of undifferentiated energy maintained by continued input, gradually dissipated by cessation of it or triggered to discharge by a change in the circuit. Likening the personifying factors to a transforming energy is not a problem, but personifying energy seems highly differentiated: there are several different kinds of it, as the phenomenology makes clear. Nor does it come at a steady rate, but in the flow of the Latin verse here and there, often both before and after the entity-word, or 'out of the blue', from the reader's store of literary and cultural knowledge. In other words, we are driven to ask, what actually happens on the microscopic level when a person is made by a combining of words and ideas? Perhaps it does not matter how this happens, but the question is genuine – and, as far as I know, unanswered.

The transforming event of capitance is discharge: a sudden release of the stored energy caused by some trigger. This is an attractive metaphor, but in the application it can play no role. The transformation is, rather, modelled by setting some arbitrary threshold value (as noted earlier, this is 10). Yet at the same time, the graphical display suggests by nature a continuum – that there is *no such threshold except as a function of how sensitively we read*. If this is so – I take it as a research question to be pursued – then the graphical display represents a genuinely more accurate form of representing and so thinking about linguistic personification than any kind of representation we have had before.

The second of the two analogies answers to the perceptual turn in the discussion. It is actually to a large group of biological and biologically based phenomena, including demographics, ecology, epidemics and sensory perception.[88] These are united by common application of the so-called Michaelis–Menten equation, originally derived to model the state-change by which a 'substrate' interacting with a catalytic enzyme is converted into another substance.[89] This equation describes the initial hyperbolic response of a system to an increasing amount of substrate. Subsequently it has been altered to model many other kinds of biological behaviour, for example response of the eye to light. This is an interesting case from the perspective of modelling because it illustrates how a model can be adapted to serve very different problems. In the modified equation,[90] the intensity of light hitting the eye is substituted for the amount of substrate. This is done by analogy: as substrate is changed into a product in the original system, so light is converted into electrical energy in the new one. Thus the model survives translation to the macroscopic level of sensory behaviour from the microscopic level of enzyme kinetics on which that behaviour depends. These kinetics, which in the original model are described in some detail, can be left to take care of themselves while we study a higher-order phenomenon that behaves in an analogical way.

The translated version is useful for modelling personification because, as with the capacitor, it allows us to formulate an analogy at the right level of detail: as light impacts on the eye, producing a sensory impression (measured as an electrical signal), so rhetorical factors affect a receptive candidate, resulting in a personification. With personification the actual event is in the reader's mind. The analogy, then, offers us the not unattractive option of interpreting the candidate metaphorically as an organ of perception – a mind's eye – and so implying identification of the reader with the candidate. Furthermore, the sensory-response model implicates the lower-level system originally studied by Michaelis and Menten, who posited an unstable, intermediate stage of interaction between enzyme and substrate, out of which the product comes. Hence a lower-level possibility for the interaction of linguistic and contextual factors with candidate entities. Once again we are driven to ask what actually happens on the microscopic level of personification. This time, however, we are offered the notion of a catalytic agent which briefly interacts with the incoming stimulus to generate the perception. What, analogically, is the catalyst? It must be the candidate entity itself, which remains itself yet triggers the perception of an ontological disturbance – which is not the entity itself but our perception of it.

The sensory response model has at least two additional advantages over the capacitance model: the stimulating agent, light, is measured by intensity, not duration, and nothing in the former model prevents there being multiple sources of light of different kinds, acting more or less at the same time, with differing individual effects.

A widely applicable biological model, especially given its perceptual form, is *prima facie* much closer to the responses of a human reader than the capacitor. But care must be taken with the conclusions we draw from closeness of this kind. Immediately the concern must be to find the most powerful heuristic tool for generating questions from the phenomenon. Thus initially analogies are selected by their display of hyperbolic behaviour to accord with a definite but ill-defined sense of it. Then each is held up for consideration with the question, 'Is personification like this?' Analogies and disanalogies that lead to the best, most fruitful questions tell us which tool to adopt. But at the same time, if by such analysis we could begin to demonstrate a strong connection between low-level perceptual mechanisms and the reader's high-level perception of our literary trope, then we could put a stronger lens on the role of creative factors in reading.

5.3.3   *Fundamental remaining problems*

Throughout my discussion of the example, the model of personification has included two simplifying assumptions which must at least
be recognized as problematic: that personifying factors do not interact
with each other, and that the duration of a personifying event may be
ignored.

As long as we can read the personifying force of the factors involved
as neither produced nor significantly affected by an interaction
between them, the first of these is not a problem, hence we can treat
this force as simply additive input to the function that models saturation. But can we do this in all cases – indeed, should we be doing it at
all? It is plausible that we should not. Some cases suggest a significant
interaction between factors, for example when one selects for a personifying sense of another (if that is what happens). The death of
Hyacinthus provides an instance. He is killed by Phoebus' rebounding
discus: *dura repercusso subiecit verbere tellus / in vultus, Hyacinthe, tuos ...*,
'the hard earth, returning the blow, hurled it up into your face,
Hyacinthus' (10.184). Here one might argue that the force of the verb
subiecit (hurled up) simultaneously personifies *tellus* and selects for the
particular sense of the adjective *dura* ('cruel' rather than 'physically
hard') that in turn also personifies *tellus*. The fundamental problem
raised here concerns the generation of meaning in language and so
points to another dimension of modelling.

The second assumption is inherited with Bloomfield's linguistic and
philological idea of personification, which as Paxson has suggested
does progressively less well as the momentary personification figure
extends into the narrative and becomes a personification character. In
fact the extending into narrative has, at least in the *Metamorphoses*,
several different forms: the character who extends over many lines but
remains clearly unrealistic (e.g. Invidia, 'envy'); the same but a fully
realized and quite plausible character (Inachus); the originally
personified character who is so well developed and integral to the narrative that he or she is accepted as an equal of any anthropomorph –
until depersonified (Cupido, 'desire'). The personification of Inachus
(lamenting father of Io, who was raped by Jupiter) suggests the possibility that factors should record not only force but also persistence, e.g.
for ontological declaratives such as the anthropocentric title *pater*
'father' and attributes such as human body-parts and related phenomena, such as Inachus' tears. But more fundamentally, perhaps, persistence may simply denote having or being part of a story, at minimum
the distinct capacity of some words to imply stories, as for example

'father' implies the story of fatherhood or 'Theseus' his story. Indeed, the boundary between referring to a story and telling one is impossible to fix except arbitrarily, so measuring persistence in the text of the *Metamorphoses* by number of lines or other metric must be qualified – but how? In other words, extension into the narrative involves us in the much larger and difficult project of modelling narrative characterization (Meister 2003).

Deep water in every direction. But is that not *exactly* what the humanities require of computing?

6 Conclusion

In his essay, 'What is Practice? The Conditions of Social Reason', Hans-Georg Gadamer writes that the modern, post-Baconian idea of science is

> no longer the quintessence of knowledge and of what is worth knowing, but a way. It is a way of advancing and penetrating into unexplored and unmastered realms ... a knowledge of manipulable relationships by means of isolating experimentation ... That is what has ultimately brought about the civilizational pattern of modernity in which we live ... This has made possible the nature of our machines, our transformation of nature, and our outreach into space. (1981/1976: 69–71)

If, as I have argued, analytical computing in the humanities *is* modelling, properly understood, and modelling is making new knowledge by manipulating hypothetical constructs, then my chosen word is key to the humanities in a digital age. Modelling strongly underscores the problematic nature of the long outmoded 'quintessence of knowledge and of what is worth knowing' – which, though neither interesting to nor authoritative among philosophers, is still eagerly given a shrine, notably in parts of computer science. Gadamer characterizes the shift from quintessence to way as a singular, diluvian change, but one has to look no further than Ovid's *Metamorphoses* to realize that such shifts have occurred before. In any case, for the humanities, computational modelling marks one of these – bringing to them, it seems, a common methodology characteristic of the sciences, and in that sense precisely, scientific. If we are to have and so hand on a digital humanities worth the name, we need to understand what modelling *does* – to the modeller as well as to the modelled thing.

This understanding begins with the natural sciences, to which I have turned just as these sciences once turned to the crafts and to industry for their analytical rhetoric (see Chapter 3.5). This is not to suggest a story of progress, rather to point out an entirely pragmatic response to the needs of a critically self-conscious *experimental* practice of modelling. In this chapter I have suggested how we might turn raw borrowings into properly cooked understandings. Making sense of something new – a half-century hardly qualifies humanities computing otherwise – begins with suitable analogies to established practices, then domesticates them. My exercise of this venerable process leaves, however, many questions. For example: What counts as *theory*, and what status do we give it in relation to the artifacts it theorizes? (I return to this question in Chapters 3 and 4.) Where and how does modelling fit in? What qualifies as a good *explanation*? What do we as computing humanists say that *knowledge* is?

On the one hand, modelling cultural artifacts treats them as something like the empirical objects of nature; on the other hand, paradoxically modelling anything is just as clearly an imaginative act. This paradox puts humanities computing in the best intellectual company anywhere to be found.

2
Genres

In these circumstances we shall render an important service to reason if we succeed in simply indicating the path along which it must travel, in order to arrive at any results – even if it should be found necessary to abandon many of those aims which, without reflection, have been proposed for its attainment.

Immanuel Kant, *Critique of Pure Reason*,
Preface to the 2nd edn (1787)[1]

1 Introduction

I turn now from analysis, which in the humanities is mostly a private affair, to synthesis of new scholarly forms and the new library in which we place and use them. As an act of communication this synthesis is public in its outcome and intention, literally as 'publication'. It is collaborative, directly or indirectly, in the sense developed in the Introduction. Ludwik Fleck argues that cognition itself is 'the most socially-conditioned activity of man, and knowledge is the paramount social creation'.[2] But for the humanities the forms we synthesize are where this social conditioning of knowledge happens. They are the interface between private knowing, to which we have no direct access, and public reception and assimilation of knowledge, which is fleeting. They constitute the evidence that I examine here for how the difference that computing makes is best to be realized.

I assume a simplified view of the community of participants within which scholarship takes place, omitting complex political questions, e.g. of motivation and reward, in order to concentrate on probing the lineaments of desire. I ask, given what we have to work with – machines, artifacts and each other – what do we want to make and to do? As a formidable challenge and call for historical self-awareness, I offer at the core of this chapter a detailed examination of a highly traditional, pre-digital scholarly form and pose the question: Can we do as well in the new media?

In the Introduction I asserted that there are many 'computings'. Chapter 1 concentrated on the computer as modelling machine. This chapter takes up the computer as communications device in the broadest sense. The further question I have in mind is this: What scholarly role does *this* computer play in the (idealized) social habitat of research?

Terry Winograd concludes from the runaway success of Internet-based applications 'that the computer is not a machine whose main purpose is to get a computing task done. The computer, with its attendant peripherals and networks, is a machine that provides new ways for people to communicate with other people' (1997: 150). He is certainly essentializing here – *his* computer is built on the accomplishment of computing tasks that identify *the* computer for others – but his is the machine I need in this chapter. For an immediate prehistory and genetic pattern for *this* computer we look chiefly to the telephone, or more precisely to the telephone network, 'by far the largest integrated machine in the world' and, in recent years, itself (one could say) the largest computer.[3] *This* computer, as we now know it, is a node in an acentric network of peers, functioning as client or server as need be. Manuel Castells' radical equation, 'technology *is* society' (2000/1996: 5), metaphorically alerts us to the dual role this device plays, as a revealing model of our own social self-understanding and as a potent model for maintaining and extending it. Thus in thinking about computer-mediated scholarly communication we may speak non-deterministically about 'the logic of the network', meaning not the inexorable force of autonomous machinery but the consequences of our own ideas talking back to us through a particular form of technological expression.

Winograd's deeper response comes by taking exception to the term 'interface', so often used to name the social boundary of computing. The idea of 'interface', he notes, 'implies that we are focusing on two entities, the person and the machine, and on the space that lies between them. But beyond the interface, we operate in an "interspace" that is inhabited by multiple people, workstations, servers, and other devices in a complex web of interactions' (1997: 153). Jerome McGann's criticism that our interfaces to new scholarly genres do not live up to the theoretical design we proclaim these digital genres should have should then come as no surprise. Winograd suggests we think of 'habitat' rather than 'interface'. Indeed, the alternative metaphor implies a social as well as holistic space; a heterogeneous environment – the kind in which we actually work (a crucial point to which I will return); and, giving a preliminary response to McGann's criticism, a plurality and complexity of engagement full of promise for the task ahead. It is in this sense, Winograd points out, that the term 'cyberspace' comes into its own.

To give the argument of this chapter reasonable scope I narrow the focus from all scholarly forms to the scholarly commentary in particular. I choose it because among reference works (themselves the most obvious, least contested candidates for digitization) the commentary is among the simplest to imagine in digital form and among the most promising.[4] I choose as my example E. R. Dodds' commentary on the *Bacchae* of Euripides. The *Bacchae* has been the subject of commentary since the Aldine edition of 1503 and so offers the commentator a very rich scholarly background from which to draw. Dodds' commentary was first published in 1944, thus coming about as close as possible to a traditional work, still in active use, that antedates any influence from computing or its culture. Hence in considering it we can isolate the scholarly, historiographical component in the work of designing a digital genre. 'Now more than ever', McGann has said, 'we want to study the complex mechanisms of book technology in order to design digital environments of comparable sophistication' (2003: 258). Understood in its own terms (and that is the rub) book technology is rich, subtle and difficult to equal, and hence a worthy adversary to our technological pride and an effective means of testing the possibilities suggested by the new medium of work. As I suggested, it is not at all clear that we can do as well with the new one as our forebears did with the old.

My tight focus on the commentary unfortunately excludes closely related problems, such as the blurring of distinction between it and a number of other genres (e.g. the lexicon) that share several of its essential characteristics.[5] I also must exclude the substantial body of speculative and theoretical work on the digital futures of the scholarly textual edition, mostly in English literary studies. This work offers a useful corrective precisely in its choice of a genre with very different material and cultural circumstances, especially in the modern period.[6] For example, in his discussion of the book as a 'machine of knowledge' particularly from the time of the Pre-Raphaelites, McGann writes persuasively of 'the signs of a culture-wide effort for the technical means to raise the expressive power of the book through visual design' (2001: 62). This effort, he argues, was pushed by the felt need for 'forms that at least approximate [the] original imaginative condition' of the originals they are attempting to re-present (67). Hence his emphasis falls on the frustrating limitations of the book as a critical tool, not on its real but neutral limits, out of which came the admirable precision and concision of Dodds' *Bacchae*. McGann's central argument is that the codex has become increasingly problematic as an instrument for the study of its own kind: 'the symmetry between the tool and its subject forces the scholar to invent analytic mechanisms that must be displayed and engaged at the primary reading level'; things get much worse 'when readers want or need something beyond the semantic content of the primary textual materials', such as images (56).

The frustration *we* feel with the book, to which commercial and institutional strictures contribute, easily answers the question of why *we* celebrate the promise of new, hyper-bookish scholarly forms. But there is real danger here of reading our frustration anachronistically back into the practices of our forebears, and so of overlooking former achievements and what they have to teach us in favour of new means for satisfying our historically conditioned objectives. Yet it is also true that at least in some cases ingenuity with codex tools – e.g. the *apparatus criticus* of the Nestle-Aland Greek New Testament – devised forbidding pathways, with the high probability of frustration for at least some potential beneficiaries.

Before I can get to my example many pages hence, in section 6 below, I must address a number of questions to give context and purpose to the detailed probing of Dodds' referential mechanisms. These are: What is commentary? How does it work mechanically? In what ways does computing promise to suit its development? What working environment best accommodates digital commentary, and what constraints does this environment place on the design? Following my close reading of a single paragraph from Dodds' commentary, I then consider the system-wide effects of what a twenty-first-century commentator might do.

2   What commentary is

Commentary practice is modern as well as ancient, widely diverse in kind and distributed across many national cultures. My example is specific to mid twentieth-century British practice in classical studies but takes into account, mostly in silence, other practices.[7] Although, as

I point out, the commentary form subsumes much variety, for purposes of discussion I begin with a simple, idealized structure comprising these major parts: (a) a scholarly introduction to the work on which commentary is offered; (b) an edited text of that work with textual apparatus; (c) the commentary itself, in the form of paragraph-length notes keyed to the text; and (d) the usual table of contents and index. This structure precisely fits the particular commentary I will consider.

The scope of commentary in general is suggested by the etymology of the word, denoting thought about something, and is documented in the variety of its historical practice. As with the index, concordance, dictionary and encyclopaedia, this variety seems to belie any single name. The fact that we have one, and that it stubbornly persists, raises the question of essential characteristics. What might these be?

For us this question immediately becomes another: What must survive into the new medium for the result to be recognizable *as* commentary? What can we do without? What must we keep? What can we add or change? Again I call on Eco's idea of translation – the interpretation of a text in two different languages, involving the culture of each – though in this case the target language (of digital commentary making) is barely emergent. The commentary as we know it is an historical product of particular 'styles of knowing' developed within the technological medium of the printed codex.[8] Other such styles are available now, and the medium has changed. How are we to define a commentary such that these styles, and others yet unforeseen, can be accommodated – alongside the old, if we choose?

Our problem is not what might happen to any given commentary, such as the one I have chosen, and is best not confined to a single tradition nor even conceived as a change from one format to another. Specific formats, which 'the shock of the new' helps us to see in detail *as* formats, have something to teach us in their effects,[9] but formats are not the point here. My focus is on the mutability of format as a new condition of work. Thus I am excluding from consideration the temporary effects of a change in media, the impermanence against which we 'back up' our precious files and the chaotic variation of approaches we develop standards to control. Rather I wish to examine what allows us perpetually to transform our resources and so keep pace with imaginative change. Hence my focus is on how we devise and stabilize the means to do so.

Asking what tools commentary-makers should have to hand is greatly complicated by the demographics of practice: who comments to whom for what set of shared concerns. Allow me, however, radically to simplify the question of what these means might be before returning to the variety against which any revised notion of commentary-making must be tested. Here I will hazard an essentialist argument for the purpose.

3 Commentary mechanics

Obviously central to the definition of commentary is its relationship to the commented object. By definition commentary depends on its object, but the relationship between the two is more complex than simple dependency suggests. The key to the relationship lies in a paradox of interpretation, which takes control of and to a varying degree remakes its object in the very act of its own subservience. The commentary is thus in a sense always primary. Some commentaries are plainly so because they straightforwardly create or constitute their objects.[10] Some are primary by default – they are all that remains of an event not otherwise recorded or an object which has not survived. Performative events, even if repeatable, are sufficiently distinct in kind from their commentaries as almost to make these commentaries entities in their own right. Such cases, though perhaps exceptional, help make the point: commentary fundamentally *refers*, but not necessarily or in any simple way *defers*, to its object. It directs our attention elsewhere, but as governor of our thinking brings attention back. It leads by following, filtering, shaping.[11] This dynamic, performative aspect of commentary, I will argue, computing promises significantly to increase.

It is convenient as well as companionable to our twenty-first-century eyes to resolve commentary reference and object into two basic mechanical processes: *citation* and *morselization*, as Simon Goldhill has named them (1999: 393). These are of course hardly sufficient to do justice to the complexities of the genre,[12] but they are the chief intellectual tools at hand. Citation (in the neutral sense of reference without deference) is particularly clear in its application other than to the commented object. Citation is often predominately to extrinsic facts, traditional sources, pre-existing arguments and secondary discussion that it not only indicates but also summons, manages and brings to bear on its text. (The point is sufficiently illustrated in Figure 2.1, below.)

Citation in turn underlies the discontinuous morselization of commentary and its sequencing of morsels according to locations in the commented object, thus its literal sub-ordination. Neither is strictly necessary, of course. A commentary essay may refer to parts of the commented object in whatever order suits its continuous argument. Graphical illustrations in literary works, such as the frontispiece to Giambattista Vico's *Scienza Nuova Seconda* (1730) or the engravings in George Sandys' translation of Ovid's *Metamorphoses* (1632), may be said to serve as commentary on their texts by spatial juxtaposition and iconographic reference to textually disjunct passages.[13] Thus we may conclude that morselization and subordination are more strong tendencies than necessary characteristics, but they are certainly normal in the commentary form with which classicists are most familiar.

Morselization of a kind is graphically expressed in 'continuous' prose by the convention of paragraphing (and before that by division of *scripta continua* into words and syntactic units), though normally counteracted by explicit transitions and implicit sequences of thought. In the usual sort of commentary these transitional devices are absent, but the implicit original sequence of the commented text determines the order in which they appear, and so supplies a continuity of thought. Thus, to the reader who knows the commented text well, these morsels may be read as continuous though stylistically choppy prose. My point, looking ahead to the shape-change, is this: once readers are allowed easily to follow or rearrange morsels in whatever sequence they wish (as in current hypertext fiction), then a further erosion of the difference between continuous prose and morselized commentary will likely begin. In particular, once commentary writers start composing for a medium in which reader-determined sequence is a possibility, those writers are likely to respond to what they can then do and so to adapt their practice.

Nothing I have said or will say undercuts citation as a fundamental characteristic of commentary, but morselization and subordination are clearly less deeply rooted in the nature and so the future of the genre. This is not at all to say that the latter two will be irrelevant, as they are hardly so in continuous prose; rather, we need to think differently about them. I will return throughout the chapter to all three characteristics, to say in more detail how I think they work and so how they might be implemented. For now, in accordance with Eco's notion of translation, we need to look directly towards the computational side and particularly at its culture to identify the recipient qualities of computing in which these characteristics may be given shape.

4 Devolution of computing power

The role of modelling in scholarly applications may now seem obvious, but it has only been so for a relatively short time. The longer-term developments that have enabled us to think in its terms deserve a brief look, since they lead us to several important consequences of what we might call the *constructive mutability* of computing. The history in question is not simply about the development of faster, cheaper and more capacious machinery. It also shows the increasing sophistication of systems towards stability and standardization on the one hand and accessibility on the other. We witness, that is, the gradual transfer of ability to construct artifacts from highly specialized technicians to ordinary users, and the simultaneously increasing technical sophistication of these users. The convergence of tools and abilities is well expressed in a recent article on the modelling of names in literary texts: 'We want to provide', the authors write, 'an interface by means of which a literary researcher is able to construct new parsing algorithms without the need to know a programming language' (Dalen-Oskam and Zundert 2004: 290). This convergence is significant to us not only for the outcome but also for the illustration of how change in equipment selectively favours (but does not determine) certain patterns of work while making others less convenient.

The history of what we might call 'DIY' ('do it yourself') computing resolves into a number of intertwined strands. First is the interrelated social development correlated to hardware, roughly from a time when maker, operator and user of experimental systems were one (into the 1950s), through the separation of distinct groups as a result of commercial manufacture of the centralized 'mainframe' (1950s to 1970s), to something like the unity lost with the mainframe, regained first with the physically isolated 'microcomputer' (1970s to 1990s), since then also via the network.[14] Second is the development of operating systems, originally an innovation to standardize and automate routine work that had been the responsibility of operators and programmers so as to free them for higher-level tasks.[15] The layered design characteristic of these systems – each layer a self-contained entity with a strictly defined range of inputs from the layer above and outputs to the one below – has allowed for steady increase in sophistication, particularly of the interface, to which I will return in a moment. Third is the change in the nature of software, from the introduction of programming languages, 'originally aimed at extending access to the computer beyond the professional programmer' (Mahoney 1990b: 329, n.9.), to their generational development towards (if not transcendence in) the still imagined ability to describe, specify or simply respond to problems in ordinary language.[16]

One particular aspect of the sophistication in operating systems deserves more attention here. This is the change from a serial computing environment to the concurrent design we now use, with its asynchronous, interactive graphical user interface (GUI).[17] Serial computing, which more or less mandated the completion of one program before the next could be run, made interaction with machines clumsy and slow. Programs therefore tended strongly to monolithic, 'black box' designs, in which the user provided the input and received the output but had little direct responsibility for the process. What scholars did on the machine thus tended strongly to diverge from their other work in both the sequentiality and opacity of the computing applications. Even custom-built software separated the conception of problems (domain of the scholar) from the computational means of working them out (bailiwick of the programmer) and so came at a significant cost. It did not just keep computing to the few. It made the importance of computing for scholarship difficult to understand by focusing attention on the necessarily expensive, relatively inflexible product rather than on the interactive, heuristic process. It thus inhibited us from understanding that at issue is a reconceptualization of our artifacts and how we relate to them, not a faster and cheaper means of producing the old kind.

In contrast, the asynchronous, concurrent design of the GUI not only permits several programs to run simultaneously, it also strongly favours the development and use of 'component' software – an aspect of the change in ideas of software noted above. These independently developed, interoperable 'primitives' designed to be used and reused in the construction of unspecified larger processes may, perhaps, be compared to alphabetic letters, which can be assembled to spell arbitrarily many words in many languages.[18]

Admittedly, the ordinary end-maker can only see hints of such a future for software applications, and many technical problems stand in the way. Currently the choice is between two constraining alternatives: either to adapt a miscellaneous collection of mostly commercial applications (seldom if ever satisfactorily) or to adopt a closed, essentially unmodifiable system of components that have been carefully designed to work with one another. Experience suggests that however we define our primitive operations, the set of them is not closed. A toolbox system that offers internal compatibility at the expense of openness seems doomed, particularly since its hidden constraints and assumptions are bound to work against the more fundamental changes in method. Scholars then need a means of inventing new primitives and building new tools easily. Some attention will be paid to this subject in Chapter 5.4.10.

Much therefore remains to be done before we can easily construct approximate computational analogues of what we do (and invent new devices) by assembling and customizing component software. But the direction of technological progress seems clearly to be opening up an opportunity for us to become designers of our own tools. As Brown and Duguid have recently noted in *The Social Life of Information*, 'We are all, to some extent, designers now' (2000: 4). This extent seems highly likely to increase. At the same time, the design of scholarly tools (as of automobiles, buildings and advertisements) encompasses a number of highly specialized skills that the average scholar is unlikely to master. But as my DIY commentary will suggest, there should be opportunity in scholarship, as in houses, for the dweller in the habitat to take a hand.

In parallel with the devolution of constructive power, large-scale, widely accessible repositories of data have been developed in the humanities and social sciences. For us the earliest examples are textual collections such as the *Thesaurus Linguae Graecae* (TLG), first on magnetic tape, then CD-ROM and now online.[19] More recently the World Wide Web has given access to lexical databases and 'archives' of images and aural data as well; for classics the primary example is the *Perseus Digital Library* (Smith, Rydberg-Cox and Crane 2000). Though wisely made for immediately pragmatic reasons, the decision of the TLG Project to produce the Greek text without software for manipulating it is paradigmatic of a fundamental division between basic resources of data on the one hand and various standard ways of transforming and combining them on the other.[20] Even when, as with the Perseus Project, both are kept under one roof, the design which cleanly separates data from software allows two important flexibilities: the development of new tools, embodying new ideas, and their straightforward application to old data; and the application of tools across data-sets, extending to otherwise very different disciplines.

5 The library[21]

Thus we find ourselves staring at a new manifestation of a very old cultural institution, the research library. In 'The Library of Babel' Jorge Luis Borges plays ironically on its visionary history as universal locus of all knowledge, paraphrasing the ancient and much quoted definition of God, *centrum ubique, circumferentia nusquam*, 'centre everywhere, circumference nowhere'.[22] Like other visionary models *for*, it is ambiguous: impossible to realize but powerfully motivating and capable of leaving an historical imprint. Thus it can be found, Roger Chartier notes in a collection appropriately celebrating the Bibliothèque de France, 'throughout the history of Western civilization. It underlay the constitution of great princely, ecclesiastical, and private "libraries"; it justified a tenacious search for rare books, lost editions, and texts that had disappeared; it commanded architectural projects to construct edifices capable of welcoming the world's memory.'[23] In the history of computing it surfaced contemporaneously at its beginning, in Vannevar Bush's Memex, and it runs through the literature on information retrieval. It appeared again with the genesis of hypertext in Ted Nelson's idea of the massively interlinked 'docuverse' and the subsequent notion of 'cyberspace', and hence is found throughout the literature of hypertext and the World Wide Web. It remains an influential pest in naïve users' unexamined and usually inarticulate belief that the Web is its realization. Since the mid-1990s researchers have known it under the rubric of 'the world-wide digital library' or, more recently, as 'the Semantic Web'.[24] Even so, with names misdleadingly suggesting imminence if not existence, it remains a dream on pragmatic grounds as well as in principle.

The genius of the library as social institution, both real and imaginary, lies in its support for diversity of reading practices through the fundamental separation of singular, relatively unchanging resources from their manifold, highly changeable uses. This diversity is its 'recombinant potential', as Lorcan Dempsey has called the digital equivalent (2003). It is a cultural archetype, in Western tradition dating to the third millennium BC (Casson 2001), imprinting us in our individual ontogeny as scholars with the ideal of aggregated, flexibly structured knowledge. No wonder, then, that in imagining the digital working environment of scholarship it is unavoidable. But my take on this much imagined institution differs from the usual, and I hope complements existing work. Nearly all of the vast literature from digital library research and related aspects of electronic publication, information retrieval, hypertext and several other fields takes either a managerial or a technical perspective, both of which are largely outside the interests of the individual scholar who, however intimately collaborating, enters the library as an individual. Here I ask instead what the still ill-defined digital library should look like at the grassroots, to the scholar as resource creator, user and end-maker – whom, after all, this library is universally declared to serve. Unfortunately this perspective is badly underrepresented in the literature.

For obvious reasons, I begin with a technological approach to scholarly work and to the social institution that situates it. But however justified, a technological approach entails the peril of losing sight of the non-computational past and present. Technological and technologically affected literature is full of examples in which a cultural artifact or institution has been crudely, ignorantly and, worst of all, silently reinvented to fit a technological mindset. In other words we face the same peril with the inherited institution as with the objects in its collection. Thus in planning for the digital library we are in peril of conceptualizing the physical institution as its digital ghost – hence the library as information storage and retrieval system. This appears to be exactly what has happened in many universities when an IT centre has merged with the library to become an 'information commons' or the like. (The word 'information' is crucial to the problem; I will return to it later.) Nor is the damage only to the library. David M. Levy and Catherine C. Marshall have argued that digital library research itself is significantly hampered 'by a largely unexamined and unintended allegiance to an idealized view of what libraries have been, rather than what they actually are or could be' (1995: 77f.). In this digital age the abstraction likely to be made from the impressions of unselfconscious experience (or dimly remembered experience of someone in professional employment) is susceptible to profound influence from the concepts and methods of computing, with the result that the abstraction becomes doubly unreal. 'By failing to question this idealization or to acknowledge the ways in which the current conception of digital libraries is based on it,' Levy and Marshall point out, 'we risk creating digital libraries that are unnecessarily limited, and, in the worst case, entirely fanciful and unusable' (1995: 78). Their worst-case scenario stops short of the worst, however: a physical library thus transformed will be a significantly damaged library.

The corrective they exemplify is a 'work-oriented perspective' – the standard social-science approach of observing what people actually do, in contemporary libraries, with the collections and with other readers. (As they note, argument from observation derives its underlying virtue from the fact that a practitioner makes a poor witness to his or her own working practices, especially the habitual and informal ones, which tend to go unrecognized and unreported.) They highlight a number of salient facts: actual researchers use heterogeneous materials, permanent and transient, paper and digital – with no indication whatever that paper, now 'the principal interpretative medium', will vanish from the scene; they take notes, sometimes annotating these materials directly; they confer and collaborate with each other and with librarians; and so forth. One could add that not only do different people do things differently, but the same people tend to vary their practices according to varying tasks – or for other reasons. Levy and Marshall conclude that 'the better word for these evolving institutions is "libraries," not "digital libraries," for ultimately what must be preserved is the *heterogeneity* of materials and practices' (1995: 83).

Heterogeneity, and so the hybrid future I mentioned, is a central lesson from studies in what Rob Kling has called 'social informatics', which can be applied to the current subject in an attempt to discover how scholars actually work in libraries – and elsewhere.[25] Part of what we learn from these studies is that libraries have in an important sense been 'without walls' for quite a long time. This phrase usually denotes the projected consequence of digitization (Chartier 1993), but in doing so it may also obscure the fact that many if not a majority of working scholars have always been mobile. Perhaps the most famous ancient example is Pliny the Elder (23–79 AD), described by his nephew as taking advantage of *every* possible opportunity for reading and note-taking – before and after his bath, in carriages and elsewhere, at all times – so that he was able to finish *tot ista volumina* 'all those volumes' of his great encyclopaedia, the *Naturalis historia* (*Epistulae* 3.5.14–17). Modern working conditions for the scholar demand as much ingenuity. There is, in other words, significant opportunity in the design of the digital library to be 'without walls' not only for scholars at home, accessing library materials electronically from yet another fixed location, but also anywhere and everywhere, as opportunity presents itself. Hence the ongoing research into digital assistance for the mobile reading and annotating practices that have always been an aspect of the library's interpenetration with the world.[26] Indeed, one of the principal benefits of the codex book was precisely for scholars like Pliny the Elder, for whom convenience on the move was crucial (Casson 2001: 133–5). Furthermore, Levy and Marshall comment, the private and ephemeral material logically rather than just physically outside the digital library also needs support 'for managing its relations with the library collections from which it is derived' (1995: 82).

Thus the 'diffuse agent' that Lougee sees the library becoming has in a very important sense always existed (2002: 4).

Since the objective of digital library research is to serve current research practice, the sociological imperative – to know as clearly and fully as possible these practices as they actually are – seems the dominant one. It is plausible to assume, however, that the incunabular digital environment we now observe is far from optimal, indeed quite confused, so a clear sight of what happens in it now is not enough. We also need the history of the library as it was to understand the inherited social institution better, e.g. in its contingent relation to the societies that have variously realized it. For example, Casson's *Libraries in the Ancient World* (2001) teaches us how rapidly the basic elements of the library came into place – how, for example, the catalogue (and so the prototype of bibliographic virtuality) arose when collections became too large to know intimately. But it also teaches us, as James J. O'Donnell says in his review of Casson's book, that we must look beyond the design and components of a particular institution to its social positioning: 'The social function of the library, ancient or modern, thus needs a careful ethnographic analysis quite beyond the scope of Casson's volume' (2001). Similarly, David M. Levy's study, 'Digital Libraries and the Problem of Purpose' (2000), addresses the question, 'Which way ought we to go in digital library research and development?', by turning to the history of public libraries in the United States to probe their social positioning historically. The direction of research, he argues, depends on who we think we are, where we are trying to go and how we have decided to go there.

The conjunction of identity and direction is not far from fundamental dreams of becoming. The question that emerges is this: What library do our efforts and the rhetoric about them show that we are trying to build, however unsuccessfully? I do not mean the specific 'deliverables' of grant applications, but rather, again, the ideal on which they triangulate, however unconsciously: their broad justification in national and social benefits to be realized; even more (with appropriate caution) what it is incautiously claimed we will have Real Soon Now; or, again, what many naïve users think they already have at their fingertips. How we might respond to the denial of what we so clearly desire is actually crucial to understand. Digitization and digital acquisition efforts to date have produced the digital libraries built up by conventional institutions and some unconventional ones, such as *JSTOR* and *Perseus*.[27] To what degree this early effort is 'in winding sheets rather than swaddling clothes' (McGann 2001: 79) depends on what we are now able to do with the ancient dream. For a moment – rushing past without brushing aside the formidable difficulties standing in its way – let us incautiously imagine such a working environment for the commentary-maker. What would a modest realization of this dream mean for him or her?

In cyberspace the conservative scholar could extract what he or she needed in order to produce commentaries, either in printed form as now or as relatively book-like packaged electronic 'products' with various improvements and extensions to the print-based form.[28] But in the envisioned world-wide digital library the devolution of constructive power would offer far more radical moves. Let me describe two closely related scenarios, both of which follow from but significantly extend what is now trivial to do on the Web. Further, let us imagine that this online library is already well stocked with primary and secondary scholarly material contributed independently by others.

You will recall that the commentary form is by nature segmented into relatively independent parts – e.g. prose introduction, text, commentary, glossary. Published online, in a medium in which sequential integrity is weak,[29] the tendency would be, as potentially with all Websites, for each part to be accessed quite separately. Hence such publication would invite (though not force absolutely) the devolution of responsibility for what is now the scholarly end-product to the end-maker, to an automatic mechanism or to some combination of these. Possibilities for the digital library equivalent of the genre thus range from the DIY commentary, more or less hand-made from online textual editions, other commentaries, lexicons, image archives, secondary literature, morphological parsers, concordancers and so forth, to what one could call 'just-in-time commentary' automatically built from such elements.[30] In any case authors, even if they were writing an entire commentary, would need to pay close attention to the possibility that the results would be so used. It seems reasonable to assume that over time authorial responsibility would tend correspondingly to shift away from preparation of whole commentaries to fashioning these bits and pieces for future combinations. The technical challenges are formidable, of course – but the question is, what formidable challenges do we want to face?

Imagining the benefits is not hard. In fact, we need little more than the work of Perseus, amplified and extended to a distributed cottage industry of scholars, to suggest them – although this is not at all to claim that the future can thus be predicted. Continuing experimental work is crucial to our understanding of what we face because our previous experience, it turns out, is in practice not as helpful as we might think. 'We have found theoretical extrapolations to be of little use in developing digital libraries', Crane and colleagues have recently written. 'A densely interlinked interactive medium has proven so different from the print environment ... that we find it hard to predict with any accuracy what will and will not work' (Crane *et al.* 2001).

One aspect of the problem is implied by an uneasiness that the reader may now be feeling: For whom are the designs intended, exactly? Who are the creators, who the audiences? What about the particular motivations of real people, their human individualities, preferences and irrationalities? The experience of past libraries will help in answering these questions, but designs for digital libraries aim in part at new creators and audiences. Indeed, that is sometimes the point of these designs. As Crane *et al.* point out, to know who is interested we have to experiment.

But what about the problem-horizon we can see? The further one moves from the DIY to the just-in-time model for commentary, the more severe becomes the core technical problem, *interoperability*,[31] which is the digital library equivalent of what the physical library achieves by combining intelligent classification with skilled librarians and users. In positive terms, interoperability, as I noted earlier, is the 'recombinant potential' of a library. The problem is achieving any significant degree of it.

Although more practically orientated studies describe a spectrum of possibilities for the ambiguous term 'interoperability',[32] I will begin with its uncompromised definition: the ability of *independently designed* components to communicate successfully *without specific knowledge of each other* and *without human intervention*. What matters here is that each component is able to handle any arbitrary input and to produce, within the domain of any intended or conceivably allowable use, an artificially intelligible response. Systems in which components have been carefully designed to work with each other are, for the moment, disqualified. Only the 'heterogeneous' or 'federated' design, as Paepcke *et al.* call it (1998: 33), yields this potential meaningfully by imitating the ancient library model in divorcing uses from resources and so allowing for their reassembly on the fly. Imagine, for example, a commentary note artificially inquiring of a heterogeneous world-wide digital library the meaning of a word-form with several homographs in a highly inflected language, such as the Latin word *maris*.

To put the matter succinctly and bluntly, no one currently knows how to achieve true interoperability. It is as elusive as the uncompromised dream of artificial intelligence that it manifests. Technical difficulties are unsolved if not insoluble for 'deep semantic interoperability' – 'a "grand challenge" research problem [that is] extraordinarily difficult, but of transcendent importance, if digital libraries are to live up to their long-term potential'.[33] These difficulties commingle with political objections to the very notion of public data, openly collaborative work and the social ideal these imply.[34] Secrecy in work, Lucy Suchman has shown, has its reasons; we need not go far afield to find and sympathize with them (1995). The history of the dream that a truly world-wide digital library inflects shows the imperial colours of domination and control repeatedly (Casson 2001); so also, closer to home, does the ongoing conflict between freedom from inspection by others and freedom to inspect others. Even if it were true and meaningful that 'information wants to be free',[35] real-world societies and governments do not want it to be – nor, if we consider the matter carefully, do we.

For technical, social and other reasons, then, it seems best to assume that there will continue to be many libraries rather than a single, unified world-wide library. Marilyn Deegan and Simon Tanner argue that the Web is not it, crucially because the Web lacks the essential characteristics of management, collection development and durability (2002: 25f.). But the distinction between digital library and Web runs into trouble from the uncertain interface between them. The individual scholar may be grateful for and use the facilities of a digital library but tends not to share the same kind of institutional focus as the librarian or designer of library facilities. The near-chaotic richness of the whole networked environment, plus all the other heterogeneous materials scholarship requires, is his or her library. The so-called 'Semantic Web' has great appeal for this reason, though on closer inspection it resolves into an uncertain triplet vexed by impossibilities and restrictions (Marshall and Shipman 2003: 57f.). Underlying all three is the fundamental problem of cataloguing, made absolute by the imperatives for consistency and explicitness. Almost invariably, Wendell Piez notes, this problem is sidestepped by a distinction between semantics that can be implemented, at least in principle, and 'a broader sense of what human beings mean when we use language or any system of signification' (2002: 1).

Common doctrine is now that the answer lies in 'metadata', that is, data about the data, classifying them. Marshall and Shipman dismiss metadata as a means of 'taming the Web' (2003: 58f.), but its DIY possibilities and so its potential importance to small scholarly groups, such as authors of commentaries, makes it relevant here.

Metadata is, simply, the digital analogue of traditional cataloguing information, the use of which dates back historically to the earliest efforts at organization and indexing of library collections (Casson 2001: 3–5). Not surprisingly, therefore, from the perspective of the classifier and publisher (both roles that the individual scholar may assume online) it is 'one of the principal concepts for the description, organization, exchange and retrieval of information in a networked environment'.[36] Given the usual ambition of such collections, it is fair to say that the ultimate aim of metadata is the structuring of recorded knowledge for practical purposes – once again, knowledge representation (Gill 1998), though not necessarily done on a massive scale. I wish to make only a few overall points about it.

The fundamental notion at play is that the intractable complexity of cultural artifacts can be reduced by appeal to interpretative consensus. But can it, on the scale that digital collections operate by nature? Return to the word shows immediately that 'all metadata is, in fact, data. Whether or not particular information functions as data or as metadata is a matter of context or perspective, and what is metadata to one person or application can be data to another.'[37] Therefore, as we saw with knowledge representation, positing a universal metadata schema as a solution to the problem of unruly data *en masse* is a fundamental error, since no universal schema exists or is even possible. Instead, an equivalent of traditional library classification schemes, developed by 'the communities of expertise', is proposed (Daniel, Lagoze and Payette 1998). With the Web, however, size and transcultural nature raise the question of how a community of interpretation is constituted, for metadata always involves interpretation (Marshall and Shipman 2003: 62). Even at the level of applying a highly flexible standard, such as the elegantly simple 'Dublin Core', we are reminded that metalanguage is only more language, which when used in the real world generates pidgins and dialects and so compromises interoperability.[38]

There can be no question that gate-keeping functions are needed; they are implicit in the word 'communities' (or whatever term we use to denote our loosely cohesive professional and disciplinary identities) and in any classification scheme. With reference to the Web, Tony Gill notes that a range of metadata standards and tools, however underdeveloped, are available – but that their proper application cannot be trusted (1998), a problem that can only get worse with widening use. But this is not only a matter of undisciplined, unprincipled or abusive applications, rampant as these would appear to be. More seriously, it extends to the creative divergence of views on how and what to classify, which means, I think, at minimum a long period of experimentation with no certain outcome. (In fact, with an eye to my argument on modelling, it means a scholarly life-form of experimentation.) Although the unreliability of much we find on the Web is easy to demonstrate, reliability is in principle defined with respect to particular views and purposes, and it comes by degrees we should be cautious in rationalizing. Better than evaluating whether something is knowledge is to ask, 'Knowledge about what?'

It may be that particularly here the concept of metadata, which we have inherited from the long history of inscribed and printed genres, is a flawed gift. 'At the limit', Geoffrey Nunberg suggests, 'we may want to think of these [new online] forms on the model of the new news services and clearinghouses: not as static compendia but rather as dynamic interfaces to an open-ended discourse ... mediated through a series of transitive personal relationships' (1996: 129f.). Nunberg's primary example is the electronic discussion group *Linguist*, which in kind and behaviour suits his point much more obviously than, say, the *Codices Electronici Ecclesiae Coloniensis, The Corpus of Romanesque Sculpture in Britain and Ireland*, the *Opere di Dante lemmatizzate* or the *William Blake Archive*. But – this *is* the point – the categories between and within genres, or broadly characterizing the indistinct entities we can hardly call genres, are blurred and blurring. The interesting question, I think, is rather how we respond to what these discussion groups began as it spreads into the bastions of achievement. 'It's not just that the lists permit the participation of interested amateurs (the "virtuosi" of the age of Pepys and Wren)', Nunberg writes. 'They also remove the burden of professionalism that was imposed in the nineteenth century to limit the published discourse of the sciences to descriptions of its "subject matter" and purge it of critical self-consideration. The amateur epistemologizing and sociologizing, the pedagogical and technical lore, the gossip and the professional politics, the anecdotal observations about curiosities that lie outside the realm of current theory – all these come bubbling back up into public view from the orality where they have been repressed for the past two hundred years' (1996: 130f.). Metadata is hardly an appropriate tool for this rich soup, so it cannot be the sole or necessary means of access to materials that include these and similar ephemera. Rather, metadata is a limited tool for limited purposes.

In an interview published in the online magazine *Ubiquity*, Terry Winograd registers his surprise as a conventionally trained computer scientist that

> superficial search techniques over large bodies of stuff could get you what you wanted. I grew up in the AI tradition, where you have a complete conceptual model, and the information retrieval tradition, where you have complex vectors of key terms and Boolean queries. The idea that you can index billions of pages and look for a word

and get what you want is quite a trick. To put it in more abstract terms, it's the power of using simple techniques over very large numbers versus doing carefully constructed systematic analysis. (2002)

He is speaking about *Google*, of course, the large-scale hypertextual search engine whose indexing method has strongly influenced how we think about finding amorphous material on the scale that the Web demands.[39] It relies on hypertextual structure to track the social status of a page as an index to relevance. The approach is rooted in the very old ideas that intentionality is revealed by action and that meaning is socially created. Perhaps the first articulation in the terms of possible machinery was by the Canadian communications engineer Gordon Thompson, who in 1979 proposed a 'serendipity machine' for connecting 'resonant' people by observing and correlating their information-seeking behaviour.[40]

Google requires a varying degree of skill to use and has some obvious and not so obvious weaknesses.[41] It hardly eliminates the need for critical judgement. How the effectiveness of its approach will fare as the size of the Web increases is difficult to predict. But its success to date suggests for our imagined commentary author/user that on-the-fly assembly of the relevant bits and pieces is not restricted to those that conform to predictable resource-description standards. Within particular disciplinary groups standardization seems more than worthy to discuss and pursue, indeed essential. But millennia of experience suggests again the paradox that the finding-power of a catalogue depends fundamentally as much on ways of circumventing as of following its routes into a collection. Winograd's observation about the complementary power of 'superficial search techniques over large bodies of stuff' is crucial if we are to heed Nunberg's exhortation that we not 'try to close off the collection in some arbitrary way, but ... provide benign [Ariadnes] (both automatic and flesh and blood) who can help users thread their way through the maze' (1996: 129). Our situation is, however, somewhat different from Theseus', as the docuverse has no centre to delimit the quest and no fixed shape or singular thread to discipline experience. It is labyrinthine, but more like Borges' infinite library or, as seen through each viewer's screen, like his Book of Sand. We may dismiss the still sometimes audible reaction of those whose minds were formed before its advent – to quote Borges' narrator's less restrained outburst, 'monstrous ... a nightmarish object, an obscene thing that affronted and tainted reality itself' (1979/1975: 91) – but the reaction is a priceless sign that we are dealing with something whose genius lies in its stubborn difference from the sturdy, reliable codex.

6 The rough ground

The DIY design favoured by emergent possibilities for a digital library implies a large number of social, technical and perhaps legal problems I am going to ignore in order to press forward with others. If my intent here were predictive, then this would be an unwise strategy, but it is not. Rather my aim is to identify a reasonably probable and promisingly effective means of acting on the fundamental scholarly desire to make new knowledge and the equally fundamental curiosity to see where it leads. What actually comes of it, possibly long after this book is remaindered and forgotten, is irrelevant. What matters now is that modelling towards a desirable future for commentary and the other scholarly genres should engage as many of us as can be persuaded.

From the individual scholar's vantage-point, DIY commentary, given sufficient raw material, seems irresistibly attractive. As Don Fowler has pointed out, scholarship and commentary are wrapped up in each other (1999). Formal commentary writing may be mainstream in only a few disciplines, but informally it permeates scholarship through practices of annotation. Thus it provides, as I noted at the beginning, a studiously concentrated opportunity to probe annotation for aspects of its potential in the digital medium. The promise of DIY technically is also to render the logical continuum between annotation and commentary easier to travel, possibly with the result that commentary becomes a more popular form of scholarly communication. Indeed, as Gregory Crane has suggested, 'the web, which tends to present "morsels" ... creates a vacuum that clamors for commentary ...'.[42] The DIY scheme implies that the hand-made commentary which bridges morsels into larger units, temporarily or otherwise, holds the greatest promise for significant interoperability, at least at the level of scholarship.

First, a brief reality check on the actual variety of commentary practice. (Preserving if not increasing this variety I take to be a fundamental goal.) It is all too easy to generalize half-consciously from a favoured commentary or one's own necessarily limited experience as a scholar, and so to proceed blindly on the assumption that the genre in question as a rule comprises some standard list of parts, such as I gave earlier. Taking a look at actual commentaries within the single discipline of classical studies, for example – even those on a single ancient text such as the *Bacchae* – quickly disabuses us of that notion.[43] The formal variety, as I said at the outset in raising the question of essentials, is sufficient to make us doubt that the same name can cover all instances. This salutary doubt casts everything that follows in a tentative light. Between the covers of a book (for any genre, in fact) there are surprisingly few constraints, and hence many choices and opportunities.

So we begin with a *tabula rasa* of components and the imperative to comment on a text to a community of its readers. (For the sake of simplicity I assume verbal commentary on verbal objects.) What components are required to engage the intended audience? Dodds on the *Bacchae* provides an instructive example that raises both of my initial questions. In his Preface to the first edition he describes two audiences: 'persons who are or wish to become professional scholars' and 'schoolboys ... reading the play for the first time'.[44] He accommodates the difference by bracketing off material addressed to the former, with a prefatory note that the latter should 'in general ignore this bracketed stuff'. The method, though simple, has much to recommend it because the reader is allowed to choose. In hypermedia we can do better with the presentation, concealing one view while revealing another, giving more possibilities and so courting a wider range of audiences – an obviously desirable goal for the less popular fields (Crane 2002). But specifically automatic methods proposed for tailoring an edition to the reader on the basis of a profile (by means of 'adaptive hypermedia'[45]) run the serious risk of closing down rather than opening up readership: individuals make poor informants about their own behaviour; they are apt, given the chance, to grow intellectually; and they may, for perfectly good reasons, need the results an otherwise accurate profile conceals from them.[46] Individuals tend not to conform well to templates, even very clever ones, so if there are to be plural views of or interfaces to a commentary, the viewer must be able quickly and easily to choose and configure.

A moment's reflection is enough to suggest that for a sufficiently diverse audience, constituting views by 'vending' components is not enough. Problems of audience pertain to the style in which each component is prepared, down to the most minute level of expression. Thus Dodds' *Bacchae* engages in a precise (and to some degree subliminal) conversation with the reader, depending on and signalling a range of social attributes that the commentary requires. In Figure 2.1 three kinds of bracketed material define the bracketed audience rather well: his spelling out the names of Latin playwrights and their plays, e.g. 'Seneca ... *Thyestes*', for the benefit of the Greek specialist, who might not bother to know the conventional abbreviations for Latin authors and works; his citing the minimum information needed by his well-informed but not mind-reading reader, e.g. 'Verrall's notion that 662 is interpolated ...', not citing or anywhere listing Verrall 1910, the only possibility; in 'ἀνεῖςαν χιόνος L. Dindorf, to avoid ...' carefully pointing to Ludwig Dindorf rather than his much better-known sibling Karl Wilhelm, both of whom were Hellenists. (Note that the commentary does not have a bibliography to make this discrimination.) Dodds' finely crafted language thereby precisely defines and maintains the community he has targeted. For a strong, illuminating contrast, compare Robert Bagg's translation and commentary, intended for the monolingual reader with no classical education whatever (1978).

My point here is that the more accurately a component of commentary addresses its audience, the less portable that component becomes. More generally, as Wendell Piez writes, 'the more particular and intimate a relation is inscribed by the medium, the more grounded in its medium is the point being made. The medium is not just a bucket of ideas; it is ... a conduit of presence, even personal presence.'[47] Hence two matters to which I will return: the responsibility of the DIY end-maker, and the problem of 'information'.

The boundedness of the codex provides a secure physical basis for such contextualization and a constant reminder of it. The commentary form, being morselized, may itself be explicitly discontinuous – as a result, one suspects, readers habitually dip into a commentary rather than read it from cover to cover – but not always (Goldhill 1999: 405f.). More important for my purposes, the effects of this formal discontinuity are counterbalanced by the habitual user's formally reinforced knowledge that he or she is consulting a specific work, e.g. Dodds. Subliminally or otherwise, such a user contextualizes any 'answer' extracted from the commentary within a coherent, recognized view of the *Bacchae* and the literary culture from which it came, with particular assumptions and implications for which there may be no direct evidence in the extract and which the user may not recognize. Even when a segment of the work has an entirely independent origin – Dodds, for example, includes the whole of Gilbert Murray's text (2nd edn, 1913) without change 'apart from correction of one or two misprints' (1960/1944: vi) – the borrowed segment, being within the covers of his book, becomes in a sense his own.

The traditional form closest to the DIY commentary, which we are now likely to see as anticipating it, is the ancient 'variorum', made by assembling for each lemma relevant notes from other sources and perhaps one's own. Its range of possibilities is very broad, from collections of criticism, learning and lore, as in the Homeric scholia and Servius' commentary on Virgil, to the comprehensive digest of scholarship, e.g. in the *Variorum Commentary on the Poems of John Milton* (1970–5) or in the ongoing *Variorum Edition of the Poetry of John Donne* (1995–).[48] A variorum by nature provides quite different choices for contextualization of included material than does a modern commentary like Dodds', though as Fowler points out, 'modern commentaries do retain something of this palimpsestic nature, in particular through their reference back to earlier commentators' (1999: 429). Much depends on the strength of the editorial hand, especially whether commentary is quoted or summarized. Roughly speaking, quotation tends to foreground multivocal comparison of morselized utterances rather than continuity of view; summary, especially in continuous prose, emphasizes comprehensiveness and perhaps historical development or continuity of scholarship. Compilers contextualize further in their choice of commentators, the order in which they are listed and by additional glossing of their own – as we saw, a responsibility of the DIY end-maker. Such glossing is in the ancient tradition of reinterpreting texts in order to rehabilitate them for a new audience, from the euhemeristic readings of Homer and medieval glossing to the use of legal precedents and contemporary spin-doctoring.

The technical path of by far the least resistance favours the ancient variorum format, in which 'the views of each successive commentator are separately registered, and the latest commentator's own contribution takes its place, if at all, at the end of the procession of learning'. This is highly significant because, Fowler notes, format shapes meaning, and this particular arrangement bodies forth the encounter with the textual object through successive layers of interpretation. 'Although commentators are often criticised for this game of pass-the-parcel,' he says, 'this is a misconceived criticism: Derrida was right, meaning *is* never fully there in the text, and the best commentaries are not those which encourage us to believe this can be evaded but those which lay bare its inevitability' (1999: 429).

The obvious current technology by which the digital variorum may first be realized is relational database design, though successors are imaginable. Two medieval literary projects in humanities computing exemplify its application: among early efforts, the Dartmouth Dante Database Project, a morselized collection of fifty-nine historical commentaries augmented, in the Princeton Dante Project, by other data, images and sound;[49] and the more recent *Stellenbibliographie zum*

Parzival *Wolframs von Eschenbach*, a line-by-line bibliographic commentary to all 24,810 lines of the oldest complete Grail romance in European literature.[50] Either project is sufficient to demonstrate the value of structurally simple rearrangement of commentary under the control of the end-user, assisted in the *Stellenbibliographie* by sophisticated classification and search tools. Each also shows a particular strength of the digital variorum. By virtue of its more than seven centuries of commentary to draw on, the Dante Project is able not simply to bring great learning to bear on an individual line of the *Divina Commedia*, but also by juxtaposing the comments, to highlight the development of the various styles of knowing in the changing styles of glossing. The published *Stellenbibliographie* covers a much smaller historical period (1984–96). Again learning is brought to bear and variations in approach can be observed, but its genius lies elsewhere. This is to provide a mechanism whereby the cottage-industry of medieval German scholarship is able to accomplish what would otherwise be beyond its reach: to publish the entirety of its scholarly dialogue on possibly the greatest and certainly the most complex work in its period – and so greatly to invigorate that dialogue.

Two additional steps lie between the digital variorum as just illustrated and a full realization of DIY commentary: modelling tools, and a rehabilitating gloss supplied by the snippet-writer and by the end-maker. These pose quite difficult technical and rhetorical problems, respectively. On the technical side, it is not at all clear how modelling tools would work over the kind of infrastructure that relational technology or its successor(s) would establish. On the rhetorical side, one imagines that DIY commentary text, written for the purpose, would differ profoundly from extracts composed for whole commentaries, such as Dodds'. Each morsel would need to contain within itself whatever context the author had in mind, or to supply a means of summoning that context. As noted earlier, for well-known authors the name would do some of this work. A major task of the commentary snippet-writer and of the end-maker, it would seem, would be to oppose the forced morselization of interconnected ideas into redistributed 'answers'. (While it is true that commentary style is not continuous in the manner of a prose essay, a traditional commentary writer, responding to a continuous primary text against a continuous mental background of ideas and in a consistent style, will not produce totally discontinuous chunks of commentary.) Again that responsibility would require glossing. Blog-writing may have something to teach us here.[51]

What can be safely assumed as constant is the communicative intentionality of the result, and so its socio-political consequences. Here historical studies of commentary practice are invaluable for their laying
open of its ingenuity and seriousness. But from my perspective the fundamental problem identified, e.g. in Simon Goldhill's brief historical
study of the genre in England, outlasts any of the actors and doubtless
will survive into the digital form. It is a problem of the interpretative
genres: how much the commentary allows or prevents consideration of
its own strategies of questioning (1999: 406). To what degree (recalling
McGann's point) can it realize Roland Barthes' 'network with a thousand entrances', in which each entrance is a strategy, and the end-user
can view them all? But wait: this is a prejudicial question coming from
a broadly postmodern agenda that may someday seem rather quaint,
or worse. For the time when, for example, main gates (and their complementary side-entrances and places where poachers scale the wall)
become fashionable again, the end-maker needs the ability to
configure one of those thousand entrances as the *only* proper entrance.
Or, perhaps, to rethink the idea of entrance. If you doubt the possibility of such a change in fashion, consider the shifting fortunes of
Hamlet, for example.

Experiments with the design of electronic textual editions suggest
that mere assembly does not avoid the problem of closing off some
views in order to open up a particular view (Robinson and Gabler 2000:
3). Physical juxtaposition is no guarantee of a comparative epistemology or even of coherence. In other words, to repeat Winograd's point,
we need to think in terms of habitats, but not merely many views
under a single roof for which a single *pater* or *mater familias* takes
charge. Habitat ('dwelling-place') means also interaction and change,
hence the modelling tools I mentioned earlier. Database design implies
not only the initial modelling of data but also modelling of the subject
the database is built to represent. A number of humanities computing
projects, the *Stellenbibliographie* in particular, demonstrate the intellectual potential. But these tools need to be in the hands of the end-
maker. In other words, what the DIY component-design has to offer is
not so much a more variegated singular view, but the ability to change
views more quickly, with less investment in any one and a greater
emphasis on comparison of them.

How far might the digital commentator go in implementing the
potential of hypertext with respect to citation? This potential, you will
recall, is to deliver what has formerly been only promised. The problem
is not if but when this should be done. The answer is *not* 'Always'.

It is, however, 'yes, please' in the trivial case of the implicit references from the primary text to the notes and for the explicit citations *ad loc.* at the beginning of each commentary note, back to the text. Exactly *why* the answer is so unproblematic is worth attention, which I will give it below. But trouble begins with the traditional citation (henceforth 'citation') to secondary literature. Citation comes into its own only where there is real need beyond the mere deictic, when the referenced material is not included within the covers of the book. Then an opportunity arises, powered by implicit demand from the reader, somehow to communicate the status that the author accords the referenced text. The citation becomes a rhetorical trope, which in the hands of a master like E. R. Dodds takes on great expressive range and subtlety. It is worth contrasting his usage, shaped by the culture of his field, to the radically simplified practice of citation in the social sciences or, indeed, in the mainline references of this book.

Here the folklore of wishing has something to teach us. It is popularly assumed that in former times, in the slow medium of print, citation was the best that one could do, but that even the simplest implementation of hypertext would be unarguably superior (hence the lack of argument on this point) because, again, it *delivers.* Even to raise the question of whether it should replace the older mechanism may thus seem odd. Those familiar with hypertext research will know that the hyperlink as most of us experience it, on the Web, is simplistic in the context not only of what is described in current specifications and typologies but also in that of stand-alone systems built decades ago.[52] This research suggests that although raising the question is not at all odd, solutions are to hand for the much more sophisticated demands of reference.

While true to a degree, the technical response does not directly address the more fundamental problem I have in mind. This problem begins with incomplete knowledge of what citations are actually for – why they promise but do not deliver – and more broadly with the historiographical error of presuming that our forebears were only trying to do what we can do, or will be able to do as soon as we implement this or that standard. Understanding the discrepancy between past and present is so important that, it would be fair to say, the future of scholarly genres in the electronic age depends on our understanding it. Nor is it an exaggeration to say that the shape of humanities computing depends on grasping the historiographical argument to which the comparison between them points. The reader will, I hope, forgive me if I seem to belabour this argument, but evidence from the popular press and much academic writing suggests that it is not as obvious as we should all hope. But now the balance may seem to tip too far towards an uncritical veneration of past practice. In the following I am concerned only to argue from my example that we must understand what this practice was in its own terms, and then ask how such a practitioner might respond using current tools. In some cases these tools will be shown to be inadequate, in others they will not.

Here I will examine a few typical citations from a single commentary paragraph, to *Bacchae* 661–2, reproduced below as Figure 2.1. This paragraph, though also typical, gives an inadequate idea of the substantial variety of the form, from the tightly focused discussion of textual variants characteristic of earlier historical examples to the discursive mini-essay with footnotes. In the later examples, such as Dodds, citation is not simply or perhaps even primarily to the text commented on but especially to the wealth of primary and secondary material conventionally brought into play. The question I wish to raise is exactly *how* this wealth has been and now might be brought into play.

The first point I wish to make is that hyperlink and citation are two distinct mechanisms whose difference is precisely that between a computationally tractable instruction and a legible statement. Where (*very* loosely speaking) the two mechanisms ultimately deliver the same object, such as a written document, they do so in different contexts with different outcomes. (In fact they deliver different things, but let that pass until later, when I discuss 'information'.) The differences should not be surprising: we are always on the familiar ground of comparing the wax apples of artificial intelligence with the real oranges of human understanding. My aim is first to establish their difference in the particular context of commentary, then to work out in somewhat greater detail their cooperative interrelation in a suitable habitat for scholarly work. To simplify matters I will take the hyperlink to be as we find it in HTML. As far as I am aware, more sophisticated forms would make no difference to the points I wish to make.

Consider first the reference in Figure 2.1 to '(Meurig-Davies, *Rev. Ét. Gr.* lxi [1948], 366)', which I transcribe fully, as we find it, in the form of a parenthetical deictic statement. For purposes of argument, let us assume that the referenced article also exists in digital form, and for the sake of simplicity let us compare the citation above to a hyperlink that might appear as '(<u>Meurig-Davies</u>)'. What, then, is the difference between these two references to the same document? The latter is as exact a translation of the former as can be managed, but as a computa-

661-2. 'Where the white snow's glistening falls never loose their grip.' If this means, as some suppose, that it never stops snowing on Citheron, the exaggeration is monstrous; it is still considerable if we take it to mean that the snow lies in places all the year round (I found none when I climbed the mountain in April). We may have here nothing more than a conventional poetic commonplace (Meurig-Davies, *Rev. Ét. Gr.* lxi [1948], 366); but I suspect that Eur. insisted on the snow because it was the right setting for a strange tale of maenadism: on Parnassus, and probably on Citheron too, the ὀρειβασία was a mid-winter rite. Like most southern peoples, the Greeks felt (and still feel) snow to be a little uncanny: to early poets the snowflakes were, like the lightning, κῆλα Διός, 'shafts of God', a threatening visitation from the skies (*Il.* 12.280, cf. Wilamowitz, *Die Ilias u. Homer*, 216). So Sophocles, describing the horror of Niobe's eternal vigil upon Sipylus, says χιὼν οὐδαμα λείπει (*Ant.* 830). βολαί, usually 'acts of throwing', can also mean 'things thrown', just as βαφαί can mean 'things dipped' (e.g. poisoned arrows, *Her.* 1190). The translation 'radiance' (L.S.⁹) is quite unjustified. For εὐᾱγεῖς, 'bright', cf. Parm. 10.2 εὐᾱγέος ἠελίοιο and other passages quoted in L.S.⁹ The original spelling may have been εὐαυγεῖς, as in διαυγής, τηλαυγής, ἐξαυγής (πώλων ... χιόνος ἐξαυγεστέρων, *Rhes.*304).¹ [Verrall's notion that 662 is interpolated, the messenger having broken off his sentence at ἵν' οὔποτε, is surely incredible. And the line seems to have been known to Seneca, who was misled by it into citing the absence of snow on Citheron as a symptom of extreme drought, *Thyestes* 117f. – ἀνεῖσαν χιόνος L. Dindorf, to avoid the tribrach composed of a single word coinciding with the foot. But this rhythm, which is rare in Aesch. and Soph. (except in the first foot), is admitted relatively often in the later plays of Eur. (Descroix, *Trim. iamb.* 159, 162). There are at least five other instances in the *Bacch.*: second foot, 18, 261, 1302; fourth, 731, 1147.]

¹ Cf. now G. Björck, *Das Alpha Impurum*, 147.

Figure 2.1: E. R. Dodds, commentary on *Bacchae* 661–2.

tional statement it perforce radically simplifies and alters its original by imposing an action not indicated and perhaps not even implied in the former. The convenience of access it represents cannot simply be interpreted as an improvement on the former because access is not simply the point of '(Meurig-Davies, *Rev. Ét. Gr.* lxi [1948], 366)'. In rough paraphrase, conceding the implicit action, this statement might read, 'if you were to look at what Meurig-Davies writes on page 366 of the

Review des Études Grecques, volume 61 for 1948, you would find confirmation of the previous statement'. This is clearly *not* identical to the mechanically deliverable offer of the full text. Even so, would the commentator have wanted this result? Would we, under our changed circumstances?

One has to be careful here, since in the print medium concision was to some degree forced on commentators by their publishers, a constraint integral to the environment in which commentators had been working for millennia. They were part of the intellectual style we must respect in attempting to understand Dodds' commentary historically in its own terms, for what it was attempting and achieving. (We might wish to be liberated from those constraints, and might be able even to demonstrate why, but that is another matter.) In the terms obtaining at Dodds' time, the hyperlink would violate rather than fulfil the author's intention, which we have no evidence to think was not perfectly and completely expressed as it stands, a deictic with at most a subjunctive action only implied. This is likely true even for those of his intended readers who as specialists in ancient Greek literature would have had easy access to the journal and so would have been able to find Meurig-Davies' *ipsissima verba* with very little trouble.

It is perhaps trivial to note that the distortion of intentionality increases as we move from explicit to implicit citation as the language of citation becomes less formal, more subtle, more like ordinary speech. Dodds' remark immediately following his translation of *Bacchae* 661–2 provides an example: 'If this means, *as some suppose*, that it never stops snowing on Citheron ...' (my emphasis) – a common rhetorical move, relegating a known opinion to anonymity, dismissing it before it becomes an objection. To hyperlink here to the actual suppositions would have close to the opposite effect of the one Dodds intended. It is of course worth asking, here as elsewhere in my discussion, how I know the intentions of a long-dead scholar. 'Shared academic culture' is an answer, but even if correct, the answer is as vague and unsatisfactory as the word 'culture' can be; 'an historical imagination' assumes a great deal but is better because it points to the most important question raised in this chapter.

In contrast to the dismissive 'as some suppose', an exact quotation in Dodds' commentary might seem safely, indeed profitably replaced by a link, since having the words themselves directly in view *is* the apparent point. Thus midway down the page: 'So Sophocles, describing the horror of Niobe's eternal vigil upon Sipylus, says χιὼν οὐδαμα λείπει (*Ant.* 830).' But a hyperlink into *Antigone* at that line would have a different effect and, as *Perseus* has shown, introduce new possibilities (including the danger of distraction). At the time of writing, Dodds could assume without thought that his quotation would recall the passage to mind, and with it the play. A leap into the full text would have been otiose at best for his intended audience – indeed might have suggested, contrary to what we know of that audience, that his readers would need the full text. Doing such things, as we know from *Perseus*, is part of a strategy for the survival of classical Greek studies, but that belongs to the present, not to mid twentieth-century Oxford.

These examples suggest how the comparison of hypertext code with human language not only establishes the difference and illuminates a subtlety and range of expression problematic to the former but also implicitly refines the question of what contribution the digital medium might make. Again my point is not to take issue with hypertext itself; rather it is first to challenge the gross misreading of natural-language citation as if it were proto-hypertext so that then their interrelation can be clearly worked out.

Now consider Dodds' reference to the Liddell and Scott *Greek-English Lexicon*: 'For εὐᾱγεῖς, "bright", cf. Parm. 10.2 εὐᾱγέος ἠελίοιο and other passages quoted in L.S.⁹' Notice two things.

The first is the understated *cf.* (L. *confer,* 'compare'),[53] which in this quoted reference invites the reader to compare Euripides' use of the adjective with that in a number of other texts.[54] Such invitations without explanation are not merely commonplace in classical scholarship, they are fundamental to the format of the commentary, 'with its rhetoric of adducing parallels' (Goldhill 1999: 403). Often they run to many citations. Usually (though not here) the choice of texts is uniquely the commentator's and so may express knowledge of the literature not available elsewhere, as is briefly illustrated by Dodds' '(*Il.* 12.280, cf. Wilamowitz, *Die Ilias u. Homer,* 216)'. But, Goldhill notes, they may also be used to close down rather than open up discussion, 'a license not to articulate, not to discuss questions of critical semantics, or of what constitutes an adequate range of questions, of what needs a gloss and what doesn't'. More innocently, accumulation may have no other motivation than unfocused generosity, passion for collecting or exhibitionism. Hence, as Goldhill says, *cf.* forms the 'grounding problem of the commentary format' (397). This old problem, kept in check by the restrictions of print, is foregrounded in the digital medium because in effect all restrictions to the amount that may be accumulated are removed. But we need to discriminate what kinds of objects are referred to. I will return to this point in a moment.

The second thing to notice is that the immediate reference is to a text the reader is almost certain to have at hand, the Liddell and Scott *Lexicon*. Here we come as close as ever in the commentary to the kind of lookup that hypertext implements. Indeed the effect of a hyperlink would be an expansion rather than contraction of meaning. As I noticed earlier for a link to the text of the *Antigone*, the danger of distraction would be there (as always when consulting a lexicon), but it is hard to imagine that the marked sense of εὐαγεῖς is not illuminated by the others within the entry and in nearby related entries. Furthermore, in contrast to the quotation from the *Antigone*, Dodds would be unlikely to have assumed his readers would know the lexicon entry well. It would seem least perilous, then, to assume that here Dodds intended the lookup, and so the accessibility of the lexicon would have suited his purpose better than any other resource we have considered – except perhaps in the references to the primary text from each lemma of the commentary. Would a hyperlink directly into the full L.S.[9] suit perfectly, or would a future Dodds wish to shape the reader's experience, e.g. by causing the first sense to appear highlighted or by selecting it exclusively? (Both suggest a more sophisticated linking technology than now available on the Web, but that is only a matter of implementation.) *Perseus* has conclusively demonstrated that a lexicon proves a very good structured portal into the literature which it cites. Dodds recognizes that fact by his citation.

A final example. Again in reference to the snow on Citheron, the commentator adds parenthetically, 'I found none when I climbed the mountain in April', and he goes on to make some anthropological observations about the Greeks. The image of Dodds climbing the sacred mountain to be *there*, at the site of the sacred Dionysiac ritual, speaks volumes about a mid twentieth-century Oxford don. It is again hard to imagine that in a digital version a more extensive note on the experience, or even a video-clip of the ascent narrated in the manner of Simon Schama or Jacob Bronowski, would not expand the value of the commentary – indeed provide a kind of appeal now eagerly sought. As for the anthropology, one can also imagine (as so often in this great commentary) wanting to go off to read much more, especially if anthropological interests brought one to the *Bacchae* in the first place. So, might the future Dodds supply a hyperlink to a monograph on uncanny meteorological phenomena or the phenomenon of the uncanny itself across many cultures?

Parts of an answer as to how a future Dodds might construct his or her commentary come from a number of sources.

We can consider a case in which the actual presence of a formerly cited object not only answers to genuine inconveniences in the historical practice but also amplifies the possibilities, including those that address our own situation. Getting to the lexicon entry from the commentary text is an example of the former, and of the latter, laying before the reader texts he or she may not have access to or even know. Additions to the commentary, for example the academically serious but entertaining video-clip, lie far beyond what the historical Dodds could have foreseen, though his offhand but arresting remark – 'when I climbed the mountain in April' – attests to his acting on an imaginative desire that we now can model.

We can also consider his desire to address multiple audiences, which we can do in many more ways than were available to him. 'In particular,' Fowler points out, 'electronic commentaries offer the prospect of "folding" comment so that not everything attached to a passage is shown at once ... Readers may be offered pathways through the material, so that only if they are interested in textual criticism need they see material relevant to that aspect of the text' (1999: 427). A database approach, as in the *Stellenbibliographie,* suggests tailor-making commentary of many different kinds, as does the closely related technology of markup.

A more challenging part of the answer comes from returning to what I argued were the least desirable amplifications and pressing them. A future Dodds should be allowed no less an expressive range than his or her predecessor, and so needs the ability to indicate e.g. that a source should be noted but need not be seen. Nevertheless, there *are* times when sources must be checked, including occasions when the reader's interests are tangential to the commentator's. Indeed, Fowler notes, the attraction of the museum-like commentaries that horde great collections of references is 'that the reader might be able to use the collected material for a different end, might be able to tell new stories on the basis of the old data: and to this end it is better to have too much than too little' (1999: 436). Given modern expectations and the difficulty of access to scholarly materials, we should provide for this need digitally as much as possible. But we also have to recognize that many if not most of the specialized printed books and articles, such as many that Dodds has cited, are unlikely ever to be digitized; marginalizing these, by failing to design for *a permanently hybrid environment,* is surely to be avoided.

Another part of the answer comes from hypertext research, notably the subfield devoted to compositional hypertext (including hypertext fiction), rhetoric and argument.[55] Creative fiction does not of course behave like commentary prose, but the writerly perspective defines an important common ground from which new forms of expression for commentary may be able to draw. I have implied that the hyperlink, when used in a referential context is, like the citation, a rhetorical trope, but fitting it to an existing trope obscures its reality as an action beyond language and so prompts suggestions of other models, e.g. cinematic and lyric, with the obvious connection to speech-act theory.[56] The question for digital commentary is, in each case of reference, what exactly is to be performed and how the reader's cooperation is to be negotiated. The intentionality of the commentary form presupposes a certain kind of negotiated interaction, which in turn must shape the emergent hyper-trope, i.e. the mechanisms, their applications and the understanding of what these signify. Deferring closure is, Fowler reminds us, the great gift of commentary, but the meander through an imaginary Nelsonian docuverse of totally interconnected documents needs the crucial element of mindful interaction.

The last part belongs to the disciplined trial-and-error of experiment, for which there is no substitute because the objective is invention of new knowledge in interaction with equipment. Here modelling commentary aims at establishing solid ground, at least for long enough to enable the practice which exploits it to move us on. The better understanding of cultural artifacts from analytical modelling is to be matched by the new commentary (or lexicon, textual edition &c.) emerging from the experiment. We need to preserve knowledge of those models that work particularly well, so they may serve *as models* for future work. This necessarily implies that particular commentaries need to be preserved. Here theoretical principles join the commonsense observation that preservation is a practical requirement in any case, since some *ad hoc* DIY assemblages will inevitably cross the fuzzy boundary between informal notes and formal publications, becoming exemplars for the field. Hence the DIY scheme begins to look suspect.

7   System-wide effects

The scholar may be forgiven for wondering – however fond his or her memories of Tinker Toys, Meccano sets or Lego may be – whether DIY is a good investment of time in any sense. The senior scholar will worry about whether the broad objective represented by end-maker DIY genres will aid or hinder the kind of scholarly world we would want to live in, about what the probable system-wide effects of these particular technological imaginings might be. The junior scholar will worry as much or more about the consequences for his or her career. The latter bundle of anxieties lie well beyond my scope here, but I will look directly at the former.

Thankfully, questions of this kind continue to receive a fair amount of attention as part of the wider debate on the 'information society' in general and electronic publishing in particular.[57] We have known for some time that electronic publishing, both formal and informal, is a source of profound disturbance to business-as-usual, even to thought-as-usual – that it is as far from a plug-and-play replacement for print as the paperless office is from reality. All scholars and many if not all aspects of scholarship are affected to some degree. Work in humanities computing obviously tends to be strongly affected, especially because its products often stretch the inherited constraints of publishing. An extensive discussion would be more than justified, but here I have space for only a few observations specifically relating to the scholarly genre on which this chapter focuses.

Scholarship as we conceive it naturally depends on our ability to document the sources we use, secondary and primary. One system-wide effect (of which we already have a foretaste from the Web) is revealed when we ask in what sense the DIY commentary *is* a document. How is the user of a temporary, perhaps even unique construct to record a meaningful, lasting reference to it? A technical answer is already available: a 'Uniform Resource Identifier' (URI) or similar device pointing to a table of contents, which would in turn list URIs for the included content.[58] The harder, ontological question remains, however. Current bibliographic references are to commonly held objects; the DIY reference would be to a potentially, even normally unique, private construct. In other words, Paul Duguid notes, we face the potentially serious intellectual and social problem of *demassification* (1996: 83ff.). If standard reference sources are replaced by idiosyncratic ones, what then happens to scholarship? Duguid observes 'the increasing ease with which socially complex technologies can be made not just for broad masses of people, but for small groups and individuals ... In brief', he declares, 'centrifugal forces of individualization and separation are coming into conflict with centripetal social needs, which were met previously and unproblematically through shared or common material objects' (84), e.g. the printed book. One outcome, already visible online, is the attempt to produce and consume information 'with less reliance on impersonal forms and more on personal warrants for legitimation', as with hypertext, especially as hypertext is

depicted in the liberationist rhetoric about it (84). Historical precedents suggest a crippling, paradoxical consequence could result: priva-
tization rather than the democratization of knowledge preached by
the liberationists.

The argument for demassification is strong enough to ward off casual
dismissal and to cast some doubt on the wisdom of end-maker scholarship. But as so often in the ongoing dialogue, the best response is not
directly to the envisioned consequence but to the assumptions implicit
in the system whose effect that consequence is. I will return to those
assumptions in a moment.

Another system-wide effect – and product of the same assumptions –
begins with Régis Debray's observation that intellectual forms supply a
'symbolic matrix ... in whose dependence we bind ourselves ... to the
world of meaning' (1996: 140f.). Earlier I raised the question briefly in
connection with individual commentary notes, which (I supposed) if
written specifically for incorporation into unknown DIY assemblages
would need to carry with them indication of whatever context the
author intended. Excepting perhaps a well-known author's name, this
would imply expressed rather than assumed context – but expressed to
whom, precisely? In other words, DIY raises the difficult question of
how pre-knowledge of digital unboundedness might affect the composition of separable components, including for example major essays.
(The short answer is, we do not know.) John Seely Brown and Paul
Duguid identify this as the emerging *disaggregation* problem: What
happens when mutually contextualizing components of a whole are
separated? The problem also turns up in one of the more popular issues
exercising those who think about writing in the hypertextual medium:
argumentation. A traditional argument, as we all know, leads the
reader through a strictly predetermined sequence. What happens, so
the question runs, when reader-determined sequencing of morselized
prose must be treated as a given, as in current hypertext fiction?[59]
Some have suggested that the matrix-change does not put an end to
argumentation but rather establishes new conditions for it and requires
corresponding rhetorical development. Wait and see?

Several closely related system-wide problems have been identified,
resulting in an altogether dark picture. Brown and Duguid have compiled them into what they call the '6-D vision' of disintegrating forces
triggered by information technology. In addition to demassification
and disaggregation, these are decentralization, denationalization,
despatialization and disintermediation (2000: 22). As they note, none
of these attributes of our supposed future is to be dismissed idly: each

reveals 'important trends and pressures in society' to which we need to attend. But my point here is the underlying error that turns such genuine social problems into a vision, bordering on paranoia, of all-encompassing disaster. One may be disinclined to such a vision, but the negating prefix (de-, dis-) common to the visionary attributes provides a clue to what is wrong: Why should the future appear entirely as negation of the present? The answer, I think, is that the future inevitably appears that way when we expect it or, need it to be the present, which it can only mirror with growing distortion. For the concerns of this chapter, the significant matter lies in the mutation of our old enemy, historical provincialism,[60] here turned around to misconstrue the future rather than the past.

Quite a different if uncertain picture appears from the creative, writerly perspective of the individual scholar. For him and her the trends and pressures of the 6-D vision imply the need to rethink contributions to commentary (and other genres) so as to anticipate their endless, unpredictable *re*aggregation by future readers – or in more familiar terms, their recontextualization. These trends and pressures apply in particular to the society that the scholarly genres respond to and maintain, pushing forward questions about how as a whole this society needs to focus its efforts, for example in helping to reconfigure how publication is managed and by whom. The reader will, I hope, forgive me for not pursuing these questions, which lie well outside the scope of the book, though roughly pointing them out does not. But well within my scope is to note what has happened here: the possibility of creative adaptation to our changed circumstances makes the system we analyse far less brittle.

8 Information

Part of the fear (and inevitably also the appeal) in the 6-D paranoia is the sense that knowledge and so the world as we know it are disembodied in the heralded transformation to digital form. For us the haunting question at the beginning of T. S. Eliot's *Choruses from 'The Rock'*, 'Where is the knowledge we have lost in information?' (I.16), speaks not only to the poverty of a reductive medium – we can turn such poverty into a powerful tool – but chiefly to its supposed intangibility. The 'shock of the new' might partially explain our sense of disorientation in the Information Age, but it cannot reach the disorientation implicit in the idea or 'impression of information', as Geoffrey Nunberg has called it. What, exactly, *is* 'information'?

For one thing, it is an astonishingly successful notion, used everywhere to characterize not only the era in which we live, the basis for its economy, prestigious social roles and so on but even the cultural *raison d'être* of education.[61] Having it is good. Being without it is bad. But its colourless, odourless, tasteless and elusive ubiquity makes the notion, however successful, exceedingly difficult to grasp critically – which fact should make us very suspicious. How can we as end-makers of the new digital environment, get a grip on whatever it is?

Part of the problem, especially in the context I am exploring here, is derived from its recent history in technical discourse, beginning with Claude Shannon's and Warren Weaver's mathematical theory of communication, in which they defined 'information' in a very special, quantifiable sense.[62] Gregory Bateson explains the central point. A unit of 'information' (in Shannon's and Weaver's sense) is 'a difference which makes a difference' (2000/1972: 315). It is quantified in negative terms, by how many alternative possibilities are excluded; hence the amount is a function of the improbability that the actual character is the right one. Consider, he says, two texts, one in English, one in Chinese. Because a given character in the latter message excludes thousands of others whereas a given one in the former excludes only twenty-five, the Chinese character is said to carry *more information* (Bateson 2000/1972: 408–9). Hence Weaver's warning in *The Mathematical Theory of Communication*: '[t]he word information ... is used in a special sense that must not be confused with its ordinary usage. In particular, *information must not be confused with meaning*' (Shannon and Weaver 1949: 8, my emphasis). Unfortunately, however, it has been. In consequence, the older sense ('Knowledge communicated concerning some particular fact, subject, or event; that of which one is apprised or told; intelligence, news') seems to have been displaced by the notion of meaning as a measurable abstract quantity without respect to the circumstances and format of its production or reception – an *essence*, wholly represented by data, that may be indefinitely transmitted and transformed.

Nunberg, in 'Farewell to the Information Age', defines the currently popular, falsely materialized sense: 'a uniform and morselized substance ... indifferent not just to the medium it resides in but also to the kind of representation it embodies ... a *noble* substance'.[63] As such the notion gains deep cultural resonances and so enormous (though quiet) authority from an old conception of the human soul, expressed for example in the Pythagorean doctrine of an essence that 'wanders, comes now here, now there, and occupies whatever body [it pleases]'.[64]

Nunberg argues in effect that the confusion of semantic with probabilistic information is not inexplicably perverse but answers to an impression already shaped by the 'information-genres' of print – newspapers, modern reference works, census reports &c. (1996: 110, 114f.). The attributed qualities of 'metaphysical haecity or "thereness", its transferability, its quantized and extended substance, its interpretative transparency or autonomy' define 'a mode of reading' (116, 123). These qualities of this 'impression of information' reify the 'material properties of the documents that inscribe it'; its semantic properties 'are the reflexes of the institutions and practices that surround the use of these documents' (1996: 120).

If the informational mode of reading is bound up with the materiality of its documents, then the 'impression of information' should be faltering with the growth of electronic forms. This seems counterintuitive: digital data, like the Pythagorean soul, are capable of indefinite transformation without change. But again, *only in the informational mode of reading are we apt to think that meaning inheres in these data and not in their embodied form.* Furthermore, Nunberg argues, computing undermines this mode and the genres which support it by failing to preserve their social and material boundaries. Hence the signs of disintegration we observed in the autochthonous forms of electronic communication are likewise artifacts of the informational perspective (1996: 124f.). Perhaps, as has been suggested, these are comparable to the anomalies in a moment of Kuhnian 'extraordinary science', when the crisis they force precipitates a major shift in how we conceptualize the world (Kuhn 1970/1962: 84–91). In any case, as a number of cogent essays have recently argued, the partiality and reductiveness of 'information' clearly do not help us with the embodied qualities of knowledge on which wise use of computational forms depends.[65]

What *is* the relation between those two aspects of the same perceived thing, its form and its content? The Pythagorean doctrine of the transmigration of souls, which I quoted above from Ovid's version of it, is appealing because like the notions of 'form' and 'content' it gives us a simple way of talking about and dealing with a central enigma of human culture. What matters, to us as to Ovid, is not the hypothetical transmigration of essence (metempsychosis) but the reality of the new thing made as much by the change of form (metamorphosis). 'Reincarnation: that's the word', Leopold Bloom remarks in *Ulysses* (II.1) – a word no less puzzling, no less indicative of genuine mystery, though it has the advantage of pointing to the crux of form.

Authorial anticipation of re-embodiment, this would suggest, should have far less to do with securing intentional meaning than with Don Fowler's 'continuing fertility of problematisation' (1999: 441), in other words, with writing for openness to new contexts. What this might mean in practice is up to practice to find out, but the lyrical quality Susana Pajares Tosca has attributed to hypertext, with its suggested alliance to creative fiction, seems a promising rhetoric with which to begin (1999; also Miles 2001). More prosaically the obvious answer is authorial metadata, which corresponds in print to titles, abstracts and keywords. Authors are unlikely to follow any fixed set of terms, but in a world where readers increasingly choose what to read on the basis of authorial metadata, sufficient standardization may obtain in practice. The question of writing in and with metadata has only recently begun to be explored.[66]

9 Conclusion

I have argued that the major difference in the offing as far as commentary is concerned – or at least the only one about which we can be confident – is the opportunity to model the commentary form. This can be done immediately, though in a very limited way, using a mixture of local and online resources.[67] In the short to medium term, major work is almost certain to be circumscribed by the localized 'big humanities' projects, such as *Perseus*. I have argued, however, that far more interesting possibilities for the future of commentary-making and for the future of other scholarly genres appear to lie elsewhere, in the convergence of user with maker of tools (thus the end-maker) in a digital library. There are numerous technical, social and political impediments I have blithely ignored, but since my aim is motivation to research, particularly experiment, I trust these are not fatal.

Earlier I recognized but postponed consideration of Glenn Most's point that purely formal analysis cannot do full justice to the complexities of the commentary (or any other) genre. Since, as Nunberg says, we have the greatest difficulty seeing which of these are contingent, we must pay attention to them all, in their cultural context as faithful translation demands, though as outsiders looking in. Whether we choose actually to implement any particular feature of old commentary practice in the new depends on a number of factors beyond my present scope, for example the theory of language that the former assumes.[68] We must, however, be able to imagine clearly what we once knew as well as what we don't know. This is the problem of the historical and ethnographic imagination, which I have touched on here but consider at greater length in the following chapter.

I fear that most of the above will repel my intended audience of working scholars with a formidable vision of unexpected difficulties, as if one were to reach out for a light-switch but encounter a untried treatise on electricity – or more accurately, its future author, still unclear about what to say. But consider what is on offer immediately: the chance not merely to rethink everything to do with scholarly genres, rather more to do so in constructivist terms. These terms are made meaningful by the tools we now have, which although primitive do allow us, 'on the threshold of what can be productively thought of as human-kind's meso-electronic period', successfully to fashion 'crude but functional electronic artifacts' (Peters 1994). This crudity notwithstanding, they are adequate enough to encourage powerful thought-experiments. In the world of computational things we tend to value intricate, complex, algorithmically sophisticated tools, and so to undervalue what we actually have, that 'stone adze in the hands of a cabinetmaker'.[69] Yet the hand-operated printing press, hand-made type, ink and paper were also 'crude but functional'; if we look to our early books we can see what inventive souls, who loved what they were doing, did with them.

I will be bold: the activity which computing greatly, newly enhances is endless, serious play. Perhaps the most important new thing for us is the prospect of dealing more imaginatively, deftly with tradition than we could before. And commentary practice in particular also looks forward in another sense, to a greatly expanded though solidly traditional role it could take. In the disaggregated docuverse, what is so clearly needed is the knowledge of how to reaggregate. Commentary, as Gregory Crane has suggested, is our expression of that knowledge.

3
Discipline

Every philosophy is tinged with the colouring of some secret imaginative background, which never emerges explicitly into its trains of reasoning.

Alfred North Whitehead, *Science and the Modern World* (1925): 11

It takes a good deal of maturity to see that every field of knowledge is the centre of all knowledge, and that it doesn't matter so much what you learn when you learn it in a structure that can expand into other structures.

Northrop Frye, *On Education* (1988): 10

Where once we thought a discipline – history, say, or politics, or even economics – was at the centre of things by having a blinkered view of humanity, now we realise that we are all on the edge of things in a great ring of viewers.

Greg Dening, *Readings/Writings* (1998): 139

1 Introduction

In his professional memoir, *After the Fact: Two Countries, Four Decades, One Anthropologist* (1995), Clifford Geertz describes his first journey into the Moroccan town of Sefrou in the early 1960s:

by then perhaps a thousand years old, [it] still had a sharpness of definition extraordinary even for Morocco, where everything seems outlined in calcium light ... The town, the oasis, the mountains, each enclosed within the next, chalk white, olive green, stone brown, each marked off from the next by a line so sharp as to seem drawn with a pen, gave a sense of deliberate arrangement. Site and settlement looked equally designed. The initial effect of going on then to descend into the body of the town was, for a foreigner anyway, the total, instantaneous, and, so it seemed for an uncomfortable period, permanent dissolution of this sense of clarity, poise, and composition. (1995: 11f.)

'The double image, clarity from a distance, jumble up close', in the years that followed, 'set a frame of perception and understanding, a Jamesian hum of buzz and implication, that could not afterward be wholly discarded, only critiqued, developed, filled out, moralized upon, and brought to bear on more exact experiences.' The 'ascending tension' which it revealed, 'between classic urban form ... and a swelling and diversifying urban life tumbling across its incised lines' (12), became Geertz's guiding conception. But the image and the creative tension of its unresolvable doubleness are more than metonyms of a particular anthropologist's fieldwork. More than signs of experience, they are vivid metaphors of the participant-observer's form of life, which is lived in relation to worlds neither closely native nor distantly foreign but uneasily and powerfully both.

Ethnography (what social anthropologists do) has informed computer science for some time in the analysis of work in offices, libraries and so on and in the design of systems to aid this work.[1] Results have prepared the ground for better knowledge of scholarly practice and for more responsive and sensitive procedures of design, e.g. of new forms and genres. While these results and the specific methodologies of approach and analysis responsible for them are important, they are not the focus here. The concern of this chapter is not how we may discover what scholars now do, wittingly or unwittingly, so that it may be improvingly retooled; rather it is how we may get to the disciplinary conditions from which specific methods arise as desire or need direct. What is required is not received technique as described in numerous textbooks of anthropology but the ethnographic *imagination*. What is required is the dynamic ability to address, move for move, the changing forms of disciplinary invention across the humanities. This imperative puts humanities computing, again and again, in that anthropological novice's shoes, with the unpredictable future immediately before him as he descends into the place of fieldwork. What matters then? Formulas only fit formulaic situations, not living ones.

But we must not go too far in the opposite direction. Describing the conventional role of observation in scientific experiment, the instrument-like 'observation-as-what-one-sees', Ian Hacking remarks that 'it is not all that important'. What matters is being *observant* and so ready to notice 'the instructive quirks or unexpected outcomes', the anomalies of a situation that signify something new (1983: 167). This is what the novice requires, and that is my concern here. Another philosopher of science, Stephen Toulmin, remarks in a slightly different context, 'This is not work for the untutored imagination. It may be an art, but it is one whose exercise requires a stiff training ... One cannot teach a man to be imaginative; but there are certain kinds of imagination which only a man with a particular training can exercise' (1967/1953: 39f.).

The training I have in mind takes two forms.

The first is to study what happens in the interdisciplinary research projects with which humanities computing is involved. Again, I do not mean what people actually do on the job or what their intentions and goals are, although these must be known and accounted for, but how engagement in these projects tends to bring about a sea-change of mind for those involved, how their intentions and goals metamorphose, and why. In what follows I adopt an ethnographic perspective in a rough and preliminary way to examine a few such projects and draw conclusions about the field from them. This change of mind is of course widely if not wildly touted, as so much is in computing's neighbourhood. My concern is to document a small bit of it, and so to make a case for the centrality of ethnographic description to the self-understanding of the field. Much more of this kind of study awaits the fortunate student.

The other, broader form of training I describe by constructing an enabling perspective on the disciplines from which humanities computing has to learn and by that learning make itself *of* as well as *in* the humanities. I argue for disciplinary kinships and illustrate how they are formed. I begin with the anthropological conceit, which I take to be true, that disciplines are social systems and so can be studied ethnographically. This kind of study proceeds through the literature of each field, attempting to construct bridging accounts, particularly with the aid of efforts within that field to achieve some form of critical self-awareness.

The purpose of both kinds of training, as of this book throughout, is to improve computing's engagement with the humanities. In Chapter 1 this engagement was located within the scholar's own individual practice, and in Chapter 2 in possible cyberspaces of communication among like-minded individuals. In this chapter it is centred directly on the meeting of humanities computing with the older disciplines. For reasons of clarity and economy I envision this meeting in the form of a paradigmatic conversation between two different kinds of specialists, designated here as 'the scholar' and 'the practitioner'. These labels are not entirely satisfactory – the practitioner of humanities computing I identify in this chapter is no less concerned with erudition or learning than the scholar is with intelligent and effective method. But 'scholar' and 'practitioner' will have to do for now. Note, however, that two serious problems underlie our unease with them: poor knowledge of how scholars do what they do (Lorraine Daston's point, developed in the Introduction) and poorly developed ability to read our machines (Michael Mahoney's point, developed in Chapter 1).

My close examination of the disciplines has two aims. The first is suggested by Clyde Kluckhohn's mischievous observation that anthropology gives the practitioner an intellectual poaching licence to go where he or she will and take what is available there (Geertz 2000/1983: 21). In the history of disciplines such poaching is actually quite common. New fields, like humanities computing, establish themselves and older ones grow with the help of figures of speech and thought taken by analogy from yet older, better understood areas of practice or from newer, promisingly vigorous ones.[2] Thus in early days the natural sciences took elements of cognitive rhetoric from the crafts and then from industry; more recently the social sciences have reached into the natural sciences, then into medicine and finally into the humanities; and literary studies has repeatedly poached from other fields, like Marxist history or Freudian psychoanalysis. This is not to recommend poaching as a way of disciplinary life – quite the opposite, in fact. Poaching signifies an empty larder and puts the poacher into an unpromising parasitic relationship with the provider, a relationship that in the long term weakens the poacher by blocking any possibility of an independent existence. A discipline thus weakened is in danger, as Northrop Frye remarks, of 'being sucked into an ideological vortex' with an entirely different nature and trajectory, and so of being denatured and thrown off course.[3] Clearly what must follow poaching as quickly as possible, as digestion must follow eating, is the transforming assimilation of foreign ideas into a native system of analysis. To paraphrase Frye's strong argument for the independence of literary criticism (1957: 6f.), the axioms, postulates and methods of a field have to grow out of that with which it deals. Its critical principles must be derived inductively; they cannot be taken as if ready-made from another discipline without making that discipline the master. But – this is my qualified point – the intellectual *raw* material is there to be taken.

The second aim of this ethnographic study has a much larger scope, though a purpose equally pragmatic and polemical. To date humanities computing has not managed to construct much of a wall around some intellectual turf in order to form itself into yet another discipline like the rest. Rather it has found, rather haphazardly, ways through existing walls and sketched out, if only in a rough and inchoate way, a methodological commons for all to draw from. Attempts have indeed been made to form a discipline as much like the rest as possible – short-term prudence recommends exactly that, to seek legitimacy. It may be that these attempts have not succeeded because the strength of will, cogency of argument and depth of pocketbook have not been readily available to overcome socio-intellectual sloth and self-interest, at least not in many places. But failure to achieve sameness with older disciplines is not my concern here, except as a *felix culpa:* a fault exceedingly fortunate because of the roaming interdisciplinary vantage point that it frees us to establish. A number of practitioners have found their way to this plural vantage point over the years. I do not lay claim to its invention or discovery. But getting and maintaining it have not been systematically examined, and that I am concerned to do in this chapter, and by doing greatly to enhance the nature, strength and purpose of the field. As an autodidact I wish for a proper curriculum.

By kinships, then, I have in mind elaborations of existing and potential family relationships that inform the interdisciplinary and largely collaborative work of the field. In this chapter I define two kinds of relations: those of *application* and those of *research*. They are represented diagramatically in Figure 3.1.[4] I will return to the details of this intellectual and disciplinary map below, but for now I wish only to make a few preliminary remarks.

The *relations of application*, indicated at the top of the figure, date from the earliest days of help desks and programming services to which scholars in the humanities could avail themselves. (Hence the origin of my paradigmatic conversation and the real or imagined desk at which it takes place.) Since then it has been clear that the analytic methods of the humanities could be modelled computationally and that these models and the software written, modified or selected to implement them are in principle independent of an individual's research, even of a particular discipline.[5] In the paradigmatic encounter

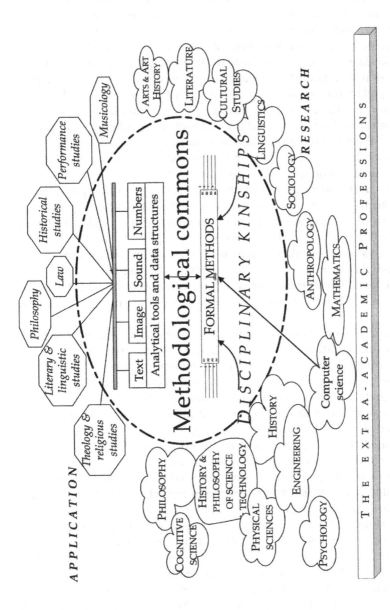

Figure 3.1:   An intellectual and disciplinary map of humanities computing

of scholar and technical expert that I imagine here, model and soft-ware-solution arise out of probing conversations from which both practitioner and scholar learn. The scholar learns what his or her problem looks like in computational form. The practitioner learns a specific but generalizable method for tackling problems of a certain kind. Experience has shown that for the scholar the encounter pro-vokes new ways of thinking about artifacts of study as well as attempts on problems heretofore beyond reach; I will say much more about this below. For the technical practitioner it yields an observer's method-ological understanding and a set of tools and technical approaches. Over time these generalize and accumulate, respectively, and the prac-titioner builds up knowledge of how and where else the fruits of labour in one discipline apply to others.

As practitioners know well, the result is far more than commodified exchange of portable techniques in a methodological 'plug-and-play', even now that some basic tools are more or less readily to hand. Crucial to success is the practitioner's incipient form of participant observation, in which insight into scholarly means and objectives combines with an outsider's objectivity. During the encounter of scholar and practitioner the latter's view from the outside is beneficial because it forces hidden assumptions to the surface. (The manifest difficulty of forcing one's own assumptions to the surface lends strong support to an argument for *collaborative separation* of the two roles into distinct persons.) Making the tacit explicit, or at least isolating it when it is unsayable, is essential to the most difficult and error-prone aspect of computerization: constructing a model that accurately reflects a given understanding of the real-world problem and so, in the modelling process that follows, is apt for exploring it.[6] There are many reasons for difficulty, e.g. problems that are poorly defined at the outset or those which evolve during the encounter as the scholar realizes what is possible. In general, as with engineering, the problems that actually are addressed, and so could be reverse-engineered from the model, develop in the field. Their shape and sub-stance are determined partly by the constraints and opportunities of the situation in which they occur, and partly by the evolving concep-tion of the problem (Wulf 2000). Hence the encounter is paradig-matic in a broader sense as well. Although a particular collaboration between scholar and technical practitioner normally has a definite conclusion, the encounter of the humanities with computing is ongoing. It defines a situation that, as Terry Winograd has said, 'is a constant co-evolution in which new tools lead to new practices and ways of doing business, which in turn create problems and possibilities for technical innovation' (1995a: 73).

The relations of research, sketched in the lower half of Figure 3.1, map out what may seem an impossibly demanding project. In the Introduction I suggested that the seemingly impossible demand changes into an opportunity when we look on this project not as every individual's task but as a *shared and conversational* undertaking. Enacting it gives meaning to 'collaboration'. If there is a fatal flaw here, then it is to be found in the presumption of sharing, that is, of regular communication across all the activities loosely delimited by Figure 3.1. Of all fields, if we measure the probability of success by the tools at hand, humanities computing should have the best chance of addressing that problem, but here I simply assume that communication is a major item on the agenda. (See Chapter 5.4.4–5.) The extent of familiarity with any particular field is meant to be variable and is to be determined. What matters at this stage is to have *a way to find a way* into each and to know that Kluckhohn's disciplinary poaching licence, granted to humanities computing *de situ*, has the potential to become a passport. Figure 3.1 is a proleptic map to accompany the initial explorations, a model *for* the field's extensions of itself into the humanities, 'a structure that can expand into other structures'.

2   Relations of application

The relations of application are established in our paradigmatic conversation. Although there are many reasons why it might take place, its primary, intellectual motivation is a bilateral curiosity. This curiosity is expressed through the exercise of analytical, methodological practices, or practices that become more and more clearly methodical as they converge in a computational model of the target problem. The meeting of the two analytical methods is where the interesting things happen.

Several years of experience on both sides of this conversation suggest that it has a discernible anatomy. Harold Short has described three phases: analysis and design; manipulation and representation; interconnection.[7]

2.1   Analysis and design phase

Typically the conversation begins in a meeting at which methodological viewpoints are exchanged: the scholar discusses the nature of his or her source material, converging on what makes it interesting and problematic; the practitioner talks about one or more ways of modelling the data, for example in a database design. For each data model the focus is on advantages and disadvantages in terms of what manipulations can be performed and what questions asked. On the basis of this initial meeting, the practitioner sketches one or more preliminary models. Then in an iterative process the best model is chosen, critiqued and modified. During this process at least three things happen: (1) the practitioner learns much more about the data and their complexity; (2) the scholar acquires better understanding of the kinds of compromises required in order that the data be manipulated computationally; (3) the scholar begins to see aspects of the data in a new light and to gain new insights into them.

It is crucial that the scholar and the practitioner are able to reach a compromise between the opposed qualities of cultural source material, rich in its complexity and ambiguity, and of computational form, mechanically rigorous. A successful design results from the convergence of these qualities. The new insights which the scholar is apt to gain from this process may influence the design, but not necessarily; they may simply be fortunate byproducts of the process.

It is quite important to avoid the common error of bestowing on this process and its results the transcendental virtues of *rigour, precision* and the like, with the implication that prior to the conversation the scholar's work and thoughts suffered from their lack. Disciplined, even simply repeated confrontation with cultural data may produce better, clearer understanding of them, especially perhaps when this confrontation takes place in such a conversation as represented here. But it is a profound mistake to think that interpretation expressed in or arising from natural language or other analogue medium is qualitatively inferior. *Rigour* is typically a quality of formal expression, as in logic, mathematics and so computing, where it signifies fitness for proof or computability; in common language it denotes strictness, even harshness, as of the law; obduracy, hardship, austerity, strict accuracy – not qualities compatible with forms of cultural expression (though what is being expressed may have them). *Precision* is much more apt, but we need to distinguish kinds of it. The telling and retelling of a history may deprive it of accuracy but increase its truth, as in an often repeated family story (Dening 1996: 49–51).

Since truth does not compute, computational and human precisions about cultural artifacts are in conflict, and it is in this conflict that the nub of the matter lies. In the language of engineering, the focus of the conversation between scholar and practitioner is design against constraints of various kinds (Wulf 2000). Facing these constraints is a matter of practical necessity, but doing so turns them into a powerful epistemological tool and defines the scope for creativity and insight.

In projects whose primary technology is database design or textual encoding, conflict most often happens over *categorization*. The scholar may come to the conversation with little to no idea of basic categories, but most often he or she will have a moderately to well articulated system in mind.

Ultimately, however, the terms in which such mental systems are defined, even if very well articulated, are not ruled by the computational imperatives of absolute consistency and total explicitness. The ambiguity and tacitness inherent to cultural artifacts (which after all are products of the human imagination) tend to survive mental categorization and so are the qualities thrown into relief by the translation that the practitioner's rigid computational structure requires. Since the scholar strives insofar as possible to disambiguate and articulate the object of study, the unbending fundamentalism proves a powerful instrument with which to prise apart his or her original categories and, perhaps, to re-examine the circumstances in which particular kinds of evidence were created, particular cases recorded.

More than concepts may be involved. In a project requiring large-scale data collection, where this is suitably done by lightly trained researchers, categories have to be simple and clear.[8] The practical matter of data reliability can thus drive an effort to simplify – not a bad thing, given the scholarly love of complex schemes – and that in turn can lead to reconceptualization of the data and to discovery of more fundamental categories.

In the *Prosopography of Anglo-Saxon England* project (2000–4), whose purpose is to provide a comprehensive biographical register of recorded inhabitants (c. 450–1066), invention of a new category, 'event', allowed automatic linking of people by the events in which they participated.[9] The well-known decoupling of presentational structure from data structure, that is, allowed new connections to be made that printed prosopographies, by the nature of their medium and technology of production, were unable to afford. Along with other such projects, the predecessor of PASE, the *Prosopography of the Byzantine World*, likewise brought about a profound change in prosopography by giving the scholarly user access to a much lower-level structuring of the primary data, hence the recombinatorial ability productive of a much expanded questioning. My point here, however, is that the scholar of our conversation, co-designer of this access, begins to think at this structural, meta-theoretical level rather than digesting the data for secondary use, a highly demanding procedure unlikely to be repeated and unable to be examined.

The combinatorial possibilities in printed reference works are constrained by the technology, but they are also half implicit: their actual use is of course not expressed and so must be puzzled out, as I illustrated in the previous chapter. In the paradigmatic conversation, the scholar is therefore likely to be surprised by the complexity of apparently simple objects. This was, for example, the case in the *Corpus Vitrearum Medii Aevi Digitization* Project, an offshoot of the International Corpus Vitrearum Project (1949–), 'dedicated to the publication of all medieval stained glass, under the auspices of the Union Académique Internationale'. For the database design, the question that had to be answered was: What is the object of study, and exactly how does one want to view it? Defining the physical object (a panel within a window, group of panels or an entire window) begins with the spatial coordinates locating it in terms of the window, church and geographical place; it extends to the material attributes of the object and its history. The object also has symbolic content, subject to a not inconsiderable amount of interpretation and classification. Furthermore, the basis of the collection is a set of photographs, which are sometimes of panels, sometimes of whole windows, sometimes of groups of panels. The complexity arises from the multiple possibilities of intersection among these coordinate types. This intersection includes a 'layering' of representations (database referring to photographs referring to objects), with a further multiplication of possibilities depending on a researcher's interest in or wish to ignore intermediate layers. Again, the cognitive change is in the meta-theoretical focus brought about by the necessity of imagining the mechanisms to enable the recombinant potential of the collection.

This potential has an additional, institutional face illustrated by CVMA and other art historical projects. Notably in all such projects surveyed for this preliminary study, the scholars involved have not wanted to use *any* of the recognized international standards,[10] consistently arguing that these were unsuitable for their methods of study. Similar resistance from scholars to the textual ontologies provided by the Text Encoding Initiative suggests that resistance is neither accidental nor perverse, nor can it be a property of the medium. Clearly it points to the felt need for maximum flexibility in the design of new scholarly forms. But that quickly becomes a question of what structures are basic or 'primitive' in the analysis of a particular cultural artifact – another meta-theoretical problem of considerable interest (discussed in Chapter 5.4.10). In other words, such ontologies are 'as if' constructs whose scholarly purpose is to raise questions, to say what might be and not what is. Practical considerations, however, point the need for standard, higher-level categories, not only to serve the impatient or other-minded scholar but also to open up the resource to wider audiences, as noted in Chapter 2. Thus an important role of the practitioner in the art historical projects surveyed here has been to insist that one or more links to existing international standards be maintained. This becomes an issue in the third phase, as noted below.

2.2 Manipulation and representation phase

In the second phase of the conversation, the scholar works with a prototype or implemented model, able to manipulate his or her data and to represent the result of queries and selections in various ways. Obviously, the earlier in the process this prototype becomes available the better, not only because many kinds of errors and infelicities will be noticed only then but also because the thinking enabled by manipulation of objects is exceedingly difficult to imagine at an earlier stage. Of all the claims for the unique significance of the computer, perhaps the most important to scholarship is, as Michael Mahoney has said, that it 'embodies a historically unique relation of thinking and doing' (1990b: 325). The scholar's project does not become real until this relation is realized. Startling insights emerge with the computational object in hand, at least partly because this is a genuinely new kind of thinking previously inaccessible to scholars.

Here the practitioner must strike a balance between delivering a working prototype early enough and delivering it with sufficient data that the use of it yields practical results. There is, of course, no hard-and-fast rule or even rule of thumb to apply, since everything depends on the nature of the data and the computational design. But everyone must keep in mind that discovering fundamental design flaws late in the development of a project can be disastrous. Manipulating the prototype may be the sole means to discover them.

Representation is both an idea that we poorly understand and a loose bundle of means for bridging digital models to the analogue world.[11] Mostly this bridging is accomplished by visualization, in images, charts and other graphical structures, such as tables. The basic means for effective visualization on screen are not much more than a decade old. Serious visualization projects still strain the capabilities of existing equipment.[12] What all these have in common, however, has been a subject of attention for many years.[13] From existing work we know that representations shape if not give meaning, that apparently slight variations in a representation can make disproportionate difference to its cognitive effects, and hence that rapid interactive play with representations, allowing for nearly costless trials, is to be encouraged.

The perfective cycle of finding and fixing problems is unremarkable, but not all problems discovered by manipulation or anticipated at an earlier stage need to be fixed immediately. Indeed, if the solution can be postponed and is likely to profit from experience with the evolving resource, it should be. In PASE, for example, the difficulty of keeping the initial categories of 'career', 'occupation' and 'status' distinct was noted early on but a solution was postponed until, with longer exposure to the data as seen through the lens of the resource, a resolution became clear. From the outset the practitioner's advice, from long experience with changing classification schemes, was to choose more rather than fewer distinctions. As long as these were made consistently, it would then be trivially easy to merge them, whereas opening up a new category would mean re-examining many cases.

The conceptual drive to simplicity – which may mean devising tools to preserve but manage complexity – may particularly belong to this phase. It is the shared contribution of both scholar and practitioner, whose intellectual work may be characterized overall as balancing the multiplicatory powers of the machine with the envisioned simplicities of mind.

In this phase as well, the result of work begins to become comparable to previous scholarly constructs, which however carefully done may be shown to be radically inadequate or incorrect. The historiographical caution worked out at length in Chapter 2 applies, but at the same time scholars in the past were as prone to error as we are, and the outcome of this phase sometimes reveals it. For example, in the process of bringing entries for clergy together in a systematic way, the *Clergy of the Church of England Database (CCED)* began quickly to demonstrate that standard reference materials were simply wrong. The fault lay not with careless work but pointed to the fact that the amount of evidence one can marshall and the flexibility in marshalling it genuinely matter to the quality of the results in history and similar disciplines. Massing more material in more imaginative ways in fact generates new questions and leads to challenging of long-held assumptions and interpretations.

2.3 Interconnection phase

There are several strong arguments against the quasi-Marxist assumption that the technocratic apparatus of humanities computing will wither away, leaving the scholarly proletariat to rule. Although there are certainly advantages to having the roles of scholar and practitioner instantiated as cognitive functions of one mind, there are very strong advantages to having them manifested in distinct persons, indeed academic departments. One of these has surfaced repeatedly in the discussion above: the collaborative power of the conversation between individuals with very different perspectives and agendas. Another, equally powerful advantage becomes possible when, as at King's College London and elsewhere, an institution has a well-established department of humanities computing (McCarty and Kirschenbaum 2003). This is the ability to interconnect projects both implicitly and explicitly.

One expression of this ability is the interdisciplinarity created through humanities computing by virtue of its methodological perspective on and collaborative participation with the disciplines, about which considerably more will be said below. Suffice it to say for the moment, however, that views on interdisciplinarity rarely if ever have a comprehensive extra-disciplinary yet academic base, as humanities computing does. The implications of what may be seen and navigated from this base remain to be worked out, but a preliminary idea may be gained from the ability of a project-active department of humanities computing to interact collaboratively across many disciplines.

An expression of this collaborative overview is the design for thematic commonalities across several projects managed by the same humanities computing department. In the projects discussed here this has in fact been done for the common focus on churches in the *CCED*, *CVMA* and the *Corpus of Romanesque Sculpture in Britain and Ireland* project, whose objective is to photograph and catalogue the wealth of surviving sculpture, both religious and secular, produced in Great Britain and Ireland within the period c. 1050–1200.

The technical synergy and collection of common approaches and tools is another type of interconnection. This leads into and overlaps with collaborative standards development.

2.4 Summary

The overall conclusion from years of experience across the three phases of project development is that the tension between scholar and humanities computing practitioner, both alert to different things, is essential and creative. On the aesthetics and dynamics of it I recommend, again, William Wulf's eloquent formula for engineering, 'design under constraint'. Like engineering in his and Walter Vincenti's view,[14] humanities computing applies formal methods from elsewhere (e.g. computer science in its use of relational database technology) but is not simply a 'humanities computer science' because the inherited methods comprise only part of the story, and perhaps not the most important part. Furthermore, as the projects cited above illustrate, the central problems in them, the focus of the intellectual interest, has only trivially to do with the computer science of the situation. Put in another way, the locus of interest is not the fundamentalist structure and its mechanisms but the conflict between it and the rich ambiguities of the cultural artifacts to which it is applied. But this is a more complex topic than it seems. I will return to it below.

The questions we ask as humanists tend to be those for which we can expect *some* kind of answer – in the sense of a response leading to better questions. Experience in project-work suggests that our new technologies of inquiry and analysis, as it were, liberate potential questions from the censure of difficulty and so allow us to go in heretofore forbidding directions. A common argument for the superiority of the interactive digital concordance over the printed one, for example, points to the multiplication of criteria one can combine in the former but not with the latter, e.g. 'life' within five words of 'death' and 'love' – a discouragingly hard question to ask with the printed kind and so (in some sense I will not attempt to define) not a question many would have thought to ask earlier. The projects discussed above also demonstrate that raising the level of complexity in the questions we can ask of our sources does better justice to them. The effect is not simply new questions but questions on a new level. But here we must be cautious: this better justice is justice *as we now conceive of it*, not by an ahistorical, absolute measure.

Back to the creative realities of collaboration. The projects suggest that these are mutually complementary to computerization not simply because more hands with different skills are needed. Rather, just as the conversation between individuals is stimulating for the challenge of different views whose integrity is shored up by their externality, so the machine externalizes scholarly methods and results, hence makes them stubbornly resistant to the human proclivity for seeing what is convenient to see. Furthermore, as the projects have shown, the massed evidence mechanically returned resists the projection of argument into evidence by giving us more than simply the examples which work.

Emphasis here has so far been one-sided, on the scholar's *metanoia* brought about by encounter with the tools and methods of humanities computing, in the relations of application. Whatever benefit this encounter may bring to traditional scholarship, however, the experienced practitioner faces the certain prospect of intellectual exhaustion unless a corresponding change-of-mind is in prospect. For this *metanoia* to be possible, we must turn to the relations of research shown in the foundational bottom half of Figure 3.1. Without them humanities computing can only be concerned with delivering goods manufactured elsewhere. With them it becomes a continual source of creative insight for the humanities and fully its own creature.

3 Relations of research

The relations of research are represented in Figure 3.1 as the 'Clouds of Knowing',[15] with some indication of important interrelationships among them. Their indefinite, cloudy shapes, in contrast to the well-defined octagons demarcating the disciplinary groups of application, are intended to suggest permeable bodies of knowledge, socially constituted but without departmental or professional aspects. The ability to read and realization of Kluckhohn's intellectual poaching licence are all the qualifications one needs.

Such relations are not new. By virtue of academic training practitioners in humanities computing have always had relationships individually with their disciplines of origin, and those who have engaged extensively with scholars across the disciplines have acquired working knowledge of several others. What *is* new is awareness of the Clouds and the comprehensiveness of the intellectual programme that their assembly maps out.[16] Seeing them thus implies their comparison, and this in turn sets the stage for the comparative epistemology that the participant observer's view defines.

The term 'comparative epistemology' I take from Ludwik Fleck. 'Whatever is known', he wrote, 'has always seemed systematic, proven, applicable, and evident to the knower' (1981/1935: 22). Thus in the ethnographic view, to the native insider of a discipline, his or her environment is all the world, or all of it that matters. Its conventions seem natural and true, if not founding principles of thought, and so tend thoughtlessly to form the matrix within which thinking is done, evaluated, indeed perceived as thought. But the pure outsider, looking in, is no better off. 'Every alien system of knowledge', Fleck continues, 'has likewise seemed contradictory, unproven, inapplicable, fanciful, or mystical.' To the outsider the interior is intellectually opaque, however perceptible to the senses, because that which informs the observables, the insider's experiential knowledge, goes without saying. Without the crucial participant understanding, an uninformed observer is apt to construe the observed in caricature as a projected self-image (cf. Winch 1990/1958: 88). 'May not the time have come', Fleck asks, 'to assume a less egocentric, more general point of view ...?'

Fleck's call has of course been variously anticipated and answered, most obviously in the social sciences, where stubbornly different ways of conceiving the world are least avoidable. Because each of us begins as native to some social environment and so is likely to regard it as unqualified reality, comparative epistemology implies defamiliarization, whose effects I have already noted in the conversational meeting of scholar and practitioner. In the social sciences more generally it is recognized as opening oneself up to otherness in fieldwork. The historian Robert Darnton has observed that, 'one thing seems clear to everyone who returns from field work: other people are other. They do not think the way we do. And if we want to understand their way of thinking' – and so our own – 'we should set out with the idea of capturing otherness' (1985/1984: 4). The opening sentence of L. P. Hartley's *The Go-Between* (1953) is frequently quoted: 'The past is a foreign country: they do things differently there.' Anthropologists at least since Claude Lévi-Strauss have noted the common disciplinary ground that Hartley's image conjures: 'Whether ... due to remoteness in time ... or to remoteness in space, or even to cultural heterogeneity, is of secondary importance compared to the basic similarity of perspective ...'[17] and the centrality of otherness to what it can reveal. 'Translated into the terms of the historian's craft ...' Darnton continues, the insistence on seeking out otherness 'may merely sound like the familiar injunction against anachronism. It is worth repeating nonetheless ... We constantly need to be shaken out of a false sense of familiarity ... to be administered doses of culture shock' (1985/1984: 4). The objective, Peter Burke explains for the sociology of knowledge, is to make 'what was familiar appear strange and what was natural seem arbitrary' (2000: 2). 'The demonstration of graspable plurality' is likewise a major duty of contemporary literary criticism. Jonathan Culler quotes William Empson: 'The central function of imaginative literature is to make you realize that other people act on moral convictions different from your own' (1988: 48).

Burke goes on to explain that defamiliarization and the comparative view it helps to establish imply a fundamental and potentially disorientating shift in our idea of knowledge. Whereas we have no trouble seeing 'ignorance', 'belief' and the like as historical, sociological or ethnographic phenomena, the term 'knowledge' commonly denotes 'our paradigm cognitive achievements' for which we tend to assume a normative, perhaps even a timeless and universal status.[18] In admitting ignorance we tend to imply a singular knowledge that would fill its void. During the past century or so, however, a number of Blakean corrosives have been working against this normative view of knowledge. Among these is, for example, the contradiction between our enormous cultural investment in the truth of natural science on the one hand, and on the other the manifest need to revise that truth in light of the continual transformation and reorganization in scientific knowledge – a point Thomas Kuhn's work has made impossible to ignore.[19] Another powerful corrosive is the confrontation with very different cultures. The beginnings of this confrontation are of course immemorial, but a new threshold seems to have been reached in Europe and North America with the beginnings of anthropology in the late nineteenth century.[20] 'One cannot read too long about Nayar matriliny, Aztec sacrifice, the Hopi verb, or the convolutions of the hominid transition and not begin at least to consider the possibility that, to quote Montaigne, '"each man calls barbarism whatever is not his own practice ... for we have no other criterion of reason than the example and idea of the opinions and customs of the country we live in"' (Geertz 2000: 45). From at least the second half of the past century that criterion has in most countries been radically, multiculturally pluralized as well. From these and other developments, there has been a steady push towards pluralized knowledge systems and processes of coming to know: to use the old terms, a shift from the context of justification according to a singular method to the highly diverse contexts of discovery in a diverse world.

Defamiliarization thus serves a fundamentally preliminary (though cyclically ongoing) janitorial function of clearing away what has become mental rubbish so that something else can happen. Once an imperial unity of knowledge has been shown to be many asymmetrically related 'knowledges', and our own more a fitful process than an achievement, we can begin to negotiate relationships among the various ways of knowing and to look once again into how our discoveries are made. Applied to the disciplines of the humanities and social sciences as ethnographic objects, this at least opens up the possibility of a coherent metadisciplinary perspective, and so of a genuine interdisciplinarity.

4 Disciplinarity and interdisciplinarity

In 'Literature as a Critique of Pure Reason' Northrop Frye quotes the passage from Alfred North Whitehead's *Science and the Modern World* used as the first epigraph to this chapter, commenting that this 'conception of philosophy as a verbal clothing worn over the indecent nakedness of something called its "imaginative background," so as to allow it to appear in public ... [is the] retreating nude that I have been trying to study all my life' (1990/1983: 169). It does not matter so much, as he says in the second epigraph, where one begins education as long as one has sufficiently maturity to catch sight of that retreating nude and follow her to the centre that is everywhere. To do this means recognizing that the received notion of disciplinarity is itself an impediment. Hence my third epigraph, which imagines getting beyond compartmentalized knowledge in a very different way.[21]

The idea of the discipline 'as an historically specific form' is actually quite recent. It is related, Shumway and Messer-Davidow argue, to developments in the sociology of knowledge but began with Michel Foucault, 'who first called attention to the discipline as "a system of control in the production of discourse"'.[22] Until recently its connotations have been 'entirely positive: to call a branch of knowledge a discipline was to imply that it was rigorous and legitimate' (1991: 202). But the very phrase 'branch of knowledge' already invokes one of the principal metaphors of legitimation, the medieval image of the 'tree of knowledge' (for example in Ramón Lull's influential *Arbor scientiae*, written ca. 1300).[23] This image implicitly legitimates an historical structure of knowledge, Peter Burke explains, by making it natural rather than artificial, and since it is a single tree, authoritative rather than contingent. It thus 'illustrates a central phenomenon in cultural history, the naturalization of the conventional, or the presentation of culture as if it were nature, invention as if it were discovery' (2000: 86). Ideas may grow organically, but once the historical contingencies are forgotten and knowledge is taken as what is known, particular growths seem inevitable, and other possibilities are excluded. Taxonomic fixity is one problem with this metaphor; another is the impossibility of anything not a branch. The panoptic view does present all branches at once, which at least implies the possibility of a multidisciplinary scampering about. But because there is by definition no knowledge apart from the tree, interdisciplinary knowing is ruled out: there is no way to represent it.

The other, now certainly more common figure of speech with the some of the same conceptual strictures is the geopolitical metaphor of 'fields', 'territories' or 'turf', with their 'boundaries', 'borders' or 'frontiers' and their 'gatekeepers'.[24] David Hilbert's introduction to 'Axiomatic Thought' (an address delivered in Zürich in 1917, as the empires of Europe were coming to a violent end) expresses the basic metaphor more robustly than many will now allow themselves, although it still comes close to representing how disciplinarity is often conceived:

Just as in the life of nations the individual nation can only thrive when all neighbouring nations are in good health; and just as the interest of states demands, not only that order prevail within every individual state, but also that the relationships of the states among themselves be in good order; so it is in the life of the sciences. In due recognition of this fact the most important bearers of mathematical thought have always evinced great interest in the laws and the structure of the neighbouring sciences; above all for the benefit of mathematics itself they have always cultivated the relations to the neighbouring sciences, especially to the great empires of physics and epistemology. (Ewald 1996: 1107)

Here the taxonomy is not naturalized: clearly it is a human construct rich in possibilities for civil, political and military expression. But all that exists or could exist is mappable, and all entities are basically of the same kind. Many of the same problematic tendencies are implicit in the much more recent 'domain' metaphor (with its quiet suggestions of dominion), used for example in computer science to conceptualize areas of knowledge.

The boundary metaphor integral to the geopolitical construct creates further problems. Disciplinary boundaries are interesting because by definition we locate them precisely where the coherence of a field becomes problematic. As Wulf has said, they mark where our knowledge fails (1995: 56). Hence the 'boundary conditions' of a discipline, theory or other construct tend to be where challenges lie – in literally marginalized problems thus hidden from view or relegated to the status of minor details, but which may have revolutionary potential if examined in a new light. Possibly the best-known example is from physics, which by 1900 appeared to have reached intellectual exhaustion, with only very minor difficulties to be tidied away before it could be said to be finished. Then, as Frye says, 'along came the first work of Planck and Einstein, and there was no more talk of physics being exhausted.'[25]

The metaphors of boundaries, walls, spaces and the like cause yet more difficulties. All depict a visible barrier, hence a reminder of confinement. But disciplinary specialization tends not to act that way;

it tends to put its limits out of mind rather than to emphasize them, and once they are out of mind, the imprisonment by them is complete. The boundary metaphor also misleads, as I suggested earlier, by implying the symmetry of the subdivided turf and formally similar entities, such as Hilbert's nation-states. These lead one to expect a similarity in outlook and method that is not borne out by the radical differences in what disciplines train specialists to see and to do.

In the most generous conception and practice of disciplinarity suggested by the second and third epigraphs to this chapter, there are no boundaries, rather expanding structures or an inner vastness that all contemplate from their own vantage points. But experience with disciplinary practices is far more often of the ethnocentric social systems described by Dening, which raise their foundational 'as ifs' from conventionality to mythic proportions, providing the 'blinding clarity' of a blinkered view. Each discipline 'claims to be distinct from all the others; each proclaims its difference from common sense; each is jealous that its partial, unreal bit of reality should belong to somebody else'. As disciplines gain social prestige, their models are transferred to the culture's mythic understanding of its environment, and their terminology enters the discourse with which reality is described. They become 'cosmological' (1996: 39f., 53). Charles Taylor cites two vivid examples, behaviourism and artificial intelligence,[26] the latter of which has proven so cosmologically successful in our own time that a computational *model* of mind is apt to be taken silently as a description of reality, not as the powerful metaphor it is.

I am not advocating an end to disciplines, nor am I concerned here directly with their reformation, necessary and desirable though that may be. They are without doubt socially constructed, therefore not beyond our power to change, but for my purposes I take them as given – they *are* remarkably resistant to change, though not unalterable. The question for humanities computing is, rather, how to deal with them as they are. The fact is that given the current dispensation, our paradigmatic conversation between practitioner and scholar, despite abundant goodwill and intelligence on both sides, is likely to happen in a conversational space strongly delimited by the scholar's particular specialism. The interdisciplinary ability to step outside that space, so as to connect the problem in question with a method, vocabulary or way of thinking uncommon to that scholar's discipline, must, then, be the practitioner's responsibility.

In an institutional world of naturalized or well-armed disciplines, researchers and teachers tend to construct their notions of interdisciplinarity in ways that reflect their own disciplinary perspectives.[27] Two senses of the term thus emerge. The first we have already encountered, although not as a supposedly interdisciplinary activity: the adventurous poaching of sources, theories, arguments and other scholarly material from another discipline for purposes of one's own. The second denotes good working relations with one's properly fenced-off neighbours towards a common end, e.g. in the Manhattan Project, studied by Peter Galison in *Image and Logic*. (Like the dean of a faculty or a head of school, the project director may be in a position to take an interdisciplinary view, but those directly involved are usually not.) Both senses can lead to good results, as is well known; both can be methodologically fruitful. But neither gives us a clue as to how disciplines might be viewed and understood systematically from without, from a truly *inter*disciplinary perspective, as humanities computing needs to do.

Conceiving disciplines as constituting 'a network of relatively autonomous practices in asymmetrical relation to each other' (Chandler 2004: 360) accords much better with experience and avoids the perils of the metaphors to which I have objected. But the sense of isolation and absence of intermediation remain. Geertz noticed more than twenty years ago that the disciplines were blurring in a *mélange* of new forms and products that may attest to the 'loosening of structures' recently called for e.g. by Pauline Yu: 'intentionally impermanent collaborations that resist institutional entrenchment and inertia ... foreground[ing] disciplinarity itself "as a *permanent question*"'.[28] Galison has argued that Michel Foucault's idea of the 'specific' intellectual lends terminology and support to the argument that grand schemes of unification (including, it would seem, disciplines with an indefinitely expanding horizon) are relics of the past.[29] The way ahead, he says, lies with 'specific' theory or criticism, whose horizon has a finite radius. Hence the disciplinary reflection of Nancy Cartwright's 'deeply dappled' physical world, 'a world rich in different things, with different natures, behaving in different ways' (1999: 1). In such a world, provincialism is forestalled, Galison says, by the incessant 'borrowing, altering, exchanging in piecemeal bits' characteristic of all forms of cultural production (2004: 382). I agree: the way ahead is constituted, at least for most of us, by combining focused depth with borrowed breadth. But I question how prevalent the borrowing actually is in the humanities, how effective and how close we actually are to the balance for which Galison argues. His celebrated metaphor of the 'trading zone' characteristically depicts the borrowing from one cultural group by another.[30] A field like what humanities computing evidently is, however, requires a *tertium quid*, neither one group nor the other but a third, middle possibility excluded by knowledge branched into trees or partitioned into turfs.

Let us be clear about the difficulty of creating this excluded middle. Thomas Kuhn, in one of the rare and most valuable discussions from actual experience of multidisciplinary work, explains what this means for deep involvement in several fields. The passage from one discipline, such as history, to another, such as philosophy, and then to another, such as physics, is no simple matter: 'each switch is a personal wrench, the abandonment of one discipline for another with which it is not quite compatible'. Each requires a quite different mental set. Nor, he says, is a compromise possible, 'for it presents problems of the same sort as a compromise between the duck and the rabbit of the well-known Gestalt diagram. Though most people can readily see the duck and the rabbit alternately, no amount of ocular exercise and strain will educe a duck-rabbit' (1977: 6).

If duck-rabbits are impossible, as I think they are, then our *tertium quid* cannot be an undifferentiated blend or a perspective defining sameness. It must be constituted by the performative ability to move in and out of disciplines, back and forth between duck and rabbit as Kuhn did – but while carrying its own proper intellectual load on its back, as he undoubtedly did. It must be migratory, itinerant – not a patch of turf but a way of travelling.

The Methodological Commons of humanities computing shown in Figure 3.1 is a visual metaphor representing the shared knowledge on which the itinerant practitioner draws – metaphorically not turf because it is common land and because it is defined by that which is wholly portable. Kuhn's Gestalt metaphor of multidisciplinary practice helps to identify the integrity of each discipline but significantly gives us that integrity as a way of looking at a world variously held in common with other ways – once again putting us in Dening's 'great ring of viewers'. Disciplines, as we know, lay claim to different source material and different approaches, but as Figure 3.1 shows, within the common workspace of humanities computing those differences are reduced to the four data types (text, image, number, sound) and a finite (but not fixed) set of tools for manipulating them. These tools are in turn derived from and their applications governed by what Short has called 'formal methods', i.e. methods formed within and reflecting the forms of the contributing Clouds of Knowing. The question for the interdisciplinary research project enabled by these relations of research is how formal methods are obtained and understood.[31]

The question is an eminently practical one: how does the practitioner of humanities computing learn his or her trade as an interdisciplinarian? The bell-wether studies and master-works of popular scholarship supply an immediate answer for which all must be grateful, but these, not always considered a priority to write, are unevenly distributed and in new or rapidly changing fields may not exist or be sufficiently current. Where does one turn, and what does one look for when guides fail?

5 Tropes and imageries of explanation

Sizing up a discipline begins pragmatically with the attempt to discover what counts by the criteria of its 'normal discourse', i.e. everything 'conducted within an agreed-upon set of conventions about what counts as a relevant contribution, what counts as answering a question, what counts as having a good argument for that answer or a good criticism of it' (Rorty 1980: 320). These conventions are rarely stated, and when stated they may be more prescriptive than descriptive. A much better source of evidence for the actual state of affairs in a discipline is, as Geertz has said, its 'tropes and imageries of explanation' – the vocabulary in which practitioners talk to each other about their practice and in so doing 'represent their aims, judgements, justifications, and so on'. These disciplinary terms, he remarks, 'take one a long way, when properly understood, toward grasping what the pursuit is all about'.[32] For comparative study of disciplines a particularly rich subset of such terms is formed by the analogical poaching to which fields resort when in need of help. Prying into the differences between old and new contexts, especially at points of semantic stress, begins to reveal the distinct identities we are after.

Geertz illustrates the point for the social sciences: seeing that in them 'society is less and less represented as an elaborate machine or quasi-organism than as a serious game, a sidewalk drama, or a behavioral text' tells one a great deal about a sea-change in analytical methods, conceptions of theory and the kinds of explanation likely to be offered. Metaphors such as 'isolating a cause, determining a variable, measuring a force, or defining a function' betray old 'dreams of social physics' from the earliest days of sociology,[33] which led to difficulties that identified essential differences separating the social from the natural sciences. More recent metaphors such as 'following a rule, constructing a representation, expressing an attitude, or forming an intention' show reasoning by analogy from the humanities.

Changes in analytical methods, conceptions of theory and kinds of explanation are strongly indicated, and with these a very different trajectory for the social sciences. But again, with this new trajectory come other sorts of problems. With the shift in attention from external measures to interpretation of meanings in their own terms, Brian Fay and J. Donald Moon argue, comes the failure 'to see the conflict, irrationality and mechanisms of repression operative in all social orders ... [and] to speak about the relevant social order in terms radically opposed to that of the participants' (1994/1977: 33).

Looking in from the outside, we can see a characteristic struggle marked by a conflicted rhetoric – nothing like the simplistic unity implied in the disciplinary label 'social science'. Yet it is a *characteristic* struggle, an identity of family resemblance formed by conflict that, once understood, orients the observer and allows for a degree of imaginative participation.

In the rapid analysis from Geertz's example I was following something like the opposite of Darnton's good advice to seek otherness by going for the most obscure aspects of an alien culture. 'When we cannot get a proverb, or a joke, or a ritual, or a poem,' he notes, 'we know we are on to something.'[34] The other side of that terminological coin is the peril of misreading an expressive form that makes sense, but *different* sense, in both cultures. The literary critic C. S. Lewis, describing how to read texts from an earlier historical period, makes the argument for language:

> When a word has several meanings historical circumstances often make one of them dominant during a particular period ... The dominant sense of any word lies uppermost in our minds. Wherever we meet the word, our natural impulse will be to give it that sense. When this operation results in nonsense, of course, we see our mistake and try over again. But if it makes tolerable sense our tendency is to go merrily on. We are often deceived ... I call such senses dangerous senses because they lure us into misreadings. (1967/1960: 12f.)

The disciplinary term 'theory' is particularly rich in such dangerous senses, as we will see in a moment, but other such words have already been cited: 'real' in Chapter 1.4.6; 'original' in 1.4.8. When a discipline adopts a crucial trope or imagery from an older, more prestigious field, the culturally prevalent meaning accompanies it. This meaning, as we will see, is often radically simplified in the borrowing: dispute and variant usage collapse into a single meaning that suits the borrower. If new usage alters meaning, then like Lewis' contemporary reader of historical texts, the disciplinary outsider may be misled and is well advised to be alert to the slightest cognitive dissonance. If specialists are wanting to adopt much more than just a word, as so often with 'science', then an additional task is to question their intentions and the consequences for their field.

The quest is still for otherness, but it is an otherness often cloaked in familiarity.

6 'Theory'

6.1 History and rhetoric

The term 'theory' is one of the most difficult terms to define and, for scholars, among the most evocative. Its power is easy to see: the general sense, a conjectural systematic account of something, defines that which makes an academic discipline disciplinary. John Lavagnino has argued that one need not always operate under the influence or direction of theory (2001), except in one important sense, to which I will return. But the ability to theorize, i.e. to have systematic ideas, would seem essential.

The importance of 'theory' within the academy goes back to the ancient Greek ideal of a life centred on systematic reflection in philosophy.[35] The Socratic challenge to the Athenian imperative of political involvement, institutionalized in Plato's Academy, marks the beginning of the opposition of theory to practice in Western tradition. Roughly speaking, two conflicting historical tendencies resulted: marginalization, as mere play, apart from the serious business of living; and, especially with the Christian ideal of the *vita contempletiva*, elevation, as the central activity of the devoted life. In the scientific revolution of the Renaissance, Galilean mathematical abstractions replaced contemplation as the primary method of knowing reality. Newton's equations of celestial mechanics secured a sense of the world as most clearly and intimately apprehended via mathematics, and a sense of the theoretical life as fulfilled in scientific research. Hence sensuous, embodied nature and the practical *vita activa* lived in relation to it became opposed to the mathematical abstractions governing that nature and the scientific *vita contemplativa* directed to their articulation.

Hence the culturally authoritative background to 'theory' that specific disciplinary uses of the term inflect. When, for example, researchers claim for a discipline that the computer has 'enabled ... theory building' (Huggett and Ross 2004), we must ask what is 'theory' that a scholar in that discipline would want to build it and which a computer would help build, if it would? Similarly, consider Allen Renear's claim that,

> the particular community which has been designing and configuring computer text-processing and encoding systems has evolved a rich body of illuminating theory about the nature of text ... [that] contributes directly to our general understanding of the deepest issues of textuality and textual communication in general. (1997: 107)

The first and primary question is not 'How rich?' or 'How illuminating?' but *'What could possibly be meant by "theory" in this context?'*[36] This question in turn drives us to ask other potentially revealing questions. We need to know, for example, what criteria are reasonable for this field in judging its conjectures; whether one can be wrong, and if so, how, and how this is shown; and, given the alliance that the claimant seeks with criteria in the sciences, what consequences for the field might follow the determined pursuit of such an alliance.

In general, a good answer will open up the aspirations of and possibilities for the discipline in question; help define the way ahead for computing in it, if there is one; and may well help the scholar to think much more clearly about what he or she is proposing to do. In any case, this is the sort of answer that a humanities computing practitioner needs. But it is unlikely to come directly from the collaborating scholar, who will tend to be too intimately committed to his or her discipline's conception of theory to be able to see it comparatively, and so to see what it implies about the discipline's particular ways of constructing the world. Rather, as I have suggested, the practitioner has to derive this answer by paying attention to the clues. Sometimes, as in the example quoted above, they will be quite explicit. Usually, however, they will be implicit and so require comparison of the idea adumbrated in conversation and in the relevant literature with standard conceptions from across the disciplines. The practitioner has to look for similarities and differences, placing the particular rhetoric of theorizing within the disciplinary spectrum, asking where the tropes and imageries of explanation belong in comparison to others, what borrowings are detected, what authority invoked or denied, what claims and assumptions made and not made.

6.2 Mathematics

I begin with mathematics for two reasons: first, that its cultural authority, principally through the natural sciences, is great, hence its influence on what we still mean by 'theory'; second, that through computer science it is strongly relevant to what we understand 'theory' to signify in the context of computing practice. I return to the mathematical background of our subject in much greater detail in the next chapter.

In mathematics 'theory' denotes 'a set of [mathematical] sentences which is closed under logical implication', that is, a self-contained system of reasoning constructed from hypothetical statements and their logical consequences.[37] Generally speaking, mathematics *is* its theories, which are not *about* anything directly but express abstract thought in 'a highly specialized language constructed to be as exact as possible' (Kilmister 1967: 1). It is, by this account, as 'pure' an expression of theory as we have, and on that basis it has often shaped our notion of what theorizing entails. As we will see in Chapter 4.3, however, the notion that mathematics enjoys a completely hermetic purity is more than a little problematic: not only is experimental mathematics now, with computing, a genuine possibility, but mathematical thought also appears to be abstracted *from* the physical world, whose ideal language it has again and again proved itself to be. Realizing that the dependency joining mathematics to science goes in both directions helps us to join it up with humanities computing, as we will see.

Theorizing in mathematics assumes consensus about the axioms of the field, i.e. its basic, irreducible, primitive and self-evident propositions. What is theorized are their implications. Dealing with axioms directly is therefore *meta*-theoretical. At this even more abstract level, theorizing concerns the identity and irreducibility of these basic statements. Since ordinary mathematics is built on this axiomatic foundation, any meta-theoretical change is revolutionary. My point for the following discussion is that before we even get to the collision of theory with the empirical world of stars, trees, nations, people, paintings, symphonies and novels, the idea of theory subdivides into two levels: the universal and the local. (To forestall an infinite regress, we go no further than two levels – no meta-meta-theoretical and so forth.) It is important to keep in mind as these surface in the following that both are conjectural and so the object of critical attention. The meta-theoretical is often problematic because, itself lacking a foundation and so having obscure origins, it tends to be treated as ultimately given and beyond examination – as what I call here, following Jonathan Culler, simply 'Theory'. But more about that later.

A second point is to be made from David Hilbert's view of mathematical theory: that it is defined by what he calls 'the axiomatic method'. This involves not simply establishing axioms but '[b]y pushing ahead to ever deeper layers of axioms ... [to] win ever-deeper insights into the essence of scientific thought itself ... ever more conscious of the unity of our knowledge' (Ewald 1996: 1115). Even if the imagined unity of knowledge is a chimera (as some, we will see, argue), what remains is the conjectural operation I have described elsewhere as modelling.

6.3 Natural sciences

With the natural sciences, nature enters directly and disruptively into the scene. Theorizing moves much closer to modelling as a result.

The coupling of theory and experiment – however understood, whether in the post-Kuhnian sense of having lives of their own, like a modern couple, or in the commonsense view, tightly and hierarchically coupled – implies that we need to ask not only what is meant by 'theory' in a given discipline but also what sort of practical activity corresponds to it, if any, and so helps to define its meaning and role. If none, we need also to ask why. A closely informed view of the sciences will show that experiment has a widely varying role and meaning, from the prominent knowledge-making manipulations of an isolated aspect of nature under controlled conditions in particle physics and molecular genetics, to the algebraic geometer's indifference to experiment in the exploration of string theory or the field biologist's meticulous comparison of plant forms, which fits badly under the standard rubric (Galison 2004: 379–80). Hence a revised, plural understanding of 'experiment' is called for if this term is to cover practical responses to theory. There is benefit in retaining a single term if doing so encourages us to ask how its meaning differs from one disciplinary context to the next. Knowing the differences, the practitioner of humanities computing can then ask, 'Which "experiment", how modified, suits the circumstance in question?'

Theory varies widely in the sciences as well, since 'the many kinds of scientists are often after different sorts of things' (Galison 2004: 380). Theory is said to perform two primary services, explanation and prediction. But the relative importance of these services varies considerably: prediction is crucial in particle physics, nearly irrelevant in evolutionary biology. Where it is crucial, prediction might seem a simple matter (a predicted event happens or it doesn't, one would think), but determining whether a happening qualifies is a matter of quantitative measurement, which is more than unprejudiced observation. Galison's work on objectivity (1999, 1998) and Poovey's on accounting practices (1998), for example, have helped to undermine anti-intellectual notions of number-magic that have made observation seem a simple affair of accuracy and so of proof. Thomas Kuhn observed more than forty years ago that 'quantitative methods have indeed been central' to many sciences for at least two centuries, but 'our most prevalent notions both about the function of measurement and about the source of its special efficacy are derived largely from myth.'[38] The interrelation of theory with measurement is particularly germane here: as Kuhn concludes, a new order provided by a revolutionary theory is a potential order; the primary function of measurement is not so much to test a theory as to make this potential into an actual order. Explanation is similarly full of surprises for the commonsense view, according to which explanatory power is immediate and persuasive. Often this is not the case: 'new canons of explanation are born with the new theories on which they are, to a considerable extent, parisitic ... The pragmatic success of a scientific theory seems to guarantee the ultimate success of its explanatory mode. Explanatory force may, however, be a long time in coming' (1977: 29) because the new canons must be understood and assimilated. Thus, by Kuhn's argument, a theory does not simply answer our questions but reworks the language in which answers are given and questions asked.

Thus Albert Einstein's famous remark to Werner Heisenberg: 'It is the theory which decides what we can observe',[39] reversing the common notion that we theorize to explain a pre-existing set of observations, to connect them into a larger pattern or law of which they become instances. Einstein was referring to 'theory' on the grand scale, or what I called 'metatheory' above: the revolutionary, paradigm-shifting act of the imagination that provides an intellectual framework within which its subject is henceforth studied. It says of its subject, 'Think about it this way' and, if 'this way' is cogent, then what Kuhn called 'normal science' takes over. We know that in the sciences 'theory' in this sense is often provoked by anomalies and so is responsive to empirical observations, but its defining feature is the discontinuous change-of-mind. It is a sense found across the other disciplines, from the foundational theories of the social sciences (e.g. of Durkheim and Weber) to what is, again, simply called Theory. As I note in the next chapter, Juris Hartmanis has suggested that Einstein's sense of 'theory' is particularly relevant to computer science, where 'theories ... help us imagine, analyze, and build the feasible'[40] and so, again, define a world to be studied. Because this 'theory' is identified with fundamental principles, it is the most dangerously attractive to fields (such as engineering or criticism) that have not or, being theoretically tangential, by nature do not state such principles explicitly.[41] They seem not to be intellectual endeavours at all in an environment where to be intellectual means, again, the demonstrable ability to theorize *in this culturally privileged sense*. Pursuing this 'theory' determinedly in those fields may be not simply mistaken but dangerous for them.

Can scientific theories be true? Are the things of science real? The belief that both are the case often seems to lie behind the transdisciplinary reach into the sciences for analytical rhetoric. Philosophers of science, however, permit themselves to be realists, or not, selectively. '*Scientific realism* says that the entities, states and processes described by correct theories really do exist ... and a genuinely correct theory would be a true one ... *Anti-realism* says the opposite: there are no such things as electrons [for example] ... The electrons are fictions. Theories about them are tools for thinking' (Hacking 1983: 21). Intermediate positions are possible, indeed come highly recommended. One may be a realist about entities but anti-realist about theories – many Fathers of the Church exemplify this, Hacking notes and agrees with them in this respect (27f.). Or one may be an anti-realist about entities but a realist about theories, arguing with Bertrand Russell (and so in a highly logico-mathematical mode) that the world is a product we construct from true theories. Much play can be had here, but the point is that when we think critically about work in a particular discipline, even when the object of study seems reliably 'out there', a variety of attitudes is possible. In other words, as I pointed out in Chapter 1.4.6, 'real' is as relative a term as 'theory'. The reach for scientific realism can be confused (by supposing naïvely that it is a singular idea) as well as wrong (contrary to the basic assumptions of the discipline).

These attitudes are not only for the philosophers to argue about but correspond to what the people involved within a discipline think is proper to do and encourage to be done. What is actually done is thus shaped if not determined. If, for example, strict realism about theories prevails, then being in error will merely seem wrong, and going from error to error evidence of useless theory. Indeed, since learning self-evidently means blundering from error to error, sometimes without apparent direction, the context of discovery tends to be of little interest and a leading role for experiment impossible when realism about theories is dominant. In developmental psychology, for example, construction of false theories and over-generalizations are central to a 'genetic epistemology', as Jean Piaget named it, and hence that field's focus on the interplay of failure with 'theory-in-action'.[42]

In Chapter 1.4 I gave some attention to the crude polarization in twentieth-century science, the positivist at one end, reasoning from the absolute dominance of pure observation and correspondingly weak, ephemeral theory; the anti-positivist at the other, reasoning from the opposite, equally absolute dominance of a theoretical agenda and (the term is characteristic) 'theory-laden' or 'loaded' experiment. I noted that positivism belongs to a faded cosmology, although remnants (such as commonsense faith in a pure observation) still persist and so need to be recognized for what they are. Anti-positivism, however, is current, and since the enemy may enter on the back of an outsider, we need to be particularly cautious. Galison and Hacking are again helpful guides. They point out that while observational and experimental data are affected by all sorts of ideas and views of the world, and while it is true that hardware and software are saturated by low-level interpretative choices, nevertheless to call these 'theory-laden' is 'grossly to misread experimental culture' – grossly, that is, to mistake the meaning of 'theory' for any sort of notion, idea or prejudice practitioners may have.[43] '[W]hen philosophers begin to teach that all observation is loaded with theory, we seem completely locked into representation', unable to escape from an idealist cul-de-sac 'and hook-up with the world'.[44] Hence *representations become the world*. When under the influence of such ideas we turn to our currently favourite means for dealing with the world, the computer, we end up inside endless projects to ontologize whatever portion of reality concerns us, rather than outside them, watching the interplay of theory and the theorized, paying attention to what doesn't fit. When 'theory' is any notion, idea or prejudice about anything, the word becomes meaningless, transdisciplinary borrowings useless and our ability to learn from its uses nil. We have a strong and vested interest in the meaningful distinctions which delimit the semantic field of scientific 'theory' from other fields of 'theory'.

6.4 Social sciences

The title of a paper by the Belgian social scientist Guillaume Wunsch, 'God has chosen to give the easy problems to the physicists, or why demographers need theory', accords with a remark attributed to Gregory Bateson, that 'there are the hard sciences, and then there are the difficult sciences'.[45] Both remarks point in two directions: towards the disciplines paradigmatic of what is 'hard', in the dual sense of *solid* reality and *difficult* methods; and towards those other disciplines, still in the shadow of the first, which in their relative softness present difficulties (so it is claimed) of a much more demanding kind. The imagery is dubious for other reasons,[46] but within its own frame, what is it saying? When softness is regarded as bad, what is the problem?

Softness resolves metaphorically into physical and emotional sensitivity, hence that which is compliant, responsive, involved – and so the rub. In his contrast of Galilean science with the humanities, Carlo Ginzburg observes (recalling in metaphor Clifford Geertz's story of Sefrou) that the 'tendency to obliterate the individual traits of an object is directly proportional to the emotional distance of the observer'.[47] Such distinctions are the rub for scientific theorizing, which aims through abstraction at universal law and so demands as great an emotional distance as possible. But the theorist of social phenomena and his or her scholarly audience are by definition intimately part of what is studied, even when large populations, macro-structures of society, culturally alien or long-dead people are the object. Hence the leitmotiv-tension of these disciplines: the scientific requirement of distance is a hermeneutical stumbling block, and the hermeneutical demand for identification with its subject is a scientific folly.

Professionally this tension surfaces in a widely noted malaise throughout the social sciences. Scholars complain, for example, about the disconnection of abstract mathematical theorizing from the social realities it supposedly addresses; about the excessive distance of much contemporary work from the meaningful questions once characteristic of these sciences; and, in general, about theoretical exhaustion.[48] Clearly a different conception of what theory should be trying to do is needed.

Wolf Lepenies has noted this tension in the historical oscillation of sociology 'between a scientific orientation which has led it to ape the natural sciences and a hermeneutic attitude which has shifted the discipline toward the realm of literature' (1988/1985: 1). Sociology began in name and scientific orientation with Auguste Comte (1798–1857), who first called it 'social physics', arguing for a 'natural science of society' based on a common framework of logic and method intended to assist in discovering the universal laws of society.[49] Lepenies has described how the discipline Comte began developed out of 'a complex process in the course of which scientific modes of procedure became differentiated from literary modes [in a] divorce ... accentuated ideologically through the confrontation of cold rationality and the culture of the feelings'. As sociology has oscillated since then from distance to intimacy, so social science method has distributed itself along a scale from the mathematical at one end to the experiential at the other. 'Theory' runs the gamut, becoming more and more difficult to recognize as scientific, or to give scientific form to, as one moves along this scale.

Ian Hacking's philosophical analysis of this history in *The Taming of Chance* reveals development of ideas that 'cleared a space for chance', as he puts it, and so made possible the revolutionary idea that from a new conception of 'law', defined in terms of probability, truths about people could be discovered (1990: 1–10). For the story I am telling the immediately important matter is that the change which enabled the dream of achieving reliable knowledge of people, and so of the ability to control them – Comte's formula, *prévoir pour pouvoir*, 'to be able to predict is to be able to control' (Giddens 1986/1982: 10), shows the ambition – also 'toppled, or at least tilted' the doctrine of causality in science (Hacking 1990: 1). In other words, the possibility of extending the certainty of physics to society came at the cost of deterministic certitude in physics – as it were, a hardening of the soft and a softening of the hard. While it is tempting to generalize beyond the case – that what is sought for is already what was there, though in a different form – Hacking's argument does support the conclusion that the disciplinary reach which created the social sciences is to be taken more seriously in the philosophical sense than otherwise we might have supposed: not merely a reach for legitimacy by Comte *et al.*, but rather a redefinition of that which legitimizes, enabling the reach and the research which followed. Thus we are prepared to ask the same question about current research: What is 'theory' now, how has it been prepared for – and, since now is *now*, what role does computing have to play?

The social sciences today begin with physical and emotional sensitivity as a fundamental postulate, hence involvement as our basic social fact: the view that, as Anthony Giddens has said, 'societies only exist in so far as they are created and re-created in our own actions as human beings', that 'we create society at the same time as we are created by it'. If we resort to the traditional metaphor of society-as-building, he notes, 'we should have to say that *social systems are like buildings that are at every moment constantly being reconstructed by the very bricks that compose them.*' And these are indeed strange bricks, which cannot be treated even in the aggregate as if they were lumps of matter. 'Atoms cannot get to know what scientists say about them, or change their behaviour in the light of that knowledge. Human beings can do so ...' Hence the ambition: not, as before, to predict and so control society for the common good, but rather to emancipate the individual. 'It is often precisely by showing that what may appear to those involved as inevitable, as unchallengeable – as resembling a law of nature – is, in fact, an historical product, that sociological analysis can play an emancipatory role in human society' (1986/1982: 11–13).

As a result of this oscillatory shift to reliance on analytic rhetoric derived from the humanities, hence to the centrality of interpretation, the primary subject of theorizing becomes *intentionality*. We now observe that human actions are what they mean and that established social codes are inadequate to explain meaning, so we turn to intention (Fay and Moon 1994/1977: 22). The reference point is still the natural sciences, but they are seen in a twisting backward glance. This uncomfortable glance remains necessary because 'social phenomena do not consist in abstract structures of meanings which can be set forth and analyzed':

> they consist in actions (and other events) which actually occur in particular places at particular times. And while we cannot even approach our subject without understanding what these actions *mean*, such understanding does not, by itself, constitute an explanation of why they *occur*. (1994/1997: 24)

Theory must say why, must account for causes. But the ground opens up from underneath the theorist, putting a great if not metamorphic strain on the meaning of 'theory'. If by that word we mean an account of rational order, then the manifest irrationality and self-contradictory behaviour observable daily in the social world of ordinary human beings presents us with enormous difficulties. Social scientists attempt to cope (much like ordinary people when confronted by irrational behaviour) by positing an underlying rationality connected to actual behaviour by some translating mechanism, as in the theories of Freud and Marx. The value of such theories can be great, but they are circumscribed by the assumption that an observer can occupy such a position of authority so as to contradict and correct those whom he or she is observing. This runs against a fundamental social scientific principle that a theory must provide an explanation true to the self-understanding of 'an ideal, fully informed and articulate participant', as Fay and Moon say (1994/1977: 31). The tendency for this already idealized participant to take on the theorizing observer's self-understanding is obvious. It is equally obvious to see why the situation thus encountered would be particularly unacceptable e.g. to anthropologists, especially in a post-colonial world, and to sociologists of multicultural societies interested in 'seeing what is', or more appropriately, in ways of seeing beyond the different horizons that accompany us: the horizons of discipline, history and culture.

Greg Dening points out that what is involved in the struggle over theory I am enacting here is less a matter of different logical systems, more of differing forms of consciousness (1998: 60). Whatever theory might be here, it expresses how the world marked out for study appears once one has entered into this world as participant-observer – once one has, in Dening's metaphor of South Pacific exploration, crossed the 'beaches of the mind' (85–92). This expression is meaningfully formal to the degree that it is *informed*, or in Geertz's terms *thickened*, by the interpretation that establishes 'familiarity with the imaginative universe within which [others'] acts are signs' (Geertz 1993/1973: 13). It is thus very much unlike the formulaic abstraction appropriate to radically thinned, uninterpreted data. Rather it takes form as inscription, in descriptive prose, appropriate to a complex, messy, polyvalent reality. But is the result theory?

Here is Geertz, in his metatheoretical essay on anthropological theory and practice from the early 1970s, 'Thick Description: Toward an Interpretive Theory of Culture':[50]

> Theoretical formulations hover so low over the interpretations they govern that they don't make much sense or hold much interest apart from them. This is so, not because they are not general (if they are not general, they are not theoretical), but because, stated independently of their applications, they seem either commonplace or vacant. One can, and this in fact is how the field progresses conceptually, take a line of theoretical attack developed in connection with one exercise in ethnographic interpretation and employ it in another, pushing it forward to greater precision or broader relevance; but one cannot write a 'General Theory of Cultural Interpretation.' Or, rather, one can, but there appears to be little profit in it, because the essential task of theory building here is not to codify abstract regularities but to make thick description possible, not to generalize across cases but to generalize within them. (1993/1973: 25f.)

With vacuous generality at one extreme and meaningless detail at the other, the theorist is unable to set down what should occupy the middle ground but can only, at the best of times, be partially glimpsed.

The problem for anthropology, Geertz avows, is 'that the terms in which such formulations can be cast are, if not wholly nonexistent, very nearly so. We are reduced to insinuating theories because we lack the power to state them' (24).

The anthropologist's frustration and the reader's impatience provoke the question of what conception of theory might be possible when formal statement is very nearly disallowed, and given this conception (if we can find it) what computing might have to offer. Considering the audience I am addressing, however, I prefer to turn this question around: Given what computing can do, how does it meet what anthropology (or any of the interpretative social sciences, including history) would recognize as activity with a theoretical trajectory?

In the same essay Geertz makes the usual move: he looks elsewhere for helpful rhetoric and finds it in medical semiotics, where likewise one generalizes within cases, inferring by means of an interpretative framework from apparent symptoms to underlying causes. These symptoms are already evident or, given the circumstances (such as a nearby epidemic), highly likely. The semiotically informed theorist, then, does not predict – prediction is blocked by its dependence on interpreted events – though for theory in this sense to survive, it must, like a physician's diagnosis, be robust enough to withstand future evidence (1993/1973: 26). The closest one gets to prediction's promised gift of control over the future is the preparatory sense that theoretical understanding confers strength, as Crombie suggests negatively in his paraphrase of George Santayana's famous dictum: 'Those who ignore history are compelled unknowingly to relive it.'[51] But how it does so, using or allowing for what sort of mechanism, is the question.

There are two answers, intimately related, both very old. The first begins with Geertz's insightful reach to medical practice, which as Ginzburg shows, transmitted to the humanities the ancient habit of mind formed by the venatic reading of clues in the spoor of beasts: 'what may be the oldest act in the intellectual history of the human race: the hunter squatting on the ground, studying the tracks of his quarry' (1989: 105). Ginzburg describes how this habit of mind, on which human survival often depended, was carried into the practices of cultural interpretation by the explicit notion of a symptom (*semeion*) to a disease always out of reach. When, as we saw earlier, Galilean science relocated true knowledge of the world to the abstractions of mathematics, and so 'could have taken as its own the Scholastic motto *Individuum est ineffabile* ("We cannot speak about what is individual")', the highly qualitative disciplines came in opposition to focus on the individuality of individual cases and so inherited the ancient habit. For this reason disciplines such as history ('a social science *sui generis*') and anthropology (about which the same might be said) 'get results that have an unsuppressible speculative margin' and manifest their theorizing as barely separable though transportable expressions of case-by-case interpretation (1989: 106).

The second answer is found in the closely analogous practice of divinatory reading, which seeks knowledge of the future *sorte* ('by lot') or by other procedural means.[52] Citing the paradigm implicit in divination texts, Ginzburg notes that formally both venatic and divinatory readings presuppose the same operation – 'minute investigation of even trifling matters, to discover the traces of events that could not be directly experienced by the observer' – and show 'great similarities in the learning processes' and intellectual operations – 'analyses, comparisons, classifications'. As the Latin word *sors* (lemma of *sorte*, above) suggests in its sense of 'one's lot, share, assigned place, category' and through the etymological sense of the English word *sort*, divinatory method became the anticipatory interpretation of patterns.

The connection with the sense of 'theory' we are after is delivered by 'modelling', which as we have seen is how with computing one looks for patterns, often in fact by sorting, in what thus becomes evidence. And so the relevance of computing to the interpretative turn of theory in the social sciences.

6.5 Humanities

In the spirit of Hacking's study of chance, it is tempting to speculate that by opening up a space for modelling, computing has something to do with this interpretative turn towards the conjectural paradigm of the humanities and puts on offer a reciprocal ability for the humanities better to reach towards establishing things that, as Fay and Moon said of social facts, 'consist in actions (and other events) which actually occur in particular places at particular times' (1994: 24). Be that as it may, on the broad and uncertain marches between the social sciences and the humanities (within which historiography and ethnography overlap), 'theory' once again undergoes a metasemiosis. The change-of-meaning is expressed as expected in differences of usage, but we also find evidence in the alternatives which become available at this point. In this section I will consider two of these, 'poetic' and 'anatomy', but first I need to dispose of what Jonathan Culler has called 'just plain "theory"' (1997) and I call 'Theory'.

This Theory, Culler notes, is not literary theory, 'not the theory of anything in particular, nor a comprehensive theory of things in general' and perhaps 'less of an account of anything than an activity' (1). Thus our unbounded, unending and universal Theory is characterized by its mind-altering effects, in particular by its challenge to commonsense notions of all kinds, showing, with the revolutionary force typical of such social constructivist revelations, that 'things could have been other than they are, had events been other than they were'.[53] Elsewhere Stanley Fish quotes Sander Gilman's typically broad definition, 'the self-conscious awareness of the methodological approaches that one uses',[54] expanding it into Theory: 'This awareness, which amounts to the historicization of the routine practices that we once regarded as the inevitable fruits of a teleological process ...' reveals social construction, but it also acts 'to raise to the level of analytical attention formative structures that lie beneath the surface of life and give it its shape' (2004: 377). In other words, it assimilates the tools of social anthropology.

The ordinary term 'theory' is thus being used not to name a particular meta-theoretical construct but as a general label for any occupant of the meta-theoretical level. It is a *meta*-meta-theoretical concept – and so offers an exceedingly slippery path of retreat beyond the critical radius into the permanence and untouchability of gospel.

Much more could be and has been said about Theory, for example its imperial tendencies, as described by Fredric Jameson, to supplant philosophy and other disciplines, police language for its ideological constructedness, indeed become the arbiter of everything (2004: 403). One can also observe that an educated imagination, with time for literature and the arts, includes all that one wants from Theory without the imperial ambitions and obfuscatory language. (This is not necessarily a criticism of any work deemed to occupy the position of Theory, rather of the occupation, though perhaps aiming at that position has ill effects.) The resemblance to natural science 'theory' is not difficult to see in broad strokes, especially given post-Kuhnian philosophy of science – the preoccupation with formality of expression; the *a priori* nature of it; the thought-revolutionary potential; the objective of defining what can be known, with the conjectural quality of this tending to weaken as it gains acceptance; and so forth. But, especially to those who, as it were, seek otherness in data, with its self-transcending potential, and who are therefore inclined to think inductively, Theory cannot be a given but must become an object to be explained – must be pulled back inside our critical radius. Hence 'theory' is not dissolved away in Theory but becomes, again, the question.

Frye, in his *Anatomy*, makes this process – the turning inside-out of the given into an object of study – the essential step in a discipline becoming what he calls there a 'science': the discovery that its real function is to interpret the very phenomena it had naïvely taken as its fundamental data (1957: 15). Thus the example of history, born when the chronicler replaces the temporal ordering of events, formerly thought to be their essential structure, with an interpretative relation connecting them to a broader and differently shaped framework. This 'inductive leap' to a new vantage ground requires assumption of total coherence through an act of what Jacob Bronowski called the 'superb optimism'[55] of the imagination: a bold act impossible by definition to actualize or to establish axiomatically. Once that leap is made it becomes possible, in Bronowski's rabbinic language I quoted earlier, to 'put a fence around the law', i.e. to delimit an area for study. This falsifies the study in absolute terms but allows us to gain some knowledge, until by another audacious act of the imagination the fence is pushed back a bit and the process continues (1978: 58–9). In scientific terms theory tells us where the fence goes until a new theory is imagined.[56] Thus the fencing governed by theorizing is always in fitful motion. Its guarantor of change is the imaginative, optimistic permanence of Bronowski's unreachable 'law', *which is clearly a human imaginative creation*.

Looking back on the *Anatomy* in 1989, in 'Literary and Mechanical Models', Frye (making Lewis' point about dangerous words) remarked that most of the misunderstanding provoked by his attempt at a systematic, progressive view of literature stemmed from his use of the word 'scientific' (and references to the natural sciences generally) to exemplify a scholarship with some direction to it. The intent in reaching out for new analytical rhetoric was not, however, to poach the soon to be discredited 'transcendental virtues' of science, rather to free criticism from dead ends so that it might 'fulfil itself in telling us something about what [literature] is' (1957: 8). 'But such conceptions as "software programming" and "computer modelling" were as yet unknown [in the humanities],' Frye commented, 'and if I were writing such an introduction today I should probably pay a good deal of attention to them and talk less about science' (1991: 6).

Frye's project would then have been modelling towards a stable conception of literature and literary practice – hence the relevance of the two conventional terms I mentioned earlier. The first of these, 'poetic' or 'poetics', is from Aristotelian literary criticism. Frye defines it in the *Anatomy* as a 'theory of criticism whose principles apply to the whole of literature and account for every valid type of critical procedure'

(1957: 14). The sense I wish to invoke here is not specifically literary, but it also bears the implicit etymological force (from Greek *poiéō*, 'make, produce, do') to suggest the transition with the humanities into a world centred on the imagination instantiated in artifacts and the skilful practices by which they are made and used. 'Poetics' and 'theory' are both contingent, but the latter conjectures towards the seen, taking on its singular authority, while the former conjectures with the made, reminding us that other constructions are possible. Thus Dening proposes that we talk not about a theory of history but 'A Poetic for Histories': an account of writing history 'concerned with the authenticity of experience rather than the credentials of the observer' and so productive of 'the most generous way to describe a reflective discourse on all the hermeneutic dimensions of histories as cultural artifacts' (1996: 35f.). Note the dialectic of anthropological engagement and meta-theoretical comprehensiveness in this poetic. Contrast the dialectic of scientific distancing and cultural exclusivity in Leopold von Ranke's powerful nineteenth-century European idea of a 'scientific history', with its sharp focus on documents – its 'mythic confidence in a text-able past', as Dening says (42). Reflect on the unsuitability of this sharp and blinkered focus for an ethno-historical understanding of any culture (such as that of recent technology) with an imperfect to non-existent or tangential to irrelevant written record. Especially given the imperial ambitions or pretensions of Theory – the unification of all under the heading of one – the generous, relativizing plurality of poetics may be preferred.

The other term on offer, 'anatomy', is one of Frye's four strands binding fiction together (novel, confession, anatomy and romance): an encyclopaedic form that denotes 'a dissection or analysis', as he says of Richard Burton's *Anatomy of Melancholy. What it is, With all the kinds, causes, symptoms, prognosticks & severall cures of it. In three Partitions, with their severall Sections, members & subsections, Philosophically, Medicinally, Historically opened & cut up* (1632). The satirical tone of Burton's title is deliberate, but what interests me here is the return through medicine again to the semiotics of the hunt. (Permit me to follow where this leads.) 'Venatic life ...' the ecologist Paul Shepard has written, 'places animals at the heart of human symbolism ... meaty thoughts and kernels of ideas in our mind-bodies' (1996: 25, 30). But not simply tracking and eating – also anatomizing, hence 'the discovery of the correspondence of similar organs in different animals, a revelation in "hidden" kinship, a paradox in which essence contradicted the external diversity of plumage and pelt' (32). This visceral theorizing, which identified animal with animal, found concealed order in evident diversity and so by extension a world-order. It is distinguished from other kinds by its precedence: not first of things 'out there' but of what lies within. 'The hunt sharpened our intelligence. And the crucial turn was the inwardness which began with the scrutiny of the opened body' (40). If, as Geertz says, ethnographic theorizing concerns a foreignness that 'does not start at the water's edge but at the skin's' (2000: 76), then this kind moves inside it to what we persist – despite the futility of the hunt through various organs for the hiding-place of mind and seat of emotions – in calling our 'inner being'.

7 Conclusion

Whether back down to earth, where Shepard would remind us that we began, or up high, where we went somewhat later, you are justified in wondering where all this leads. What does all this have to do with the *practice* of humanities computing? Why must we care? What comes of such an arduous, costly project as I have sketched here?

Hacking's simple observation that being observant is key to productive experimental work applies with equal force in the analogous situations of humanities computing, whether traditionally solitary or paradigmatically conversational. The central questions around which the entirety of this chapter turns are first *how one becomes observant* in the ways required by the practice, and second *what one does and where one goes* when that odd, out-of-place, anomalous or missing something is observed in the course of work.

The answer to the first question, implied throughout, requires us to make the connection between being observant and having what Frye called an 'educated imagination' (1963) – the trained ability to conjure what is not present to the senses. In humanities computing, that is, how do we obtain through whatever data are in question ready intercourse with 'the forms of things unknown'? The words are Theseus', from *A Midsummer Night's Dream*:

And as imagination bodies forth
The forms of things unknown, the poet's pen
Turns them to shapes, and gives to airy nothing
A local habitation and a name. (V.i)

On the technical level – a subject for the next chapter – the migrant practitioner must of course have ready access to the forms of the technical imagination. But the challenge that has been this chapter's concern is how the imagination is trained first to see potential in a problem and then to inform and nurture it. This potential is not *brought to* the conversation but *created in* it by the intersection of methods and interpretation. For that intersection properly to happen both practitioner and scholar should be able to see into the other's conceptual area. Experience suggests that the general assimilation of computing has educated the scholar, possibly to or closely approaching a point of equilibrium. Much more needs to be done for the humanities computing practitioner, as detailed here. But as much or more of my purpose in this chapter has been to enable the practitioner to inform and nurture the potential thus created with the help of methods from other disciplines. Although the scholar may of course contribute, this is primarily the practitioner's responsibility, since methods are his or her particular concern. Thus the answer to the second question.

To put the matter negatively, I am arguing against a pair of corresponding errors. The first is that technical expertise and scholarly expertise, separated by a desk, social distinction or whatever, meet and under direction of the latter solve a problem posed by the latter. The second is that all the fuss is quite unnecessary because soon all scholars will do for themselves, and so no more conversation. On the one hand, to assert the first is to misunderstand what has to some degree or other always been happening in our paradigmatic conversation and expresses the real potential of the field itself. (What is envisioned is a genuine conversation rather than two people talking at each other.) On the other hand, to assert the withering away of the humanities-computing state is greatly to underestimate the two quite different but conspiring difficulties of maintaining technical competence and of freely taking another point of view on one's own problem. It is to ignore the essential (rather than historically contingent) value of collaborative exchange. It is, again, to sanction an impediment. No, the conversation *is* paradigmatic, and for it to do what it can do requires an intellectually migrant and multicultural practitioner at the ready.

Allow me in conclusion to propose a deeply familiar analogy. The project of making these disciplinary kinships is like learning another language, say a difficult, complex one such as ancient Greek. Apart from the hard work, the first and almost immediate truth one perceives is that the rewards are all out of proportion to the effort. The effort is great, but the rewards are much, much greater: a whole new world opens up more quickly than expected, though dealing in it competently takes time and further effort. The second truth is that one is *learning* within a structure that expands into all others, peering into the inner commons from the great ring of viewers. But let the last words be Aristotle's, from the beginning of *De partu animalium*:

Every systematic science [*theoría kaì méthodos*], the humblest and the noblest alike, seems to admit of two distinct kinds of proficiency; one of which may be properly called scientific knowledge of the subject [*èpistéme toû prágmatos kalôs*], while the other is a kind of educational acquaintance [*paideía*] with it. For an educated man [*pepaideuménos*] should be able to form a fair offhand judgment as to the goodness or badness of the method used by a professor in his exposition. To be educated is in fact to be able to do this; and even the man of universal education we deem to be such in virtue of his having this ability. It will, however, of course, be understood that we only ascribe universal education to one who in his own individual person is thus critical in all or nearly all branches of knowledge, and not to one who has a like ability merely in some special subject. For it is possible for a man to have this competence in some one branch of knowledge without having it in all.[57]

4
Computer Science

The blind people who had been shown the head of the elephant replied, 'The elephant, your majesty, is just like a water jar.' Those who had been shown the ear of the elephant replied, 'The elephant, your majesty, is just like a winnowing basket.' Those who had been shown the tusk of the elephant replied, 'The elephant, your majesty, is just like an iron rod.' ... Those who had been shown the body of the elephant replied, 'The elephant, your majesty, is just like a granary.' ... Those who had been shown the tail of the elephant replied, 'The elephant, your majesty, is just like a pestle.' ... Saying, 'The elephant is like this, it's not like that. The elephant's not like that, it's like this,' they struck one another with their fists ...

Udana 66, trans. Thanissaro Bhikkhu[1]

... every tool carries with it the spirit by which it has been created.

Werner Heisenberg, *Physics and Philosophy* (1990): 15

1 Introduction

If we presume computer science to be *the* science of computing, then it would seem reasonable to conclude that humanities computing must converge on this science to become genuinely grounded: its technical methods must be computer science methods. But the presumption is flawed twice over: both computer science and computing are incorrigibly plural. In the Introduction and variously throughout the preceding chapters I have argued that there are in fact many computings. Here I will show why we have very good reason to think that this multiplicity is neither accidental nor convergent but essential, and that it is limited in principle only by human ingenuity. In this chapter my initial project, however, will be to deconstruct the unitary notion of computer science so that, with both false unities gone, we can ask what aspects of the rich plurality of concerns might be relevant to the humanities, and so to humanities computing. At the same time I assume that names must be respected – that they correspond to something and serve some purpose (be it actual or imagined), or they cease to be uttered. I reason that a powerful disciplinary label like 'computer science', while not naming a coherent set of beliefs, methods or practices, must identify *something*. While it is possible to argue, as Immanuel Wallerstein does for sociology, that computer science is only a 'corporate structure' (1998: part I), the evidence of intellectual vigour argues otherwise: there are no calls to 'unthink' its culture, but rather to build and indeed to extend it. In any case, I prefer to assume if not a singular identity then an intellectual centre – a centre of many orbits, we might say. In this chapter I triangulate on that centre in order to distinguish these orbits from humanities computing. In that way, again, it becomes possible to ask what among them might be of interest.

My second purpose here is to exemplify in detail the kind of close-up study that I described broadly in the previous chapter and the kind of kinship that is its primary result. My perspective will again be ethnographic rather than either disinterested or deferential. While humanities computing is no satellite of computer science, it certainly is part of the same large intellectual system and has much to gain from the right kind of relationship with its powerful neighbour.

2 Diversity and relations

No discipline would seem better to exemplify the ethnographic double-vision than computer science: 'clarity from a distance, jumble up close'. Yet the definiteness and singularity implied by its singular name is far more problematic than the anthropologist's perception of that distant North African town, partial though it was. The problem is not just that the assumed unity is largely projected, and so more like one of those blind men's unjustified extrapolations in the Buddhist parable from which I have quoted. More importantly, unlike the situation the parable depicts, we are all blind: there is no one authority to whose clear vision of the whole we can refer – and no natural whole independent of our collective groping efforts to construct it. Hence despite the pervasive feeling within computer science, often also voiced in similar discussions of humanities computing, that as Richard Hamming said in the late 1960s, that 'we should ignore the discussion and get on with *doing* it', the attempt to define computer science matters (1969: 4). Then it mattered to the field because, as Hamming explained in his Turing Award lecture, granting agencies often did not know whom to ask for evaluations. Thinking that computer science was simply a branch of applied mathematics, they often turned to mathematicians, as a result of which, he feared, computing would never get beyond number crunching. But by then some mathematicians had begun to realize that computing was 'applied' in a new, theoretically interesting sense (Mahoney 2000b: 27–31). There can be no doubt of this now, but even distant outsiders know that only one part of the beast is mathematical and that several conflicting views of this beast remain. Hence the attempt at definition still matters within the field because what a field becomes tends to be what people think it is, and computer science is still very much becoming what it might be. The openness, turmoil, uncertainty and sense of an unbounded, unpredictable future attested in its literature, though indicating problems to be solved, are the virtues of a living field with which we can engage. In presenting computer science as a site of anxieties and conflicts, my intention here is, again, precisely to further such engagement.

But why do we, on the outside of the field, need to go further than the famously generous definition of computer science by Allen Newell, Alan Perlis and Herbert Simon: 'the study of computers' and the 'varied, complex, rich' phenomena surrounding them (1967: 1373f.)? Why not simply make use of the products?

Deconstructing cultural monoliths is generally good for one's mental health, especially in the case of an entity with enormous cultural authority and social power. The illusion of monolithic authority is apt to engender veneration more than understanding, whereas resolved into a sharp image of diversity the former monolith of computer science becomes a variety of genuinely interesting and relevant trajectories of research. In particular, knowing the multiple referents of the singular name helps us to clarify the natures and purposes of humanities computing by identifying both the similarities and especially the contrasts. (Where two practices on such different paths have come to the same conclusions, these conclusions are strengthened. Where they differ, useful questions are raised.) Obviously humanities computing is indebted to the products of computer science, but without taking a close look we cannot see how far the indebtedness extends, nor with what consequences. We cannot see if our indebtedness extends or should extend further than the products into the core of a putative science.

Like computer science in its early days, humanities computing is also subject to misapprehension as not only inferior to but also permanently dependent on the 'real thing'. In such a relationship the most damaging dependency is on the superior field's construction of its inferior's identity: the more alike the concerns, the more they are foregrounded; the less alike they are, the less likely to receive attention, even to be visible at all. If, for example, we look at humanities computing from the perspective of those who formulate algorithms (abstract computable procedures), then something like the following hierarchy results:[2]

1. Creation of algorithms to analyse data stored on a computer;
2. Self-conscious, knowing use of algorithmic processes to analyse such data;
3. Creation of such data from artifacts of a discipline;
4. Use of such data to address problems in the discipline;
5. Use of computers for any common purpose.

In this view humanities computing at its very best has an elite, core group who devise algorithms, presumably of specific relevance to problems in the humanities; a larger group of technically well-grounded, algorithmically literate scholars; and so on, until we reach the users of applications, who cannot properly be included at all. The problem here is not the strong emphasis on intellectual work, which unobjectionably ranks designing algorithms high above pushing buttons, nor is it direct involvement in the creation of basic tools, which is an essential component of the field. Rather it is the implicit framing of the possibilities according to extrinsic criteria, which are in fact not even those of computer science as a whole. This view silently relegates humanities computing to the role of a poor relation, a 'computer science for poets', in which the science is diluted and nothing of poetry remains.

I postpone detailed consideration of how humanities computing relates to computer science to the end of this chapter. Meanwhile I intend to take a look into the uncertainly dimensioned black box of the latter and into some of the black boxes within it, such as the concept of 'algorithm'. Seeing what there is, we can ask where the ideas and practices came from. This not only gives us a better idea of where the field might be going but also a means of relating to its history. Computer science has a great deal more of it than humanities computing. We can learn from this history. I will look in particular at the nature of formal methods and the meaning of 'theory'.

3 Parts, origins and focus

There are two facts with which to begin worrying the problem that computer science presents to the outsider: first, that it is internally diverse, spanning 'an enormous intellectual distance', from theoretical mathematics to application programming;[3] and second, that it is thriving. Computer science comprises 'an extensive network of practitioners in industry, academia, and private practice' that together with molecular biology constitutes 'the fastest growing sector of academia' (Mahoney 2002: 27). It would seem reasonable, at least as a first approximation, to assume that the field somehow coheres, or is at least cohesible, and then attempt to determine how. But that attempt must begin with the diversity.

Roughly speaking, the major fault-line within computer science corresponds to the division between the older disciplines that collaborated in its making: mathematics on the one hand, engineering on the other. Michael Mahoney has pointed out that originally the physical device had no theory and computing no agenda of its own. 'Rather, computers and computing posed a constellation of problems that intersected with the agendas of various fields' and stimulated the development of many agendas. 'Theories are about questions, and where the nascent subject of computing could not supply the next question, the agenda of the outside field often provided it' (1997: 619). The cycle of engagement and transformation continues, in both directions across the divide between computer science and the now many disciplines with which it interacts. 'Every time that computer scientists have approached a new problem domain,' William Wulf observes, 'we've discovered new things about computers' (2000) and vice versa. Continual innovation is in such accord both with how we think and with the nature of computing that new problems and new domains of application seem unlikely to find a limit.

A few terminological qualifications before we proceed. In accord with usage, I will reserve the term 'computation' for the mathematical sense current in theoretical computer science, that is, the abstract scheme of what it means to compute something. I will use 'computing' for all the activities involving the physical machine(s) derived from this scheme, that is, for what we want to do with the actual device(s).

The adjective 'computational' and the associated adverb I will take as more or less neutral. 'Truth' should be understood here in the context of mathematics, where it is a common, uncontentious term (although the truth of something in particular may be quite contentious). By 'knowledge' I mean human cognitive achievements, which however qualified I do not presume can be unproblematically represented in a computer. Finally, 'the computer' I take to be a convenient collective noun that does not in any way imply a singular essence.

My effort here must also be qualified. Because many of the activities and subjects of concern to computer science already outstrip my scope, I do not attempt anything like a comprehensive portrait of the field. Nor do I attempt even superficially to cover all historical developments that led to the device itself. Even to achieve my limited objectives I must take many shortcuts. Here, with the help of secondary literature, I confine myself to brief glimpses, with two goals in mind. One, with which I conclude this chapter, is a provisional notion of a productive relationship between humanities computing and computer science. The other, constitutive of it, is my attempt throughout this chapter to delineate what computing, as it has come to be understood in theory and practice through computer science, has to teach the humanities. There are other worthy goals. These are mine.

My first shortcut to the essence we require is to strike for the origins of the field, my second to consider selected aspects.

Contrary to the singular line of development presented by the primitive chronicles of 'firsts' in computing, historical research has shown that its convergent origins are not coincident. These origins lie, *inter alia*, in the design of automatic mechanical calculators and the development of mathematical logic; in efforts in programmable automation, such as the Jacquard loom, and devices for office automation; in the culture of human 'computers', i.e. persons 'employed to make calculations in an observatory, in surveying, etc.'; and in the development of feedback and control mechanisms in engineering.[4] The first computers in the modern sense, Mahoney explains, were the joint product of quite separate groups in electrical engineering and theoretical mathematics, 'whose expertise intersected in the machine and overlapped on the instruction set' (1990b: 327). As long as the devices they constructed remained specialized instruments for scientific research, programming was unproblematic. Those most intimately involved with computing in its early days 'apparently looked upon programming as incidental to their respective concerns'. What changed the picture radically was application beyond science to the commercial, social and military worlds, which brought about an explosive growth in problems for computing to address. This in turn required the rapid adaptability of machine to circumstance that software could provide. Once software became important to computing, computing became much more than its diverse but convergent roots. It became, increasingly, the many parts of everyday life that we subsume under the abstraction 'computer' and that in their diversification reflect life in all of its barely controllable messiness.

These origins of computing demarcate a familiar division between engineering and science, making and studying, doing and thinking, with tensions as old as the argument between Ajax and Odysseus over the arms of Achilles. But the computer, 'the first machine for doing thinking' (Mahoney 1990b: 325) – or for doing thinking *with* – has again and again demonstrated the confounding of categories such as these. The locus of confounding is in software, where the more theoretical side of computer science meets the world through systems engineered to serve and interact with it. Humanities computing and computer science stand together at this locus, so if common intellectual ground is to be located, it seems likely to be here. In this chapter I propose to inspect this ground by looking first to the theoretical component, then to the practical. Both, as we will see, attest that neither is sufficient on its own and that together they make for an exceedingly rich situation.

The story of computing more or less sorts into three versions. The first or standard story, told from a logico-mathematical perspective, takes the algorithm as its central idea and so tends to ignore not simply the physical and social aspects of computing but also its manifestations in other disciplines insofar as they deviate from exercise of algorithmic, formal thought. The second version is told by those who qualify this story theoretically. They note the inability of the algorithmic account to explain the evident power and potential of computing, then either argue for a more comprehensive idea, such as Peter Wegner's 'interaction machine', or question the nature of mathematics and logic philosophically, as Brian Cantwell Smith does in exploring an 'intentional science'.[5] The third version likewise questions the standard account but does so on the basis of its empirical and historical inadequacies, focusing on the effects, politics and policies of computing in business, industry, the military, government and society at large.[6] Each of these versions has something to teach us. In this chapter I give the standard account centre-stage because it is simultaneously best known among specialists and least accessible to everyone else. Though inadequate, it has a strong claim on our attention for what it can tell us about analytic applications of computing. I take the second version as direct critique of the first and so weave elements of it into the first story. My response to the third is my account of modelling in Chapter 1, which approaches computing as an experimental activity. I regard this aspect of computing as so important for the humanities that I have given it pride of place in the book, even at the risk of colouring the account here.

4 Mathematics

Mathematics is at the centre of the standard account of computing. To give even a brief survey of its role would require us to explore several interrelated agendas comprising that branch of our subject commonly known as theoretical computer science. Unfortunately the historiography of computing is at too primitive a stage to have enabled the writing of such explanatory, bridging accounts for the theoretical branch as have for generations made the physical sciences accessible to scholars in the humanities.[7] Since undertaking such a task here is not possible, I must at this juncture hazard another short-cut: to strike for the historical roots of computational theory in mathematics from Gottfried Wilhelm von Leibniz (1647–1716) to Alan Turing (1912–54), on the eve of implementation.[8] Fortunately for my project, this history is well enough known and sufficiently blessed with learned commentary that it can safely be retold in summary and reshaped for my purposes. The question at which I propose to direct this history is what mathematics and mathematical computer science can teach the humanist about computing. There are in fact several lessons to be learned; I will conclude this section with a review of them.

The following analogy is sometimes made: just as knowledge of the internal combustion engine is irrelevant to driving, it is said, so the principles of computation do not matter to even the most demanding user of computers. The analogy would seem to be strengthened by the layered design of computing systems, discussed at the end of this chapter. This design, e.g. in the graphical user interface, allows us to operate in ignorance of the complexity that each apparently simple move subsumes. But neither automobile nor computer supports the point that the analogy was devised to make once we become more than mere users operating within standard parameters. Once we begin to theorize the nature of computing or even to speculate on what in principle we can do with it, its mathematical basis becomes distinctly relevant.

Hence a serious, critical treatment of computing cannot avoid its mathematics, at least to the extent of acquiring some fundamentals. This is no less true for the humanities – indeed, even more so than for the sciences, whose imaginative language is mathematics. At the same time we need to be clear that by 'basic' or 'fundamental' we mean 'serving as the foundation on which understanding is built'. One of the services that asking for such explanation can perform is to probe what foundations there are, and perhaps then to identify basic problems that the architects have ignored in designing the superstructure.

For those whose focus is on the artifacts to which computing techniques are applied, one of the most important explanations to require of foundational knowledge is how to characterize and so come to grips with the special quality that computing brings to non-computational problems. Common usage, as I noted in the previous chapter, suggests that this quality is its *formality*, as attested e.g. by the so-called formal methods of everyday work in applied computing, such as relational database design or textual markup. What is this, exactly? Defining formality, as we will see, is very difficult despite the fact that it is everywhere asserted and seems to make intuitive sense. Its persistence in discussions of computing and its general accord with experience suggest that it points to something quite important, however vaguely. As a working notion it certainly serves a purpose, but the time has come to probe it. Since formality has been nowhere more thoroughly explored than in mathematics (long regarded as the science of the formal *par excellence*) we need to ask: What is the outcome of the study of formal methods in mathematics? This turns out to be quite a good question, since historically pursuit of formality there led to the discovery of strong constraints on what formal systems can do. The mechanism of this discovery in fact led to computing, but we need to know why this historical fact remains philosophically consequential.

My much reduced story of mathematics begins with Leibniz's articulated vision 'of human reason reduced to calculation' – an inspiring and significant failure – and 'of powerful mechanical engines to carry out calculations' – a magnificent achievement (Davis 2000: 146). Early in his career, Leibniz outlined ideas for a universal symbolic language and a mechanical means of reasoning. 'Given a "calculus", or procedure for solving problems,' Campbell-Kelly and Russ explain,

> Leibniz was well aware of the possibility of mechanical implementation. In the early 1670s, he designed and built a working mechanical calculator ... and he was the first to explore and exploit the

formal affinity between logic and mathematics. He suggested that logic could be developed into 'a sort of universal mathematics', and he applied mathematical methods to derive some syllogistic forms using the algebraic methods of symbolism. (1994: 702)

The Baconian point was, Leibniz said in a characteristic mixture of Latin and German, *Theoricos Empiricis felici connubio zu conjungiren*, 'to join theorists and empirics in a happy marriage' (Burke 2000: 16f.). The connubial metaphor is itself a happy one, and especially close given the contemporary ideals of theory and experiment on the one hand and of conjugal relations on the other. We may claim a beginning for this marriage in the physical computer, but only a beginning which, to follow the metaphor, becomes what it is by creating a deepening history of negotiated differences. We need to ask the standard questions: what each is like separately; what together they produce that otherwise would not be; and in what their fulfilment consists? But perhaps most important of all, we need simply to keep this metaphor, *as a metaphor*, in mind.

More than a century later, George Boole (1815–64) completed part of Leibniz's project by making classical syllogistic logic into a branch of mathematics.[9] This work is recalled by its instantiation in the 'Boolean logic' of computational query languages and in the design of electronic circuitry, where 'logic circuits' perform Boole's fundamental operations (Feynman 1999/1996: 20–30). But Boole did more than enlarge mathematics: in applying mathematical reasoning to domains other than numbers, he simultaneously turned mathematics towards logic and so initiated a central preoccupation with a formal, abstract approach to the foundations of mathematics. This in turn directed attention to the philosophical questions of what underlies and supports mathematical reasoning, what gives it strength – and ultimately whether there are limits to what may be known by any means.

In the story I am telling the chief proponent of the formal approach was David Hilbert (1862–1943),[10] whose ruling concern was with the axioms of mathematics – that is, its self-evident propositions or foundational statements.[11] In such a meta-mathematical view, Solomon Feferman explains, '*all* notions used in an axiomatic system and *all* assumptions concerning these must be fully spelled out' (1999: 101). For the history of computing Hilbert's primary contribution was precisely to make this truly rigorous demand and to pursue it with persistence and clarity of mind. It came in two stages, both of which had early expression in his lecture 'Mathematische Probleme', famous for setting the agenda of mathematics in a series of unsolved problems then at the leading edge of research.[12] The first stage of his contribution emerged in the second of these problems, in which he asked whether the axioms of mathematics can be shown to be both complete and free from contradictions, i.e. consistent among themselves. 'Without pursuing the many foundational issues here,' as Campbell-Kelly and Russ explain, Hilbert thought to ground his science not on the basis of logic,[13] properly so called, 'but on the idea of a formal system' that had these properties of *consistency* and *completeness* (1994: 702).[14]

Hilbert developed this problem seriously only in the 1920s, culminating in a lecture in Bologna in 1928. But his fundamental conjectures of consistency and completeness were dashed three years later by the young Austrian mathematician Kurt Gödel,[15] who showed that mathematical truth 'goes beyond what can be proved in any given formal system'.[16] Kilmister explains the overall result:

insight and deduction give sets of consequences which are certainly overlapping, but neither contains the other. On the one hand deduction is so powerful that it can ... produce many complicated results which are beyond the power of insight. This is not so surprising as the situation on the other hand ... that deduction will always be unable to prove all the truths which are accessible to insight. (1967: 102)

Although mathematicians continue to work towards a version of Hilbert's goal, his programme as originally set forth was effectively demolished.[17] Seeing it as a sharply defined failure is necessary in order to realize how it bore fruit in Gödel's decisive separation of the larger realm of truth from smaller one of proof. Furthermore, from that separation comes the crucial question of exactly *how* unproved things are known, which as we will see was to preoccupy Gödel in his later years. Indeed, as I emphasized in Chapter 1, this question is what drives research, gives it direction and so makes it progressive. It is, of course, a familiar question – indeed, it is the central question of research in humanities computing because Gödel's result demonstrates *the inherent limitation of formal systems and methods*. Writing a decade later (in a rejected article not published until 1965), Emil Post came to the obvious conclusion 'that *mathematical thinking is, and must be, essentially creative*', and hence that with 'a reversal of the entire axiomatic trend of the late 19th and early 20th centuries, with a return to meaning and truth ... [formal] thinking will then remain as but one phase of mathematical thinking' (Davis 1993/1965: 343). Quoting this passage, Meurig Beynon and Steve Russ comment that Post 'would find much in contemporary computing to endorse his perception of the future for formal systems', namely the failure of theoretical computer science, inheritor and propagator of formality, to speak to computing in the wild, 'by and large an activity that defies formalisation, in which all manner of informal and heuristic techniques are used to construct programs with primary reference to their intended meaning and function' (2004). We must, then, look very carefully at our pride in formal approaches – but, as my argument for modelling goes, not abandon them, rather use them instrumentally.

Hilbert's second and more obvious contribution to the history of computing developed out of another major question regarding human reasoning to which he had also sought a positive answer. This appeared first in the tenth of Hilbert's problems: given a particular kind of equation (known as Diophantine, after the third-century Greek mathematician Diophantus), Hilbert called for 'a process according to which it can be determined by a finite number of operations whether the equation is solvable ...'[18] In the 1920s similar problems were emerging, with the implication that it was simply impossible to decide whether certain equations were solvable. Hilbert and his student Wilhelm Ackermann, in *Grundzüge der theoretischen Logik*, identified the underlying situation as the fundamental problem of mathematical logic and named it the *Entscheidungsproblem* or 'decision-problem' (1928: 73–4). In essence this problem leads to the question, 'does predicate logic admit a "decision procedure" ... to determine whether a given formula is valid or not?'[19] The Cambridge mathematician G. H. Hardy observed that if there were such a procedure, 'we should have a mechanical set of rules for the solution of all mathematical problems, and our activities as mathematicians would come to an end' (Gandy 1995/1994: 62). In other words, the question was whether in the case of mathematics – and so by extension in other fields as well – exhaustion was genuinely possible. Once again, as we noted in the previous chapter for physics some three decades earlier, the answer turned out to be negative. Again a negative answer had very great theoretical and practical consequences.

These emerged in the work of Alan Turing, particularly in his remarkable 1936 paper 'On Computable Numbers, with an Application to the Entscheidungsproblem'. Although there were four responses to this problem in that year, Turing's is the best remembered and by far the most intellectually productive.[20] Because the answer was negative, Turing had to show that in principle no such procedure was possible. To do this required that he define exactly what was 'effectively computable', as he named what we would now call an algorithm. He did this by comparing 'a man in the process of computing a real number to a machine which is only capable of a finite number of conditions' (1936: 231). Davis outlines the steps: a shift in focus 'from the rules to what the person actually *did* when carrying them out'; a reduction of the operations 'to a few extremely simple basic actions'; substitution of a correspondingly simple machine for the person; finally, proof that no such machine 'performing only those basic actions could determine whether a given proposed conclusion follows from given premises' using the rules of logic. 'As a byproduct,' Davis remarks, 'he found a mathematical model of an all-purpose computing machine' (2000: 147f.).

Allow me to draw out the implications of two points in Davis' remark: the computer as *by-product*, and the *all-purpose* nature of Turing's imaginary machine.

The notion of computer as by-product is perhaps ironic,[21] but it alerts us to the essential interplay between failure and productive work in computing. Turing's fame does not rest principally on his *via negativa* demonstration of failure in Hilbert's programme, as Alan Perlis remarked in the first Turing Award lecture, rather for 'the model he invented and employed' in his proof (1967: 1). But importance is not the same thing as fame, and inquiring into the import of Turing's work leads from the productive failure of Hilbert's project in the *Entscheidungsproblem* to the productive failures of that which does not compute, as we have seen. Perlis makes this point himself, though as it were in reverse, when he notes that, 'a most fruitful consequence of the Turing machine has been with the creation, study and computation of functions which are computable, i.e., in computer programming. This is not surprising *since computers can compute so much more than we yet know how to specify'* (1, my emphasis). In other words, when we look from the machine, we see that what can be done with it is greater than we know how to describe mathematically. When we look from cultural artifacts, we see that what we know of them is greater than we know how to describe computationally. These two 'greater thans' each echo Gödel's result, that 'there are true statements which cannot be proved'. Their isomorphism recalls Leibniz's connubial intention and so strengthens it.

In his 1936 paper Turing imagined a machine comprising two parts. The first is a read-write head with a 'state-table' in which a finite number of machine-states is recorded, thus called the 'finite state machine' (Feynman 1999/1996: 55–65). The second part, positioned under it, is a moveable tape divided into cells, in each of which a symbol may be written or read. Feynman describes what this machine does:

> The action of the machine is simple ... it starts off in a certain state, looking at the contents of a cell. Depending on the state, and the cell contents, it might erase the contents of the cell and write something new, or leave the cell as it is ... Whatever it does, it next moves one cell to the left or right, and changes to a new internal state. (1999/1996: 66)

The machine, which became known as the Turing Machine (TM), is single-purpose. Like a hard-wired physical device, it performs a specific task – Feynman's example is a TM that counts right and left parentheses on its tape to make sure they balance. But two of its properties, simplicity and recursiveness, allowed Turing to transform the TM into a 'universal' machine capable of performing any computable task, hence his proof. Mahoney explains:

> Since a state may be described in terms of five symbols (current state, input, output, shift right/left, next state), a computation may itself be expressed as a sequence of symbols, which can also be placed on the tape, thus making possible a universal machine that can read a computation and then carry it out by emulating the machine described by it.[22]

This is the all-purpose computer or Universal Turing Machine (UTM). Turing obtained his main result by using the UTM to show that a hypothetical machine capable of computing in a finite number of steps that it would halt leads to a logical contradiction, so that no decision-procedure is possible.

Hence the by-product of which Davis spoke. Quite independent of Turing's intention in devising the UTM is its fundamental nature as 'an open schema for a potentially infinite range of particular applications' (Mahoney 1990b: 326). The protean quality of the result is attributable to the physical 'stored-program principle', which specifies not only that the program is stored but that it is stored *as data*, so that it is modifiable during the course of a computation. Because a Turing Machine can write on its own tape, the UTM is possible. Thus software turns one physical device 'into an indefinitely large variety of *virtual machines*' (Edwards 1998: 94). Hence, as I argued in the Introduction, 'it is a mistake to view the computer as a single technology. More appropriately, each application is a new technology harnessing information processing capability, much as the electric motor, the locomotive, and the jet plane all harnessed energy-transforming capability' (Landauer 1997: 104). 'It has taken historians a long time to understand this point,' Edwards comments. 'The main paradigm in computer historiography has been device history, focusing on machines, engineers, and the computer industry' (1998: 94). As a result we have an increasingly detailed picture of the physical manifestations of computing, but from the historical perspective fundamental to a humanistic understanding, the less physical our object of attention the less clear this picture appears. Historians have tended to neglect software, but even more the role of the entirely abstract schema described by the Universal Turing Machine and the mathematics behind it. In historical discussions, the emphasis on the fact that programs are *stored* has obscured what is new about Turing's machine, since there are prior claims to the storing of programs, e.g. in the Jacquard loom. His innovation lies in the self-modifying nature of the TM design.

In the UTM, Davis comments, the sharp distinction between hardware, software and data vanishes (2000: 164f.): the values defining a machine, and so virtually equivalent to its hardware, can function as what we might call software for another machine, which reads it as data. Herbert Simon, in *The Sciences of the Artificial*, notes that to a very high degree (as long as we are operating within normal parameters) the behaviour even of real computers betrays almost nothing of their physical reality other than their organizational properties (1996/1969: 17). Hence the suitability of computing to functional description and our strongly reinforced tendencies to think functionally and methodologically. With computing it becomes much more practical not only to describe and find patterns in nature and culture but also *almost* – a quantum qualification of the greatest importance – to detach them from their contexts and give them independent life. It becomes possible to study the mechanical, as an abstraction, in itself.

Functioning, then, as a creolized dialect of mathematics, computation joins its areas of application rather more directly than before with the theoretical side of the sciences, complementing the experimental side bestowed on us via the manipulatory powers of computing. Because of the intimacy that this joining effects, we must pay attention to mathematics not simply as the offstage labour by which Turing's universal by-product came to be and as the footnoted explanation for the open plurality of computings. In fact the mathematicians' *agon* from Hilbert to Turing speaks directly to the concern of the humanities and so is worth a second, deeper look. Once again a standard story, though important to tell, needs to be qualified.

It is most important to realize that Hilbert was not simply proved wrong by Gödel and Turing, nor did his successors simply triumph, despite words like 'demolish' and the finality suggested by the mathematical terms 'proof', 'result' and 'truth'. Rather Hilbert gave particularly significant articulation to a set of mathematical and philosophical questions that these successors developed and that remain at the core of computation as we know it. Hilbert's programme was founded, Michael Detlefsen explains, on a concern for paradox in mathematics originating in 'a discrepancy between the laws according to which the mind of *homo mathematicus* works, and the laws governing objective mathematical fact' (1986: ix). In his own words, Hilbert's aim was 'to describe the activity of our understanding, to make a protocol of the rules according to which our thinking actually proceeds.'[23] Hilbert's language makes quite clear that he was after objective, *a priori* mathematical truth. His meta-mathematical attention to the rules of thought rather than to the constructive thinking they supposedly govern identifies his lifelong preoccupation 'with the form, as distinguished from the matter, of reasoning'. For that reason the label 'formalist' is commonly applied to his programme, but several of his remarks speak to the insufficiency of formalism. His lecture 'Axiomatic Thought' (1918), for example, demonstrates beyond doubt that 'Hilbert viewed formal axiom systems instrumentally, as a powerful tool for mathematical research. ... But he nowhere suggests that the whole of mathematics can simply be *identified* with the study of formal systems ...'[24]

With Hilbert, then, we address the limits of a programme within which the tool of formalism was central and which was, as Gödel later said, attempting to chart a middle course between *a priori* truth and historically contingent understanding (1995/ca. 1961: 381). In 'Axiomatic Thought', Hilbert argued that once a field is sufficiently mature to have discovered its own axioms, the 'axiomatic method' comes into play. This method 'amounts to a [continual] *deepening of the foundations* of the individual domains of knowledge' when critical analysis of current axioms discovers that they are in fact composites of still deeper propositions (Ewald 1996: 1109). In a lecture he gave the day after Gödel announced his devastating result, Hilbert famously proclaimed, 'Wir müssen wissen, / Wir werden wissen' ('we must know, we will know') – words later inscribed on his tombstone (Gandy 1995/1994: 58). This expresses a vain faith unless the middle course of deepening foundations through analysis is open. 'For any specific given formalism', Martin Davis points out,

> there are mathematical questions that will transcend it. On the other hand, in principle, each such question leads to a more powerful system which enables the resolution of that system. One envisions hierarchies of ever more powerful systems each making it possible to decide questions left undecidable by weaker systems. (2000: 124)

Hence my invocation of modelling to set the failure of Hilbert's programme into a broader and positive context. The most rewarding commentary of all on the situation is Gödel's, in the ca. 1961 lecture (which Gödel wrote, but never gave) to which I have alluded, 'The modern development of the foundations of mathematics in the light of philosophy'.[25] In this lecture Gödel sets foundational research in mathematics against world-views prevailing over time, from the conservatively idealistic, spiritual, theological and *a priori* beliefs in an absolute order on the right to the radically sceptical, materialistic, positivist and empirical on the left. The overall shift since the Renaissance, he argues, has been from right to left, with the result that secure knowledge of objective states has been progressively denied, leaving us with prediction of results and a greatly weakened sense of theory (hence the growth of positivism). Mathematics is by nature an *a priori* science, Gödel declares. Therefore in opposition to this trend it has developed continually away from empiricism towards ever more abstract generalizations. Hilbert's intervention, Gödel argues, was in response to exaggerated inroads of the prevailing *Zeitgeist*, which would deny any truth of mathematics that could not be established empirically. 'And thus came into being', Gödel comments, 'that curious hermaphroditic thing [*jenes merkwürdige Zwitterding*] that Hilbert's formalism represents, which sought to do justice both to the spirit of the time and to the nature of mathematics.' He attempted to strike a middle course, Gödel notes, 'but one obviously too primitive and tending too strongly in one direction.'(Gödel 1995/ca. 1961: 378–81). Formalism, in other words, was not the right instrument.

Jean Piaget points out that Gödel's course-correction meant moving away from formalism and towards the intuitive. Thus his famous result demonstrated the limits of formalization, raising for logical, axiomatic systems in particular the question, 'What does logic formalize?'; that is, 'what lies underneath the undemonstrable axioms and undefinable notions' out of which such a system is constructed? Piaget continues: 'This ... is a problem that shows the inadequacy of formalization as the fundamental basis', however many times axiomatization is iterated. 'It shows the necessity for considering thought itself as well as considering axiomatized logical systems, since it is from human thought that the logical systems develop and remain still intuitive' (1970/1968: 11). For Gödel the way ahead was exactly such a consideration of thought itself – hence his turn to the phenomenology of Edmund Husserl in 1959, late in his career, and his use of it prominently in the 1961 lecture.[26] The purpose of this turn 'was to find, by such "inquiry into essences"' as Husserl's philosophy described, 'a deeper notion of rationality' than, for example, had been available to Hilbert.[27] Gödel found in Husserl two fundamental points of connection: a conceptual realism, so that mathematical ideas could be treated objectively; and a perceptual intuition, by which we see and describe these independent objects.[28] He rejected the *via positiva* of computation, for he thought it was 'not by proving certain properties by a projection onto material systems – namely, the manipulation of physical symbols' that a way ahead would be found,

but rather by cultivating (deepening) knowledge of the abstract concepts themselves which lead to the setting up of these mechanical systems, and further by seeking, according to the same procedures, to gain insights into the solvability, and the actual methods for the solution, of all meaningful mathematical problems. (1995/ca. 1961: 383)

Gödel's Husserlian idea of acting on concepts as one would on objects and his shifting of attention from them to the acts by which they are perceived accord well with Turing's approach to mathematics via the mechanical procedure of 'effective computability', in which he turned the *Entscheidungsproblem* into an object and studied its actions.[29] But for Gödel intuition seemed to indicate that 'the mind is not mechanical, in the sense that it ought not to be viewed as a finite, discrete, combinatorial syntax manipulator' (Tieszen 1992: 192). His intentions, recorded in an interview for a popular book on mathematics, suggest where this is going. Gödel is quoted by his interviewer: '"Either mathematics is too big for the human mind," he says, "or the human mind is more than a machine." He hopes to prove the latter.'[30]

What, then, are the lessons for the humanities to learn from a history of formal systems and of computation?

The first is the intention behind Leibniz's dream, 'to join theorists and empirics in a happy marriage' and so to resolve the tension that, Gadamer argues, has been inherent in Western culture since Galileo. The lesson, however, is in particular *how* that tension is resolved, or rather used. Unlike the musical metaphor of harmony, which would have supplied part of what we need, the connubial metaphor implies creation of a new, independent entity alongside its progenitors, the *tertium quid* (which I described in the previous chapter) that does not subsume their identities but fulfils them. I will return to this lesson below.

The second is David Hilbert's attempt, in response to the tension between *a priori* mathematics and a *Zeitgeist* with strong *a posteriori* inclinations, to relate the two – in effect to bring about Leibniz's connubial arrangement, although purely within mathematics. We have been concerned with two expressions of his project: first the demand for consistency and completeness in the axioms, and second the demand for decidability of propositions. Both are attempts to relate the theoretical to the empirical in the sense that they recognize the need to ground intuitive thought in something stubbornly external and objective – indeed, to identify 'objective' as a virtue and define what it might mean in mathematics. Gödel's criticism that the result was hermaphroditic (rather than connubial) points out its weakness with metaphorical precision, but Hilbert's aspiration and the powerful, enduring way in which he formulated it comprise a lesson worth learning – the lesson of modelling and its relation to truth. As a corollary, we see that the brilliant failure of Hilbert's project is its enduring success.

The third lesson is Gödel's negative result of 1931, establishing that there are true statements which cannot be proved. By separating the larger realm of truth from the smaller one of proof, he accomplished the sort of creative act that Milton attributed to God in *The Doctrine and Discipline of Divorce*: 'when by his divorcing command the world first rose out of Chaos, nor can be renew'd again out of confusion but by the separating of unmeet consorts' (1.10). Being creative, this separation generated the fertilizing question of how, exactly, unsolvable problems are dealt with, which is indeed the principal question to which computing always returns. As we saw, Gödel pointed into a way of answering, or rather, what he called 'a systematic method for such a clarification of meaning' via Husserlian phenomenology. Although research in this area is quite young, we can already see in the philo-sophical combination that attracted Gödel – of conceptual realism with a procedural, almost interventionist perception – the basis for common ground with those who address the context of discovery. Chapter 1 was concerned with sketching that common ground.

The fourth lesson is Turing's similarly negative response to Hilbert's demand for decidability. Turing's contribution, we might say, is to raise the question of how two different kinds of statement relate: the theoretical, expressed in the existential rhetoric of classical mathematics (e.g. x = 1, read 'x *is* equal to 1'), and the computable, expressed in the procedural rhetoric of algorithms (x = 1, read '*set* x equal to 1'). Turing showed that certainty belongs to, indeed is defined by the 'effectively computable', the mechanical. Here the creative outcome is, as Perlis and Mahoney both noted, the schema for an indefinite number of physical machines for 'doing thinking with' and so, since that is paradoxical, for exploring the question raised by Gödel. But because they are for doing thinking *with*, they escape Perlis' 'Turing tar-pit in which everything is possible but nothing of interest is easy' (54, 1982: 10) and become computings whose wilds we are just begin-ning to explore.

Finally, two additional lessons or, rather, reiterations of lessons that run throughout this book. First, the way of productive research is a carefully crafted, demanding *via negativa*. Second, the old displacement of definitive knowledge by continual coming to know is re-enacted in computing.

5   Software engineering

With Turing's universal machine we reach the forecourts of software, in which the algorithmic meets the socially rule-governed.[31] Turing's focus was on what his machine could *not* do rather than what it could. It was clear even before software got very far into the world that his design was an inadequate guide: 'workers in the field ...' Michael Rabin and Dana Scott observed in 1959, 'have felt more and more that the notion of a Turing machine is too general to serve as an accurate model of actual computers.'[32] Under the pressure of a demand for empirical adequacy, their observation has been applied to algorithms in general. Peter Wegner, for example, has memorably declared that 'algorithms are metaphorically dumb and blind because they cannot adapt interactively while they compute. They are autistic in performing tasks according to rules rather than through interaction' (1997: 82). He has offered several models, such as the 'interaction machine', for recognizing formally the many kinds of computing that Turing's schema is not adequate to describe.[33] The most generous and so most demanding of views is, perhaps, due to Terry Winograd and Fernando Flores, who wrote years ago that 'in designing tools we are designing ways of being' (1986: xi). Indeed, large portions of computer science are now devoted to implementing ways of being, or forms of life, as well as addressing questions of usability. But the problems begin at a much lower level, in what we now call, inappropriately according to some, 'software engineering'. These are the problems I will consider here.

Software as we find it is itself enigmatically dual, reflecting the opposition of engineering-like and mathematics-like aspects. On the one hand, it is embodied in concrete textual expressions, which are built up from primitive elements; on the other, it is abstractly mechanical, following a rigorous logical process. Viewed philosophically rather than historically, that is, software is problematic.[34] In a preliminary philosophical sketch, Brian Cantwell Smith finds profound difficulties with computation, which he presents under seven distinct 'construals' (2002: 28–43). He argues that the entire debate is vexed by muddled terms, as a result of which we run directly into an 'ontological wall' of recalcitrant theoretical issues. Common usage of our word 'formal', for example, betrays a confusing proliferation of 'different readings ... : *precise, abstract, syntactic, mathematical, explicit, digital, a-contextual, nonsemantic*, among others' (2002: [15]). Thus the term acts as 'a lightning rod for a cluster of ontological assumptions, methodological commitments, and social and historical biases' that make a clear sight of our subject very difficult. Picking these apart, Smith argues that 'no standard construal of formality ... is both (i) substantive and (ii) true of extant computational practice.' The problem is that in interacting with the world, computing inevitably mingles meaning and form, with the result that formality in any well-defined sense is violated. The muddle results from transposing a term meaningful in one context into others where it is not. If formality is perfectly defined by Turing's effective computability, that is, then mathematics and history demonstrate that imagination and reality both escape it.

Now that we have a context for formality, we can see why the error so stubbornly persists. Gregory Bateson explains:

> whenever we pride ourselves upon finding a newer, stricter way of thought or exposition; whenever we start insisting too hard upon 'operationalism' or symbolic logic or any other of these very essential

systems of tramlines, we lose something of the ability to think new thoughts. And equally, of course, whenever we rebel against the sterile rigidity of formal thought and exposition and let our ideas run wild, we likewise lose. As I see it, the advances in scientific thought come from *a combination of loose and strict thinking*, and this combination is the most precious tool of science. (2000/1972: 75)

Another way to think about the enigma of software is to consider the role software plays in the relation between an operational computing system and the world to which this system corresponds. As we saw in Chapter 1, this correspondence is resolved by the idea of modelling into two relationships. Here I have redrawn these schematically in Figure 4.1.[35] The left-hand relationship, between a properly formulated model and the computing system it defines, is governed by mathematical 'model theory' and is well understood (Hodges 1998). The right-hand relationship, between the world and the computational model, is where the difficulties lie for any straightforward account. It is where, Mahoney notes, 'the science of software moves away from the computer into the wider world and interacts with the sciences (if they exist) pertinent to the systems to be modeled computationally. There it becomes a question of how to express those sciences computationally and of how to evaluate the fit between the target system and the computational model' (2002: 38). It is where computing intersects for example with the humanities. Thus, in Chapter 1, I have described how we express the humanities computationally in terms of a philosophically informed modelling practice. In this intimately interactive, hands-on practice, the misfit between model and target not only points a way forward but is the point of the exercise, as Bateson's observation suggests.

In the standard account, however, computer science has a rather different set of concerns that develop from the fundamental question, 'what can be automated?'[36] Hence designing and building systems in this account resembles what I have called 'modelling', but the goal is quite different. Rather than research that privileges non-computational insight and develops towards knowledge by interaction with provisional constructs, the goal 'is all about getting something to do something', as Feynman says.[37] The right-hand side therefore becomes the serious, practical issue of discovering how to get from a statement of requirements to a program that may said to be working, then to verify whether it will work under all conceivable circumstances. Before the program can be written, the system it is designed to automate must be

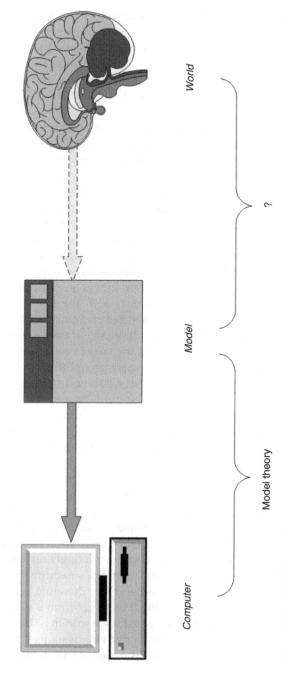

Figure 4.1:   World, model and computer

understood *as a system*, and that in itself is a major stumbling block. Already by 1967 the problems in this fraught process had reached the point that a major international conference on the subject was called. At the conference the standards of engineering practice were put forward as a solution. 'The phrase "software engineering" was deliberately chosen as being provocative, in implying the need for software manufacture to be [based] on the types of theoretical foundations and practical disciplines that are traditional in the established branches of engineering.'[38] But, as Mahoney points out, the provocation generated questions rather than standard approaches, since for example it was not at all clear what theory and practice might be relevant nor what the software equivalents might be. Now, in the fourth decade of the so-called software crisis, with software engineering still 'a term of aspiration', as Wayt Gibbs politely puts it (1994), more than an explanation is required. The hard problem is not individual failures as such, for as James Tomayko and others point out, failure is central to the epistemology of engineering.[39] But the problem is indicated by the fact that software engineers seem unable to learn from failures. What in the nature of software prevents them?

Ready-made governing principles for computer science are available neither from engineering nor from mathematics, where we might expect chiefly to find them. John Holland argues they can *only* come from mathematics, but, Mahoney comments, *this* mathematics is as yet undiscovered, and when discovered it 'will be about software' (2002: 41f.). If the complex amalgam we call 'computer science' has a science to it, then mathematics *is* the principal candidate, but what is meant by 'science' is hardly straightforward. Its meaning is formed in a struggle over the claims that practitioners have made and are making for this prestigious disciplinary term. Richard Feynman, a physicist, has for example denied the term 'science' to mathematics as well as to computer science because, he said, unlike physics neither field studies natural objects (1999/1996: xiii). Feynman's assertion is, however, not a matter of fact but a very interesting question that puts old truths to the test. On the one hand, Eugene Wigner's and Richard Hamming's observations of 'the unreasonable effectiveness of mathematics' in the natural world, the philosophical argument for its empirical origins, its growth in modern times 'almost entirely out of the problems of science' and the continuing stimulus of interaction with empirical research, including the rise of an experimental branch, suggests that as the logical side of science mathematics is strongly dependent on the material side.[40] On the other hand, the history of technology shows that we have repeatedly projected our inventions onto the world, then enlarged science to include the study of the world these projections have reshaped: thermodynamics from the steam engine, information theory from communications systems and so on. Mathematics has again and again proved to be the ideal form of the resulting science. But with computing we may be witnessing an historical rupture.[41]

Gödel's sight of mathematics beyond its own axiom systems makes room for computing. But from a mathematical perspective 'the computer has proved elusive, as central concerns of programming remain beyond the effective reach of mathematics ...'[42] Referring to 'a continuing dissonance' between the two fields, Mahoney quotes *What Can Be Automated: the Computer Science and Engineering Research Study* (Arden 1980): 'even though all the levels of the hierarchy which comprise computer systems can be interpreted as algorithms, the *study of algorithms* and the *phenomena related to computers* are not coextensive, since there are important organizational, policy and non-deterministic aspects of computing that do not fit the algorithmic mold' (2002: 37).

I will postpone the question that Mahoney raises, 'of what mold those aspects do fit', until we are ready to look at the relationship of computer science to humanities computing, which is directly concerned with encompassing 'the phenomena not covered by algorithms'. For now we can certainly learn from the shared failure of engineering and mathematics to provide ready-made governance. Not surprisingly, what we learn is that computer science is not just more than its historical roots; it is different from them even when the signs of inheritance are most evident. If we agree to call it a science (resistance *is* futile), then it is certainly science in a new sense, with a whole new relationship to theory and practice.

6   Significant terms: 'theory' and 'experiment'

As in the previous chapter, I propose here to approach the disciplinary question of *this* science by considering what happens when the crucial scientific terms 'theory' and 'experiment' enter the domain of computing. For obvious reasons these terms tend strongly to be influenced by their common meanings in mathematics and physics (or engineering), respectively.

Not surprisingly, theory came to computing from mathematics, or more specifically, Robin Milner explains, the 'hard theoretical core to computation' directly out of the Church–Turing thesis, which states that the known ways of defining what Turing called 'effectively computable' produce equivalent results.[43] It ramified through 'recursion theory, showing that certain things are essentially harder to compute than others', into modern complexity theory, which explains what can be computed on the basis of the mathematical relationship between the size of the job and the time required to compute it (Milner 1987: 58). To some computer scientists, 'this study ... simply *is* computation theory. To them, everything else is engineering of one kind or another ...'

The partition of computer science into a mathematical high ground and a vaguely defined lowland of engineering – or, from another point of view, a bedrock of practice from which flights of exploration (or of fancy, depending on the speaker) may be attempted – is obviously anti-Leibnizian and retrograde. Mahoney points out that comparisons to mathematics and contrasts with it date from the early period of computer science, with emphasis on effective procedures and feasible computation (1997: 618). Nevertheless the inclination to prefer mathematics rather less critically is to be expected from the fact of allegiance with a strong and prestigious external authority, which privileges the part of computer science most like itself and renders the rest tangential. As we have already seen, this flight to the high ground of mathematics runs into serious difficulties even for most theoretical parts of the field: reasoning with a thought-experimental machine is simply not the same as computing with a physical one. However much we may at any one moment ignore their physicality, machines are technological objects embedded in a social world (cf. Simon 1996/1969: 18–21). Hence they develop and proliferate, and in so doing continually alter the problem-horizon of theorists. They present a 'moving target – strange behaviour for mathematical objects' (Mahoney 2002: 35). Theoreticians in computer science may 'tend to prove theorems [with] standards for demonstrating correctness ... very similar to those traditionally used in mathematics' (ACECSE 1994: 25), but for an ethnographic understanding of computer science, the dissimilarities and the strange behaviours are crucial clues.

So also, for example, is the rootlessness Jeffrey Ullman finds characteristic of much computer science theory. He argues that an over-reliance on unsupported promise (so characteristic of computing generally) has led in many cases to a regress of papers commenting on each other, as a result of which the original problem is lost in a welter of speculation (1995: 43). He calls for a *reinvention of theory*, to move most of it 'much closer to practice' (44). Calls for such a move express a common reaction to the anti-Leibnizian flight of theorist from empiric.

One strong candidate for what this might mean is implied by a telling use of our term in one of the roles attributed to knowledge representation by Davis, Shrobe and Szolovits: to be 'a fragmentary *theory* of intelligent reasoning'.[44] What is 'theory' that a knowledge representation (or, perhaps, other computational construction) could be a means of coming upon or coming up with an adequate expression? They explain that a theory in this sense is fragmentary and often implicit: fragmentary because representations typically capture only part of the insight that motivates them, which itself is partial; implicit because it emerges in the representation, although it may be 'made more evident' through analysis. Such a conception of theorizing resembles modelling as discussed in Chapter 1, but it is not the same thing: modelling as defined there is the recursive and perfective manipulation of constructs; theorizing, in the sense developed here, is in contrast the process of understanding and explaining the world emergent in modelling. Theorizing, in other words, is the abstraction of modelling, not artifactual but artifact-driven in the way that the technological development of the computer has enlarged our idea of what computation itself means (May 1980: 17). And note: we speak here of *theorizing* – a way of acting, not an achievement.

Milner similarly argues that theorizing in computer science should be conceived as an activity proceeding outward from the central core of mathematical theory by stitching together a patchwork from whatever theories prove useful in the process of building and working with large systems (1987: 58). Thus 'one arrives at concepts ... not just by thinking about systems but by building them' (59); theoretical growth is stimulated and guided by the experiential work theory articulates. The old but persistent notion that theory necessarily comes first – 'that the conceptual frame for design already exists and that we only need to animate it by the right formal methodology' – is shown to be mistaken by the productive interaction of mathematics with 'application demand, often from the physical sciences'. Hence the argument for an 'experimental computer science' by analogy to these sciences. The difference he finds is that whereas the physical sciences experiment to discover *what is true*, experimental computer science does it to discover *how to design* (cf. Hartmanis 1995: 13). This is, he suggests later, a weak distinction for computing: as in the enigma of software, the procedural *how* (realized in execution) and the descriptive *what* (expressed as an object) are better conceived as two sides of the same meta-theoretical coin, distinct but inextricably together, just as theory and experiment are when the activity of science is viewed from an historical and philosophical distance. Again, it's a matter of emphasis. Juris Hartmanis, for example, argues from the fact that systems begin in ideas, which set their course and so determine what may be experienced with them – that theory defines what may be done. He invokes Albert Einstein's remark to Werner Heisenberg (which I quoted in the previous chapter) that '[i]t is the theory which decides what can be observed',[45] and goes on to comment that, 'even more than in physical sciences, the theory ... will determine what can be observed and what is worth observing'. The danger here for computer science, Milner notes, is sharpened by the popularity of the term 'formal methods' and the consequent elevation of method to the old status of theory, as an historically *a priori* conceptualization. (Once again the term 'formal' shows its uncertain colours.) Such methods then become fixed tools in a finite toolkit rather than a way of making or adapting tools for needs determined by the changing conditions of research. In so doing they attenuate rather than express the potential of computing.

In his conversation with Heisenberg, Einstein is arguing against the positivistic view that a theory may be founded 'on observable magnitudes alone': 'Only theory, that is, knowledge of natural laws,' Einstein declares, 'enables us to deduce the underlying phenomena from our sense impressions.' The important point for us to extract here is that Einstein is talking about the phenomena of nature *whereas we are considering artifacts of the imagination* – precisely Feynman's argument for denying the status of science to computer science, as previously noted. The difference in how we make sense of these things, as John Unsworth has pointed out, is attested by where we invest our intelligence in applications of computing: in software, to interpret data of the natural sciences, meaningful only in a large aggregate; or in markup, to render the semantically dense data of human artifacts computationally tractable.[46] To borrow a metaphor from medieval Christianity, the Book of Nature requires a very different act of reading than the Book of Man.[47] Theory in Einstein's sense familiarly defines the former; theory in computing struggles towards a scientific form of the latter – and in the process is deriving what 'scientific' means for that 'theory'. If it is not a contradiction in terms to say so, it is an *embedded theory*, not just a theory of the embedded, that we must be trying to define.

In moving mathematical theory and an equipment-centred practice closer together, the obvious model is physics, a science joining mathematics to the world through experiment. Engineering, of course, offers an equally rich and possibly a longer history of such engagement, though with a more consistently practical focus, as do the crafts that preceded engineering. In fact a useful distinction between 'experiment' in the sciences and in engineering is quite difficult to maintain (if, indeed, it can be made clearly at all), because, again, in the context of artifacts *what is true* and *how to design* are but weakly distinguishable. As Wulf reminds us, the connections from computer science to the physical sciences and to engineering are only analogical, with no commitment and no criteria other than the emerging purposes of the new field (1995: 55). Again, this field is a 'science', and so characterized by 'theory' and (if not too mathematical) 'experiment', insofar as it struggles to become one, and in the process redefines the terms of engagement. In particular, then, 'experiment' enters the mix as a set of possibilities to be adapted.

We have seen that in general such imported senses tend to be the most conservative and least informed by the relativizing effects of philosophical and historical studies. Thus, for example, references to 'the scientific method', supposed to govern experiment, are not uncommon (e.g. Tichy 1998: 33), even though the idea of a single scientific method has long been discredited. Claims of a 'new relation between theory and experiments' (El-Kadi 1999: 27) are likely to be at least in part rediscoveries of the fact that wherever practised, these modes of inquiry – theory for representing, experiment for intervening, to use Hacking's terms – need to be coupled as equals, tightly or loosely, in order for research to progress. Similarly, one finds the idea of 'demonstration' (i.e. a 'demo') measured against the already outdated theory-first notion that experiment for computer science should mean 'collection of data to show that the technology adheres to some underlying model or theory of software development' (Zelkowitz and Wallace 1998: 23). The distinction between 'demo' and 'experiment' is better made on other grounds: although demos can provide 'proof of concept' in the engineering sense, they 'critically depend on the observers' imagination and willingness to extrapolate; they do not normally produce solid evidence.'[48] One wonders whether it would be preferable to think not in such black-and-white terms but rather of a sliding scale of cogency in demonstrations, from the sales-pitch unsupported by more than show, to the conclusive proof *quod erat demonstrandum*. In any case, the exploratory, heuristic sense of experiment goes beyond what a demo is literally supposed to accomplish. It expresses the intellectual leading edge of trying things out.

But what is this heuristic sense applicable to computing, and what does it imply? In building large, complex systems, John Plaice comments, 'we often have no idea what these tools will offer until they are actually used' (1995: 33) – until we interact with them in a disciplined way and so learn something new. The question, of course, is what the discipline in question might be like. Gödel comments in his 1961 lecture that, 'one may view the whole development of empirical science as a systematic and conscious extension of what the child does when it develops' (1995/ca. 1961: 383). Hence we can learn from the developmental idea of 'theory-in-action' proposed by Genevan psychologists to explain how children build up knowledge of the world from their direct experience with it,[49] suggesting 'experiment' as the experiential process, 'theory' as its evolving expression. Bonnie Nardi's phrase for anthropology, an 'experiential science' rather than an experimental one, further suggests what happens to the idea of experiment as the focus becomes ever more strongly anthropocentric.[50] If 'in designing tools we are designing ways of being', as Winograd and Flores have said, then experiment in computer science can be quite deeply experiential and ultimately takes place in an experiential context, however technical the problem. Hence experiment, though ranging *from* highly technical trials of computing mechanisms, ranges *to* the uncertain marches where computer science encounters the social sciences and related aspects of engineering. Theory, as the evolving expression of experiment, likewise. To paraphrase Juris Hartmanis' Turing Award lecture, theory is judged on the one hand by the mathematical insights it yields about computational models and on the other by the utility of these models in applications of computing (1995: 12). The highly technical manner in which the work is most often expressed should not, however, deflect our ethnographic gaze from the human 'ways of being' that distantly or directly comprise its goal. Neither can the ethnographic outsider, needing to understand the discipline to construct a relation to it, afford to overlook its technical basis, since that too imposes constraints and opens up equally human questions, such as preoccupied Leibniz, Boole, Hilbert, Gödel, Turing and the rest.

7   Amalgam from a distance

I began this chapter by invoking, once again, Clifford Geertz's initial, unresolved double-vision, 'clarity from a distance, jumble up close'. By doing so I implied that like him I would be offering something like a 'general conception of what it is that [drives] things' in computer science (1995: 13). Despite the diversity within its uncertain and expanding bounds, it remains possible to use the term 'computer science' meaningfully. Having seen something of the 'jumble up close', we need now to pull back to see if the vision from a distance has become clearer.

With respect to cultural artifacts, the limits of computing define where humanities computing does its primary scholarly work. Mahoney has observed that the continuing preoccupation of theoretical computer science with these limits offers little help in resolving the problems that lie within the bounds of what can be computed. 'For that reason,' he says, 'computer science remains an *amalgam* of mathematical theory, engineering practice, and craft skill' (1997: 632), just as humanities computing would seem to be an *amalgam* of computer science theory, software engineering practice, craft skill and scholarship. The metallurgical metaphor is apt: 'An intimate (plastic) mixture or compound of any two or more substances', with etymological echoes, through Greek and Arabic, of healing and marriage (*OED*). I do not want to load one scholar's use of a single word with the weight of an entire argument, but the recurrent echo of Leibniz's connubial figure of speech, here with medical or alchemical properties, gives us something to work with. Like the definition of computer science by Newell, Perlis and Simon, it avoids the extremes of essentialism and separatism, but it goes considerably further by suggesting that the diversity we observe, seemingly impossible to resolve into a rational continuum, is the diversity of a unity that can only be inferred. As with Ovid's *Metamorphoses* we first apprehend a singular entity, then in becoming familiar with it we see every construction of the supposed whole crumble away, each tempting us to make one more attempt at closure. Eventually we realize that *the perpetual impetus to construct a permanently elusive whole is the point.* Is this not what one would expect from a science of computing?

This point is shared by all living disciplines, of course, but as already observed the open-ended schema of computings established by the Universal Turing Machine gives it special force and shape. This schema is provocation to progress, answering to the prevalent epistemology of knowing rather than of knowledge – Gadamer's way rather than quintessence. To paraphrase Heisenberg, in the amalgam of spirit by which the physical computer was created, the Galilean component is strong. So also, of course, is mathematical logic in all its precision and radical incompleteness. These two components together establish modelling in my sense as axiomatic to computing. But, Piaget observed, logic brings the question of what formalizing formalizes, and so the history of mathematics as briefly recounted here comprises more: the driving passion for truth, Gödel's deepening of the way towards it and Piaget's own attention to the context of discovery. The spirit of the physical machine is also shaped by the fact that it *is* a physical machine beyond the logical design. So we also need to consider the problem of 'mind in matter' from its elaboration in the reading of static cultural artifacts, experiment and other physically enacted events, particularly human–machine interaction design.[51] The computer is less a special case than might seem to follow from its articulate prehistory in the language of mathematics, and software less an exception than programming languages might suggest. The distinction between verbal and non-verbal artifacts is hardly an empty one, but as I noted earlier 'all the arts are dumb' on the metalinguistic level, including poetry as much as the art of computer programming.[52] Some form of criticism must speak to us for them. Thus criticism – not in the least an inappropriate term, given the intensely interpretative nature of designing 'ways of being' – is another component of that spirit.

This criticism, like literary criticism, has two besetting sins: the theorist's flight into abstraction, which obscures what are ultimately the most challenging problems; and the engineer's machine-myopic view, shared by the scholars of device-history, who likewise put these problems out of sight.[53] Richard Hamming, in his 1968 Turing Award lecture, comments:

> At the heart of computer science lies a technological device, the computing machine. Without the machine almost all of what we do would become idle speculation ... I still believe that it is important for us to recognize that the computer, the information processing machine, is the foundation of our field. (1969: 5)

Hamming put his finger on the former sin, perhaps the strongest tendency to error in computer science. It would be wrong to interpret his recommendation as a turning away from theory; he was doing no more than asserting with many others that computing is principally about acting on and within the world, about Feynman's 'getting things done', studying the consequences, learning from them and devising ever better means.[54] At the same time Hamming's strong aversion to 'the bragging of uselessness and the game-playing that the pure mathematicians so often engage in' is typical of how one end of a polarized field looks from the standpoint of the other. This is the difficulty: every statement about the importance of one aspect to such a field seems to imply dismissal or downgrading of others and so must be carefully qualified.

Hamming's criticism is now more than thirty years old, as is Minsky's attack in his Turing Award lecture on an 'excessive preoccupation with formalism' across computer science (1970: 197). Mahoney's recent analysis shows, however, that if there has been a decline in such public statements from '[o]ur young and slightly paranoid discipline', as Wulf has called it (1995: 56), diminished hand-wringing does not reliably indicate a resolution to the difficulties that still keep theorist and empiric, computational mathematician and software engineer, beyond kissing-distance.

But what they have in common continues to point the way forward. Perhaps the most promising singular formulation of the common concern is Minsky's. At the end of his Turing Award lecture he describes the computer scientist's responsibility to education: not to build teaching machines, not to teach mathematics, but to show the teachers 'how to help the children to debug their own problem-solving processes'. He concludes that, 'The computer scientist is the one who must study such matters, because he is *the proprietor of the concept of procedure ...*' (1970: 214, my emphasis). For Minsky this concept is, of course, algorithmic and so goes back through Turing's idea of effective computability to Leibniz's dream. It is a common enough reduction of computing.[55] But putting it into the context of childhood education sets, again, the context of discovery (or invention, or the making of knowledge) as the common ground where theorist and empiric come together. What is most important in this move is the question being asked: *How do we come to know what we somehow know?* For the humanities, the procedure to which Minsky refers is an instrument to assist us in asking this question.

8   Computer science and humanities computing

The universal machine's open-ended schema gives to computer science a licence for indefinite expansion. In the 1968 Turing Award lecture from which I have previously quoted, Richard Hamming saw this licence as a mandate for survival. He observed that long-term support of a discipline needing 'large sums of money' would require social approval, which in turn implies that 'we had better give a practical flavour to our field'. One way to do this, he said, was 'to require a strong minor in some field *other* than computer science and mathematics' in order to gain 'real experience in using the computer to get useful results'. He did not mention the humanities nor seems to have had them in his sights, but making the case for experience in application pointed to a door we are opening.

Since Hamming's lecture, and especially since the last decade of the twentieth century, the expansion of computer science towards the humanities has accelerated. In 1972 Robert Oakman (Computer Science, South Carolina) noted that 'the computer constitutes a powerful new educational tool for imaginative creativity and insight in all the arts and humanities'; in 1987 he saw 'no clear answers' to the urgent question of how, exactly, humanists might be taught computing so that they could enjoy its benefits and give their badly needed guidance to its application.[56] In 1991 Christian Koch (Computer Science, Oberlin) noted that in the US 'there is not yet an applied computer science specialization' (289). In 1992, a US National Research Council report, *Computing the Future: a Broader Agenda for Computer Science and Engineering*, mentioned the humanities twice. A decade later, another such report, *Beyond Productivity: Information, Technology, Innovation, and Creativity*, gave the humanities forty-seven mentions, identified art and design as 'forms of CS research and development' (96), proposed a model of 'transdisciplinarity' to account for the interrelations among fields (99–102) and subsumed all of these under 'the exciting new domain of information technology and creative practices – ITCP' (1).[57]

As these publications suggest, high-level discussion of the relationship between computer science and the humanities (for the Anglophone world, especially in the United States) has been largely dominated by the former or by official bodies for which computer science is the primary source.[58] The tendency has been to relate computer science and the humanities according to their separate concerns as these are imagined by those peripheral to humanistic scholarship: on the one hand, interesting problems for the computer scientists from the more challenging data of the humanities and help from its wealth of 'domain-specific knowledge';[59] on the other, better tools for the humanists via a distillation of scholarly work, by observation of behaviour and by interview, into a '"humanities process," analogous to various business processes', as one contributor to CHSRM 1998 put it. (The assumed passivity of humanists in such a relation is not atypical; it is implicit in the words of one recent proposal for collaboration 'driven by *humanist values* and conducted according to proven, collaborative, *scientific methods and principles*'. The transdisciplinary model proposed in *Beyond Productivity* is the least constrained by inherited structures and most in touch with recent thinking on disciplinarity: in this model, 'the disciplines not only apply their methods in a new context but also are receptive to fundamental changes in knowledge and methodology based on their interaction.'[60]

In all of these construals of relationship, however, the active role of the humanities remains unspecified and unclear. Indeed no agency is identified to represent their perspective or interests. One may charitably infer the assumption that scholars will flock to the task, but it would be unreasonable to assume so: in general they have neither the time nor the training to contribute useful insights into their working methods. It is unreasonable to expect them to 'imagine what they don't know' without an imagination educated by active involvement with computing and its culture; and it is unrealistic to expect them to do all this on their own, spontaneously. Similarly, it is unreasonable to expect computer scientists to volunteer the design, programming and debugging efforts required to produce a usable tool, since they are not programmers for hire (if they were few could afford them) but researchers with their own agenda(s).[61] In other words, humanities computing is not in this equation. *But it needs to be.*

There are, of course, brilliant exceptions to the overall lack of success individual scholars have had in attracting the attention of computer science on their own terms.[62] Linguistics is exceptional as a field, fitting Hamming's mandate for practical as well as theoretical involvement, but here there are particular reasons. Again I quote Carlo Ginzburg:

> The quantitative and antianthropocentric orientation of natural sciences from Galileo on forced an unpleasant dilemma on the humane sciences: either assume a lax scientific system in order to attain noteworthy results, or assume a meticulous, scientific one to achieve results of scant significance. Only linguistics has succeeded, during the course of the twentieth century, in escaping the quandary, subsequently posing as a more or less finished model for other disciplines. (1989/1986: 124)

The linguistic model behind the disciplinary one is the formalization of grammar by Noam Chomsky and his school, which laid the basis for the subdiscipline of computational linguistics. Nancy Ide has remarked that due to superior technical know-how, computer science was able to 'steal' much of the linguistic work going on in humanities computing for itself.[63] A better explanation for the success of the theft, however, is that computer science took on those aspects of language that are most intelligible when seen from its perspective and used for its purposes. *It took on language understood in a particular way.* Much more can be derived from the less computationally orientated subfields of linguistics. The close relationship between humanities computing and corpus linguistics and the slowly accumulating successes of statistical approaches to literary problems (noted in the Introduction) demonstrate a different perspective and different purposes. In any case neither the theft nor its failure to take the abundant remainder brings us any closer to understanding what a desirable relationship between computer science and humanities computing would be. A channel for communication is clearly open, but neither theft in one direction nor mere poaching in another is the basis for a healthy relationship. Indeed, theft provides the wrong metaphor; the parable of the Loaves and the Fishes comes much closer.

If, as Tito Orlandi has rightly said, a humanities computing application unsupported by technical knowledge is the work of a *charlatan*,[64] then someone who in their technical competence uses cultural artifacts primarily as a means of exercising skill, however extensive, is an *idiot savant* or *computnik* – these are Richard Hamming's terms (1969: 6). In both cases, as Orlandi pointed out long before this, the problem arises in consequence of the false conclusion that the humanist and the computer scientist embody irreconcilable views of the world and therefore can at best exploit each other. The problem, rather, is separated understandings, which *are* different but by being separated are not able to generate the cognitive *tertium quid* (the child of Leibniz's connubial dreams) that defines humanities computing – as we would like it to be if not as it is.

Hence this book and, in particular, this chapter. But in the generic and chiefly non-Anglophone sense of the 'humane sciences' (*sciences humaines, scienze umanistiche, Geisteswissenschaften* and so on), my efforts here are preceded by others, for example Jean-Claude Gardin, Tito Orlandi and Manfred Thaller,[65] who have emphasized the science in computing and involvement with some of the core activities commonly assumed to belong to computer science.

The logicist programme of Gardin, for example, has since 1980 sought to reconstruct processes of reasoning in the humane sciences by comparing the structures to which their argumentation is actually reducible by logical methods to the output of expert systems that embed the structures these arguments are supposed to follow. It is, in other words, a study of disciplinary rhetoric with two results: appraisal of this rhetoric and, by implication, recovery of the steps taken in the discovery phase of the research but omitted from the final argument. His programme aims to explore, as he says, 'where the frontier lies between that part of our interpretive constructs which follows the principles of scientific reasoning and another part which ignores or rejects them' (1990: 26). It is the opposite of modelling in my sense in that it privileges the logical schema rather than imperfectly articulated knowledge, but the point here is his use of basic computer science to illuminate how we know (or not) what we say we know.

Orlandi's interest is in the processes of thought in the work rather than in arguments about it. Referring to Gardin and others, he describes the essential act of rendering a cultural artifact into computationally tractable data as 'the conscious individuation of discrete elements in a continuous universe'. Using a philological example, he observes that this is 'precisely the kind of formalization required by the Turing machine' (2000). He raises the question of 'the formal way of thinking' that the universal machine brings (2002: 57), arguing along with Thaller that what joins computing to the humanities is method: on the one hand, 'a core of computer science methods' elaborated within each discipline according to its special nature (55); on the other, 'the historical and philological methodologies proposed by the great (mainly German) tradition of the late XIX century' (51f.). Although one might wish to question the applicability of nineteenth-century ideas of history and text to twenty-first-century scholarship – indeed, to question whether any discipline is or should be reducible to a canon of methods, as claimed (Orlandi *et al.* 1999: 2.3.1) – again the point not to miss is the use of basic computer science to articulate a new way of thinking about traditional materials and problems.

Thaller asserts in addition that 'information as occurring within the Humanities' – for example the historical records preserved in manuscript, with the typical problems of dating, format, language, script or other graphical features – 'has inherent properties, which from the narrowly focused point of view of a more general computer science ... do not merit closer study' and therefore are not adequately represented, if at all (2001). For this reason a 'humanities computer science' (*Historisch-Kulturwissenschaftliche Informationsverarbeitung*), which actively pursues the design and construction of adequate data-models and processes, is required. The argument is made primarily in and through the programme Thaller established at Cologne.[66] By raising the question of properties inherent to humanities data, Thaller has already made the point that a comparison of what computer science recognizes with that on which the scholar focuses is an essential move in the development of humanities computing. In each case the theoretical and meta-theoretical questions stirred up by these contributions remain in and of the humanities: not only how argument is done and what crucial steps of discovery are omitted, but whether logic is the aim or merely an instrument; not only how methods may be formalized, but whether a formal canon of methods is the point, indeed what 'formal' can possibly mean and what form method can take there; not only what distinguishes the data of the humanities from other kinds, but how far we can get as a result of having tools adequate to these data and what exactly such tools would be like.

9 Conclusion

The design of computing systems attests to a fundamental habit of mind, elaborated chiefly through the sciences, by which we have attributed a layer-structure to the world 'from the point of view of intelligibility. This ... structure,' Giuseppe Del Re comments, 'may or may not have an ontological import, but it is essential for the "existence judgments" which science is expected to pronounce' (2000). Thus we see, infer or hypothesize physical objects in hierarchical groups roughly by size, from galaxies to subatomic particles, each a component of the next. We organize the biological, social and psychological worlds similarly, by species, classes and so forth. 'We understand walls in terms of bricks, bricks in terms of crystals, crystals in terms of molecules etc.'[67] At any one level, the abstractive structure allows us in theory to ignore all but those characteristics of the layer below that are recognized as input by the layer above.[68] Thus the laws of planetary motion ignore the individuality of rocks, dirt, trees and so forth.

As I suggested, artificial systems tend to implement this habit of mind, none more prominently than computing systems.[69] Winograd and Flores have called the principle of design 'opacity of implementation' because the one below each level and the one above it are *opaque* to it (1986: 87, 90–2). A typical system comprises a physical machine as the bottom layer, itself comprising several sublayers from hardware to firmware; next a logical machine, including virtual components; then an operating system, whose growing number of sublayers support a growing range of functions; finally application programs, themselves multi-layered, that elaborate these functions. Feynman explains this structure using the metaphor of a file-clerk: as we move up the structure, the clerk becomes more competently featured; as we move down, we discover what the clerk is made of; moving sideways we stay at the same level of detail but see what things would be like in a differently organized system (1999/1996: 19). In consequence of the UTM principle, there is no fixed limit as to how many layers can be added. 'Clearly, one can keep going up in level,' Feynman explains, 'putting together new algorithms, programming languages, adding the ability to manipulate "files" containing programs and data, and so on.' The tacit if not explicit objective is a machine like us (but not necessarily looking like us). Hence the rising importance of the social sciences to computer science, the occasional glances towards the humanities and in general the increasing interdependency of computing and most other aspects of life.

Programming may therefore be described in much the same way, although in reverse order, from some real-world problem at the top, where we are, down to its implementation in hardware at the bottom. (In practice a programmer stops at an intermediate level, where he or she encounters the compiler of the high-level language he or she is using, but in principle we can view the creation of a computing system as a single but staged top-down act.) Hence the layered design of systems gives rise to W. W. Royce's well-known 'waterfall' diagram of software development. Although it is no longer thought to describe what does or should happen, it remains useful for the point I wish to make. Figure 4.2 is a waterfall-like structure adapted from Mahoney's variation on Royce's diagram (2002: 37). Its purpose is, in conclusion, to suggest the relation of humanities computing to computer science and to raise some questions about it.

Mahoney's version illustrates the basic point that the more the domain of application diverges from a deductive structure, 'the less we can say in principle and the more we have to rely on empirical means of verifying that the program is working as planned.'[70] My version suggests that by reducing the application to such a structure and confronting the performance of this structure empirically, we can learn. *How* this reductive translation occurs is, for us in particular and for software engineers as a whole, inside a black box we have not yet been able to open. Chapter 1 is my attempt to take a look.

In Figure 4.2 I illustrate this translation through three recursive levels, to the point at which its conceptualization reaches the stage of becoming a model, where the confrontation occurs. The recursive loop at each of these levels indicates the usual scholarly reconsideration of

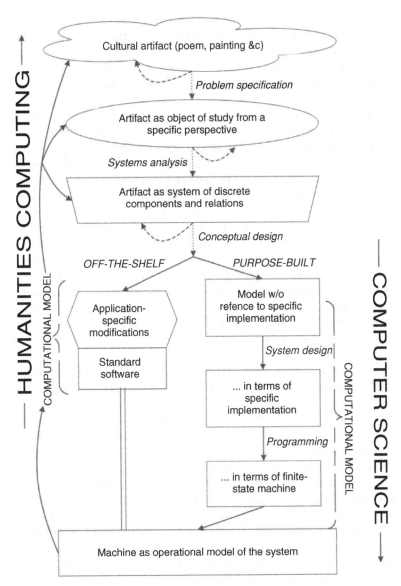

Figure 4.2: Stages of modelling

the interpretative act; the dotted arrows indicate that in each case reduction means a significant loss. The solid arrows and the absence of these loops from the fourth level on to the bottom denote that the translations are unproblematic and that no loss occurs. At the fourth level I show a choice: either to the right, for construction of a purpose-built system, or to the left, for use of general-purpose modelling software, such as a spreadsheet or database system. (My extensive example of modelling in Chapter 1.5 illustrates exactly such an application of both.)

The results from the operational model at the bottom of the diagram are, of course, problematic to the scholar of the cultural artifact, hence the arrows returning to the model and from it back to the top. The real source of difficulty here is not a discrepancy between mistaken or insufficient ideas and what the results genuinely show. Rather it is whether the results are genuine at all. At each recursive stage prior to the computational model, 'good enough' decisions are made that overlook or deliberately sacrifice aspects of the developing conception. 'Trade-offs' are made that are, as Minsky has pointed out (1970: 197ff.), in general not well understood but unavoidable, by Wulf's principle of 'design under constraint' (2000). They are acts of modelling, heuristic, experimental, subject to the recursive comparing of results to reality. Compromises made in how a problem is formulated, the perspective chosen, the components and relations defined and the model constructed from them sum together into a result that in general is impossible to validate in any absolute sense against the real-world object. For the humanities the *only* possibility is comparison between the result and the scholar's own interpretation, hence the privileging of that interpretation from the beginning.

In another of his delightful epigrams, Alan Perlis has written, 'The goal of computation is the emulation of our synthetic abilities, not the understanding of our analytic ones' (45, 1982: 9). That is why throughout this book discussion orbits modelling, which I discussed in Chapter 1 for its analytic capabilities but which gains them synthetically. Once fundamentals of mathematics have clarified the picture and the experiential science of engineering has reaffirmed the epistemology and achievement of design under constraint, attention comes to focus on the waterfall's middle, where humanities computing and computer science have the most directly to say to each other. The question asked there in the form that makes most sense to both sides is, in Steve Russ's words, 'what automated processing can be integrated with human processing?'[71]

5
Agenda

The task of the law is to devise a set of incentives that will determine conduct in a fashion that produces the most good.

Louis Michael Seidman, 'Points of Intersection' (1996: 105)

1 Introduction

I began this book with questioning – 'the piety of thought' – and I end it that way: not by attempting to conclude what must surely be inconclusive but by aiming out beyond the end of the story I tell here, with the question of agenda. The job of this chapter is to recommend action. Though most often foolish in our context, future-talk is unavoidable because computing has no significance whatsoever for research in the humanities other than in *what is to be done* with it, concretely and immediately. We might expect from the machine whose heritage is universal that innumerable directions may be taken. The question is, which do we take? We must ask not 'So what?' but 'So what is to be done?'

Before filling out an agenda for humanities computing, however, it is prudent to look at what other fields do and how they do it. For some the idea of an agenda is natural, for others strange. This should give us due warning that once again, a field must ultimately grow its own vocabulary from its own way of being.

2 What are agendas?

A definition of *agenda* is simple enough: a 'list of things to be done'. It pertains to 'matters of practice, as distinguished from matters of belief' or knowledge. The agenda of a scholarly field, which exists for knowledge of its subject, would seem then to be a straightforward notion of how its practitioners have collectively imagined that their subject is to be pursued. Common usage suggests, however, that not all fields have an agenda or have one in the same sense, unless we blanket all of them with a unifying social purpose or attribute to each a hidden agenda. We might, for example, say that a group of art historians or literary critics sharing a particular set of beliefs about their subject share an agenda, but rarely would we say that the field as a whole has one. Sociology has a strong social agenda, some have argued, because it deals with problems of pressing concern to us all and cannot avoid getting involved (Giddens 1986: 2f.). David Hilbert's list of mathematical problems constituted an agenda for his field, likewise calling for communal action – proving theorems may be done in solitude but is very much a group activity. The latter, however, has a very different character from the social activist's.

In short, then, no uniform definition of 'agenda' will take us very far because its function, form and content speak to the community of practice it organizes. An agenda expresses how practitioners conceptualize and pursue their work.

At the same time a common urgency and commitment underlies all these very different uses. No practice worthy of survival is so abstract, remote and self-sufficient that it does not need to frame its question of what is to be *done* in terms of its wider social responsibilities and ambitions. The title of a recent lecture by Jerome McGann (2004a), echoing the title of a pamphlet by Vladimir Lenin (1902),[1] sounds the basic question running through all questions of agenda: 'Culture and Technology: the Way We Live Now, What Is To Be Done?'

Thus the very idea of an agenda buzzes with impatience, and beneath that a passion for something and a suffering of its absence. An agenda is all about *concernful* action, even when the desire for doing is expressed by the fact of a social system rather than by any who are part of it. (Think of all those boring meetings.) But in the practice that ideally motivates the practitioner, an agenda is *desiderata* acted on, bringing about that 'for which a desire or longing is felt'. Gaston Bachelard's proclamation comes to mind: 'Man is a creation of desire, not a creation of need' (1964/1938: 15f.). In the sense I am developing here, an agenda is not a list of items to be ticked off before sleep, or retirement or the end of everything, but a consensual plan for doing what we want to do in aid of what we want to bring about. Hence politics always figures in, though with pronounced stylistic variation: very quietly but no less passionately in the case of mathematics, for example; much more noisily and publicly in the case of civil engineering. Agendas can be private, but here the concern is for disciplines as social systems, hence the importance of influence and control. This poses interesting problems for humanities computing as a collegial service, but more about that later.

For all disciplines affected by computing, it should be clear that to the degree they are affected they become concerned with 'getting something to do something', as Feynman said, and so implicitly if not explicitly with forming an agenda. The question of agenda is in consequence central to humanities computing, but for the reason just given we cannot simply begin adding items to the list. We must first ask what form this list might take for a field that mixes computing with several quite different disciplines.

Once again a good place to start is with computer science. Michael Mahoney has the following to say about agendas in the context of its theoretical branch:

The *agenda* of a field consists of what its practitioners agree ought to be done, a consensus concerning the problems of the field, their order of importance or priority, the means of solving them, and perhaps most importantly, what constitutes a solution. Becoming a recognized practitioner means learning the agenda and then helping to carry it out. Knowing what questions to ask is the mark of a full-fledged practitioner, as is the capacity to distinguish between trivial and profound problems; 'profound' means moving the agenda forward. One acquires standing in the field by solving the problems with high priority, and especially by doing so in a way that extends or reshapes the agenda, or by posing profound problems. The standing of the field may be measured by its capacity to set its own agenda. New disciplines emerge by acquiring that autonomy. Conflicts within a discipline often come down to disagreements over the agenda: what are the really important problems?

As the shared Latin root indicates, agendas are about action: what is to be *done*? By emphasizing action, the notion of agendas refocuses attention from a body of knowledge to a complex of practices. Since what practitioners do is all but indistinguishable from the way they go about doing it, it follows that the tools and techniques of a field embody its agenda. When those tools are employed outside the field, either by a practitioner or by an outsider borrowing them, they bring the agenda of the field with them. Using those tools to address another agenda means reshaping the latter to fit the tools, even if it may also lead to a redesign of the tools, with resulting feedback when the tool is brought home. What gets reshaped and to what extent depends on the relative strengths of the agendas of borrower and borrowed. (2002: 28)

Mahoney's analysis may be resolved into what I will call 'the four p's': *p*roblems, *p*ractitioners, *p*ractices and *p*rogram. Let me draw out a few consequences from each.

1. *Problems.* An agenda of a field in the above sense is not simply a list of problems, rather it is a conceptualization of the field such that it has problems. It is seeing the field *as problems*. For disciplines that conventionally work on them, like mathematics or computer science, the qualification is obvious, but for those that do not ordinarily define their work in that way, like art history or literary criticism, the assumption it carries along is a large one.

The problem with 'problem' is revealed by its usage in logic and throughout most other contexts, in its loosely formal sense of 'a question propounded for solution, a set task'. Hence we can resolve the idea of 'problem' into three qualities: enigmatic, formal and public. Once again the telling point is the implied if not expressed formality, and once again its effect varies according to the field. Roughly speaking, as we move away from mathematics towards the humanities, 'problem' (as distinct from challenge, difficulty or enigma) becomes increasingly less useful as a way of describing intellectual work.[2] Thus, on the one hand, Hilbert's list remains a standard point of reference for mathematics, but on the other, it is difficult to imagine anything like such a list in any of the humanities, despite the fact that speaking of a 'problematic' or of 'problematizing' is common in those disciplines. Paradoxically, then, the first item on the agenda of humanities computing is the question of whether an agenda in this sense is useful, and if so, where and for what. Surely there are problems in the field, even some that can be solved. The question is, what else? What does an agenda omit by nature?

2. *Practitioners.* The question here is their training. Thomas Kuhn describes education in the natural sciences as a process of working through textbook exemplars, i.e. standard problems already solved in the course of normal science. These, he notes, guide learning as

paradigms guide research, but it is the manner of the guidance that concerns us here. Again, in the passage from *Structure of Scientific Revolutions* where Kuhn makes contact with Polanyi's tacit knowing, he emphasizes that this guidance may be 'aided by but does not depend upon the formulation of rules and assumptions' (1970/1962: 44). Rather the novice is guided by following examples of how things have been done. Often the crucial point is not what the rules are but which rule to apply. This surprises us to the degree that we assume such rules dominate, less so the more we take account of the tacit or seemingly unsystematic aspects of work. It is not in the least strange for the (anti-Galilean) humanities and social sciences, e.g. history, where the student learns by imitating as well as analysing examples of historical writing; anthropology, where fieldwork is the norm; or philosophy, where particular thought-styles are learned by engaging imaginatively with those who have practised them. In none of those disciplines is any explicit set of rules remotely desirable. Hence the question: How are practitioners of humanities computing to be trained? Another item on our agenda, this time recursive, is thus curriculum. If 'learning the agenda and then helping to carry it out' does not delimit the whole of this curriculum, then what else is there, and how is it taught?

3. *Practices*. Mahoney's observation that an agenda refocuses attention 'from a body of knowledge to a complex of practices' recommends agenda-thinking strongly. This is not, however, the same thing as saying that (to use his distinction) knowledge belongs to the discipline of application, practices to the technical field. Roughly speaking the results by which these practices are ultimately judged do belong to that discipline, which by assessing these results to some degree assesses the practices that produced them. But the paradigmatic collaboration at the core of humanities computing suggests that knowing and practising are too tightly coupled for a clean separation of responsibilities. It is as if in a race the runner and the judge jointly designed the contest and rethought it while it was being run. The goals of the two may never precisely coincide, but they are convergent when the collaboration is successful. An agenda of humanities computing is, then, likewise a joint project, with the consequence that the identity of the field, at least in its details, is a negotiated (and renegotiated) identity. To recall the ethnographic metaphor, crossing the 'beaches of the mind' is a creative act, not something that simply goes according to plan. In practice, in

specific settings, relationships endure, but there cannot be any long-term convention guaranteeing them or isolating the agenda from strong collaborative influence. I emphasize the paradigmatic encounter because the point *is* in the crossing and in being observant of the conditions of work wherever practitioners find themselves. The difficulty that I am touching on is the old difficulty inherent in collaboration. What is new is the centrality of it to a scholarly practice; and this implies that we really do need to understand what 'collaboration' means, not simply to assert its putative benefits.

4. *Program.* An agenda brings us to the means for carrying it out, i.e. to the tools and techniques that, Mahoney argues, embody the agenda of a field and so act as carriers of it wherever they go. How much of an agenda survives a migration of its tools may be questioned; one can, for example, use a spreadsheet in ways entirely new to the maker and to the tradition from which the tool was derived. As we saw in Chapter 1.4.6, some intentionality survives the transfer of objects across cultures. The notion of 'technology transfer' thus assumes both too much and too little: you don't get everything, and what you get has other trajectories. Hence my word for Mahoney's fourth criterion of agendas: their manifestation as something like programs within the tools we use, i.e. programmes in the sense specific to computing.

There are several quite complex problems here, some of which I have already discussed at length. For the question at hand, however, the important matter is how the agenda of humanities computing is influenced by the very means used to carry out the work.[3] As things stand, the implication is that humanities computing is permeated at root by bits of several agendas, from computer science, industry, the military and so forth. (This gives one cause to investigate the history and theory of the inherited tools in the contexts that have shaped them.) More important because more immediately influential, however, is the collecting and exchanging of agenda micro-items that humanities computing manages, distributes and shapes among the disciplines – for example, the fragments of the corpus linguistics agenda brought to any field that uses a KWIC concordance. Borrowing will of course happen in any case. That is not new. But the sustained attention to it is, and so is the quantity of interchange, whose consequences for the disciplines remain to be seen.

I conclude, then, that for humanities computing 'agenda' has the following broad characteristics.

It is, first of all, *incomplete in principle*. To paraphrase Gödel, there will always be things to be done for which no specific agenda item can be formulated. Serious, undirected play is of the essence, and so also the freedom to choose problems no one else regards as important, to imagine and act upon ideas that cannot be anticipated from a current list of them, or to arrive at a result before its time. The formal nature of the problems on an agenda and of the methods that help define them means furthermore that a list is *conceptually poor* as a means of communicating practice. Hence the vanishing point of agenda opens up into curriculum, taught through a quasi-apprenticeship like that in the similarly equipment-orientated sciences. Agenda must also denote something *open and fluid* because it is a momentary product of an ongoing collaborative negotiation, *plural* because this negotiation happens across several disciplines simultaneously, and in that plurality *competing* because these disciplines themselves have differing interests.

3   Defining an agenda

If heavily qualified as an instrument for guiding the field, an agenda for humanities computing so defined remains far too generous in scope and includes far too many participants for me to give the whole a fair treatment. I must begin by subtracting large areas of the topic so that I can come to grips with what I regard as the core set of concerns.

The major challenge I avoid here is to examine the large areas of overlap between a research agenda for humanities computing and those of many other closely related groups: e.g. communities in computer science and related technical areas,[4] library research[5] and cultural heritage,[6] as well as the initiatives of national academies and funding bodies. Allow me merely to note these and the need to keep in touch with the research they signify. (Keeping in touch with them is an agenda item.) The international Text Encoding Initiative provides perhaps the best example of large-scale contribution from humanities computing to a shared technical agenda of widespread interest and influence.[7] Another is the Arts and Humanities Data Service in the UK, which connects the agenda of humanities computing to multidisciplinary problems of 'discovery, creation and preservation of digital resources in and for research, teaching and learning'.[8] Two recent national initiatives in the Anglophone world, the Commission on Cyberinfrastructure for the Humanities and Social Sciences in the US and the ICT in Arts and Humanities programme in the UK,[9] have involved the field on a broader scale to articulate the requirements of a research agenda across the disciplines. For many years humanities computing has contributed to the research agenda of the European language industries through ties between the Association for Literary and Linguistic Computing and the Istituto Linguistica Computazionale (Pisa).[10] A map of the interrelationships among these organizations and individuals would show in detail the overlapping I can only sketch briefly here.

By subtracting these areas of overlap and removing everything to do with purely local concerns, we are then left with what the individual is in a position to do that falls within the common range of interests. This is not to detract from the importance or achievement of the large-scale efforts, broad initiatives and grand programmes. Indeed, without them many of us would be disabled or significantly poorer. But my emphasis on the small-scale – on the individual and what he or she can do with little or no external funding – is quite deliberate. For one thing, it heeds the urgent worries about sustainability, which is as serious a problem for academic initiatives as for urban development and broader social and economic projects (Zorich 2003). It also recognizes that in the humanities the particularity and individuality of the cultural artifact, the individual who studies it and the result of that study are primary. Scholarly helps to scholarship, such as lexicons, encyclopaedias and other reference works, have often been collaborative but primary studies seldom so, and for good reason. At the same time, as I emphasized in the Introduction and in Chapter 2, the solitary work of the humanities is deeply social, so the individual's enaction of the much reduced agenda I sketch here is to be envisioned very much within a social network, serving communal purposes. Indeed, the theme of communication runs throughout.

4 A preliminary agenda

The following provisional list, meant to be illustrative rather than exhaustive, begins with three fundamental items for which I have argued in this book, given in the order in which I discussed them in previous chapters. It is followed by seven others arising from them.

4.1 Analysis

The first item is to understand how computing affects analysis in the humanities beyond simply fetching, counting and formatting data –

how, in other words, it affects analysis itself rather than its scope, speed or convenience. These latter effects are demonstrably important – in the foreground of what has become digital library research – but prior to them is the problematic relationship between the artifact of study and the actual data fetched, counted or formatted. I have placed this question first on the agenda because otherwise we elide the profound difference between artifact and data and so are in no position to understand the significance and reception of the results we obtain from these data. We need to know what that difference is, and how an analysis based on it might differ from what we have been doing all along. Otherwise we are not only in the dark ourselves but also have very little to say to those who ask what all the fuss is about – what new questions may be formulated and what old ones more interestingly answered, or answered at all. The imperative to answer such questioners is an agenda item on its own, to which I return below.

Although the question is asked in principle, it is asked from the crucial experience of anomalies: the stubborn residue of items not fetched that should have been; the counts strangely unrepresentative of a reading; the heuristically powerful though seemingly arbitrary changes in format. From an analytic point of view, a successful answer to an old question asked in an old way is of little interest because it gives us no immediate insight into our computational methods and techniques. In particular it gives us no way of understanding the significance of these anomalies in the context of what has made them anomalous, which is to say, no way to recognize anything methodologically new. The point I am making has been sporadically and intuitively grasped, to be sure; I am hardly the first to make it. We have not, however, raised the question at a sufficient level of generality to embrace all the disciplines.

4.2 Genres and contexts of scholarship

The second item arising from this book is to study the primary genres of scholarly communication within and among the disciplines – the synthetic output of these disciplines rather than their analytic tools and methods. Scholarly communication is a broad and diverse topic, many aspects of which are of direct concern to humanities computing. In this book I have taken up the primary question of the formal scholarly genres, concentrating in particular on shared problems in re-imagining the genres of reference and the contexts into which they fit. I have paid particular attention, as a matter of some urgency, to historical analysis of inherited exemplars. My earlier point was that as builders of systems to replace or move alongside them, we need to know in great detail how these exemplars were intended to work lest we aim lower out of ignorance. A further point, not made earlier, is that as builder-scholars we are potentially well equipped to write the intellectual histories of which earlier scholarly devices were a part. An intellectual history of the concordance would, for example, contribute substantially to many areas.[11]

But this is only the beginning. The rest is emerging all around us through experimental designs for scholarly publication. The time is ripe for fundamental questions to be asked from within the disciplines as to the audience, purpose and fitness of their publications. It is not surprising that the best kind of response is illustrated by those most concerned with works of reference. Gregory Crane, for example, argues that the lexicon we are now attempting to imagine must aim to serve not the specialists in the mold of a century ago, whose interests were mirrored in the great Liddell–Scott–Jones *Greek–English Lexicon*, but the non-lexicographic readers of the twenty-first century. McGann makes the general point noted earlier, that the failure of our interfaces to represent how we now think about our artifacts indicates where the attention of theoretically inclined scholars must be. Adrian Miles makes the specific point for artifacts with a significant temporal component (2003). This is not at all to deny the benefits of presentation on a far greater scale, reaching larger, more diverse audiences. But the rigid, old-fashioned structuring of many digital products, reflecting the limitation of printed exemplars without the manifest virtues of the codex, cannot be denied. Hence we must add to our agenda the search for ways to implement theoretical designs already in sight and those emergent in experimental work.

The obvious context for digital publication is now the Web, and in the foreseeable future seems likely to be something close to it. In greater, more adequate detail, this context has been imagined in an ideally interoperable 'world-wide digital library', which I discussed in Chapter 2. Libraries on such a scale are not restricted to the humanities, but humanists have a great deal to contribute, including how the history of the library may inform its future. Here the primary topic for humanities computing would seem to be the nature of digital referentiality – how documents of many kinds, including the digital equivalent of marginalia, might interconnect in a docuverse. The actual experience of imagining and constructing individual scholarly works against the resistance of ideas, materials and colleagues is essential.

4.3 Disciplinary relations and kinships

The third agenda item explored in this book, in Chapters 3 and 4, is how humanities computing relates or might relate to the disciplines already on the scene: what it may derive from them, what it has to give them and how it stands and moves with respect to them, as what kind of entity. In this context disciplinarity is a critical question for the nascent field and a fact with which it has to deal somehow. The relevant literature tells us clearly in its many conflicting voices that the inherited division of learning is itself a problem, reflected in the problem of how the university responds to the larger society of which it is a part. Familiarity with the debate advises us strongly to resist the lunge for disciplinary status before understanding what the consequences of being in the conventional mold would be. At the same time it alerts us to the possibility that humanities computing might itself contribute significantly to the debate by exemplifying a new mode of action. This new mode, I have argued, comes directly out of the experience of dealing with the disciplines as they are: social systems to be approached as the anthropologist approaches any such system. In addition, several of these older fields offer disciplinary kinships from which humanities computing has a great deal to learn. I have illustrated some of the benefits throughout the book. Many others remain to be discovered by informed, sensitive explorers.

Valuable contributions may be expected from practitioners who have strayed far enough from their disciplines of origin so that they can see them from the outside but not so much that they cannot participate in their imaginative forms of life – who are 'lapsed', as Deegan and Tanner say (2002: xii), but not forgetful. It seems to me a distinct possibility (not just the projection of a autobiographical fact) that the expatriate relationship between the humanities computing practitioner and his or her discipline of origin is an exemplar on the basis of which advanced training in the field could well be based.

4.4 Developing the forms of publication

Practitioners of humanities computing need to pay increasing attention to their own output and other communicative practices. Humanities computing draws on two distinct traditions of publishing: on the one hand, the informal if not ephemeral kinds characteristic of technical work, which suit rapid development of ideas expressed primarily in things rather than in words; on the other, the much more slow-paced, expansive, historically and philosophically minded critical discourse suitable to the humanities. This book, clearly in the latter mode, represents a conscious choice based on the conviction that to deserve the first half of its name humanities computing must be able to support such discourse – which requires the scope and consequent generosity of mind allowed by the monograph. The second half of the name is, of course, also to be earned, by a corresponding development of technical writing, by far the greater challenge if the field is to address an audience of humanists.

The problem on the technical side is not so much one of clear, straightforward exposition. Although that is difficult and crucial to achieve, professional journals and conferences have already established standards of clarity and bibliographic care demanded by this audience. Rather, the agenda items here are first to make publication a priority for technical work in humanities computing, with consequent partial redefinition of responsibilities in the job; and second to extend the mantle of recognizable scholarship to cover both the published writings and the software arising from this work. As I have noted, humanities computing is joined by historians of experimental science and technology in an attempt to reach beyond the secondary written record – which for technical work in humanities computing is woefully scanty to begin with – to the primary source in equipment, in software. We need, as Michael Mahoney has pointed out, to be able to *read our machines*. Because the subject of technical writing exists in the present, a scholarship of systems also faces the problem of dealing with the highly contingent reality of recent things. Again help is to be found from the historians of science and technology (McCarty 2004a).

4.5 Becoming more conversational

Communication must also be taken far more seriously in its informal mode, not just as something practitioners do but, remembering Socrates, as a primary mode of serious work. *Humanist* and its kind are one form of written conversation as yet insufficiently exploited, however great the volume of correspondence may be. (Significant parts of this book were developed through conversations in *Humanist*. I very much hope others are doing or will do the same.) The basic problem is not this or that form, its characteristics, how it is managed and so forth. Rather it is the partly unrealized, partly misunderstood shift from monumental to conversational modes of work that has occurred during the past century. Northrop Frye wrote of the change in his lifetime, from stately leather-bound books of authority – in his case, 'portly theological tomes in black bindings' – to almost disposable paperbacks, offprints and photocopies (1976: 49–53). We have obviously gone much further in this direction, but without at the same time sorting the difference between two basic requirements of the humanities: on the one hand, to write and read in the generous, sustained, confident and leisurely manner most perfectly served (so far) by the codex; on the other, to recognize that our work is a temporary offering in the long conversation of scholarship. The 'anxiety of continuity', as Frye has called it (1983/1971: 37), finds expression in the ideal of definitive scholarship effectively parodied by David Lodge in the life's ambition of his comic villain, Morris Zapp: beginning with Jane Austen to write the commentary of commentaries on each author in English literature, 'fixing' them definitively so that '[a]fter Zapp, the rest would be silence' (1978/1975: 44f.). This book has been written with the opposite idea in mind: that however great the risk, what matters is that the conversation expand, diversify and flourish. Hence the venturing of ideas gathered far afield and brought into view so that in questioning and challenging them the reader may enlarge the field and make it stronger. Just as the compositional principle of *in medias res* once used the linearity of epic narrative against itself as leverage to the inexpressibly non-linear, so provoking controversy may function within a monumental-seeming codex to topple monumentalizing readings so that we may salvage components for the next provisional structure.

Risk-taking belongs on the agenda of all the humanities, of course, but humanities computing requires the adventurous spirit more than most.

4.6   Doing the ethnography

In Chapter 3, I described the paradigmatic conversation of scholar and practitioner, made assertions about it, and used the paradigm to support an argument for an ethnographic perspective on the disciplines. Now, considering what is to be done, the opportunity for primary ethnographic work derived from such conversations should strike us as urgent. The observations made in Chapter 3 are anecdotal, though derived from years of experience across a team of practitioners. Clearly we need proper studies of how thinking has been changed, or not, in the collaborations on both sides. Evidence in the daily project work of humanities computing centres is freely available, though exceedingly difficult to recover if not recorded as projects develop. Observational methods have been developed in parallel studies of laboratory science, so these would not have to be wholly invented. We would do well to consider the traditional scientific practice of keeping laboratory notebooks – a crucial resource for the history of science.

I have remarked above on the need to study the effect of the formalizing nature of computing on analysis, which the proposed ethnography would of course greatly aid. But the ethnography would also be directed at its effect on synthesis, complementing recent attention to the recurrent forms of scholarship, e.g. by historians of the book and sociologists of knowledge. Looking outward, into the disciplines, practitioners of humanities computing are in an excellent position to investigate how the new forms they are helping to build, express and shape the scholarly imagination. Much – but not all – of that shaping to date has simply gone unreported.[12]

Ethnography would also need to address the nature of collaboration itself, as it actually happens, paying attention to the failures as well as the successes. Studies of collaboration in the sciences are virtually unknown to practitioners in the humanities, where they would provide illuminating precedents. But collaboration *in the humanities* is the question – and it *is* a question. Certainly an outcome we do not want is to establish the word as a euphemism for an old and invidious social distinction. The 'total university network of support services for research', Jaroslav Pelikan declared more than a dozen years ago,

> must be seen as a free and responsible community if it is to be equal to the complexities that are faced by university-based research. Indeed, even such a term as 'providers of support services' is becoming far too limited to describe both the skills and the knowledge required of those who hold such positions. Scholars and scientists in all fields have found that the older configurations of such services, according to which the principal investigator has the questions and the staff person provides the answers, are no longer valid, if they ever were; as both the technological expertise and the scholarly range necessary for research grow, it is also for the formulation and refinement of the questions themselves that principal investigators have turned to 'staff', whom it is increasingly necessary – not a matter of courtesy, much less as a matter of condescension, but as a matter of justice and of accuracy – to identify instead as colleagues in the research enterprize. (1992: 62)

4.7 Writing history

Such ethnographic studies as I have called for would help to answer the question of 'impact', which annoys practitioners like a nervous tic. But the common framing of this question as one of *impact* actually precludes a meaningful answer. It implies what we might call the Billiard

Ball Theory of History, according to which important things have *impact* but unimportant things do not even make a dent.[13] The problem with this theory when extended beyond snooker to people is that it makes worse than monkeys of them. It makes them quite literally into reactive blockheads – like billiard balls, but not as round, smooth and resilient. Despite the obvious defect, this theory is commonly used by otherwise intelligent people struggling to quell the natural anxiety over whether their work has made a genuine difference. So they ask, has computation had an *impact* on what centrally concerns us? Have a sufficient number of colleagues been suitably *impressed* (intellectually dented) by it? Clearly these questions are all wrong, however prudent it may feel to entertain them. But we do need a way of answering the critics. Money not spent on humanities computing could be spent elsewhere. Indeed, money that might be support humanities computing *is* being spent elsewhere.

As my satirical account suggests, the core problem is historiographical. To date we have chronologies, not histories – chiefly lists of 'firsts' with the people who achieved them, structured mostly by the temporal order in which they occurred.[14] As I noted in Chapter 3, quoting Frye, a history is born for a subject when the historian replaces this temporal ordering, formerly thought to be the essential structure of events, with an interpretative relation connecting them to a broader and differently shaped framework. One would think that such an 'inductive leap' to a new vantage point would find abundant support within the humanities, as it certainly does from ongoing, closely parallel work in the history of technology and specifically the history of computing. But our lack of an epistemology based on what humanists do (Lorraine Daston's point, discussed in the Introduction) means that the only substantial tradition on which we can draw is the history and philosophy of the natural sciences. These fields are, as I hope I have demonstrated, very helpful, although not quite what we need. But here is an opportunity that humanities computing is well positioned to address in its preparatory study of artifacts and practices. An audience for its epistemology is ready and waiting.

4.8   Writing for non-specialists

Enacting the first item on the agenda I have sketched – to explore the difference between cultural artifact and computational data – aims at a robust and persuasive answer to the fundamental question of humanities computing: In the simplest terms, what *is* all the fuss about? John Unsworth points out that the question hangs not over access to information, about which nearly everyone is persuaded, but over what can be done with this information once we have it: 'what new questions we could ask, what old ones we could answer' (2003b). Unless we can respond intelligently to the satisfaction of the most demanding questioners, he notes, there is very little reason for the field to continue and a dim prospect for its sustainability. The point here is that the case given substance by successful pursuit of the first agenda item must be persuasively made to those questioners. They should of course include *all* humanities computing practitioners, but more especially the scholarly community as a whole and the public at large. Colleagues, including the administrators who are in a position to enable research, need to hear in some detail 'that there's more to digital libraries than searching and browsing', more to publication than simply putting up Web pages. Response to the general public and to the governmental bodies that represent it is to an old question given new inflection by computing: whether, as Unsworth says, 'the problems humanities scholars care about are specific cases of more general problems, and solutions to the special cases will address the general cases as well' (2003b). By addressing the latter question humanities computing could take an important lead for the humanities as a whole.

Here, once again, humanities computing would do well to look to the natural sciences, where for many decades the 'public understanding of science' (or, better, 'public engagement' with it) has been promoted through books by prominent scientists, programmes of government agencies, university departments and journals.[15] These efforts complement works from the history and philosophy of science and from science studies such as I have drawn on throughout – the fields that by making scientific practice the subject of humanistic inquiry pave the way for incorporating scientific understanding within the humanities and vice versa. Although humanities computing faces a much smaller public with its incomparably more modest needs, in an age of accountability, public understanding is equally necessary for its survival, as Unsworth has explained. Such understanding is also in the nature of the humanities to build, although in general they have not done it often or well. Their complacency was famously pilloried by C. P. Snow, as I noted in the Introduction. Humanities computing might not have so much opportunity to be complacent, but by pursuing the so-what question in every article, book, lecture and course, if only briefly, practitioners can take an active, even prominent role in the argument of justification. Simple answers are needed not only to open up the minds of others but also as approximations in the constant reach for simplicity of understanding.

4.9 Doing the homework

Much of the above would seem to turn on far better handling of one of the greatest difficulties humanities computing scholarship has faced world-wide: the bibliographic problem. Great efforts have been made at comprehensive gathering of international publications, scholars and projects, notably by Joseph Raben (1977), Ian Lancashire (1988, 1991) and Giovanni Adamo (1994). But as Russon Wooldridge correctly perceived, a significant percentage of relevant work takes place at an intermediary stage 'at which questions of computer methodology ... are of interest to the scholar before the computer disappears into the background'.[16] One strongly suspects, however, that without unrealistically heroic efforts no journal such as the one he founded to help capture such work, the online *Computers and the Humanities Working Papers*, would have a chance of publishing more than a minuscule proportion of that intermediary work – because most of it will never have been written down at all, because those doing it have failed to understand how important it is. My own involvement in such efforts suggests as well that outside the usual disciplinary channels, identifying relevant publications is at best haphazard. If, for example, words such as 'computer' or 'digital' (or their equivalents in other languages) are not mentioned in the title of a relevant article published in a journal outside the field, then it is highly unlikely that this article will be identified.

The bibliographic problem is further complicated by the several languages in which work is published, with differences not only of language but also of culture – which is to say, of intellectual and social conventions more than skin-deep. Multiculturalism leaves open the question of a common language in all senses of the term. Since in fact few of those working in humanities computing in the Anglophone world can handle more than one language (i.e. the one in which I am writing), too hard a push for multilinguistic competence can be damagingly exclusionary. The fragility of the field would recommend encouragement rather than exclusion. This is not, however, an attempt to dilute in any way the humanist scholar's sharply felt need to take on more languages. 'Monolingualism can be cured!' is as good as slogans get.

Under the present dispensation the bibliographic problem would then seem insolvable. But the problem is subject to at least two serious qualifications.

The first is that online publication has somewhat redefined the nature of the problem since the last of the major bibliographies was published. Although informal online publication is still relatively rare in some fields, in others articles and book chapters are often co-published online or working drafts made freely available. Online *curricula vitae* are common across all fields; everyone has e-mail, and many will respond. Web searching tools allow us to circumvent whatever classification schemes may be imposed, making possible a degree of interdisciplinary exploration previously inconceivable. Talk of a 'semantic web' has highlighted the obvious limitation imposed by character-string searches, however clever the tools. But my own experience, particularly in the writing of this book, confirms Winograd's: that the massiveness of the resource combined with a reasonable degree of bibliographic cunning is sufficient for very effective gathering on-the-fly.

Work on a semantic web (whatever that may turn out to be) will proceed in any case because of demand from more highly conventionalized user-communities and the inherently interesting nature of the technical challenges involved. Humanists, it seems to me, would be more highly rewarded by investing their efforts in two directions. The first is simply to put as much scholarly literature online as possible, either themselves directly or through publishers, consortia and the like. In many if not most areas of research across the humanities, the tide has turned in favour of online resources, at least as the first stop in locating relevant secondary literature. Self-interest alone would suggest a vigorous pursuit of online publication by whatever means. The second direction to take is equally unoriginal but effective: to give priority to and so encourage surveys, summaries and annotated bibliographies of current scholarship across the disciplines wherever it might be relevant to the field.

The second qualification is itself twofold: first, for some time we have not been in any position to expect of ourselves or of others that each work will build on all that preceded it; second, and more importantly, the strictly cumulative idea of scholarship is a long-discredited product of an older cosmology. We think differently now. Rather than the sense that we advance by 'standing on the shoulders of giants',[17] we are more likely to construe ourselves archaeologically, as building on the rubble and bones of the past, incorporating into a layered whole the relics still visible to us. But I may seem here to be in contradiction, arguing on the one hand, in support of my own heavily referential practice, that humanities computing demands wide recognition of existing work in many disciplines; on the other hand, both practically and theoretically, that there is no need. My argument, however, is really that the principle of selection is different.

4.10   Re-tooling

By far the item most often placed on the agenda of humanities computing, the last on my provisional list, is making better tools, especially for text-analysis. This problem returns us to the question of primitives raised in Chapter 2.5 in the context of the devolving ability to design and build computational tools. It involves us in several complicated social as well as intellectual issues.[18]

The conventional approach to design of computing tools for the humanities is exemplified by the Tübingen System of Text Processing Programs (TUSTEP), whose interoperable set of modules expresses and has influenced the preparation of numerous editions, bibliographies, indexes, dictionaries and encyclopaedias since the late 1960s.[19] The design of TUSTEP resolves this preparation into relatively low-level mechanical primitives, e.g. capture, retrieval, collation, analysis, sorting, rule-based manipulation and output in digital or printed form. For several reasons – including perhaps chiefly the language of documentation, the complexity of its interface and the somewhat differing style of scholarly work in the Anglophone world – calls in English for 'better tools' have unfortunately often been made in ignorance of it. This is a costly ignorance, since TUSTEP's performance demonstrates a cogent and practical design, which in turn raises questions we need to be asking: Are these the right sort of primitives? Are they at the right level of abstraction?

A second ignorance concerns some of the most promising work to date, at the intersection of statistics and literary criticism. The great promise of analytic textual computing, John Unsworth has pointed out, is 'to uncover in reams of mute data the aesthetically and intellectually apprehensible patterns on which understanding depends' (2003a). That is certainly what John Burrows, Hugh Craig, Richard Forsyth, David Holmes, David Hoover, Fiona Tweedy and others have been patiently doing.[20] 'The most decisive conceptual event of twentieth-century physics', Ian Hacking argues, 'has been the discovery that the world is not deterministic' (1990: 1). In the space thus 'cleared for chance' do art and nature imitate each other?

Constructive responses to the calls for better tools have been short-lived and unproductive. Unsworth points out in his analysis of the situation that little seems to have come of past efforts to mobilize programming talent (2003b). Partly, he says, the fault lies in the failure 'to demonstrate the usefulness of all the stuff we have digitized over the last decade and more'. Two requirements are implied: first, that we know what computing can do for us in our asking and answering of significant questions; second, that the benefits can be demonstrated. These requirements are the first and eighth of my agenda items, respectively. Two additional challenges and related agenda items arise from the specific call for better tools. I list these in reverse order of importance, though all are crucial.

The first challenge comprises a bundle of social issues stirred up by any attempt to organize an adequate response to the call. In Unsworth's words, these include 'how to structure a successful collaboration; how to engage end-users in design; how to sustain such a project over the long run, through inevitable changes in institutional priorities, computing environments, and personnel' (2003b). These unpack into deeper problems: collaboration in the humanities; transformation of the scholar from passive end-user to active end-maker; and identification of principles for humanities computing that make projects sustainable by grounding them in fundamental concerns. The first of these I have discussed above as an aspect of agenda item 6; the second I consider immediately below; the third, again, is the central subject of this book, included in agenda item 1.

The second challenge is to question the failure of tool-making itself, not as a result of ignorance, a problem of social organization nor a lack of funding or possibilities, but rather as effort in the wrong direction. Thus Unsworth recommends redirecting attention from what computers can do (again, already exemplified for a large area of scholarship) to what 'humanists want to do', with the aim of producing 'a modular, extensible toolkit ... that actually helps us ask new questions, and answer old ones'.[21] The functional primitives of scholarship he has in mind are thus very different from TUSTEP's – in his provisional list, discovering, annotating, comparing, referring, sampling, illustrating, representing. TUSTEP's concrete response to the old question of tools has, of course, the advantage of immediate, proven applicability; its approach, still open to further development, derives practical appeal and technical strength from well-developed expertise in data processing. Unsworth's approach responds by asking a different kind of question from a perspective unique to humanities computing. It sets an agenda for experimental research with very few constraints.

In a remarkable paper developed along compatible lines, John Bradley compares a typical exercise in literary critical close-reading to text-analysis as usually implemented, in which a text is transformed algorithmically into results that affect how a critic views it (2003). Criticism, he argues, is not actually centred on words, though words are important to it, but rather on constructing a 'mental model' of the text. (Once again we must be careful not to attribute to pre- or non-computational thinking an idea domesticated by the computer, though the analogy between interpretation and modelling is strong.) Criticism is thus poorly supported by batch-orientated software, which being a 'black box' is by nature peripheral to what the scholar actually does – and so peripheral, if present at all, to his or her scholarly writing. Rather, Bradley argues, text-analysis needs to follow Douglas Englebart's move, described in *Augmenting Human Intellect* (1962), away from batch-processing to interactive modelling. In this way the computer becomes central to the work by corresponding more perfectly to how the worker thinks. Vannevar Bush's famous paper, 'As We May Think' (1945), implies the same argument, and much of the work in hypertext and human–computer interaction design likewise.

Bradley notes potential consequences. Although non-verbal aids have been used in the scholarly analysis of text, the primary medium of thought and sole means of expression outside the classroom has been prose. 'If a suitable environment for the development and manipulation of conceptual models was available,' he speculates cogently, 'one can imagine that the analyst might choose to publish not a conventional paper *describing* the model, but the model itself as a digital object' (2003: 204). It is at least conceivable that in some cases such a model would communicate the author's interpretative intentions better than a written argument, and it seems obvious that if well designed it would do so better than any description of the model. Some digital products already demonstrate the superiority of modelling over conventional scholarly forms.[22] But it should be noted that a strong and instructive precedent is to be found in textual editions and other scholarly reference works taken as meta-theoretical statements – devices, if you will, with which many interpretative structures may be built.

Unlike their printed and bound predecessors, forms of expression *in silico* easily accommodate graphical components. Should models become a primary form of scholarly communication, graphics seem highly likely to enter the mainstream of humanities scholarship, with consequences to be watched. This is a particularly strong possibility for text-analysis, which has been graphical almost *ab ovo*, from the visually significant KWIC display (in which the design shapes interpretation) to distribution charts and statistical plots. Devising graphical forms and conventions to support or express scholarly argument is an agenda item already well underway. Learning to design and to read graphical displays poses a major challenge for the primarily textual humanities, opening them up to kinships with art history, aesthetics, design, the creative arts and with those disciplines in the social and natural sciences where graphical display, e.g. under the rubric of 'scientific visualization', has been primary for a long time. Investigating these is clearly also to be done. In his paper Bradley thus points with reservations to software in social scientific 'qualitative analysis' (2003: 201–4).

Two qualifying remarks by way of conclusion.

First, the idea that thinking is reducible to primitives or fundamental modules is philosophically controversial, challenged on the one hand by Heideggerian phenomenology, vigorously and variously pursued on the other by analytic philosophers and linguists.[23] In humanities computing we should at least be clear that we are modelling thinking, however subversive of the entire project that may be.

Second, much can be and has been done, at least in the analysis stage, with existing software. Very little of the agenda sketched above needs to wait on the tools we would have. Indeed, deferral is, as I have noted, a perilous trap.

5   Epilegomena

In summary form I have argued for the following agenda items:

(1) Discover, confirm and exemplify how computing affects analysis, so that the basic case for humanities computing is clear and persuasive across the disciplines.

(2) Explore the realization of scholarly forms in the digital medium, attempting both the historical achievements of print as these remain desirable and the potential of the digital medium to implement new theoretical designs.

(3) Identify and cultivate kinships with the disciplines, so that humanities computing is informed by the collective ways of knowing they have cultivated.

(4) Redefine both 'scholarship' and 'publication' in theory and practice so as to include all of the work within the purview of the field, particularly with respect to software.

(5) Develop as a prevalent habit and as a serious, essential aspect of work the strongly conversational mode of scholarly publication exemplified by *Humanist* and other Internet forums.

(6) Write the ethnography of collaborative engagements to document how successful collaborations happen and how perceptions change in the encounter of the humanities with computing.

(7) Develop a genuine historiography of humanities computing from existing chronologies; begin writing histories of the field.

(8) Cultivate and exercise the ability to explain the essentials of humanities computing to non-specialist colleagues and to the general public.

(9) Devise appropriate bibliographic mechanisms and online publishing habits; change the notion of cumulative scholarship in the field so that a bibliographic imperative can realistically be followed.

(10) Propose and investigate programmable scholarly primitives for the construction of better tools.

At the beginning of this chapter I argued that any agenda we might construct for humanities computing, including the above, will to a significant degree be (a) incomplete and (b) partially dependent on the priorities of the disciplines in its purview. Allow me to summarize these qualities and then to speculate on where an incomplete, partly dependent agenda might lead us.

Incompleteness, I have argued, follows from the inadequacy of the concept 'problem' (in the sense that agendas have them) to capture the humanistic aspects of what its practitioners do. Humanists problematize, but not to make or discover that which is to be *solved*. Rather the aim is to recontextualize or renew understanding of the stubborn, recurrent 'problems' that are more the fabric of post-Edenic life than rips in it we may hope to mend. Of course solvable problems occur and are solved meanwhile, but they are incidental to the main purpose. Hence, however we construe the work of the humanities, including that of humanities computing, it cannot be cleanly resolved into an agenda.

Dependency of the agenda on external objectives is a necessary consequence of interdisciplinarity as I have defined it. Denied (which is to say, liberated from) both ownership and boundedness of its area of operations, humanities computing cannot turn to any of the common geopolitical metaphors. There is no way of saying precisely where the 'field' stops and something else begins, who owns or belongs to it and who does not. Membership is loose and inclusive. Some, such as the author of this book, spend all their time in it. Speaking for them, I might summarize our experience by comparing it more nearly to crewing a ship of exploration in an archipelago of disciplines – wandering within something like James Chandler's 'network of autonomous practices in asymmetrical relation to each other'.[24] But, as I suggested in Chapter 3, if we take this 'wand'ring bark' of disciplinary exploration and assistance seriously, we can see in it a clue to a better, more generous conception of disciplinarity that suits humanities computing well and may be more broadly applicable. The problem with Chandler's postmodern network sleeps in his metaphor: nodes may be asymmetrical; their relationships may be changeable; but once again there are only nodes and relationships, just as there are only branches on the *arbor scientiae*. This network is thus a stylistic variant of the old scheme, still committed to its basic structure.

As epigraph to Chapter 3 I quoted Greg Dening's metaphor of 'a great ring of viewers' from his powerful collection of meditations on a lifetime as an ethnographic historian of the South Pacific. In a series of lectures on the Australian imagination, David Malouf speaks of two visions blended in his culture: Aboriginal land-dreaming of the island-continent and the latecomers' sea-dreaming from its edge.[25] Dening elsewhere writes as a scholar of sea-dreaming explorers. Here, I think, he is thinking as a land-dreamer, suggesting that we re-imagine the disciplines looking inward to a vast, primeval and mostly unknown commons, towards the centre which is everywhere. Alain de Lille's paradox is wise European counsel, on offer for centuries to help us prise open the 'blinkered view of humanity' that is the price of thinking ourselves at the centre of things, and which results in warring states.

So what is to be done? One thing is to act on Malouf's 'spirit of play' *within* Dening's great disciplinary ring, where humanities computing's scholarly walkabout must surely be located.

An agenda for humanities computing may recognize the imperative to negotiate among the viewers, but it can hardly specify very much about these negotiations. All who are served by the playful spirit I have just imagined are changing with respect to computing as computing is changing with respect to them. Basic familiarity can now be expected from colleagues and students in most places where computers are found, often accompanied by an implicit, largely uncritical belief in the virtues of computing, a tendency to identify it with the Web and an end-user's rather than an end-maker's perspective. Analytic methods and synthetic forms remain mostly a *terra incognita* on the horizon. Exhaustion, as we saw, is never a possibility. But my point here is that because of the machine's universality, humanities computing remains perpetually at that horizon. The practitioner is therefore always having to revise the pidgin with which he or she intermediates between scholar and computer, in person or in software, among distinct individuals or within a single skin. What must be done is mostly learned in the doing, as with all fieldwork.

The computer scientist Edsger Dijkstra noted that the question of whether machines can think is about as interesting as the question of whether submarines can swim.[26] We laugh at the absurd image of a swimming submarine, but as I have argued throughout this book, humanities computing orbits Dijkstra's fundamental absurdity. Thus we make computers work for us analytically by refining crude instances of mechanically expressed thought to the point at which we can no longer specify a stubborn difference we somehow otherwise know. We make them work for us synthetically to the degree that an end-maker is able to build and refine many such swimming submarines from a common assembly of parts. But what in all this is *new*? In his Turing Award lecture Dijkstra declared that computers in their capacity as tools 'will be but a ripple on the surface of our culture ...' but that in their capacity as intellectual challenge they are 'without precedent in the cultural history of mankind'.[27] We can quibble with the common idiom of his assertion. Nothing, Mahoney points out, is really unprecedented (1990b: 325). There are always precedents: those things that come before in time, that we fashion into histories and so make the sense we require from them. But if we must quibble with the great Dijkstra, we must do so sympathetically. The feeling of the etymologically monstrous (L. *monstruosus*, portentous, unnatural, strange) persists, which I take to portend that we are still in process of constructing a precedent. This book is in a sense precisely dedicated to doing just that.

Dijkstra points specifically to the fundamental challenge of programming in 'an environment where highly hierarchical artefacts are both possible and necessary': layered systems spanning a temporal granularity from the very small to the very large, with an upper end-point that would seem by virtue of the universal machine to be undefinable. In consequence we become makers of our own hierarchical world – an artificial 'great chain of being', as Arthur O. Lovejoy described the ontological tradition of Western culture. More than one irony tempers the enthusiasm of becoming *fabricator operis immensi*,[28] hence 'as gods'. There is the historical come-uppance visited on the hubristic technologist who, having Archimedes' lever and a place to stand, threatens to prise life as we know it out of its orbit. (Some computing system failures have in fact come close to a bungling enactment of Archimedes' boast.)[29] But the more interesting irony, of profit to the humanities, is that this artificial chain shows the cosmological projection of a hierarchical world for what it has always been. Thus it gives us, in the ability to remake and the responsibility to maintain the hierarchy, constant reminder of both. Knowing the world is constructed and that we have constructed it gets us only so far, however. To my mind the precedent whose inchoateness gives us the uncanny sense of the unprecedented lies in our being thrown back onto the primacy of the real – and since that always escapes the net, to questioning. We contemplate the difference between the submarines we fashion and the swimmers we are: the one powerful and efficient in taking us boldly where no one has gone before, because imagination has made it so; the other lithe, alive, within a deep calling unto deep.

Notes

Introduction

1. See the compilation and anatomy of activities in McCarty and Kirschenbaum 2003.
2. See in particular the professional journals, especially *Literary and Linguistic Computing* and *Computers and the Humanities*; the ALLC/ACH conference proceedings referenced at www.allc.org and www.ach.org; Hockey 2000 for textual scholarship. For the bibliographic problem as a whole see Chapter 5.4.9.
3. Both strategies may be found e.g. in Newell 1991; compare the adjacent Winograd 1991. Often, however, the dismissal must be implied from the invisibility of the field to those with a strongly technical background. For the italicized phrase see Raymond 1996/1991, a.k.a. *The Jargon File*, www.catb.org/~esr/jargon.
4. Bush 1945: 105 and 1967: 92.
5. For help with the latter and renewed insights into skill, I am indebted to Nigel Bontoft, master builder.
6. Eddington 1949/1939: 18. Hamming's apparent quotation is a paraphrase of an argument well worth considering in the original.
7. The quoted phrase is Ian Hacking's, said 'nonchalantly' but meant seriously; for an example see Hacking 1983: 186–209.
8. See especially Becher and Trowler 2001/1989: 23f., also Hutcheon and Hutcheon 2001: 1367f.; for the term 'epistemic culture', Knorr Cetina 1999; for a fine example of making the relation between culture and mode of communication, Lederberg 1996.
9. Galison 1997: 628 and *passim*; see also Biagioli and Galison 2003; Pickering 1992.
10. See the series of articles under 'Theories and Methodologies' in *PMLA* 116.2-5 and their references.
11. Stillinger 1991: 202, quoted by Inge 2001: 623.
12. Cf. Inge 2001: 629 to Hirschfeld 2001: 619f.
13. Snow's lecture has been continuously in print since 1959 and is occasionally the subject for reassessment; see Collini 1998; Rorty 2004.
14. Gilman 2004: 387, my emphasis.
15. The multiple authorship of publications in the sciences is almost always a convenient fiction, i.e. it denotes the multiple authorship *of the work* on which the single-authored 'write-up' reports; see Biagioli and Galison 2003.
16. See e.g. Vessey 2004.
17. See Ben Jonson, *Timber, or Discoveries* (1640); George Orwell, 'Politics and the English Language' (1946). This ideal remains dominant, however badly individual writings live up to it. The Latin, 'not for oneself but for all', is from Lucan, *Pharsalia* 2.383, referring to Brutus' Stoic selflessness.

18. For the first see Norman 1998 and Weiser 1996; for the second, Winograd's argument, discussed in Chapter 2.1.
19. McGann 2001: 74. Cf. *The Valley of the Shadow* project, which tells 'no "one" story', valley.vcdh.virginia.edu/usingvalley/valleyguide.html.
20. Veblen 1906. Papal Bull, 'Quasi lignum vitae', 14 April 1255, number 247 in Denifle and Châtelain 1889: 279. The echoes through medieval and patristic literature are numerous, back e.g. to *lignum vitae* in Revelations 22: 2 and *lucerna fulgoris* in Luke 11: 36.

1 Modelling

1. 'Je genauer wir die tatsächliche Sprache betrachten, desto stärker wird die Widerstreit zwischen ihr und unsrer Forderung. (Die Kristallreinheit der Logik hatte sich mir ja nicht *ergeben*; sondern sie war eine Forderung.) Der Widerstreit wird unerträglich; die Forderung droht nun zu etwas Leerem zu werden. – Wir sind aufs Glatteis geraten, wo die Reibung fehlt, also die Bedingungen in gewissem Sinne ideal sind, aber wir eben deshalb auch nicht gehen können. Wir wollen gehen; dann brauchen wir die *Reibung*. Zurück auf den rauhen Boden!' *Philosophische Untersuchungen*, trans. G. E. M. Anscombe.
2. Weil 1978: 116; see Peter Winch's comments in the Introduction (1978: 3).
3. For the work of Don Ihde see note 43, below; see also Borgmann 1984; note the Society for Philosophy and Technology, www.spt.org, and its journal, *Techné: Research in Philosophy and Technology*, scholar.lib.vt.edu/ejournals/ SPT/.
4. On the significance of metamorphosis in literature and the arts, see Warner 2002; in classical mythology, Forbes Irving 1990. See also Ransmayr 1990/1988; Malouf 1978.
5. For 'embodied knowledge' and its literature see Lakoff and Johnson 1999, Gardner 1993/1983; 'multimodal reasoning', Craig, Nersessian and Catrambone 2002, Markman and Dietrich 2000 and in computing specifically Dourish 2001; 'distributed cognition' in the context of modelling, Giere 2002.
6. Geertz 1993/1973: 93. Cf. Goodman's distinction between 'denotative' and 'exemplary' models, respectively (1976/1969: 172–3); Groenewold's 'more or less poor substitute' and 'more or less exemplary ideal' (1961: 98). Similar distinctions are quite common in the literature.
7. Minsky 1995/1968; Shanin 1972: 10; Lloyd 1998; for the mediating role of models, Morrison and Morgan 1999.
8. Minsky 1995/1968; cf. Wegner 1997: 88.
9. Daston suggests that gaining methodological self-awareness is one of the central projects of 'where to go and what to do next' in the humanities (2004: 363, 361). See the Introduction.
10. Robin Gandy quotes Ludwig Wittgenstein: 'And this is how it is: if only you do not try to utter what is unutterable then nothing gets lost' (1995/1994: 85 n. 43).
11. For the significance of error in humanities computing see Unsworth 1997; in scientific research, Wimsatt 1987 (biology), Mayo 1996 and esp. Kuhn

1977: 128–74 (experimental physics) and in general Allchin 2001. For the epistemology of approximation see Ramsey 1992.
12. Minsky 1997/1991. The difference made by speed must be qualified, however; cf. pre-computational DNA modelling (Watson 2001/1968) with the 'spring and ball' technique in chemistry (Del Re 2000) and early lexicographic practice (Murray 1977: 203): the latter two offer kinaesthetic as well as visual feedback impractical to impossible with current computers.
13. Smith 1995: 460 (my emphasis); cf. Fetzer 1999: 23.
14. Gadamer 2000/1960: 4–9; Kuhn 1977: 137. See section 4.4, below, and Chapter 3.6.4.
15. See Fodor 1995, Winograd 1991: 207–8 and below.
16. Goodman 1976/1969: 171; Groenewold 1961: 98; Achinstein 1968: 203; Ziman 2000: 147; see also Chapter 4.5.
17. For 'map' see Ziman 2000: 126–32, 147–51 and Toulmin 1967/1953: 94–109 and section 3.4, below; for 'diagram', Goodman 1976/1969: 171–3 and section 3.3, below.
18. For the often conflated ideas of 'ratio' (*logos*) and 'proportion' (*analagon*) in Greek mathematics see Fowler 1999/1987: 15f. For analogy in imaginative language and thought see Gibbs, R. 1994 (reviewed by Turner 1995), Turner 1996; in computer science, Hoffman 1995; in cognitive science, Mitchell 1993, Holyoak and Thagard 1997; in the philosophy of science, Achinstein 1968, Leatherdale 1974, Gentner 2002, Shelley 2002; in relation to modelling Bailer-Jones 2002, Bailer-Jones and Bailer-Jones 2002. I do not deal here with metaphor in relation to modelling, for which see Black 1962 and 1993/1979; Johnson 2002.
19. Goodman argues that representation is not mimetic but symbolic: object X is always *represented as* Y, which means that Y is selective with respect to X and stands in symbolic relationship to it. See also Elgin 1998; Hopkins 2004.
20. Possibly the best and least problematic overview is Davis, Shrobe and Szolovits 1993; see also Sowa 2000; Barr and Feigenbaum 1981. Lenat 1998 illustrates the problematic tendencies in this field; Winograd 1991 and Dreyfus 1985 provide an antidote. For KR in a philosophical context see Agre 1997: 222–40 and *passim*; Agre 2003.
21. www.cyc.com/; note the publications under 'Technology'.
22. Frye 1991: 4f; cf. Winograd's analysis of the 'almost childish leap of faith' made by such projects (1991: 204–7).
23. Winograd and Flores 1986: 97–100, 131–3, 174–7; Dreyfus 1985. See also Brooks 1991.
24. Shin and Lemon 2002; note the extensive bibliography.
25. Monmonier 1996/1991; Wood 1992; Turnbull 1994/1989 and 2000.
26. Bateson cites Alfred Korzybski's principle that 'the map is not the territory' (1933) but points out its contradiction by 'the natural history of human mental process': we regularly identify map and territory, name and thing named (2002/1979: 27–8). See also Goodman 1972: 15; Kent 2000/1978: xix.
27. For the cognitive role of perceptual simulation, replaying kinaesthetic memories e.g. in diagramming and physical modelling, see Markman and Dietrich 2000, Davies and Stone 2000. The idea that such simulations play

a significant role in cognition leads to the preference for animations as more *knowledgeable* than static diagrams (Craig, Nersessian and Catrambone 2002).

28. For the epistemological aspects of automata see Riskin 2003.
29. This is known as a 'stochastic' or 'guessing' approach; see Bateson 2002/1979: 137–74.
30. Galison 1997: 690f. Mahoney notes that when 'John von Neumann changed [the] traditional view [of modelling] by arguing against the need for a physical model to mediate between nature and mathematics ...', the job of the scientist became 'to build models that matched the phenomena, without concern for whether the model was "true" in any other sense' (2002: 39).
31. Rowe 1994, quoted by Burch 2002: 245; see also Winsberg 2001.
32. Beacham and Denard 2003 and the 3D Visualization Centre, www.warwick.ac.uk/3d/; publications of the Cultural Virtual Reality Lab, UCLA, www.cvrlab.org; the Crystal Palace model, *Monuments and Dust* project, IATH (Virginia), www.iath.virginia.edu/london/; the *3D Virtual Buildings Project*, 3dlearning.iit.nrc.ca/3DVirtualbuildings, for which see Bonnett 2004.
33. See esp. Ian Hacking's discussion of the Michelson–Morley experiment (1983: 253–61). See Gooding 2000 and Morrison 1998 for an overview; the triplet of articles Hacking 1988, Heelan 1988 and Galison 1988, Franklin 2002.
34. See also Brown 2002; Gooding 1998; and note esp. the careful argument in Kuhn 1977: 240–65.
35. Hesse 1963: 1–6. In *La Théorie physique* (1914) Duhem had admitted they could be 'useful psychological aids' but declared them to be 'incoherent and superficial' in relation to theory. In *Physics, the Elements* (1920), Campbell argued for their epistemological value, stressing in particular their ability to accommodate the dynamical nature of knowledge.
36. I rely primarily on Galison 1987, Hacking 1983 and Nickles 2000.
37. 1938: 6–7; cf. Feyerabend 1993/1975: 147–58.
38. Popper 2000/1959: 7; see Nickles 2000: 87.
39. Hanson 1961, which reproduces in interrogative form the title of Popper's *Logic of Scientific Discovery*.
40. McGann 2001: 101–3, quoting Samuels 1997.
41. For the 'residue' metaphor see Sperberg-McQueen 2002; it is related to if not derived from the now commonplace metaphor of the 'problem space', a standard conceptual tool used in automated problem-solving. See Newell 1980; Cheng 2004; see also Chapter 3.4.
42. See William Carlos Williams, 'Landscape with the Fall of Icarus' (1962).
43. For the philosophy of technology, see esp. Ihde 1991, the collected essays in Achterhuis 2001/1997 and Tiles 2000. For computing in particular see Dourish 2001, Winograd 1995b, Winograd and Flores 1986, and the concluding discussion in this section.
44. See e.g. Hacking 1983, 2002; Rorty 1991.
45. References to *Sein und Zeit* (*Being and Time*) will use the abbreviation *SZ* followed first by the page numbers of the German edition, then of the Macquarrie and Robinson translation. Here I limit myself here to the

nearest contact-points as these have been identified by Winograd and Flores, and then only in briefest summary. On *SZ* see Dreyfus 1991; on Heidegger as a whole, Sheehan 1998; on his significance for the philosophy of science, Rouse 1998; for computer science see below. See also Ihde 1991: 50ff. Heidegger's famous essay on technology, 'Die Frage nach der Technik' (Heidegger 1978, trans. 1997), has other concerns; see Dreyfus 1995.

46. For Heideggerian phenomenology in recent computer science see Winograd 1995b; Sheridan 2000; Clear 1997; West 1997; Dourish 2001; Denning 1998b, s.v. 'Practices'; Capurro 1992; Mallery, Hurwitz and Duffy 1992.

47. See Winograd 2000 and Suchman 1987: xii, 53f.

48. Dreyfus identifies gradations of breakdown, in increasing order of seriousness: malfunction, temporary breakdown and total breakdown (1991: 70–83; *SZ* 73–4/102–5).

49. For Polanyi's philosophical roots see Polanyi 1969: 155 and Jha 2002: Chapter 3, who also deals with his very important use of Gestalt psychology.

50. His most succinct statement is Polanyi 1983/1966. On his work see Jha 2002. More generally see Barbiero 2004, Delaney 2000, Molander 1992; for computer science Ennals 1990: 61f.

51. The idea of the tool as an extension of the body (i.e. a prosthetic, in the etymological sense, 'of the nature of addition, giving additional power') is immemorial since, as Polanyi argues, it is inherent. Thus Aristotle in his general theory of animal activity remarks that 'the staff is like a separable limb' (*de motu animalium* 702b4f., trans. M. C. Nussbaum). See note 72.

52. This is Gilbert Ryle's distinction, for which see Ryle 2000/1949: 28–32 and Daniel C. Dennett's introduction, ix–xix. Note John Shotter's discussion of 'knowing from' as a third kind (1984: 188–9, 212), reviewed briefly in Goudsmit 1998: 57.

53. On Peirce generally see Burch 2001; on his importance to the philosophy of science see Misak 2000.

54. See Wirth 1998; Aliseda-LLera 1997; Magnani 2001; Burch 2001; Lipton 2000.

55. Harman 1965, where he analyses several alternatives; Lipton 2000.

56. See Hacking 1990: 207 for a discussion of the terminology. His choice is for 'hypothesis', though he notes that philosophers are divided as to which term they use. 'Abduction' seems the most common in current literature.

57. For Holmes see the several essays in Eco and Sebeok 1988/1983; for Darwin see Lipton 2000.

58. Ginzburg 1989/1986: 104, 204. Note also the context of an earlier version, in Eco and Sebeok 1988/1983.

59. For science and medicine see Galison 1998 and 1999; for commerce see Poovey 1998.

60. For the centrality of the intentional artifact to computing, see Smith 1998/1996.

61. Geertz 1993/1973: 15f. This is Hayden White's territory; see White 1987.

62. Black 1962: 219–43; see also Black 1993/1979. He finds in the imaginative dimensions of modelling the possible convergence of the sciences and the humanities (1962: 242f.).

63. On the narratological and computational, see Meister 2003.

64. 1966: 75. Laudans notes the influence of Descartes' hypotheticalism on e.g. Boyle, Glanvill and Locke. Note that Vaihinger distinguishes the hypothetical, by which we try to establish a reality, from the fictional, which is purely expedient (1924: 85–90).
65. For the layered design of operating systems, see Chapter 4.9; for archetypes Frye 1957.
66. Hacking traces the implication of 'discovery' to theory-dominated philosophy; see 1983: 225f.
67. For span see Sinclair 1966: 415; cf. Sinclair 1991: 109–21. For the concordance and H. P. Luhn's KWIC format, see McCarty 1993: 57.
68. Referring to an ingenious experiment on quarks, in which positrons and electrons are sprayed onto a niobium ball, Hacking declares, '*So far as I'm concerned, if you can spray them then they are real*' (1983: 23).
69. Cf. George Miller's delightfully playful statement on the reality of the cognitive span for which he has argued (1956: 97).
70. See also Ferguson 1994; Mahoney 2003.
71. Vincenti is paraphrasing the psychologist Donald T. Campbell, whose theory is the basis for his model (Vincenti 1990: 48); this is developed extensively in the final chapter (241–57) with the support of several historical studies from aeronautical engineering that form the bulk of the book. For Campbell's central notion of 'evolutionary epistemology', see Campbell 1974; Bradie and Harms 2004.
72. Vincenti 1990: 242. The metaphor is common in discussions of perception and tool-use. In the context of phenomenology see e.g. Merleau-Ponty 1962/1945: 14; Polanyi 1962/1958: 59 and 1983/1966: 13, 14, 29, where he discusses probes, such as the cane, and tools, such as the hammer, found also in Heidegger (e.g. *SZ* 69f./98–100). Note also Descartes, *Optics*, Discourses 1, 4 and 6 (1985/1637: 153, 166, 169). Bateson, discussing concepts of the self, draws a parallel between skilled felling of a tree and a blind man's locomotion with a stick, arguing that user, tool and object must be considered as a total, closed system (2000/1972: 317f.). See Ihde 1991: 11–44 and *passim*, where he argues for the applicability of such thinking to instrumentation. Suchman 1987: 53f. quotes Dreyfus, as above; see Vera and Simon 1993: 17–18 for a critique of her 'situated action' theory.
73. Again to anticipate the discussion of disciplinary terminology in Chapter 4.4, the status and meaning of 'original' (as illuminated by the status of 'copy') varies significantly across the humanities. Ginzburg's telling examples are literary and textual studies on the one hand, art history and aesthetics on the other (1989: 105–8).
74. Gani 1972: 83; see also Black 1962: 242.
75. See esp. Paxson 1994: Chapter 1.
76. Davie 1981: 92 summarizes F. W. Bateson's argument that 'personification is inherent in the very grammatical structure of our language, hence ... we "personify" when we're not aware of doing anything of the sort.'
77. See Bloomfield 1963 and 1980; Davie 1967 and 1981; Levin 1981. Bloomfield outlines five 'grammatical tests' for personification but argues these in the abstract rather than against particular texts (1963: 163); as a result they are of little help in practice.

78. 1957: 11. See Anna Wierzbicka's discussion of linguistics in the wake of Leonard Bloomfield and Noam Chomsky (1996: 3–9).
79. See the Introduction to the online prototype at www.kcl.ac.uk/humanities/cch/wlm/analyticalonomasticon/intro.htm.
80. In the bilingual Loeb edition revised by G. P. Goold, capitalization is used to mark those entities the editor regarded as personified; from the grammatical perspective his consistency is certainly no better than the first stage I describe.
81. I discuss McGann's criticism in the Introduction.
82. See www.kcl.ac.uk/cch/wlm/analyticalonomasticon/.
83. The design is, as just noted, work-in-progress. Note that several entities are shown with attributes that are either not used at all or that serve as reminders and notes. Thus START LOCATION and END LOCATION in the INSTANCE entity are there to allow for duration to be computed in some future version of the database; NOTES in the CONTEXTS-TO-WEIGHT entity and DEFINITION in the FACTOR-TO-WEIGHT entity serve as space for annotation; APTITUDE FACTOR in the PERSONS entity has simply been abandoned in preference to a value set in the spreadsheet.
84. If, for example, I decide that the past indicative active form of *speak* in '*She spoke* to the tree' personifies the tree, I should not therefore be committed to assigning the same personifying force to the perfect passive participle in 'the words *spoken* to the tree', even if it is clear in context that the same person spoke the words.
85. Examples of parallels are between Orpheus' severed head and the banks of the stream down which it floats 11.52f., and between chance and desire in attributing the cause of Phoebus' love for Daphne, 1.452f. Examples of groups are the constellations Phaethon encounters on his ill-conceived journey 2.80–3; the catalogue of entities to whom Medea refers in her incantation of the natural powers, 7.192–219.
86. Patrick Juola <juola@mathcs.duq.edu> in a series of e-mails, May 2003.
87. One common equation is $v(t) = V * (1 - e^{(-t/RC)})$, where V is the maximum value to be reached, e a real-number constant (the 'Euler number', approximate value 2.72), t time and RC the impedance. The charging current is assumed to be constant; time is the variable. In my application I have assumed that time (i.e. duration of the event) is negligible; rather it is the arithmetic sum of the personifying weight that varies. I use the impedance value simply to adjust the shape of the curve. For the chart I have set $V = 20$, to signify a provisional hypothesis that no amount of personifying force will ever amount to more than twice the threshold. I have set RC such that for weights up to the threshold the calculated effect is as close to linear as possible; this allows me to declare by setting an individual weight or perhaps two that an entity is in fact personified.
88. See the references in Thieme and Yang 2000: 256.
89. The equation is: $V = V_{MAX} * ([S]) / (K_M + [S])$, where V is the rate at which an enzyme reacts with the 'substrate' S (the substance to be changed; [S] denotes its quantity), V_{MAX} its maximum value, K_M the 'Michaelis constant' (the concentration at half of V_{MAX}, in effect expressing the affinity of the enzyme for the substrate). See Michaelis and Menten's paper in Teich and Needham 1992: 54–9 and the lucid explanation by Willmott 2001.

90. This equation is: $V = V_{MAX} * (I^n) / (I^n + \sigma^n)$, where I is the intensity of light, σ is the translated version of K_M, i.e. the half-saturation intensity, and n is an exponent used to adjust the slope of the hyperbolic curve (Valeton and van Norren 1983: 1540).

2   Genres

1. '... es ist schon ein Verdienst um die Vernunft, diesen Weg wo möglich ausfindig zu machen, sollte auch manches als vergeblich aufgegeben werden müssen, was in dem ohne Überlegung vorher genommenen Zwecke enthalten war.'
2. Fleck 1981/1935: 42; see Thomas Kuhn's Preface; cf. Smith 2000: 1092.
3. Cherry 1977: 123. On the telephone see Pool 1977; see also McCarty 1992.
4. On reference works see Deegan and Tanner 2002: 74–6; Lynch 2001; on commentaries, Fowler 1999 and Goldhill 1999; note also Bolter 1993. On the commentary form more broadly, see Most, ed. 1999; Gibson and Kraus 2002.
5. On the lexicon and its futures, see the work of Gregory Crane and others at the Perseus Digital Library, www.perseus.tufts.edu, Publications.
6. See, for example, the essays in Unsworth, O'Keeffe and Burnard 2005 (forthcoming); Smith 2004; McGann 2001; Robinson and Gabler 2000; Hockey 2000, esp. chapter 7; Bornstein and Tinkle 1998; Sutherland 1997; Lavagnino 1997; Shillingsburg 1996; Finneran 1996; see also the journal *TEXT* (Society for Textual Scholarship), www.textual.org/text.
7. My primary points of reference are Most, ed. 1999 (essays on commentary in the Babylonian, Hebrew, Late Antique, Buddhist, Islamic, Greek, European medieval and modern traditions); Fraade 1991 (Hebrew); Gibson and Kraus 2002 (Greco-Roman).
8. Goldhill 1999: 402.
9. Hughes 1991/1980; Fowler 1999: 428.
10. See Vallance 1999 on the 'non-submissive commentary'; von Staden 2002: 114 on Galen's 'recuperative elucidation of the obscure ancient voice'.
11. See esp Fraade 1991: 10–12, on Philonic commentary as a guided journey of the soul to perfection.
12. Most 1999: vii argues the point for all formal descriptions of commentary.
13. For the visual arts see section C in Most, ed. 1999; for marginal mss. imagery Camille 1992; for page as image Parkes 1991, Martin and Vezin 1990; Bornstein and Tinkle 1998. For computational techniques see Graham 1991 and Kirschenbaum 2002.
14. See Campbell-Kelly and Aspray 1996 and Ceruzzi 1998 for a far more detailed account.
15. On the early development of operating systems see Ceruzzi 1998: 96–101. On their layered design, see Chapter 4.9.
16. On the development of software and computing systems, see Wegner and Goldin 1999; Frankston 1997; Alan C. Kay's remarks in Bergin *et al.* 1997: 16f.; Winograd 1979; Milner 1987. On the related development of computer science see Feigenbaum 1996. On Fourth Generation Languages, reusable code, object-oriented programming and the related 'programming

without programmers' movement, see Schach 2002/1990: 440–3; Winograd 1995a; Martin 1982. On new social theories of computer use see Lyman and Wakeford 1999.

17. See Winograd 1997 on 'interaction design'; Bradley on the mismatch between criticism and text-analytic tools, discussed in Chapter 5.4.10.
18. Note the particular example of the development in hypertext systems from monolithic design to so-called 'open hypertext', for which see Wiil, Nürnberg and Leggett 1999.
19. Brunner 1993 and references in n. 40, p. 31; Berkowitz 1993 esp. n.3, p. 53.
20. For the relationship between 'object-orientated' design and the library model of aggregated sources separated from any particular uses of them, see Bradley 2004b.
21. See esp. Deegan and Tanner 2002; Hawkins and Battin 1998; Arms 2000. Note also *LC21: a Digital Strategy for the Library of Congress* (2000); publications of the Council on Library and Information Resources (CLIR), www.clir.org. The standard journals, listed in the headnote to the Bibliography, are *D-Lib, First Monday, CACM, JoD* and *Ariadne;* see also *Representations* 42 (Spring 1993). Publications in library and information science, such as the *Annual Review of Information Science and Technology* and the *Journal of the American Society for Information Science*, are obviously relevant. For an historical overview of computing in libraries see Rayward 2002.
22. The idea is found in numerous versions, including those of Nicholas of Cusa (ca. 1400–64) and Blaise Pascal (1623–62); here I quote from the French theologian and poet Alain de Lille (Alanus de Insulis, 1128–1202); see Alverny 1965: 297.
23. Chartier 1993: 38; see also Deegan and Tanner 2002: 58. For the history of ancient libraries see Casson 2001.
24. For the early history of digital library research in information retrieval see Deegan and Tanner 2002: 22–5; Fox, Akscyn, Furuta and Leggett 1995. For the several things called 'the Semantic Web', see Marshall and Shipman 2003.
25. See e.g Brockman, Neumann, Palmer and Tidline 2001; Kling 1999; Suchman 1995; Hearst 1996 and Hearst, Kopec and Brotsky 1996; Paepcke 1996.
26. Marshall, Golivchinsky and Price 2001.
27. See Fox and Marchionini 2001. *Perseus* is explicitly a digital library in this sense (Crane *et al.* 2001), though not the creature of a conventional library.
28. Many if not most of the CD products we now have are historically conservative in this sense, e.g. the *OED on CD-ROM*, the *CETEDOC Library of Christian Latin Texts* or *The Wife of Bath's Prologue on CD-ROM*: self-contained entities that marry source material to the means for its analysis.
29. By sequential integrity I mean the degree to which a predetermined, intended sequence of access imposes itself on the person consulting the source. Compare scroll and codex (for which see Diringer 1953: 13–52) to Website.
30. I am following Deegan and Tanner's basic typology (2002: 65f.).
31. See esp. Paepcke *et al.* 1998; the following note for discussions of kinds of interoperability. Among the many discussions of problems, see Doerr, Hunter and Lagoze 2003 on a 'core ontology'; Renear 1997 for the 'theoretically

deep' issue of document structure; the Stanford Digital Libraries Group, www-diglib.stanford.edu, for an 'abstraction layer' allowing users and diverse materials to interact (1995). Crane 1998, Crane *et al.* 2001 and Rydberg-Cox *et al.* 2000 discuss the problem from the perspective of a single, integrated set of diverse resources; Smith *et al.* 2003 describe *DSpace*, a dynamic digital repository for the wide range of materials produced within a single university.

32. See e.g. Lynch and Garcia-Molina 1995; Arms *et al.* 2002, who discuss schemes that can be implemented.

33. Lynch and Garcia-Molina 1995; see also Piez 2002.

34. Paepcke *et al.* 1998: 34. For the problem in the history of written commentary see Most 1999.

35. As battle-cry this is usually attributed to Stewart Brand; Clarke 2001 traces its lineage tellingly to John 8:32 – and note the crucial differences. See also Duguid 1996: 65, Clarke 1999.

36. Deegan and Tanner 2002: 112, who provide the best overall summary of the research (112ff.); see also Lagoze and Payette 2000; Gill, Gilliland-Swetland and Baca 1998.

37. Wendler, quoted by Deegan and Tanner 2002: 112–13.

38. Baker 1998. The problem also shows up in Renear 2001, in his turn to speech-act theory.

39. Brin and Page 1998; note also the method of association implemented by amazon.com. For a survey of retrieval mechanisms for the Web see Kobayashi and Takeda 2001.

40. Thompson 1979: 43–6, discussed in McCarty 1992: 208; see also note 45, below.

41. An obvious weakness is the inability to discriminate among kinds of popularity, which is a problem for subjects that cannot be characterized by relatively specific terms. A less obvious weakness is its preference for sites to which many link because they are part of an institutional infrastructure. See, however, Google Scholar, scholar.google.com/.

42. He continues: '[T]he comment attached to the fragment one is reading will become more and more prominent, because *that* is how text is going to be experienced and because it's *easy* to link text to commentary' (e-mail 5/6/01).

43. See Most, ed. 1999. I think it is both invalid and unwise to consider only 'serious' commentaries; I am also very cautious to label any instance of the variety we find as meaningless.

44. 1960/1944: vi; see also Gibson 2002.

45. Wu, de Kort and De Bra 2001; McCarty 2001b, III.C.2 'Adaptive and dynamic hypermedia'; De Bra, Brusilovsky and Houben 1999. Note also the regular sessions on the topic at the ACM Hypertext conferences, www.sigweb.org.

46. Fowler 1999: 437.

47. Personal e-mail, 31/1/04.

48. A 'variorum edition' may, as in the case of the Donne, include a variorum commentary, but not necessarily, e.g. the *The Poems of Emily Dickinson, Variorum Edition* (1998). Note also the in-progress Electronic Variorum Edition of *Don Quixote*, for which see www.csdl.tamu.edu/cervantes/V2/CPI/variorum/index_new.htm.

49. See the Princeton Dante Project, etcweb.princeton.edu/dante; Hollander 1989; Hollander 1993: 235f.
50. Yeandle 2002, reviewed by McCarty 2005 (forthcoming), with references.
51. On the 'blog' (or 'web-log') see Walker 2005 (forthcoming); Serfaty 2004; Keren 2004; Miller and Shepherd 2004; Nilsson 2004; Spangenberg 2002; Mortensen and Walker 2002. On the related rhetorics of hypertext, see McCarty 2001b: B.2.
52. For technical specifications and standards, see McCarty 2001b: II.A, esp. DeRose 1989. The superior sophistication of several early systems is a commonplace; see DeRose and Van Dam 1999, Van Dam 1988.
53. Goldhill 1999: 397; see 393–409 for an extensive unravelling of another case; Gibson 2002 for discussion and a typology.
54. Dodds cites the first reference given by L.S.[9], to Parmenides, so we may conclude he is not selecting any particular references for attention.
55. See McCarty 2001b, IV.B., and more recently esp. Miles 2001; Saïd and Evrard 2001. See also Shields 2000 and Kaplan 2000 and the section below.
56. Miles 2001; Tosca 1999. For the connection to speech-act theory and pragmatics see Tosca 2000.
57. The best work so far is Nunberg, ed. 1996; as the collected essays suggest, recent work in the history of the book overlaps. See also Brown and Duguid 2000; Hawkins and Battin 1998; and the sources in note 21.
58. Multiple tables of contents for a single pool of online articles is now a commonplace; indeed the idea is a natural consequence of hypertext. A more complex implementation would be required in a DIY scheme but could be solved with no great technical effort.
59. See Carter 1997; the other references in McCarty 2001b, III.B.2. The argument that sequences of logical or structural entitles in hypertextual documents are less rigidly determined than those in a codex is a subtler and more difficult one to make that would appear. I assume it here but argue the essence of the case below.
60. 'If the last 150 years of social thought has taught us anything,' Steve Fuller notes, 'it is that our understanding of normality is more a product of historical provincialism than any universal intuitions' (2000: 188). This applies to the future with particular force.
61. See the discussion in Capurro and Hjørland 2002, section 3, and *passim*; Machlup and Mansfield 1983; Denning 1995; Floridi 2004. See also Guillory 2004.
62. Shannon 1948; Shannon and Weaver 1949; Mahoney 1990a: 537–40.
63. Nunberg 1996: 116f. (my emphasis); cf. *OED* s.v. 'noble' a, 7b.
64. Ovid, *Met* 15.165f.: ... *errat et illinc / huc venit, hinc illuc, et quoslibet occupat artus.*
65. See Nunberg, ed. 1996; Zeitlyn, David and Bex 1999; Brown and Duguid 2000. For visualization see the discussion of VR in Chapter 1.3.5.
66. The *Orlando Project*, www.ualberta.ca/ORLANDO, has notably made the composition of a literary history coincide with the tagging of it. The publications of this project are germane to the issue raised here; see esp. Grundy *et al.* 2000; Brown and Clements 1998. Similarly *Perseus* is focusing on 'ways in which documents can be designed from the start to interact with other objects in the digital library' (Crane *et al.* 2001).

67. See, for example, the *Stellenbibliographie* (Yeandle 1998); my own *Analytical Onomasticon*, www.kcl.ac.uk/humanities/cch/wlm/analyticalonomasticon/.
68. Boyarin 1999; Goldhill 1999.
69. Bush 1967: 92, quoted in the Introduction.

3   Discipline

1. See Fields and Wright 2000; Suchman *et al.* 1999 and Suchman 1995; Kling 1999; Lyman and Wakeford 1999; Nardi 1997; Landauer 1997; Winograd 1995a; Denning and Dargan 1994; Denning 1994; Medina-Mora, Winograd, Flores and Flores 1992; Norman 1986. For the application to market-research see Bell 2001. For the broad background and theoretical questions see Edwards 1995; Winograd and Flores 1986; numerous papers by Peter Wegner and colleagues, of which the most accessible is Wegner 1997. For ethnography and science studies see Knorr Cetina 1995: 141.
2. Geertz 2000/1983: 22. For the same in computer science, but with negative results, see Smith 1998/1996: 32–42.
3. Frye 1991: 5; see also 1957: 3–29.
4. See note 16 below on the origins of this figure; a previous version was published in McCarty 2003.
5. The dependency would seem to be on the basis of the type of data and a very broadly and openly defined set of basic operations largely independent of topic, historical period or theoretical approach; this is represented in Figure 3.1. See Chapter 5 for a further discussion of the primitives.
6. See Chapter 5.4 and the argument of Chapter 1.
7. Many of the insights of this section are Short's, based on the author's interview with him on 25/3/04. The more recent experience concerns projects centred at King's College London for which he has been technical director. These are as follows: the *Clergy of the Church of England Database* (CCED), the *Corpus of Romanesque Sculpture in Britain and Ireland* (CRSBI), the *Corpus Vitrearum Medii Aevi Digitisation Project* (CVMA), the *Prosopography of Anglo-Saxon England* (PASE), *Relics and Selves: Iconographies of the National in Argentina, Brazil and Chile, 1880–1890* and others, all listed at www.kcl.ac.uk/humanities/cch/projects.html.
8. This was the case in the *Clergy of the Church of England Database* project, which dispatched numerous lightly-trained researchers to archives across the country.
9. Pelteret and Burghart 2002.
10. E.g. Iconclass, www.iconclass.nl; the Getty Art and Architecture Thesaurus, www.getty.edu/research/conducting_research/vocabularies/aat/; the Princeon Index of Christian Art, ica.princeton.edu.
11. Chapter 1.3.2; Smith 1998/1996: 42–9.
12. See the discussion of VR in Chapter 1.3.5.
13. Arnheim 1969; Tufte 1990; Kirschenbaum 2002.
14. Wulf 2000; Vincenti 1990; Chapter 1.4.7.
15. The term is Harold Short's, with apologies to the anonymous fourteenth-century author of the collection of mystical treatises known as *The Cloud of Unknowing*.

16. To my knowledge first explicit recognition of this kind was made by the author and Harold Short at the 'Roadmap' meeting convened by Antonio Zampolli at Pisa, April 2001, for which the map shown as Figure 3.1 was first developed; see www.allc.org/reports/map/ for reports on this meeting.
17. Lévi-Strauss 1963: 16. On the convergence of history and anthropology see also Comaroff and Comaroff 1992: 3–48; note Berger's inclusion of sociology as occasioning '"culture shock" minus geographical displacement' (1991/1963: 35; see 32–6).
18. Williams 2001: 11–12, quoted in Chapter 1.3.2.
19. On the changing nature of truth in the natural sciences, see Piaget 1970/1968: 1–19, which charts the path from the fact of knowledge-change into the psychology of coming to know; on Kuhn's debt to Piaget, see Kuhn 1977: 21–3.
20. Note, for example, Edward B. Taylor, *Primitive Culture* (1871); and most prominently Sir James George Frazer's *The Golden Bough: a Study in Magic and Religion* (1890–1936) and his massively commented edition of Pausanias' *Description of Greece* (1898).
21. Sociological descriptions of the academic cultural landscape such as Becher and Trowler 2001/1989 are insufficient for my purposes because they never seriously question the figures of thought (such as those of Becher's and Trowler's title) within which their sociology of knowledge operates.
22. Shumway and Messer-Davidow 1991: 201, in a special issue of *Poetics Today* devoted to disciplinarity; they refer to Foucault 1972/1969: 224. See Collini 1998: xliii–lv.
23. The irony of the transposition of this image in Lull's treatise to the cover of Sowa 2000 should not be lost on us.
24. Shumway and Messer-Davidow 1991: 208–9; Burke 2000: 86.
25. 1991: 5. See my discussion of the 'residue' and the 'problem space' in Chapter 1.4.1.
26. On behaviourism as originally an 'as if' assumption and the successes that followed, see Pearson 1972: 99; on the research significance of what it excluded and the parallel with AI, Taylor 1985: 1.
27. Cf. Klein's more detailed taxonomy, cited by Shumway and Messer-Davidow 1991: 213.
28. Geertz 2000/1983: 19–35; Yu 1997: 28f.
29. Galison 2004; Foucault 1980: 126–8, summarized by Chandler 2004: 357f. as a history of disciplinarity.
30. Galison 1997, esp. chapter 9 but also chapter 1 and sections 3.11, 6.7, 6.11, 8.1, 8.5, 8.7.
31. See the discussion of formality in Chapter 4.3 and following.
32. 2000/1983: 22, 157f.; also Crombie 1994: 11.
33. The phrase 'social physics' is still in active use; see section 6.4.
34. Darnton 1985/1984: 5; cf. Geertz 2000/1983: 157.
35. For this account I rely on Gadamer 1998/1983.
36. Cf. Caton 2003; the rejoinder in Renear 2004a and Renear 2004b.
37. Weisstein; cf. Hilbert's definition in Ewald 1996: 1107f.
38. Kuhn 1977: 179 and the entirety of 'The Function of Measurement in Modern Physical Science', 178–224.

39. Heisenberg 1971/1969: 63. Gerald Holton notes from conversation with Heisenberg that, 'While the theory determines what can be observed, the uncertainty principle showed him that a theory also determines what cannot be observed.' Holton comments that, 'Einstein, whose development away from positivistic instrumentalism to a rational realism had escaped Heisenberg's notice, went on to explain at length how complicated any observation is in general, how it involves assumptions about phenomena that in turn are based on theories' (2000).
40. Traub 1981: 353; see also Hartmanis 1995: 12, and Chapter 4, below.
41. See, for example, Simon 1996/1969: 111–14; Schön 1983; Tomayko 2002. Essentially the problem is for fields or aspects of fields in which tacit knowing is central; see Chapter 1 for a detailed discussion.
42. Piaget 1970/1968; Karmiloff-Smith and Inhelder 1974: 209; Inhelder, Sinclair and Bovet 1974.
43. Galison 1997: 544; cf. Hacking 1983: 171.
44. Hacking 1983: 130 (original order of the quoted segments is reversed).
45. Wunsch 1995. The latter is attributed without source to Bateson by James Funaro, www.icase.edu/workshops/hress01/presentations/funaro.pdf and by Nardi 1997: 363.
46. For the implicit sexism in disciplinary metaphors of hard vs. soft, see Melnick 1999; Keller 1996/1985 and 1992; Spender 1998/1980. Cf. Becher and Trowler 2001: 36.
47. Ginzburg 1989: 112. The term 'emotional' requires comment about its cognitive function, for which see Damasio 1994.
48. See Franck 2002: 1; Berger 1992: 12; Glaser and Strauss 1967: 10f. See also Loftus 1991; Stehr 1996; Boron 1999.
49. Giddens 1986/1982: 10f.; Hacking 1990: 35–46.
50. 1993/1973: 3–30; see the recent reflections on 'The State of the Art' (2000: 89–142).
51. Crombie 1994: 89; Santayana, *Reason in Common Sense* (1905: 284).
52. Ginzburg 1989/1986: 103; cf. Shepard 1996.
53. Fuller 1997: 247; Hacking 1999: 6f.
54. Fish 2004: 377, quoting Gilman 2004: 384.
55. Bronowski 1978: 86; likewise in Gödel's spectrum of world-views (1995/ca. 1961: 375).
56. More recent philosophy of science complicates the picture with a plurality of fenced-off areas, as noted above, but in the broad strokes of my depiction the process remains the same.
57. trans. William Ogle. I am indebted to Dr Hartmut Krech (Bremen) for pointing me to this passage.

4   Computer science

1. *Udana* ('Exclamations') is the third book of the *Khuddaka Nikaya*, from the Pali Buddhist canon; see www.accesstoinsight.org/canon/sutta/khuddaka/udana/ud6-04.html. See also Case 2004 and cf. John Godfrey Saxe (1816–87), 'The Blind Men and the Elephant'.
2. A revision of Ide 2001; cf. the three-level structure in Orlandi *et al.* 1999: 2.3.2, which maps easily on to Ide's. See section 7, below.

3. Wulf 2000; cf. Thaller's characterization in Orlandi 2002: 55.
4. Mahoney 1990b: 327; Essinger 2004; Campbell-Kelly and Aspray 1996: 29–52 and 9–10; Mindell 2002.
5. Fant 1993; cf. Mahoney 2002: 38. For Wegner's work, see below; for Smith's see esp. 1998/1996 and 2002, and note also Naur 1995.
6. For historical accounts see Campbell-Kelly and Aspray 1996 and Mahoney 1998; Ceruzzi 1998 and Mahoney 2000a; Edwards 1995; Mahoney 2002.
7. For mathematics see, however, Mahoney 1997, and for theoretical computer science Mahoney 2002: 28–32.
8. For von Neumann's contributions see Aspray 1990; Ulam 1980; Mahoney 2002; for Shannon see Mahoney 1997: 620.
9. Campbell-Kelly and Russ 1994: 702; Davis 2000: 21–40. See Davis' account of the work intervening between Boole and Hilbert in Chapters 3 and 4.
10. Reid 1996; en.wikipedia.org/David_Hilbert.
11. For the intellectual style that Hilbert exemplifies, see Crombie 1994: 93–182; Hacking 1985.
12. Hilbert 1902 gives the publishing history in a note on page 407; for a discussion of the lecture and subsequent mathematics see Feferman 1998.
13. See von Neumann's comments quoted by Mahoney 1997: 662.
14. Note that parallel effort of Russell's and Whitehead's *Principia Mathematica* (1910–13), employing formal logic, did not touch Hilbert's second problem.
15. Davis 2000: 101f.; Feferman 1999: 103.
16. Davis 2000: 118; see also Feferman 1998: 6, 14–16.
17. Davis 2000: 122–4 and notes; Feferman 1998: 6, 14–16; Boyer 1989/1968: 679-89; Detlefsen 1986.
18. Hilbert 1902: 421; see Feferman 1998: 4–5.
19. Campbell-Kelly and Russ 1994: 703. A fuller account is given by Davis 2000: 146f. and note 8.
20. Gandy 1995/1994; Feynman 1999/1996: 54.
21. Davis himself notes that Turing was not only 'interested in the possibility of actually constructing a machine on [the] lines' of his own design, as his teacher Max Newman wrote, but actually built one (2000: 169–70).
22. 1997: 620, corrected according to the online version of July 2004; cf. Feynman 1999/1996: 66–75.
23. 'The Foundations of Mathematics' (1927: 475), quoted by Detlefsen 1986: x. Contrast the 'intuitionism' of L. E. J. Brouwer (1881–1966), who denied any prior authority in logic or *a priori* axioms; see Davis 2000: 95.
24. Ewald 1996: 1106f.
25. 1995/ca. 1961: 374–87. This lecture was unpublished until recently, hence the delayed attention to Gödel's phenomenology and philosophical reflections on Hilbert's programme. See Dagfin Føllesdal's introduction to the lecture (1995/ca. 1961: 364–73), Føllesdal 1995; Tieszen 1992; van Atten and Kennedy 2003.
26. See Tieszen 1992: 183 on Husserl's mathematical training and concerns. For Gödel's use of Husserl see esp. Føllesdal 1995.
27. van Atten and Kennedy 2003: 450. Gödel's understanding of Husserl, Føllesdal argues, is 'extraordinary, placing him among the foremost interpreters of Husserl' (1995: 428).

28. See Føllesdal's summary (Gödel 1995/ca. 1961: 438–40).
29. Tieszen 1992: 180; van Atten and Kennedy 2003: 462.
30. David Bergami, *Mathematics* (Time Life Books, 1980), quoted by van Atten and Kennedy 2003: 460.
31. This is where computer science meets the social sciences. See Winch 1990/1958: Chapters 1 and 2; Fay and Moon 1994/1977; Winograd 1991.
32. Rabin and Scott 1959: 114, quoted in Mahoney 1997: 621.
33. See his numerous papers on the limitations of the Turing Machine model, the latest of which are available from www.cs.brown.edu/people/pw/home.html.
34. Colburn, for example, draws a parallel with the mind/body problem (2000: 198–209).
35. Based on Figure 1 in Smith 1995: 462.
36. Denning 1985: 16, ref. to Arden 1980; 2004; Knuth 1974.
37. Feynman 1999/1996: xiii; cf. Forsythe 1968: 454.
38. Naur, Randell and Buxton 1976, quoted in Mahoney 1990b: 326.
39. Tomayko 2002: 72f; Petroski 1992; Vincenti 1990: 49f.
40. Wigner 1960 and Hamming 1980; Ernest 1998; Kline 1990/1972: 230; Mahoney 2002: 27, 1997: 618 and Campbell-Kelly and Russ 1994: 705f. On experimental mathematics, see also Pagels 1988: 44 and the journal *Experimental Mathematics*, www.expmath.org.
41. Michael Mahoney, personal e-mail, 9/9/04.
42. Mahoney 2002: 27 and *passim*; see also Feynman 1999/1996: 90, Smith 1998/1996, Fant 1993.
43. This thesis, from the proofs of Alonzo Church and Alan Turing, has several formulations; see Copeland 2002.
44. 1993: 21, my emphasis; cf. Unsworth 2001.
45. Hartmanis in Traub 1981: 354, referring to Heisenberg 1971/1969: 63 (with slight change of wording); unfortunately Hartmanis' highly abbreviated version partially obscures Einstein's argument. See Chapter 3.6.3 for Gerald Holton's commentary on this remark.
46. E-mail, 15/8/01; the note is transcribed in McCarty 2001a: 182, n. 44.
47. For the metaphor see Crombie 1994: 719 n. 1; Foucault 1972/1966: 35.
48. Tichy 1998: 36, *contra* Hartmanis 1995: 13, who argues for 'a dramatic demonstration rather than a dramatic experiment'.
49. See Chapter 3.6.3.
50. Nardi 1997: 362; cf. Smith's conclusion that software manifests 'the full-fledged social construction and development of intentional artifacts' (2002: [20], emphasis removed).
51. See especially Prown 1988 and the discussion of experiment in Chapter 1.3.6; see also McCarty 2004a: 167–9.
52. Chapter 1.4.3, quoting Frye 1957: 4.
53. Tichy 1998: 32; Edwards 1998: 94. See also Hartmanis in Traub 1981: 354.
54. Hartmanis in Traub 1981: 353. See also Forsythe 1968; Denning 1998a.
55. See e.g. Hartmanis 1995: 14; Fant 1993: 4.
56. Oakman 1987: 227, 229, 232; see also 1984/1980.
57. *Beyond Productivity* (Mitchell, Inouye and Blumenthal 2003) is an outcome of the Roundtable Meeting in Washington DC , 28 March 1997, for which see *Computing and the Humanities: Summary of a Roundtable Meeting* 1998 (hereafter CHSRM).

58. In the US the Commission on Cyberinfrastructure for the Humanities and Social Sciences, www.acls.org/cyberinfrastructure/cyber.htm, in progress at the time of writing, has been preceded by the Roundtable Meeting, mentioned above; a Computer Science and the Humanities initiative and a Building Blocks Workshop organized by the National Initiative for a Networked Cultural Heritage (NINCH), www.ninch.org; a conference, 'Transforming Disciplines: Computer Science and the Humanities', www.carnegie.rice.edu/ (Janet Murray's paper remains unpublished, but see Murray 2003.). See also Numerico and Vespignani 2003; Fiormonte 2003; Roncaglia 2002; Aarseth 1997.
59. Cf. the genial expression of this interest in Wulf 2000; note the development from technique (how) to object (what), hence the dependency on 'domain experts', charted in Feigenbaum 1996.
60. Mitchell, Inouye and Blumenthal 2003: 99. For transdisciplinarity see Somerville and Rapport 2003.
61. The best work along such lines has been done under the rubric of digital library research, discussed in Chapter 2; see also the 1995 conference 'Reconnecting Science and Humanities in Digital Libraries', www.uky.edu/~kiernan/DL/symp.html.
62. Note, for example, the Digital Atheneum Project, www.digitalatheneum.org; the Institute for Advanced Technology in the Humanities, www.iath.virginia.edu; the Centre for the Study of Ancient Documents, www.csad.ox.ac.uk.
63. Ide 2001: 13; for Chomsky's place in theoretical computer science, see Mahoney 2002: 28–32.
64. Quoted and discussed by Unsworth 2002: 72.
65. In addition to the publications cited below, see the following: Gardin 1987, 1991; for Orlandi those listed at rmcisadu.let.uniroma1.it/~orlandi/pubinf.html and 2003. For Thaller see the items listed at www.hki.uni-koeln.de/people/thaller/mt.html and 2004.
66. www.hki.uni-koeln.de/.
67. Dijkstra 1972: 866; I have quoted from EWD340.
68. See Simon 1996/1969: 6ff. and 183–216. As he points out, normal operating conditions are assumed; the more robust the system, the more inclusive these conditions will be.
69. On the layered design of computing systems see Winograd and Flores 1986; Denning 1994; Chapter 2.4.
70. Michael Mahoney, personal e-mail, 9/9/04.
71. Steve Russ, personal e-mail, 3/6/04.

5   Agenda

1. www.marxists.org/archive/lenin/works/1901/witbd/.
2. A prominent exception is analytical philosophy, in which practitioners conventionally use the term as an organizing principle of their work. But the idea of a 'philosophical problem' is not without difficulty, and its influence not without objections; see Hacking 2002: 37f., 59–61.
3. Manfred Thaller makes this point, for which see Chapter 4.8.
4. E.g. the World Wide Web Consortium (W3C), w3c.org; the Special Interest Group on Hypertext, Hypermedia and the Web, www.sigweb.org, and the

Association for Computing Machinery (ACM), www.acm.org, of which it is a part; the Association for Computational Linguistics, www.aclweb.org; the European Language Resources Association (ELRA), www.elra.info; the Society for Imaging Science and Technology, www.imaging.org.

5. See *D-Lib Magazine*, www.dlib.org, and esp. its listing of projects, agencies and activities.

6. See the National Initiative for a Networked Cultural Heritage (NINCH), www.ninch.org; the J. Paul Getty Trust, www.getty.edu.

7. www.tei-c.org.

8. www.ahds.ac.uk.

9. www.acls.org/cyberinfrastructure/cyber.htm; www.ahrb.ac.uk/ict.

10. www.ilc.cnr.it.

11. For some ideas towards that history, see McCarty 1993.

12. For some exceptions and a discussion, see *Humanist* 18.334, 338, 345, 348, 355–6, 359, 361, at www.kcl.ac.uk/humanities/cch/humanist/, Volume 18.

13. See Edwards 1995 on the billiard-ball imagery, which 'nicely encapsulates what is probably the most common view of the relationship between information technology and the social world' (257).

14. Susan Hockey has recently begun asking the questions that need to be asked (2004: 3).

15. Note e.g. Bronowski 1965/1956 and 1978; Einstein 1982/1954; Heisenberg 1971/1969 and 1990/1958; Oppenheimer 1953; Whitehead 1925; Ziman 1991/1978 and 2000. See also the journals *Public Understanding of Science* and *Interdisciplinary Science Reviews*. For the remainder see *psi-com: a Gateway to Public Engagement with Science*, psi-com.ac.uk.

16. www.chass.utoronto.ca/epc/chwp/.

17. For the history of this expression, see Merton 1993; Crombie 1994: 25, esp. n. 37.

18. See Hockey 2000, esp. Chapters 4–9.

19. The TUSTEP site (www.tustep.de directs one to www.uni-tuebingen.de/zdv/zrlinfo/tustep-des.html), lists the reference works prepared by its means; see also Bradley 2004a: 519–21; Ott 2000; Hockey 2000: 131f. Compare the 'UNIX philosophy' of the toolbox, for which see Raymond 2004, section 1.6.

20. See Burrows 2004, Craig 2004 and their references.

21. Unsworth 2000; cf. Unsworth 2003b.

22. Bradley cites a number of prosopographical projects in which the traditional biographical digest is replaced by collations of the relevant primary data (2003: 205).

23. For Heidegger see Dreyfus 1991: 60, quoted in Chapter 1.4.2. For the philosophical modularists see Hacking 2004: 15; for linguistics see Wierzbicka 1996.

24. Chandler 2004: 360, quoted in Chapter 3.4.

25. Malouf 1998: 8; see also Winton 1998/1993: 36 and McCarty 2005 (submitted).

26. EWD898-2, in the *E. W. Dijkstra Archive*, www.cs.utexas.edu/users/EWD/.

27. EWD340, published as Dijkstra 1972: 866.

28. Quintilian, *Declamatio maior* IV.14.

29. Smith 1995 discusses some of these; more importantly, he connects the hybris of computational perfection with the problem of modelling.

Bibliography

Abbreviations are used for *ACH* (*Association for Computers and the Humanities*); *ALLC* (*Association for Literary and Linguistic Computing*); *ACLS* (*American Council of Learned Societies*); *CACM* (*Communications of the Association for Computing Machinery*); *CHum* (*Computers and the Humanities*); *CI* (*Critical Inquiry*); *D-Lib* (*D-Lib Magazine*); *JACM* (*Journal of the Association for Computing Machinery*); *JoDI* (*Journal of Digital Information*); *JEP* (*Journal of Electronic Publishing*); *LLC* (*Literary and Linguistic Computing*); *PMLA* (*Publications of the Modern Language Association of America*). URLs are omitted for the following open resources: ACLS Occasional Papers series, www.acls.org/aclspubs.htm; *Ariadne*, www.ariadne.ac.uk; *Bryn Mawr Classical Review*, ccat.sas.upenn.edu/bmcr/; *Dictionary of the Philosophy of Mind*, artsci.wustl.edu/~philos/MindDict/; *D-Lib*, www.dlib.org; *First Monday*, www.firstmonday.org; *Jahrbuch für Computerphilologie*, computerphilologie.uni-muenchen.de/ejournal.html; *JoDI*, jodi.ecs.soton.ac.uk; *JEP*, www.press.umich.edu/jep/; *Stanford Encyclopedia of Philosophy*, plato.stanford.edu; *Ubiquity*, www.acm.org/ubiquity/. Items originating from the *Association for Computing Machinery* (ACM) will be found in its Digital Library, www.acm.org/dl/. The *Routledge Encyclopedia of Philosophy* has been consulted in its online form, www.rep.routledge.com.

Aarseth, Espen. 1997. 'The Field of Humanistic Informatics and its Relation to the Humanities'. *Human IT* 4. www.hf.uib.no/hi/espen/HI.html.

ACECSE. *Academic Careers for Experimental Computer Scientists and Engineers*. 1994. National Research Council. Washington DC: National Academies Press. www.nap.edu/html/acesc/.

Achinstein, Peter. 1968. *Concepts of Science: a Philosophical Analysis*. Baltimore MD: Johns Hopkins University Press.

Achterhuis, Hans, ed. 2001/1997. *American Philosophy of Technology: the Empirical Turn*. Trans. Robert P. Crease. Indiana Series in the Philosophy of Technology. Bloomington IN: Indiana University Press.

Adamo, Giovanni. 1994. *Bibliografia di informatica umanistica*. Informatica e discipline umanistiche 5. Roma: Bulzoni Editore.

Agre, Philip E. 1997. *Computation and Human Experience*. Cambridge: Cambridge University Press.

———— 2003. 'Writing and Representation'. In *Narrative Intelligence*. Ed. Michael Mateas and Phoebe Sengers. 281–303. Advances in Consciousness Research 46. Amsterdam: John Benjamins. polaris.gseis.ucla.edu/pagre/ni.html.

Aliseda-LLera, Atocha. 1997. 'Seeking Explanations: Abduction in Logic, Philosophy of Science and Artificial Intelligence'. PhD dissertation, Stanford University. ILLC Dissertation Series 1997-4. Amsterdam: Institute for Logic, Language, and Computation, University of Amsterdam. www.illc.uva.nl/Publications/reportlist.php?Year=1997.

Allchin, Douglas. 2001. 'Error Types'. *Perspectives on Science* 9.1: 38–58.

Alverny, Marie Thérèse d'. 1965. *Alain de Lille. Textes inédits.* Études de philosophie médiévale 52. Paris: Librarie Philosophique J. Vrin.

Arden, Bruce W., ed. 1980. *What Can Be Automated? The Computer Science and Engineering Research Study (COSERS).* Computer Science 3. Cambridge MA: MIT Press.

Arms, William Y. 2000. *Digital Libraries.* Digital Libraries and Electronic Publishing. Cambridge MA: MIT Press.

_____ Diane Hillman, Carl Lagoze, Dean Krafft, Richard Marisa, John Saylor, Carol Terrizzi and Herbert Van de Sompel. 2002. 'A Spectrum of Interoperability: the Site for Science Prototype for the NSDL'. *D-Lib* 8.1.

Arnheim, Rudolf. 1969. *Visual Thinking.* Berkeley: University of California Press.

Aspray, William. 1990. *John von Neumann and the Origins of Modern Computing.* Cambridge MA: MIT Press.

Bachelard, Gaston. 1964/1938. *The Psychoanalysis of Fire.* Trans. Alan M. Ross. Boston MA: Beacon Press.

Bagg, Robert, trans. 1978. *The Bakkhai by Euripides.* Amherst: University of Massachusetts Press.

Bailer-Jones, Daniela M. 2002. 'Models, Metaphors and Analogies'. In *The Blackwell Guide to the Philosophy of Science.* Ed. Peter Machamer and Michael Silberstein. 108–27. Oxford: Blackwell.

_____ and Coryn A. L. Bailer-Jones. 2002. 'Modeling Data: Analogies in Neural Networks, Simulated Annealing and Genetic Algorithms'. In Magnani and Nersessian 2002: 147–65.

Baker, Thomas. 1998. 'Languages for Dublin Core'. *D-Lib* 4.12.

Barbiero, Daniel. 2004. ' Knowledge, Tacit'. In *Dictionary of Philosophy of Mind.*

Barr, Avron and Edward A. Feigenbaum. 1981. 'Representation of Knowledge'. In *The Handbook of Artificial Intelligence*, vol. 1. 142–222. Ed. Avron Barr and Edward A. Feigenbaum. 4 vols. London: Pitman.

Bateson, Gregory. 2000/1972. *Steps to an Ecology of Mind.* Rev. edn. Chicago: University of Chicago Press.

_____ 2002/1979. *Mind and Nature: a Necessary Unity.* Advances in Systems Theory, Complexity, and the Human Sciences. Cresskill NJ: Hampton Press.

Beacham, Richard and Hugh Denard. 2003. 'The Pompey Project: Digital Research and Virtual Reconstruction of Rome's First Theatre'. *CHum* 37.1: 129–39.

Becher, Tony and Paul Trowler. 2001/1989. *Academic Tribes and Territories: Intellectual Enquiry and the Culture of Disciplines.* 2nd edn. Buckingham: Society for Research into Higher Education and the Open University Press.

Bell, Genevieve. 2001. 'Looking Across the Atlantic: Using Ethnographic Methods to Make Sense of Europe'. *Intel Technology Journal* Q3. developer.intel.com/technology/itj/q32001/articles/art_1.htm.

Bender, Thomas. 1997. 'Locality and Worldliness'. In *The Transformation of Humanistic Studies in the Twenty-First Century.* 1–10. ACLS Occasional Paper 40. New York: ACLS.

Berger, Peter L. 1991/1963. *Invitation to Sociology: a Humanistic Perspective.* London: Penguin Books.

_____ 1992. 'Sociology: a Disinvitation?' *Society* 30.1: 12–18.

Bergin, Tim *et al.* 1997. 'The History of Programming: Does Our Present Past Have a Future?' *ACM SIGPLAN Notices* 32.9: 15–37.

Berkowitz, Luci. 1993. 'Ancilla to the *Thesaurus Linguae Graecae*: the TLG Canon'. In Solomon 1993: 34–61.

Beynon, Meurig and Steve Russ. 2004. 'Redressing the past: liberating computing as an experimental science'. Grand Challenges for Computing Research, Newcastle-upon-Tyne, 29–31 March 2004. www.nesc.ac.uk/esi/events/Grand_ Challenges/gcconf04/submissions/26.pdf.

Biagioli, Mario and Peter Galison, eds. 2003. *Scientific Authorship: Credit and Intellectual Property in Science*. London: Routledge.

Black, Max. 1962. *Models and Metaphors: Studies in Language and Philosophy*. Ithaca NY: Cornell University Press.

_____ 1993/1979. 'More About Metaphor'. In *Metaphor and Thought*. Ed. Andrew Ortony. 19–41. 2nd edn. Cambridge: Cambridge University Press.

Bloomfield, Morton W. 1963. 'A Grammatical Approach to Personification Allegory'. *Modern Philology* 60.3: 161–71.

_____ 1980. 'Personification-Metaphors'. *The Chaucer Review* 14.4: 287–97.

Bolter, Jay David. 1993. 'Hypertext and the Classical Commentary'. In Solomon 1993: 157–71.

Bonnett, John. 2004. 'New Technologies, New Formalisms for Historians: the 3D Virtual Buildings Project'. *LLC* 19.3: 273–87.

Borges, Jorge Luis. 1979/1975. 'The Book of Sand'. Trans. Norman Thomas di Giovanni. In *The Book of Sand*. 87–91. London: Penguin.

Borgmann, Albert. 1984. *Technology and the Character of Contemporary Life: a Philosophical Inquiry*. Chicago: University of Chicago Press.

Bornstein, George. 1998. 'Yeats and Textual Reincarnation: "When You Are Old" and "September 1913"'. In Bornstein and Tinkle 1998: 223–48.

_____ and Theresa Tinkle, eds. 1998. *The Iconic Page in Manuscript, Print, and Digital Culture*. Ann Arbor MI: University of Michigan Press.

Boron, Atilio A. 1999. 'A Social Theory for the 21st Century?' *Current Sociology* 47.4: 47–64.

Boyarin, Daniel. 1999. 'The Bartered Word: Midrash and Symbolic Economy'. In Most, ed. 1999: 19–65.

Boyer, Carl B. 1989/1968. *A History of Mathematics*. 2nd edn. New York: John Wiley & Sons.

Bradie, Michael and William Harms. 2004. 'Epistemology, Evolutionary'. In *Stanford Encyclopedia of Philosophy* (Spring 2004 edition).

Bradley, John. 2003. 'Finding a Middle Ground Between "Determinism" and "Aesthetic Indeterminacy": a Model for Text Analysis Tools'. *LLC* 18.2: 185–207.

_____ 2004a. 'Text Tools'. In Schreibman, Siemens and Unsworth 2004: 505–22.

_____ 2004b. 'Tools to Augment Scholarly Activity: an Architecture to Support Text Analysis'. In *Augmenting Comprehension: Digital Tools and the History of Ideas. Proceedings of a Conference at Bologna, 22–23 September 2002*. Ed. Dino Buzzetti, Giuliano Pancaldi and Harold Short. 19–47. London: Office for Humanities Communication, King's College London. pigeon.cch.kcl.ac.uk/ docs/papers/bologna/.

Brin, Sergey and Lawrence Page. 1998. 'The Anatomy of a Large-Scale Hypertextual Web Search Engine'. *Computer Networks and ISDN Systems* 30: 107–17. www-db.stanford.edu/pub/papers/google.pdf.

Brockman, William S., Laura Neumann, Carole L. Palmer and Tonyia J. Tidline. 2001. *Scholarly Work in the Humanities and the Evolving Information Environment*. Washington DC: Digital Library Federation, Council on Library and Information Resources.

Bronowski, Jacob. 1965/1956. *Science and Human Values*. 2nd edn. Perennial Library. New York: Harper and Row.

_____ 1978. *The Origins of Knowledge and Imagination*. Mrs Hepsa Ely Silliman Memorial Lectures. New Haven CN: Yale University Press.

Brooks, Rodney A. 1991. 'Intelligence Without Representation'. *Artificial Intelligence* 47: 139–59. www.ai.mit.edu/people/brooks/papers/representation.pdf.

Brown, James Robert. 2000. 'Thought Experiments'. In Newton-Smith: 2000: 528–31.

_____ 2002. 'Thought Experiments'. In *Stanford Encyclopedia of Philosophy* (Summer 2002 edition).

Brown, John Seely and Paul Duguid. 2000. *The Social Life of Information*. Boston MA: Harvard Business School Press.

Brown, Susan and Patricia Clements. 1998. 'Tag Team: Computing, Collaborators, and the History of Women's Writing in the British Isles'. *Computing in the Humanities Working Papers* A.8 and *TEXT Technology* 8.1. www.chass.utoronto.ca/epc/chwp/orlando/.

Brunner, Theodore F. 1993. 'Classics and the Computer: the History of a Relationship'. In Solomon 1993: 10–33.

Burbules, Nicholas C. 1997. 'Rhetorics of the Web: Hyperreading and Critical Literacy'. In *Page to Screen: Taking Literacy Into the Electronic Era*. Ed. Ilana Snyder. London: Routledge.

Burch, Robert. 2001. 'Peirce, Charles Sanders'. In *Stanford Encyclopedia of Philosophy* (Fall 2001 edition).

Burch, Thomas K. 2002. 'Computer Modelling of Theory: Explanation for the 21st Century'. In Franck, ed. 2002: 245–65.

Burke, Peter. 2000. *A Social History of Knowledge from Gutenberg to Diderot*. Vonhoff Lectures, University of Groningen. Cambridge: Polity Press.

Burrows, John. 2004. 'Textual Analysis'. In Schreibman, Siemens and Unsworth 2004: 323–47.

Bush, Vannevar. 1945. 'As We May Think'. *Atlantic Monthly*, July: 101–8. www.ps.uni-sb.de/~duchier/pub/vbush/vbush.shtml.

_____ 1967. 'Memex Revisited'. In *Science is Not Enough*. 75–101. New York: William Morrow and Company.

Camille, Michael. 1992. *Image on the Edge: the Margins of Medieval Art*. Cambridge MA: Harvard University Press.

Campbell, Donald T. 1974. 'Evolutionary Epistemology'. In *The Philosophy of Karl Popper*. Ed. Paul A. Schilpp. Vol. 1. 413–63. The Library of Living Philosophers XIV. 2 vols. LaSalle IL: Open Court.

Campbell-Kelly, Martin and William Aspray. 1996. *Computer: a History of the Information Machine*. New York: Basic Books.

_____ and S. B. Russ. 1994. 'Computing and Computers'. In *Companion Encyclopedia of the History and Philosophy of the Mathematical Sciences*. Vol. 1. 701–7. Ed. I. Grattan-Guiness. 2 vols. London: Routledge.

Capurro, Rafael. 1992. 'Informatics and Hermeneutics'. In *Software Development and Reality Construction*. Ed. Christiane Floyd, Heinz Züllighoven, Reinhard Budde and Reinhard Keil-Slawik. 363–75. Berlin: Springer Verlag.

_____ and Birger Hjørland. 2002. 'The Concept of Information'. *Annual Review of Information Science and Technology* 37: 343–411. http//www.capurro.de/info-concept.html.

Carter, Locke Mitchell. 1997. 'Arguments in Hypertext: Order and Structure in Non-Sequential Essays'. PhD dissertation, University of Texas at Austin 1997. labyrinth.daedalus.com/dissertations/carter.pdf.

Cartwright, Nancy. 1983. *How the Laws of Physics Lie*. Oxford: Clarendon Press.
_____ 1999. *The Dappled World: a Study of the Boundaries of Science*. Cambridge: Cambridge University Press.
Case, Peter. 2004. 'The Blind People and the Elephant'. In *Myths, Stories, and Organizations: Premodern Narratives for our Times*, ed. Yiannis Gabriel. 49–65. Oxford: Oxford University Press.
Casson, Lionel. 2001. *Libraries in the Ancient World*. New Haven CN: Yale University Press.
Castells, Manuel. 2000/1996. *The Rise of the Network Society*. 2nd edn. The Information Age: Economy, Society and Culture 1. Oxford: Blackwell.
Caton, Paul. 2003. 'A Critique of "Theory" in Text Encoding'. Athens, GA: ACH / ALLC Joint Conference.
Cecire, Natalia. 2012. 'When Digital Humanities was in Vogue'. *Journal of Digital Humanities* 1.1: 54–9. http://journalofdigitalhumanities.org/1-1/ (24/2/14).
Ceruzzi, Paul E. 1998. *A History of Modern Computing*. History of Computing. Cambridge MA: MIT Press.
Chandler, James. 2004. 'Critical Disciplinarity'. *CI* 30: 355–60.
Chartier, Roger. 1993. 'Libraries Without Walls'. *Representations* 42: 38–52.
Cheng, P. C.-H. 2004. 'Scientific Discovery, Computational Models of'. In *International Encyclopedia of the Social and Behavioral Sciences*, ed. Neil J. Smelser and Paul B. Baltes. 13731–3. Amsterdam: Elsevier.
Cherry, Colin. 1977. 'The Telephone System: Creator of Mobility and Social Change'. In Pool 1977: 112–26.
Chomsky, Noam. 1957. *Syntactic Structures*. The Hague: Mouton.
Clarke, Roger. 1999. 'Freedom of Information? The Internet as Harbinger of the New Dark Ages'. *First Monday* 4.11.
_____ 2001. '"Information Wants to be Free ..."' ww.anu.edu.au/people/ Roger.Clarke/II/IWtbF.html.
Clear, Tony. 1997. 'The Nature of Cognition and Action'. *Inroads: ACM SIGCSE Bulletin* 29.4: 25–9.
Colburn, Timothy R. 2000. *Philosophy and Computer Science*. Explorations in Philosophy. Armonk NY: M. E. Sharpe.
Collingwood, R. G. 1993/1946. *The Idea of History*. Rev edn. Ed. Jan van der Dussen. Oxford: Oxford University Press.
Collini, Stefan. 1998. 'Introduction'. In Snow 1998/1959: vii–lxxi.
Comaroff, John and Jean Comaroff. 1992. *Ethnography and the Historical Imagination*. Studies in the Ethnographic Imagination. Boulder CO: Westview Press.
Computing and the Humanities: Summary of a Roundtable Meeting. 1998. Computer Science and Telecommunications Board, National Research Council and Coalition for Networked Information and National Initiative for a Networked Cultural Heritage and Two Ravens Institute. ACLS Occasional Paper 41. New York: ACLS.
Computing the Future: a Broader Agenda for Computer Science and Engineering. 1994. National Research Council. Washington DC: National Academies Press. books.nap.edu/html/ctf/
Copeland, B. Jack. 2002. 'The Church-Turing Thesis'. In *Stanford Encyclopedia of Philosophy* (Fall 2002 edition).

Craig, David L., Nancy J. Nersessian and Richard Catrambone. 2002. 'Perceptual Simulation in Analogical Problem Solving'. In Magnani and Nersessian 2002: 167–89.

Craig, Hugh. 2004. 'Stylistic Analysis and Authorship Studies'. In Schreibman, Siemens and Unsworth 2004: 273–88.

Crane, Gregory. 1998. 'The Perseus Project and Beyond: How Building a Digital Library Challenges the Humanities'. *D-Lib* 4.1.

_____ 2002. 'Cultural Heritage Digital Libraries: Needs and Components'. In *Research and Advanced Technology for Digital Libraries. Proceedings of the 6th European Conference on Digital Libraries, ECDL 2002, Rome, Italy, September 16–18*. 626–37. Ed. Maristella Agosti and Costatino Thanos. Berlin: Springer Verlag.

_____ Robert F. Chavez, Anne Mahoney, Thomas L. Milbank, Jeffrey A. Rydberg-Cox, David A. Smith and Clifford E. Wulfman. 2001. 'Drudgery and Deep Thought'. *CACM* 44.5: 35–40. Abbreviated version of www.perseus.tufts. edu/Articles/cacm2000.html.

_____ and Elli Mylonas. 1991. 'Ancient Materials, Modern Media: Shaping the Study of Classics with Hypermedia'. In *Hypermedia and Literary Studies*. Ed. Paul Delaney and George P. Landow. 205–20. Cambridge, MA: MIT Press.

Crombie, A. C. 1994. *Styles of Scientific Thinking in the European Tradition. The History of Argument and Explanation especially in the Mathematical and Biomedical Sciences and Arts*. 3 vols. London: Duckworth.

Culler, Jonathan. 1988. *Framing the Sign: Criticism and its Institutions*. Oxford: Basil Blackwell.

_____ 1997. *Literary Theory: a Very Short Introduction*. Very Short Introductions. Oxford: Oxford University Press.

Dalen-Oskam, Karina van and Joris van Zundert. 2004. 'Modelling Features of Characters: Some Digital Ways to Look at Names in Literary Texts'. *LLC* 19.3: 289–301.

Damasio, Antonio R. 1995. *Descartes' Error: Emotion, Reason and the Human Brain*. London: Picador.

Daniel, Ron, Jr., Carl Lagoze and Sandra D. Payette. 1998. 'A Metadata Architecture for Digital Libraries'. In *IEEE International Forum on Research and Technology Advances in Digital Libraries. ADL'98 Proceedings, April 22–24, 1998, Santa Barbara, California*. 276–88. Piscataway NJ: IEEE Computer Society Press. www.cs.cornell.edu/lagoze/papers/ADL98/dar-adl.html.

Darnton, Robert. 1985/1984. *The Great Cat Massacre and Other Episodes in French Cultural History*. New York: Vintage.

Daston, Lorraine. 2004. 'Whither CI?' *CI* 30.2: 361–4.

Davie, Donald. 1967. *Purity of Diction in English Verse*. London: Routledge & Kegan Paul.

_____ 1981. 'Personification'. *Essays in Criticism* 31.2: 91–104.

Davies, Martin and Tony Stone. 2000. 'Simulation Theory'. In *Routledge Encyclopedia of Philosophy*.

Davis, Martin. 2000. *The Universal Computer: the Road from Leibniz to Turing*. New York: W. W. Norton and Company.

_____ ed. 1993/1965. *The Undecidable: Basic Papers on Undecidable Propositions, Unsolvable Problems and Computable Functions*. Corr. edn. Mineola NY: Dover Publications.

Davis, Randall, Howard Shrobe and Peter Szolovits. 1993. 'What Is a Knowledge Representation?' *AI Magazine* 14.1: 17–33. www.aaai.org/Library/Magazine/Vol14/14–01/vol14-01.html.

De Bra, Paul, Peter Brusilovsky and Geert-Jan Houben. 1999. 'Adaptive Hypermedia: From Systems to Framework'. *ACM Computing Surveys* 31.4es: 1–6.

Debray, Régis. 1996. 'The Book as Symbolic Object'. In Nunberg, ed. 1996: 139–51.

Deegan, Marilyn and Simon Tanner. 2002. *Digital Futures: Strategies for the Information Age*. London: Library Association Publishing.

Del Re, Giuseppe. 2000. 'Models and Analogies in Science'. *Hyle – International Journal for the Philosophy of Chemistry* 6.1: 5–15. www.hyle.org/journal/issues/6/delre.htm.

Delaney, C. F. 2000. 'Knowledge, Tacit'. In *Routledge Encyclopedia of Philosophy*.

Dempsey, Lorcan. 2003. 'Interoperability: recombinant potential'. www.oclc.org/research/presentations/dempsey/imlsdiglibresearch.ppt.

Denifle, Henricus and Æmilio Châtelain, eds. 1889. *Chartularium Universitatis Parisiensis ...* Vol. 1. Paris: Université de Paris.

Dening, Greg. 1996. *Performances*. Chicago: University of Chicago Press.

_____ 1998. *Readings/Writings*. Melbourne: University of Melbourne Press.

Denning, Peter J. 1985. 'The Science of Computing: What is Computer Science?' *American Scientist* 73.1: 16–19.

_____ 1994. 'The Fifteenth Level (Keynote Address)'. In *Proceedings of ACM SIG-METRICS Conference on Measurement & Modeling of Computer Systems*. 1–4. New York: ACM Press. cne.gmu.edu/pjd/PUBS/15level.pdf.

_____ 1995. 'Can There Be a Science of Information?' *ACM Computing Surveys* 27.1: 23–5.

_____ 1998a. 'Computing Science and Software Engineering: Filing for Divorce?' *CACM* 40.8: 128.

_____ 1998b. 'Computing the Profession'. *Educom Review* 33.6: 26–30, 46–59.

_____ 2004. 'The Great Principles of Computing'. *Ubiquity* 4.48.

_____ and Pamela A. Dargan. 1994. 'A Discipline of Software Architecture'. *Interactions* 1.1: 55–65.

DeRose, Steven J. 1989. 'Expanding the Notion of Links'. In *Proceedings of the Second Annual ACM Conference on Hypertext*. 249–57. New York: ACM Press.

_____ and Andries Van Dam. 1999. 'The Lost Books of Hypertext'. *Markup Languages* 1: 7–32.

Descartes, René. 1985/1637. 'Optics'. In *The Philosophical Writings of Descartes*. Trans. John Cottingham, Robert Stoothoff and Dugald Murdoch. Vol. 1. 152–75. 3 vols. Cambridge: Cambridge University Press.

Detlefsen, Michael. 1986. *Hilbert's Program: an Essay on Mathematical Instrumentalism*. Synthese Library 182. Dordrecht: D. Reidel.

Dijkstra, Edsger W. 1972. 'The Humble Programmer'. *CACM* 15.10: 859–66. www.cs.utexas.edu/users/EWD.

Diringer, David. 1953. *The Hand-Produced Book*. New York: Philosophical Library.

Dodds, E. R. 1960/1944, ed. and comm. *Euripides Bacchae, Edited with introduction and commentary*. 2nd edn. Oxford: Clarendon Press.

Doerr, Martin, Jane Hunter and Carl Lagoze. 2003. 'Towards a Core Ontology for Information Integration'. *JoDI* 4.1.

Dourish, Paul. 2001. *Where the Action Is: the Foundations of Embodied Interaction.* Cambridge MA: MIT Press.

Dreyfus, Hubert L. 1985. 'From Micro-Worlds to Knowledge Representation: AI at an Impasse'. In *Readings in Knowledge Representation.* Ed. Ronald J. Brachman and Hector J. Levesque. 71–94. Los Altos CA: Morgan Kaufmann.

―――― 1991. *Being-in-the-World: a Commentary on Martin Heidegger's Being and Time, Division I.* Cambridge MA: MIT Press.

―――― 1995. 'Heidegger on Gaining a Free Relationship to Technology'. In *Technology and the Politics of Knowledge.* Ed. Andrew Feenberg and Alastair Hannay. 97–107. Indiana Series in the Philosophy of Technology. Bloomington IN: Indiana University Press.

Duguid, Paul. 1996. 'Material Matters: the Past and Futurology of the Book'. In Nunberg, ed. 1996: 63–101.

Eco, Umberto. 2001. *Experiences in Translation.* Trans. Alastair McEwen. Toronto Italian Studies. Toronto: University of Toronto Press.

―――― and Thomas A. Sebeok. 1988/1983. *The Sign of Three: Dupin, Holmes, Peirce.* Advances in Semiotics. Bloomington IN: Indiana University Press.

Eddington, Sir Arthur. 1949/1939. *The Philosophy of Physical Science.* Tarner Lectures 1938. Cambridge: Cambridge University Press.

Edwards, Paul. 2004. *Heidegger's Confusions.* Amherst NY: Prometheus Books.

Edwards, Paul N. 1995. 'From "Impact" to Social Process: Computers in Society and Culture'. In *Handbook of Science and Technology Studies.* Ed. Sheila Jasanoff, Gerald E. Markle, James C. Petersen and Trevor Pinch. 257–85. Rev. edn. Thousand Oaks CA: Sage Publications.

―――― 1998. 'Virtual Machines, Virtual Infrastructures: the New Historiography of Information Technology'. *Isis* 89.1: 93–9. www.si.umich.edu/~pne/PDF/isis_review.pdf.

―――― 2001. 'Making History: New Directions in Computer Historiography'. *IEEE Annals of the History of Computing* 23.1: 86–8. www.si.umich.edu/~pne/PDF/makinghistory.pdf.

Einstein, Albert. 1982/1954. *Ideas and Opinions.* Ed. Carl Seelig. Trans. Sonja Bargmann. New York: Three Rivers.

El-Kadi, Amr. 1999. 'Stop That Divorce!' *CACM* 42.12: 27–8.

Elgin, Catherine Z. 1998. 'Goodman, Nelson'. In *Routledge Encyclopedia of Philosophy.*

Englebart, Douglas C. 1962. *Augmenting Human Intllect: a Conceptual Framework.* Summary Report AFOSR-3223 under Contract AF 49(638)-1024, SRI Project 3578 for Air Force Office of Scientific Research. Menlo Park CA: Stanford Research Institute. www.bootsrap.org/institute/bibliography.html, item 3.

Ennals, Richard. 1990. 'Interpretation and Code-Breaking'. In *Interpretation in the Humanities: Perspectives from Artificial Intelligence.* Ed. Richard Ennals and Jean-Claude Gardin. 60–78. Boston Spa: British Library.

Ernest, Paul. 1998. *Social Constructivism as a Philosophy of Mathematics.* Reform in Mathematics Education / Science, Technology & Society. Albany NY: State University of New York Press. www.ex.ac.uk/~PErnest/soccon.htm.

Essinger, James. 2004. *Jacquard's Web: How a Hand-loom Led to the Birth of the Information Age.* Oxford: Oxford University Press.

Ewald, William, ed. 1996. *From Kant to Hilbert: a Source Book in the Foundations of Mathematics*. Vol. 2. 2 vols. Oxford Science Publications. Oxford: Clarendon Press.

Fant, Karl M. 1993. 'A Critical Review of the Notion of the Algorithm in Computer Science'. In *Proceedings of the 1993 ACM Conference on Computer Science*. 1–6. New York: ACM Press.

Fay, Brian and J. Donald Moon. 1994/1977. 'What Would an Adequate Philosophy of Social Science Look Like?' In *Readings in the Philosophy of Social Science*. Ed. Michael Martin and Lee C. McIntyre. 21–35. Cambridge MA: MIT Press.

Feferman, Solomon. [Online versions of the following are at math.stanford.edu/~feferman/papers.html.]

———— 1998. 'Deciding the Undecidable: Wrestling with Hilbert's Problems'. In *In the Light of Logic*. 3–27. Logic and Computation in Philosophy. Oxford: Oxford University Press.

———— 1999. 'Does Mathematics Need New Axioms?' *American Mathematical Monthly* 106: 99–111.

Feigenbaum, Edward A. 1996. 'How the "What" Becomes the "How"'. *CACM* 39.5: 97–104.

Feinstein, Elaine. 1994/1971. 'Introduction'. In *Selected Poems*, by Marina Tsvetaeva. Trans. Elaine Feinstein. 4th edn. New York: Penguin.

Ferguson, Eugene S. 1994. *Engineering and the Mind's Eye*. Cambridge MA: MIT Press.

Fetzer, James H. 1999. 'The Role of Models in Computer Science'. *The Monist* 82.1: 20–36.

Feyerabend, Paul K. 1993/1975. *Against Method*. 3rd edn. London: Verso.

Feynman, Richard P. 1999/1996. *Feynman Lectures on Computation*. Corrected edn. Ed. Tony Hey and Robin W. Allen. Oxford: Westview.

Fields, Robert and Peter Wright. 2000. 'Editorial: Understanding Work and Designing Artefacts'. *International Journal of Human–Computer Studies* 53: 1–4.

Finley, M. I. 1986. *Ancient History: Evidence and Models*. New York: Elisabeth Sifton Books / Viking.

Finneran, Richard J., ed. 1996. *The Literary Text in the Digital Age*. Editorial Theory and Literary Criticism. Ann Arbor: University of Michigan Press.

Fiormonte, Domenico. 2003. *Scrittura e filologia nell'era digitale*. Nuova Didattica: Arte e letteratura. Torino: Bollati Boringhieri.

Fish, Stanley. 2004. 'Theory's Hope'. *CI* 30.2: 374–8.

Fleck, Ludwik. 1981/1935. *Genesis and Development of a Scientific Fact*. Ed. Thaddeus J. Trenn, Robert K. Merton. Trans. Fred Bradley and Thaddeus J. Trenn. Intro. Thomas S. Kuhn. Chicago: University of Chicago Press.

Floridi, Luciano. 2004. 'Information'. In *The Blackwell Guide to the Philosophy of Computing and Information*. Ed. Luciano Floridi. 40–61. Oxford: Blackwell.

Fodor, Jerry. 1995. 'West Coast Fuzzy'. Review of *The Engine of Reason, the Seat of the Soul, Philosophical Journey Into the Brain*, by Paul M. Churchland. *Times Literary Supplement*, 25 August.

Føllesdal, Dagfinn. 1995. 'Gödel and Husserl'. In *From Dedekind to Gödel: Essays on the Development of the Foundations of Mathematics*. Ed. Jaakko Hintikka. 427–46. Synthese Library 251. Dordrecht: Kluwer.

Forbes Irving, P. M. C. 1990. *Metamorphosis in Greek Myths*. Oxford Classical Monographs. Oxford: Clarendon Press.

Forsythe, George E. 1968. 'What to Do Till the Computer Scientist Comes'. *American Mathematical Monthly* 75.5: 454–62.

Foucault, Michel. 1972/1966. *The Order of Things: an Archaeology of the Human Sciences.* World of Man. London: Tavistock.

―――― 1972/1969. *The Archaeology of Knowledge.* Trans. A. M. Sheridan Smith. London: Tavistock.

―――― 1980. 'Truth and Knowledge'. *Power/Knowledge: Selected Interviews and Other Writings 1972–1977.* Trans. and ed. Colin Gordon. London: Harvester Wheatsheaf.

―――― 2000/1967. 'On the Ways of Writing History'. In *Aesthetics, Method, and Epistemology,* Vol. 2. 279–95, ed. James Faubion, trans. Robert Hurley. *Essential Works of Foucault 1954–1984.* 3 vols. London: Penguin Books.

Fowler, David. 1999/1987. *The Mathematics of Plato's Academy: a New Reconstruction.* 2nd edn. Oxford: Clarendon Press.

Fowler, Don. 1999. 'Criticism as Commentary and Commentary as Criticism in the Age of Electronic Media'. In Most, ed. 1999: 426–42.

Fox, Edward A., Robert M. Akscyn, Richard K. Furuta and John J. Legett. 1995. 'Digital Libraries'. *CACM* 38.4: 22–8.

―――― and Gary Marchionini. 2001. 'Digital Libraries'. *CACM* 44.5: 31–2.

Fraade, Steven D. 1991. *From Tradition to Commentary: Torah and its Interpretation in the Midrash Sifre to Deuteronomy.* SUNY Series in Judaica: Hermeneutics, Mysticism and Religion. Albany NY: State University of New York Press.

Franck, Robert. 2002. 'General Introduction'. In Franck, ed. 2002: 1–8.

―――― ed. 2002. *The Explanatory Power of Models: Bridging the Gap between Empirical and Theoretical Research in the Social Sciences.* Methodos Series, Vol. 1. Boston: Kluwer Academic.

Franklin, Allan. 2003. 'Experiment in Physics'. In *Stanford Encyclopedia of Philosophy* (Summer 2003 edition).

Franklin, Ursula. 1990. *The Real World of Technology.* CBC Massey Lectures Series. Montreal: CBC Enterprises.

Frankston, Bob. 1997. 'Beyond Limits'. In *Beyond Calculation: the Next Fifty Years of Computing.* Ed. Peter J. Denning and Robert M. Metcalfe. 43–57. New York: Copernicus.

Frye, Northrop. 1957. *Anatomy of Criticism: Four Essays.* Princeton NJ: Princeton University Press.

―――― 1963. *The Educated Imagination.* Toronto: Canadian Broadcasting Corporation.

―――― 1976. 'The Renaissance of Books'. In *Spiritus Mundi: Essays on Literature, Myth, and Society.* 49–65. Bloomington IN: Indiana University Press.

―――― 1983/1971. *The Critical Path: an Essay on the Social Context of Literary Criticism.* Brighton: Harvester.

―――― 1988. *On Education.* Markham ON: Fitzhenry & Whiteside.

―――― 1990/1983. 'Literature as a Critique of Pure Reason'. In *Myth and Metaphor: Selected Essays 1974–1988,* ed. Robert D. Denham. Charlottesville VA: University of Virginia Press.

―――― 1991. 'Literary and Mechanical Models'. In *Research in Humanities Computing 1. Selected Papers from the 1989 ACH-ALLC Conference.* Ed. Ian Lancashire. 3–12. Oxford: Clarendon Press.

Fuller, Steve. 1997. 'Who's Afraid of the History of Contemporary Science?' In *The Historiography of Recent Science and Technology*. Ed. Thomas Söderqvist. 245–59. Studies in the History of Science, Technology and Medicine 4. Amsterdam: Harwood Academic Publishers.

Gadamer, Hans-Georg. 1981/1976. 'What Is Practice? The Conditions of Social Reason'. In *Reason in the Age of Science*. 69–87. Trans. Frederick G. Lawrence. Cambridge MA: MIT Press.

_____ 1998/1983. 'Praise of Theory'. In *Praise of Theory: Speeches and Essays*. 16–36. Trans. Chris Dawson. New Haven CT: Yale University Press.

_____ 2000/1960. *Truth and Method*. 2nd edn. Trans. Joel Weinsheimer and Donald G. Marshall. New York: Continuum.

Galison, Peter. 1987. *How Experiments End*. Chicago: University of Chicago Press.

_____ 1988. 'Philosophy in the Laboratory'. *Journal of Philosophy* 85.10: 525–7.

_____ 1997. *Image & Logic: a Material Culture of Microphysics*. Chicago: University of Chicago Press.

_____ 1998. 'Judgment Against Objectivity'. In *Picturing Science, Producing Art*. Ed. Caroline A. Jones and Peter Galison. 327–59. New York: Routledge.

_____ 1999. 'Objectivity is Romantic'. In *The Humanities and the Sciences*. 15–43. ACLS Occasional Paper 47. New York: ACLS.

_____ 2004. 'Specific Theory'. *CI* 30.2: 379–83.

Gandy, Robin. 1995/1994. 'The Confluence of Ideas in 1936'. In *The Universal Turing Machine – A Half-Century Survey*. Ed. Rolf Herken. 51–102. Computerkultur II. 2nd edn. Wien: Springer Verlag.

Gani, Joseph. 1972. 'Model-building in Probability and Statistics'. In Shanin, ed. 1972: 72–84.

Gardin, Jean-Claude. 1987. *Expert Systems and Scholarly Publications*. Fifth British Library Annual Research Lecture. London: British Library.

_____ 1990. 'L'interprétation dans les humanités: réflexions sur la troisième voie / Interpretation in the Humanities: some thoughts on the third way'. In *Interpretation in the Humanities: Perspectives from Artificial Intelligence*. Ed. Richard Ennals and Jean-Claude Gardin. 22–59. Boston Spa: British Library Publications.

_____ 1991a. *Le calcul et la raison. Essais sur la formalisation du discours savant*. Recherches d'histoire et de sciences sociales. 46. Paris: Éditions de l'École des hautes études en sciences sociales.

_____ 1991b. 'On the Way We Think and Write in the Humanities: a Computational Perspective'. In *Research in Humanities Computing 1. Papers from the 1989 ACH-ALLC Conference*. Ed. Ian Lancashire. 337–45. Oxford: Clarendon Press.

Gardner, Howard. 1993/1983. *Frames of Mind: the Theory of Multiple Intelligences*. 10th edn. New York: Basic Books.

Geertz, Clifford. 1993/1973. *The Interpretation of Cultures: Selected Essays*. London: Fontana Press.

_____ 1995. *After the Fact: Two Countries, Four Decades, One Anthropologist*. Jerusalem-Harvard Lectures. Cambridge MA: Harvard University Press.

_____ 2000/1983. *Local Knowledge*. New York: Basic Books.

_____ 2000. *Available Light: Anthropological Reflections on Philosophical Topics*. Princeton University Press: Princeton.

Gentner, Dedre. 2002. 'Analogy in Scientific Discovery: the Case of Johannes Kepler'. In Magnani and Nersessian 2002: 21–39.

Gibbs, Raymond W., Jr. 1994. *The Poetics of Mind: Figurative Thought, Language, and Understanding.* Cambridge: Cambridge University Press.

Gibbs, W. Wayt. 1994. 'Trends in Computing'. *Scientific American* September: 86.

Gibson, Roy K. 2002. '"Cf. E.G.": a Typology of "Parallels" and the Role of Commentaries in Latin Poetry'. In Gibson and Kraus 2002: 331–57.

_____ and Christina Shuttleworth Kraus, eds. 2002. *The Classical Commentary: Histories, Practices, Theory.* Mnemosyne: Bibliotheca Classica Batava. Leiden: Brill.

Giddens, Anthony. 1986/1982. *Sociology: a Brief but Critical Introduction.* 2nd edn. London: Macmillan.

Giere, Ronald N. 2002. 'Models as Parts of Distributed Cognitive Systems'. In Magnani and Nersessian 2002: 227–41.

Gill, Tony. 1998. 'Metadata and the World Wide Web'. In Gill, Gilliland-Swetland and Baca, eds. 1998.

Gill, Tony, Anne Gilliland-Swetland and Murtha Baca. 1998. *Introduction to Metadata: Pathways to Digital Information.* Los Angeles CA: Getty Research Institute. www.getty.edu/research/conducting_research/standards/intrometadata/

Gilman, Sander L. 2004. 'Collaboration, the Economy, and the Future of the Humanities'. *CI* 30.2: 384–90.

Ginzburg, Carlo. 1989/1986. 'Clues: Roots of an Evidential Paradigm'. In *Clues, Myths, and the Historical Method.* 96–125. Trans. John and Anne Tedeschi. Baltimore: Johns Hopkins University Press.

Glaser, Barney G. and Anselm L. Strauss. 1967. *The Discovery of Grounded Theory: Strategies for Qualitative Research.* New York: Aldine de Gruyter.

Gödel, Kurt. 1995/ca. 1961. 'The Modern Development of the Foundations of Mathematics in the Light of Philosophy'. In *Unpublished Essays and Lectures.* Ed. Solomon Feferman, John W Dawson, Jr., Warren Goldfarb, Charles Parsons and Robert M. Solovay. 364–87. Vol. 3 of *Collected Works.* 3 vols. Oxford: Oxford University Press.

Goldhill, Simon. 1999. 'Wipe Your Glosses'. In Most, ed. 1999: 380–425.

Gooding, David. 1990. *Experiment and the Making of Meaning: Human Agency in Scientific Observation and Experiment.* Science and Philosophy 5. Dordrecht: Kluwer Academic Publishers.

_____ 1998. 'Thought Experiments'. In *Routledge Encyclopedia of Philosophy*
_____ 2000. 'Experiment'. In Newton-Smith 2000: 117–26.

Goodman, Nelson. 1972. *Problems and Projects.* Indianapolis: Bobbs-Merrill.

_____ 1976/1969. *Languages of Art: an Approach to a Theory of Symbols.* 2nd edn. Indianapolis IN: Hackett.

Goudsmit, Arno L. 1998. 'Towards a Negative Understanding of Psychotherapy'. PhD dissertation, Rijksuniversiteit Groningen 1998. www.ub.rug.nl/eldoc/dis/ppsw/a.l.goudsmit/thesis.pdf.

Graham, David. 1991. 'Putting Old Wine in New Bottles: Emblem Books and Computer Technology'. *Emblematica* 5.2: 271–85.

Groenewold, H. J. 1961. 'The Model in Physics'. In *The Concept and the Role of the Model in Mathematics and Natural and Social Sciences.* Ed. Hans Freudenthal. 98–103. Dordrecht: D. Reidel.

Grundy, Isobel, Patricia Clements, Susan Brown, Terry Butler, Rebecca Cameron, Greg Coloumbe, Susan Fisher and Jeanne Wood. 2000. 'Dates and

ChronStructs: Dynamic Chronology in the Orlando Project'. *LLC* 15.3: 265–90. www.ualberta.ca/ORLANDO/.

Guala, Francesco. 2002. 'Models, Simulations, and Experiments'. In Magnani and Nersessian 2002: 59–74.

Guillory, John. 2004. 'The Memo and Modernity'. *CI* 31.1: 108–32.

Hacking, Ian. 1983. *Representing and Intervening: Introductory Topics in the Philosophy of Natural Science*. Cambridge: Cambridge University Press.

_____ 1984. 'Five Parables'. In *Philosophy in History: Essays on the Historiography of Philosophy*. Ed. Richard Rorty, J. B. Schneewind and Quentin Skinner. 103–24. Ideas in Context. Cambridge: Cambridge University Press.

_____ 1985. 'Styles of Scientific Reasoning'. In *Post-Analytic Philosophy*, ed. John Rajchman and Cornell West. 145–65. New York: Columbia University Press

_____ 1988. 'On the Stability of the Laboratory Sciences'. *Journal of Philosophy* 85.10: 507–14.

_____ 1990. *The Taming of Chance*. Ideas in Context. Cambridge: Cambridge University Press.

_____ 1999. *The Social Construction of What?* Cambridge MA: Harvard University Press.

_____ 2002. *Historical Ontology*. Cambridge MA: Harvard University Press.

_____ 2004. 'Mindblind'. Review of *In Gods We Trust: the Evolutionary Landscape of Religion*, by Scott Atran. *London Review of Books* 26.20: 15–16.

Hamming, Richard W. 1969. 'One Man's View of Computer Science'. *JACM* 16.1: 3–12.

_____ 1980. 'The Unreasonable Effectiveness of Mathematics'. *American Mathematical Monthly* 87.2: 81–90.

Hanson, Norwood Russell. 1961. 'Is There a Logic of Scientific Discovery?' In *Current Issues in the Philosophy of Science. Symposia of Scientists and Philosophers*. Ed. Herbert Feigl and Grover Maxwell. Proceedings of Section L of the American Association for the Advancement of Science. 20–35. New York: Holt, Rinehart and Winston.

Harman, Gilbert. 1965. 'The Inference to the Best Explanation'. *Philosophical Review* 74.1: 88–95.

Hartmanis, Juris. 1995. 'On Computational Complexity and the Nature of Computer Science'. *ACM Computing Surveys* 27.1: 7–16.

Hawkins, Brian L. and Patricia Battin, eds. *The Mirage of Continuity: Reconfiguring Academic Information Resources for the 21st Century*. Washington: Council on Library and Information Resources and the Association of American Universities.

Hearst, Marti A. 1996. 'Research in Support of Digital Libraries at Xerox PARC. Part I: the Changing Social Roles of Documents'. *D-Lib* 2.5.

_____ Gary Kopec and Dan Brotsky. 1996. 'Research in Support of Digital Libraries at Xerox PARC. Part II: Paper and Digital Documents'. *D-Lib* 2.6.

Heelan, Patrick A. 1988. 'Experiment and Theory: Constitution and Reality'. *Journal of Philosophy* 85.10: 515–24.

Heidegger, Martin. 1962. *Being and Time*. Trans. John Macquarrie and Edward Robinson. Oxford: Blackwell.

_____ 1977/1955. 'The Question Concerning Technology'. In *The Question Concerning Technology and Other Essays*. Trans. William Lovitt. 3–35. New York: Harper & Row.

_____ 2001/1927. *Sein und Zeit*. 18th edn. Tübingen: Max Niemeyer.

Heisenberg, Werner. 1971/1969. *Physics and Beyond: Encounters and Conversations*. Trans. Arnold J. Pomerans. New York: Harper and Row.

_____ 1990/1958. *Physics and Philosophy: the Revolution in Modern Science*. London: Penguin Books.

Hesse, Mary B. 1963. *Models and Analogies in Science*. London: Sheed and Ward.

_____ 1974. *The Structure of Scientific Inference*. London: Macmillan.

Higgins, Hannah B. and Douglas Kahn, eds. 2012. *Mainframe Experimentalism: Early Computing and the Foundation of the Digital Arts*. Berkeley: University of California Press.

Hilbert, David. 1902. 'Mathematical Problems'. *Bulletin of the American Mathematical Society* 37.4: 407–36.

_____ and W. Ackermann. 1928. *Grundzüge der theoretischen Logik*. Berlin: Springer Verlag.

Hirschfeld, Heather. 2001. 'Early Modern Collaboration and Theories of Authorship'. *PMLA* 116.3: 609–22.

Hockey, Susan. 2000. *Electronic Texts in the Humanities*. Oxford: Oxford University Press.

_____ 2004. 'The History of Humanities Computing'. In Schreibman, Siemens and Unsworth 2004: 3–19.

Hodges, Wilfred. 1998. 'Model Theory'. In *Routledge Encyclopedia of Philosophy*.

Hoffmann, Robert R. 1995. 'Monster Analogies'. *AI Magazine* 16.3: 11–35. www.aaai.org/Library/Magazine/Vol16/16–03/Papers/AIMag16-03-002.pdf

Hollander, Robert. 1989. 'The Dartmouth Dante Project'. *Quaderni d'Italianistica* 10: 287–98.

_____ 1993. 'Dante and His Commentators'. In *The Cambridge Companion to Dante*. Ed. Rachel Jacoff. 226–36. Cambridge University Press.

Holton, Gerald. 2000. 'Werner Heisenberg and Albert Einstein'. *Physics Today Online* 53.7. www.physicstoday.com/pt/vol-53/iss-7/p38.html.

Holyoak, Keith J. and Paul Thagard. 1997. 'The Analogical Mind'. *American Psychologist* 52.1: 35–44.

Hopkins, R. D. 2004. 'Depiction'. In *Routledge Encyclopedia of Philosophy*.

Huggett, Jeremy and Seamus Ross. 2004. 'Introduction'. *Internet Archaeology* 15. intarch.ac.uk/journal/issue15/inf_index.html.

Hughes, Robert. 1991/1980. *The Shock of the New: Art and the Century of Change*. Rev. and enlarged edn. London: BBC Books.

Hughes, Ted, trans. 1997. *Tales from Ovid. Twenty-four Passages from the Metamorphoses*. London: Faber and Faber.

Hutcheon, Linda and Michael Hutcheon. 2001. 'A Convenience of Marriage: Collaboration and Interdisciplinarity'. *Publications of the Modern Language Association* 116.5: 1364–76.

Ide, Nancy. 2001. 'What Humanists Need to Know About Computing (and Computer Science)'. www.cs.vassar.edu/~ide/transparencies/HC-vancouver.ppt.

Ihde, Don. 1991. *Instrumental Realism: the Interface between Philosophy of Science and Philosophy of Technology*. Indiana Series in the Philosophy of Technology. Bloomington: Indiana University Press.

Inge, M. Thomas. 2001. 'Collaboration and Concepts of Authorship'. *PMLA* 116.3: 623–30.

Inhelder, Bärbel, Hermine Sinclair and Magali Bovet. 1974. *Learning and the Development of Cognition*. Trans. Susan Wedgwood. Cambridge MA: Harvard University Press.

Jameson, Fredric. 2004. 'Symptoms of Theory or Symptoms for Theory?' *CI* 30: 403–8.

Jha, Stefania Ruzsits. 2002. *Reconsidering Michael Polanyi's Philosophy*. Pittsburgh: University of Pittsburgh Press.

Johnson, Mark. 2002. 'Metaphor-Based Values in Scientific Models'. In Magnani and Nersessian 2002: 1–19.

Kaplan, Nancy. 2000. 'Literacy Beyond Books: Reading When All the World's a Web'. In *The World Wide Web and Contemporary Cultural Theory*. Ed. Andrew Herman and Thomas Swiss. 207–34. London: Routledge.

Karmiloff-Smith, Annette and Bärbel Inhelder. 1974. 'If You Want to Get Ahead, Get a Theory'. *Cognition* 3.3: 195–212.

Keller, Evelyn Fox. 1991. 'Language and Ideology in Evolutionary Theory: Reading Cultural Norms into Natural Law'. In *The Boundaries of Humanity: Humans, Animals, Machines*. Ed. James J. Sheehan and Morton Sosna. 85–102. Berkeley: University of California Press.

_____ 1992. *Secrets of Life / Secrets of Death: Essays on Language, Gender and Science*. London: Routledge.

_____ 1996/1985. *Reflections on Gender in Science*. 10th edn. New Haven CT: Yale University Press.

_____ 2002. *Making Sense of Life: Explaining Biological Development with Models, Metaphors, and Machines*. Cambridge MA: Harvard University Press.

Kenner, Hugh. 2005/1968. *The Counterfeiters: An Historical Comedy*. Normal IL: Dalkey Archive Press.

Kent, William. 2000/1978. *Data and Reality*. 2nd edn. Bloomington IN: 1st Books.

Keren, Michael. 2004. 'Blogging and the Politics of Melancholy'. *Canadian Journal of Communication* 29.1. www.cjc-online.ca/viewarticle.php?id=856.

Kilmister, C. W. 1967. *Language, Logic and Mathematics*. London: English Universities Press.

Kirschenbaum, Matthew, ed. 2002. 'Image-Based Humanities Computing'. Special issue of *CHum* 36.3.

Kline, Morris. 1990/1972. *Mathematical Thought from Ancient to Modern Times*. Vol. 1. 3 vols. Oxford: Oxford University Press.

Kling, Rob. 1999. 'What Is Social Informatics and Why Does It Matter?' *D-Lib* 5.1.

Knorr Cetina, Karin D. 1995. 'Laboratory Studies: the Cultural Approach to the Study of Science'. In *Handbook of Science and Technology Studies*. Ed. Sheila Jasanoff, Gerald E. Markle, James C. Peterson and Trevor Pinch. 140–66. Rev. edn. Thousand Oaks CA: Sage Publications.

_____ 1999. *Epistemic Cultures: How the Sciences Make Knowledge*. Cambridge MA: Harvard University Press.

Kobayashi, Mei and Koichi Takeda. 2000. 'Information Retrieval on the Web'. *ACM Computing Surveys* 32.2: 144–73.

Koch, Christian. 1991. 'On the Benefits of Interrelating Computer Science and the Humanities: the Case of Metaphor'. *CHum* 25.5: 289–95.

Kuhn, Thomas S. 1970/1962. *The Structure of Scientific Revolutions*. 2nd enlarged edn. Chicago: University of Chicago Press.

_____ 1977. *The Essential Tension: Selected Studies in Scientific Tradition and Change*. Chicago: University of Chicago Press.

Lagoze, Carl and Sandra Payette. 2000. 'Metadata: Principles, Practices, and Challenges'. In *Moving Theory into Practice: Digital Imaging for Libraries and Archives*. Ed. Anne R. Kenney and Oya Y. Rieger. 84–100. Mountain View CA: Research Libraries Group.

Lakoff, George and Mark Johnson. 1999. *Philosophy in the Flesh: the Embodied Mind and its Challenge to Western Thought*. New York: Basic Books.

Lancashire, Ian. 1991. *The Humanities Computing Yearbook 1989–90. A Comprehensive Guide to Software and other Resources*. Oxford: Clarendon Press.

——— and Willard McCarty. 1988. *The Humanities Computing Yearbook 1988*. Oxford: Clarendon Press.

Landauer, Thomas K. 1997. 'Behavioral Research Methods in Human-Computer Interaction'. In *Handbook of Human-Computer Interaction*. Ed. Martin G. Helander, Thomas K. Landauer and Prasad V. Prabhu. 203–27. 2nd edn. Amsterdam: Elsevier.

Laudan, Laurens. 1966. 'The Clock Metaphor and Probabilism: the Impact of Descartes on English Methodological Thought, 1650–65'. *Annals of Science* 22.2: 73–104.

Lavagnino, John. 1997. 'Reading, Scholarship, and Hypertext Editions'. *Journal of Electronic Publishing* 3.1.

——— 2001. 'Forms of Theory: Some Models for the Role of Theory in Humanities Computing Scholarship'. In *Philologien und Informationstechnologien – Philology and Information Technology*. Proceedings of the fourth seminar *Computers, Literature and Philology*. Gerhard-Mercator-Universität Duisburg 06. 09.12.2001. Ed. Elisabeth Burr. In preparation. www.uni-duisburg.de/FB3/CLiP2001/abstracts/Lavagnino_en.htm

LC21: A Digital Strategy for the Library of Congress. 2000. Committee on an Information Technology Strategy for the Library of Congress, Computer Science and Telecommunications Board and Mathematics Commission on Physical Sciences, and Applications. Washington DC: National Academies Press. web.archive.org/web/20011128064711/books.nap.edu/html/lc21/.

Leatherdale, W. H. 1974. *The Role of Analogy, Model, and Metaphor in Science*. Amsterdam: North Holland Publishing.

Lederberg, Joshua. 1996. 'Options for the Future'. *DiLib* 2.5.

Leff, Gordon. 1972. 'Models Inherent in History'. In Shanin, ed. 1972: 148–60.

Lenat, Douglas B. 1998. 'From 2001 to 2001: Common Sense and the Mind of HAL'. In *HAL's Legacy: 2001's Computer as Dream and Reality*. Ed. David G. Stork. 193–209. Cambridge MA: MIT Press. www.cyc.com/cyc/technology/halslegacy.html.

Lenoir, Timothy. 2002. 'Science and the Academy of the 21st Century. Does Their Past Have a Future in the Age of Computer-Mediated Networks?' In *Ideale Akademie: Vergangene Zukunft oder konkrete Utopie?* Ed. Wilhelm Voßkamp. Berlin: Akademie Verlag.

Lepenies, Wolf. 1988/1985. *Between Literature and Science: the Rise of Sociology*. Trans. R. J. Hollingdale. Ideas in Context. Cambridge: Cambridge University Press.

Lévi-Strauss, Claude. 1963. *Structural Anthropology*. Trans. Claire Jacobson and Brooke Schoepf. New York: Basic Books.

Levin, Samuel R. 1981. 'Allegorical Language'. In *Allegory, Myth, and Symbol*. Ed. Morton W. Bloomfield. 23–38. Harvard English Studies 9. Cambridge MA: Harvard University Press.

Levy, David M. 2000. 'Digital Libraries and the Problem of Purpose'. *D-Lib* 6.1.

——— and Catherine C. Marshal. 1995. 'Going Digital: a Look At Assumptions Underlying Digital Libraries'. *CACM* 38.4: 77–84.

Lewis, C. S. 1967/1960. *Studies in Words*. 2nd edn. Cambridge: Cambridge University Press.

Lipton, Peter. 2000. 'Inference to the Best Explanation'. In Newton-Smith 2000: 184–93.

Liu, Alan. 2012. 'Where is the Cultural Criticism in the Digital Humanities?' In *Debates in the Digital Humanities*. Ed. Matthew K. Gold. 490–509. Minneapolis MN: University of Minnesota Press.

Lloyd, Elisabeth A. 1998. 'Models'. In *Routledge Encyclopedia of Philosophy*.

Lodge, David. 1978/1975. *Changing Places: a Tale of Two Campuses*. London: Penguin Books.

Loftus, Geoffrey. 1991. 'On the Tyranny of Hypothesis Testing in the Social Sciences'. Review of *The Empire of Chance: How Probability Changed Science and Everyday Life*, by Gerd Gigerenzer, Zeno Swijtink, Theodore Porter, Lorraine Daston, John Beatty and Lorenz Krüger, Cambridge University Press 1990. *Contemporary Psychology* 36.2: 102–5.

Lougee, Wendy Pradt. 2002. *Diffuse Libraries: Emergent Roles for the Research Library in the Digital Age*. Washington DC: Council on Library and Information Resources. www.clir.org/pubs/abstract/pub108abst.html.

Lyman, Peter and Nina Wakeford. 1999. 'Introduction: Going Into the (Virtual) Field'. *American Behavioral Scientist* 43.3: 359–76.

Lynch, Clifford. 2001. 'The Battle to Define the Future of the Book in the Digital World'. *First Monday* 6.6.

_____ and Hector Garcia-Molina. 1995. *Interoperability, Scaling, and Digital Libraries Research. A Report on the May 18–19, 1995 IITA Digital Libraries Workshop*. Stanford CA: Stanford Digital Library Technologies.

Machlup, Fritz and Una Mansfield, eds. 1983. *The Study of Information: Interdisciplinary Messages*. Knowledge: Its Creation, Distribution and Economic Significance 4. New York: Wiley.

Magnani, Lorenzo. 2001. *Abduction, Reason, and Science. Processes of Discovery and Explanation*. New York: Kluwer Academic / Plenum Publishers.

_____ 2002. 'Epistemic Mediators and Model-Based Discovery in Science'. In Magnani and Nersessian 2002: 305–29.

_____ and Nancy J. Nersessian, eds. 2002. *Model-Based Reasoning: Science, Technology, Values*. New York: Kluwer Academic / Plenum Publishers.

Mahoney, Michael S. [For online versions of the following see www.princeton. edu/~mike/; exceptions noted as *.]

_____ 1990a. 'Cybernetics and Information Technology'. In *Companion to the History of Modern Science*. Ed. R. C. Olby, G. N. Cantor, J. R. R. Christie and M. J. S. Hodge. 537–53. London: Routledge.

_____ 1990b. 'The Roots of Software Engineering'. *CWI Quarterly* 3.4: 325–34.

_____ 1997. 'Computer Science: the Search for a Mathematical Theory'. In *Science in the Twentieth Century*. Ed. John Krige and Dominique Pestre. 617–34. Amsterdam: Harwood Academic Publishers.

_____ 1998. 'Review of Martin Campbell-Kelly and William Aspray, *Computer: a History of the Information Machine*'*. *IEEE Annals of the History of Computing* 20.2: 86–7.

_____ 2000a. 'Review of Paul E. Ceruzzi, *A History of Modern Computing*'. *IEEE Annals of the History of Computing*'*. 22.3: 93–4.

_____ 2000b. 'The Structures of Computation'. In *The First Computers – History and Architectures*. Ed. Raúl Rojas and Ulf Hashagen. 17–32. Cambridge MA: MIT Press.

_____ 2000c. 'Historical Perspectives on Models and Modeling'*. Zürich: XIIIth DHS–DLMPS Joint Conference on 'Scientific Models: Their Historical and Philosophical Relevance'.

_____ 2002. 'Software as Science – Science as Software'. In *History of Computing: Software Issues. International Conference on the History of Computing ICHC 2000, April 5–7, 2000, Heinz Nixdorf MuseumsForum, Paderborn, Germany.* Ed. Ulf Hashagen, Reinhard Keil-Slawik and Arthur L. Norberg. 25–48. Berlin: Springer Verlag.

_____ 2003. 'Reading a Machine'. Rev. edn.

_____ 2005 (forthcoming). 'The Histories of Computing(s)'. *Digital Scholarship, Digital Culture.* Special issue of *Interdisciplinary Science Reviews* 30.2.

_____ 2011. *Histories of Computing*. Ed. Thomas Haigh. Cambridge MA: Harvard University Press.

Mallery, John C., Roger Hurwitz and Gavan Duffy. 1992. 'Hermeneutics: From Textual Explication to Computer Understanding?' In *The Encyclopedia of Artificial Intelligence.* Ed. Stuart C. Shapiro. 596–611. 2nd edn. New York: John Wiley. www.ai.mit.edu/people/jcma/papers/1986-ai-memo-871/memo.html.

Malouf, David. 1978. *An Imaginary Life.* London: Chatto and Windus.

_____ 1998. *A Spirit of Play: the Making of Australian Consciousness.* Boyer Lectures 1998. Sydney: Australian Broadcasting Corporation Books. www.abc.net.au/rn/boyers/index/BoyersChronoIdx.htm#1998.

Markman, Arthur B. and Eric Dietrich. 2000. 'Extending the Classical View of Representation'. *Trends in Cognitive Sciences* 4.12: 470–5.

Marshall, Catherine C., Gene Golivchinsky and Morgan N. Price. 2001. 'Digital Libraries and Mobility'. *CACM* 44.5: 55–6.

_____ and Frank M. Shipman. 2003. 'Which Semantic Web?' In *Proceedings of the Fourteenth ACM Conference on Hypertext and Hypermedia, Nottingham UK* 57–66. New York: ACM Press.

Martin, Henri-Jean and Jean Vezin. 1990. *Mise en page et mise en texte du livre manuscrit.* Paris: Éditions du Cercle de la Librarie – Promodis.

Martin, James. 1982. *Application Development without Programmers.* Englewood Cliffs NJ: Prentice-Hall.

Maxwell, James Clerk. 1911. 'Diagram'. In *Encyclopedia Britannica.* 11th edn.

May, Kenneth O. 1980. 'Historiography: a Perspective for Computer Scientists'. In Metropolis, Howlett and Rota 1980: 11–18.

Mayo, Deborah G. 1996. *Error and the Growth of Experimental Knowledge.* Science and its Conceptual Foundations. Chicago: University of Chicago Press.

McCarty, Willard. [For online versions of the following see www.kcl.ac.uk/humanities/cch/wlm/publications.html.]

_____ 1992. 'HUMANIST: Lessons From a Global Electronic Seminar'. *CHum* 26: 205–22.

_____ 1993. 'Handmade, Computer-Assisted, and Electronic Concordances of Chaucer'. In *Computer-Based Chaucer Studies,* Vol. 3. 49–65, ed. Ian Lancashire. Toronto: Centre for Computing in the Humanities.

_____ 2001a. 'Looking Through an Unknown, Remembered Gate: Interdisciplinary Meditations on Humanities Computing'. *Interdisciplinary Science Reviews* 26.3: 173–82.

_____ 2001b. 'A serious beginner's guide to hypertext research'. www.kcl.ac.uk/humanities/cch/wlm/essays/diy/hyperbib.html.

_____ 2002. 'A Network with a Thousand Entrances: Commentary in an Electronic Age?' In *The Classical Commentary: Histories, Practices, Theory*. Ed. Roy K. Gibson and Christina Shuttleworth Kraus. 359–402. Leiden: Brill.

_____ 2003. 'Humanities Computing'. In *Encyclopedia of Library and Information Science*. New York: Marcel Dekker.

_____ 2004a. 'As It Almost Was: Historiography of Recent Things'. *LLC* 19.2: 161–80.

_____ 2004b. 'Modelling: a Study in Words and Meanings'. In Schreibman, Siemens and Unsworth 2004: 254–70.

_____ 2005 (forthcoming). 'Complexity and Simplicity'. Review of *Stellenbibliographie zum 'Parzival' Wolframs Von Eschenbach für die Jahrgänge 1984–1996*, by David Yeandle. *LLC* 20.1.

_____ 2005 (submitted). 'Tree, Turf, Centre or Archipelago? Poetics of Disciplinarity for Humanities Computing'.

_____ and Matthew Kirschenbaum. 2003. 'Institutional Models for Humanities Computing'. *LLC* 18.3: 465–89. www.allc.org/imhc/.

McGann, Jerome. 2001. *Radiant Textuality: Literature after the World Wide Web*. New York: Palgrave.

_____ 2003. 'Textonics: Literary and Cultural Studies in a Quantum World'. In *The Culture of Collected Editions*, ed. Andrew Nash. 245–60. Basingstoke: Palgrave Macmillan.

_____ 2004a. 'Culture and Technology: the Way We Live Now, What Is To Be Done?' Invited lecture, 'Digital Scholarship, Digital Culture', King's College London, May 2004.

_____ 2004b. 'Marking Texts of Many Dimensions'. In Schreibman, Siemens and Unsworth 2004: 198–217.

_____ et al. 2000. *The Complete Writings and Pictures of Dante Gabriel Rossetti. A Hypermedia Research Archive*. [First Installment] Charlottesville VA: Institute for Advanced Technology in the Humanities, June. www.iath.virginia.edu/rossetti/.

Medina-Mora, Raúl, Terry Winograd, Rodrigo Flores and Fernando Flores. 1992. 'The Action Workflow Approach to Workflow Management Technology'. In *Proceedings of the 1992 ACM Conference on Computer-Supported Cooperative Work. Toronto, 1992*. 281–8. New York: ACM Press.

Meister, Jan Christoph. 2003. *Computing Action: a Narratological Approach*. Narratologia: Contributions to Narrative Theory / Beiträge zur Erzähltheorie 2. Berlin: Walter de Gruyter.

Melnick, Burton. 1999. 'Cold Hard World / Warm Soft Mommy: Gender and Metaphors of Hardness, Softness, Coldness, and Warmth'. *PSYART: a Hyperlink Journal for the Psychological Study of the Arts*. Art. 990918. www.clas.ufl.edu/ipsa/journal/articles/psyart/1999_melnick01.shtml.

Merleau-Ponty, Maurice. 1962/1945. *Phenomenology of Perception*. Trans. Colin Smith. London: Routledge & Kegan Paul.

_____ 1964/1947. 'The Primacy of Perception and Its Philosophical Consequences'. In *The Primacy of Perception and Other Essays on Phenomenological Psychology and the Philosophy of Art, History and Politics*, ed. and trans. James M. Edie. 12–42. Northwestern Studies in Phenomenology and Existential Philosophy. Evanston IL: Northwestern University Press.

Merton, Robert K. 1993. *On the Shoulders of Giants: a Shandean Postscript. The Past – Italianate* Edition. Chicago: University of Chicago Press.

Metropolis, N., J. Howlett and Gian-Carlo Rota, eds. 1980. *A History of Computing in the Twentieth Century: a Collection of Essays*. New York: Academic Press.

Miles, Adrian. 2001. 'Hypertext Structure as the Event of Connection'. In *Proceedings of the Twelfth ACM Conference on Hypertext and Hypermedia. Aarhus, Denmark.* 61–8. New York: ACM Press.

_____ 2003. 'Softvideography'. In *Cybertext Yearbook 2002–2003, Vol. 77.* Ed. Markku Eskelinen and Raine Koskimaa. 218–36. Jyväskylän: Research Center for Contemporary Culture.

Miller, Carolyn R. and Dawn Shepherd. 2004. 'Blogging as Social Action: a Genre Analysis of the Weblog'. *Into the Blogosphere: Rhetoric, Community, and Culture of Weblog.* blog.lib.umn.edu/blogosphere/blogging_as_social_action.html.

Miller, George A. 1956. 'The Magical Number Seven, Plus or Minus Two: Some Limits on Our Capacity for Processing Information'. *Psychological Review* 63: 81–97. www.well.com/user/smalin/miller.html.

Milner, Robin. 1987. 'Is Computing an Experimental Science?' *Journal of Information Technology* 2: 58–66. www.lfcs.inf.ed.ac.uk/reports/86/ECS-LFCS-86-1/.

Mindell, David A. 2002. *Between Human and Machine: Feedback, Control, and Computing before Cybernetics.* Johns Hopkins Studies in the History of Technology. Baltimore MD: Johns Hopkins University Press.

Minsky, Marvin L. 1970. 'Form and Content in Computer Science'. *JACM* 17.2: 197–215.

_____ 1997/1991. 'Conscious Machines'. *Proceedings, National Research Council of Canada, 75th Anniversary Symposium on Science in Society, June 1991.* Rev. edn. web.media.mit.edu/~minsky/papers/Conscious_Machines [?]

_____ 1995/1968. 'Matter, Mind and Models'. Rev edn. web.media.mit.edu/~minsky/papers/MatterMindModels.html.

Mironesco, Christine. 2002. 'The Role of Models in Comparative Politics'. In Franck 2002: 181–95.

Misak, Cheryl. 2000. 'Peirce'. In Newton-Smith 2000: 335–9.

Mitchell, Melanie. 1993. *Analogy-Making as Perception: a Computer Model.* Neural Network and Connectionism Series. Cambridge MA: MIT Press.

Mitchell, William J., Alan S. Inouye and Marjory S. Blumenthal, eds. 2003. *Beyond Productivity: Information Technology, Innovation, and Creativity.* Washington DC: National Academies Press. books.nap.edu/html/beyond_productivity/.

Molander, Bengt. 1992. 'Tacit Knowledge and Silenced Knowledge: Fundamental Problems and Controversies'. In *Skill and Education: Reflection and Experience.* Ed. Bo Göranzon and Magnus Florin. 9–31. Artificial Intelligence and Society. Heidelberg: Springer Verlag.

Monmonier, Mark. 1996/1991. *How to Lie with Maps.* 2nd edn. Chicago: University of Chicago Press.

Morgan, Mary S. 2002. 'Model Experiments and Models in Experiments'. In Magnani and Nersessian 2002: 41–58.

_____ and Margaret Morrison, eds. 1999. *Models as Mediators: Perspectives on Natural and Social Science.* Ideas in Context. Cambridge: Cambridge University Press.

Morrison, Margaret C. 1998. 'Experiment'. In *Routledge Encyclopedia of Philosophy.*

_____ and Mary S. Morgan. 1999. 'Introduction', 1–9; 'Models as Mediating Instruments', 10–37. In Morgan and Morrison, eds. 1999.

Morrison, Toni. 1970. *The Bluest Eye*. New York: Washington Square Press.

Mortensen, Torill and Jill Walker. 2002. 'Blogging Thoughts: Personal Publication as an Online Research Tool'. In *Researching ICTs in Context*. Ed. Andrew Morrison. 249–79. Intermedia Reports. Oslo: University of Oslo.

Most, Glenn W. 1999. 'Preface'. In Most, ed. 1999: v–xv.

_____ ed. 1999. *Commentaries – Kommentare*. Aporemata: Kritische Studien Zur Philologiegeschichte 4. Göttingen: Vandenhoeck und Ruprecht.

Murray, Janet H. 2003. 'Inventing the Medium'. In *The New Media Reader*. Ed. Noah Wardrip-Fruin and Nick Montfort. 3–11. Cambridge MA: MIT Press.

Murray, K. M. Elizabeth. 1977. *Caught in the Web of Words: James A. H. Murray and the Oxford English Dictionary*. New Haven CN: Yale University Press.

Nardi, Bonnie A. 1997. 'The Use of Ethnographic Methods in Design and Evaluation'. In *Handbook of Human-Computer Interaction*. Ed. Martin G. Helander, Thomas K. Landauer and Prasad V. Prabhu. 361–6. 2nd edn. Amsterdam: Elsevier.

Naur, Peter. 1995. *Knowing and the Mystique of Logic and Rules*. Studies in Cognitive Systems 18. Dordrecht: Kluwer Academic.

Netz, Reviel. 1999. *The Shaping of Deduction in Greek Mathematics*. Ideas in Context 51. Cambridge: Cambridge University Press.

Newell, Allen. 1980. 'Reasoning, Problem Solving, and Decision Processes: the Problem Space as a Fundamental Category'. In *Attention and Performance VIII*. Ed. Raymond S. Nickerson. 693–718. Hillsdale NJ: Lawrence Erlbaum.

_____ 1991. 'Metaphors for Mind, Theories of Mind: Should the Humanities Mind?' In *The Boundaries of Humanity: Humans, Animals, Machines*. Ed. James J. Sheehan and Morton Sosna. 158–97. Berkeley CA: University of California Press.

_____ Alan J. Perlis and Herbert A. Simon. 1967. 'Computer Science'. *Science* N.S. 157.3795: 1373–4.

Newton-Smith, W. H., ed. 2000. *A Companion to the Philosophy of Science*. Blackwell Companions to Philosophy. Oxford: Blackwell.

Nickles, Thomas. 2000. 'Discovery'. In Newton-Smith 2000: 85–96.

Nilsson, Stephanie. 2004. 'The Function of Language to Facilitate and Maintain Social Networks in Research Weblogs'. Umeå universitet, 2004. www.humlab. umu.se/exjobb/files/LanguageBlogs.pdf.

Norman, Donald A. 1986. 'Cognitive Engineering'. In *User Centered System Design: New Perspectives on Human–Computer Interaction*. Ed. Donald A. Norman and Stephen W. Draper. 31–61. Hillsdale NJ: Lawrence Erlbaum.

_____ 1998. *Invisible Computer: Why Good Products Can Fail, the Personal Computer is So Complex and Information Applicances are the Solution*. Cambridge MA: MIT Press.

Numerico, Teresa and Arturo Vespignani, eds. 2003. *Informatica per le scienze umanistiche*. Itinerari. Bologna: il Mulino.

Nunberg, Geoffrey. 1996. 'Farewell to the Information Age'. In Nunberg, ed. 1996: 103–38. ecot.rice.edu/~Tony.Gorry/NunbergFarewell.pdf.

_____ ed. *The Future of the Book*. Berkeley: University of California Press.

O'Donnell, James J. 2001. Review of *Libraries in the Ancient World*, by Lionel Casson. *Bryn Mawr Classical Review 2001.04.25*.

Oakman, Robert. 1984/1980. *Computer Methods for Literary Research.* 2nd edn. Athens GA: University of South Carolina Press. University of Georgia Press.
_____ 1987. 'Perspectives on Teaching Computing in the Humanities'. *CHum* 21: 227–33.

Ogden, C. K. and I. A. Richards. 1949/1923. *The Meaning of Meaning: a Study of the Influence of Language upon Thought and of the Science of Symbolism.* 10th edn. International Library of Psychology, Philosophy and Scientific Method. London: Routledge & Kegan Paul.

Olsen, Mark. 1993. 'Signs, Symbols and Discourses: A New Direction for Computer-Aided Literature Studies'. *Computers and the Humanities* 27: 309–14.

Oppenheimer, J. Robert. 1953. *Science and the Common Understanding.* New York: Simon and Schuster.

Orlandi, Tito. 2000. 'Ideas for a Theoretical Foundation of Humanities Computing'. Invited lecture, 'Humanities computing: formal methods, experimental practice', King's College London, 13 May. rmcisadu.let.uniroma1.it/~orlandi/saggiomio.pdf.

_____ 2002. 'Is Humanities Computing a Discipline?' *Jahrbuch für Computerphilologie* 4: 51–8.

_____ 2003. 'Per un curriculum europeo di informatica umanistica'. In *Informatica umanistica – Dalla ricerca all'insegnamento.* Ed. Domenico Fiormonte and Giulia Buccini. 19–25. Informatica e discipline umanistiche XI. Bulzoni Editore.

_____ Joseph Norment Bell, Lou Burnard, Dino Buzzetti, Koenraad de Smedt, Ingo Kropac, Jacques Souillot and Manfred Thaller. 1999. 'European Studies on Formal Methods in the Humanities'. In *Computing in Humanities Education: a European Perspective.* Ed. Koenraad de Smedt, Hazel Gardiner, Espen Ore, Tito Orlandi, Harold Short, Jacques Souillot and William Vaughan. 13–62. Bergen, Norway: University of Bergen. helmer.aksis.uib.no/AcoHum/book/.

Ott, Wilhelm. 2000. 'Strategies and Tools for Textual Scholarship: the Tübingen System of Text Processing Programs (TUSTEP)'. *LLC* 15.1: 93–108.

Paepcke, Andreas. 1996. 'Digital Libraries: Searching is Not Enough. What We Learned on-Site'. *D-Lib* 2.5.

_____ Chen-Chuan K. Chang, Héctor García-Molina and Terry Winograd. 1998. 'Interoperability for Digital Libraries Worldwide'. *CACM* 41.4: 33–43.

Pagels, Heinz R. 1988. *The Dreams of Reason: the Computer and the Rise of the Sciences of Complexity.* New York: Simon and Schuster.

Parkes, M. B. 1991. *Scribes, Scripts and Readers: Studies in the Communication, Presentation and Dissemination of Medieval Texts.* London: Hambledon Press.

Passarotti, Marco. 2013. 'One Hundred Years Ago. In Memory of Father Roberto Busa SJ'. In *Proceedings of the Third Workshop on Annotation of Corpora for Research in the Humanities (ACRH-3).* Ed. Francesco Mambrini, Marco Passarotti and Caroline Sporleder. 15–24. Sofia: The Institute of Information and Communication Technologies, Bulgarian Academy of Sciences. www.bultreebank.org/ACRH-3/ACRH-3Proceeding.pdf (24/2/14).

Paxson, James J. 1994. *The Poetics of Personification.* Literature, Culture, Theory 6. Cambridge: Cambridge University Press.

Pearson, Geoffrey. 1972. 'Comment [on Nevil Moray, "Models in Experimental Psychology"]'. In Shanin, ed. 1972: 98–101.

Pelikan, Jaroslav. 1992. *The Idea of the University: a Reexamination.* New Haven CT: Yale University Press.

Pelteret, David A. E. and Alex Burghart. 2002. 'Describing Events in Database Terms: an English Charter of AD 804'. In *DRH 2001 and 2002*. Ed. Jean Anderson, Alastair Dunning and Michael Fraser. London: Office of Humanities Communication. www.kcl.ac.uk/humanities/cch/pase/pase.htm.

Perlis, Alan J. 1967. 'The Synthesis of Algorithmic Systems'. *JACM* 14.1: 1–9.

―――― 1982. 'Epigrams on Programming'. *ACM SIGPLAN Notices* 17.9: 7–13. www.cs.yale.edu/homes/perlis-alan/quotes.html.

Peters, Paul Evan. 1994. 'Keynote speech'. College Station TX: First Annual Conference on the Theory and Practice of Digital Libraries. csdl.tamu.edu/csdl/DL94/peters.keynote.html.

Petroski, Henry. 1992/1982. *To Engineer is Human: the Role of Failure in Successful Design*. New York: Vintage.

Piaget, Jean. 1970/1968. *Genetic Epistemology*. Trans. Eleanor Duckworth. Woodbridge Lectures 8. New York: Columbia University Press. www.marxists.org/reference/subject/philosophy/works/fr/piaget.htm.

Pickering, Andrew, ed. 1992. *Science as Practice and Culture*. Chicago: University of Chicago Press.

Piez, Wendell. 2002. 'Human and Machine Sign Systems'. Montreal, Quebec: Extreme Markup Languages 2002. www.piez.org/wendell/papers/signsystems.pdf.

Plaice, John. 1995. 'Computer Science is an Experimental Science'. *ACM Computing Surveys* 27.1: 33.

Polanyi, Michael. 1962/1958. *Personal Knowledge: Towards a Post-Critical Philosophy*. Corr. edn. Chicago: University of Chicago Press.

―――― 1969. *Knowing and Being: Essays by Michael Polanyi*. Ed. Marjorie Grene. London: Routledge & Kegan Paul.

―――― 1983/1966. *The Tacit Dimension*. Gloucester MA: Peter Smith.

Pool, Ithiel de Sola, ed. 1977. *The Social Impact of the Telephone*. MIT Bicentennial Studies. Cambridge MA: MIT Press.

―――― Craig Decker, Stephen Dizard, Kay Israel, Pamela Rubin and Barry Weinstein. 'Foresight and Hindsight: the Case of the Telephone'. In Pool, ed. 1977: 127–57.

Poovey, Mary. 1998. *A History of the Modern Fact: Problems of Knowledge in the Sciences of Wealth and Society*. Chicago: University of Chicago Press.

Popper, Karl R. 1935. *Logik der Forschung*. Wien: Verlag von Julius Springer.

―――― 2002/1959. *The Logic of Scientific Discovery*. Trans. Karl R. Popper, with Julius and Lan Freed. London: Routledge.

Post, Emil. [1941]. 'Absolutely Unsolvable Problems and Relatively Undecidable Propositions: Account of an Anticipation'. In Davis 1993/1965: 338–406.

Prown, Jules David. 1988. 'Mind in Matter: an Introduction to Material Culture Theory and Method'. In *Material Life in America 1600–1860*. Ed. Robert Blair St George. 17–37. Boston MA: Northeastern University Press.

Putnam, Hilary. 1988. 'Much Ado About Not Very Much'. *Daedalus* 117.1: 269–81.

Raben, Joseph. 1977. *Computer-assisted Research in the Humanities. A Directory of Scholars Active*. New York: Pergamon.

Rabin, Michael O. and Dana Scott. April 1959. 'Finite Automata and Their Decision Problems'. *IBM Journal of Research and Development* 3.2: 114–25.

Ramsey, Jeffry L. 1992. 'Towards an Expanded Epistemology for Approximations'. In *Proceedings of the Biennial Meeting of the Philosophy of Science Association*. 154–64. Chicago: University of Chicago Press.

Ransmayr, Christoph. 1990/1988. *The Last World.* Trans. John E. Woods. New York: Grove Press.

Raymond, Eric S. 2004. *The Art of UNIX Programming.* Boston MA: Pearson Education. www.faqs.org/docs/artu/.

——— ed. 1996/1991. *The New Hacker's Dictionary.* 3rd edn. Cambridge MA: MIT Press.

Rayward, W. Boyd. 2002. 'A History of Computer Applications in Libraries: Prolegomena'. *IEEE Annals of the History of Computing* 24.2: 4–15.

Reichenbach, Hans. 1938. *Experience and Prediction: an Analysis of the Foundations and the Structure of Knowledge.* Chicago: University of Chicago Press.

Reid, Constance. 1996. *Hilbert.* New York: Copernicus.

Renear, Allen. 1997. 'Out of Praxis: Three (Meta)Theories of Textuality'. In Sutherland 1997: 107–26.

——— 2001. 'The Descriptive/Procedural Distinction is Flawed'. *Markup Languages: Theory and Practice* 2.4: 411–20.

——— 2004a. 'Text Encoding'. In Schreibman, Siemens and Unsworth 2004: 218–39.

——— 2004b. 'Theory Restored'. Göteborg, Sweden: ALLC/ACH Joint Conference. www.hum.gu.se/allcach2004/AP/html/prop149.html.

Riskin, Jessica. 2003. 'The Defecating Duck, or, the Ambiguous Origins of Artifical Life'. *CI* 29: 599–633.

Robinson, Arthur H. and Barbara B. Petchenik. 1976. *The Nature of Maps: Essays Toward Understanding Maps and Mapping.* Chicago: University of Chicago Press.

Robinson, Peter and Hans W Gabler. 2000. 'Introduction. Making Texts for the Next Century'. *LLC* 15.1: 1–4.

Roncaglia, Gino. 2002. 'Informatica Umanistica: Le Ragioni Di Una Disciplina'. *Intersezioni* 3: 353–76. www.merzweb.com/testi/saggi/informatica_umanistica.htm.

Rorty, Richard. 1980. *Philosophy and the Mirror of Nature.* Princeton NJ: Princeton University Press.

——— 1991. *Essays on Heidegger and Others.* Vol. 1 of *Philosophical Papers.* 2 vols. Cambridge: Cambridge University Press.

——— 2004. 'Being That Can Be Understood Is Language'. In *Gadamer's Repurcussions: Reconsidering Philosophical Hermeneutics.* Ed. Bruce Krajewski. 21–9. Berkeley: University of California Press.

Rosen, Robert. 1995/1994. 'Effective Processes and Natural Law'. In *The Universal Turing Machine: a Half-Century Survey.* Ed. Rolf Herken. 485–98. 2nd edn. Computerkultur II. Wien: Springer Verlag.

Rouse, Joseph. 1998. 'Heideggerian Philosophy of Science'. In *Routledge Encyclopedia of Philosophy.*

Rowe, Glenn W. 1994. *Theoretical Models in Biology: the Origin of Life, the Immune System, and the Brain.* Oxford: Oxford University Press.

Rydberg-Cox, Jeffrey A., Robert F. Chavez, David A. Smith, Anne Mahoney and Gregory R. Crane. 2000. 'Knowledge Management in the Perseus Digital Library'. *Ariadne* 25.

Ryle, Gilbert. 2000/1949. *The Concept of Mind.* Rev. edn. London: Penguin Books.

Saïd, Tazi and Fabrice Evrard. 2001. 'Intentional Structures of Documents'. In *Proceedings of the Twelfth ACM Conference on Hypertext and Hypermedia. Aarhus, Denmark.* 39–40. New York: ACM Press.

Samuels, Lisa. 1997. 'Introduction, to the Special Issue on Poetry and the Problem of Beauty'. *Modern Language Studies* 27.2. wings.buffalo.edu/epc/authors/samuels/beauty.html.

Schach, Stephen R. 2002/1990. *Object-Oriented and Classical Software Engineering.* 5th edn. WCB/McGraw-Hill.

Schön, Donald A. 1983. *The Reflective Practitioner: How Professionals Think in Action.* New York: Basic Books.

Schreibman, Susan, Ray Siemens and John Unsworth, eds. 2004. *A Companion to Digital Humanities.* Blackwell Companions to Literature and Culture 26. Oxford: Blackwell.

Sculley, D. and Bradley M. Pasanek. 2008. 'Meaning and Mining: The Impact of Implicit Assumptions in Data Mining for the Humanities'. *Literary and Linguistic Computing* 23.4: 409–24.

Searle, John. 1991/1984. *Minds, Brains and Science.* Reith Lectures 1984. London: Penguin Books.

Seidman, Louis Michael. 1996. 'Points of Intersection: Discontinuities at the Junction of Criminal Law and the Regulatory State'. *Journal of Contemporary Legal Issues* [San Diego] 7.1: 97–163.

Sells, Michael A. 1994. *Mystical Languages of Unsaying.* Chicago: University of Chicago Press.

Serfaty, Viviane. 2004. *The Mirror and the Veil: an Overview of American Online Diaries and Blogs.* Amsterdam Monographs in American Studies 11. Amsterdam: Rodopi.

Shanin, Teodor. 1972. 'Models in Thought'. In Shanin, ed. 1972: 1–22.

_____ ed. 1972. *Rules of the Game: Cross-Disciplinary Essays on Models in Scholarly Thought.* London: Tavistock.

Shannon, Claude. 1948. 'A Mathematical Theory of Communication'. *Bell System Technical Journal* 27: 379–423, 623–56.

_____ and Warren Weaver. 1949. *The Mathematical Theory of Communication.* Urbana IL: University of Illinois Press.

Sheehan, Thomas. 1998. 'Heidegger, Martin (1889–1976)'. In *Routledge Encyclopedia of Philosophy.*

Shelley, Cameron. 2002. 'Analogy Counterarguments and the Acceptability of Analogical Hypotheses'. *British Journal for the Philosophy of Science* 53: 477–96.

Shepard, Paul. 1996. *The Others: How Animals Made Us Human.* Washington DC: Island Press / Shearwater Books.

Sheridan, Thomas B. 2000. 'Interaction, Imagination and Immersion: Some Research Needs'. In *Proceedings of the ACM Symposium on Virtual Reality Software and Technology.* 1–7. New York: ACM Press.

Shields, Rob. 2000. 'Hypertext Links: the Ethic of the Index and Its Space-Time Effects'. In *The World Wide Web and Contemporary Cultural Theory: Magic, Metaphor, Power.* Ed. Andrew Herman and Thomas Swiss. 145–60. New York: Routledge.

Shillingsburg, Peter. 1996. *Scholarly Editing in the Computer Age: Theory and Practice.* 3rd edn. Ann Arbor: University of Michigan Press.

Shin, Sun-Joo and Oliver Lemon. 2003. 'Diagrams'. In *Stanford Encyclopedia of Philosophy* (Winter 2003 edition).

Shotter, John. 1984. *Social Accountability and Selfhood.* Oxford: Blackwell.

Shumway, David R. and Ellen Messer-Davidow. 1991. 'Disciplinarity: an Introduction'. Special Issue of *Poetics Today* 12.2: 201–25.

Simon, Herbert A. 1996/1969. *The Sciences of the Artificial*. 3rd edn. Cambridge MA: MIT Press.

Sinclair, John. 1966. 'Beginning the Study of Lexis'. In *In Memory of J. R. Firth*. Ed. C. E. Bezell, J. C. Catford, M. A. K. Halliday and R. H. Robins. 410–30. London: Longmans, Green and Co., Ltd.

_____ 1991. *Corpus Concordance Collocation*. Describing English Language. Oxford: Oxford University Press.

Smith, Barbara Herrnstein. 2000. 'Netting Truth'. *Publications of the Modern Language Association* 115.5: 1089–95.

Smith, Brian Cantwell. 1995. 'The Limits of Correctness in Computers'. In *Computers, Ethics & Social Values*. Ed. Deborah G. Johnson and Helen Nissenbaum. 456–69. Englewood Cliffs NJ: Prentice Hall.

_____ 1998/1996. *On the Origin of Objects*. Bradford Book. Cambridge MA: MIT Press.

_____ 2002. 'Foundations of Computing'. In *Computationalism: New Directions*. Ed. Matthias Scheutz. Cambridge MA: MIT Press.

_____ 2005. 'Meaning of Digital'. *Digital Future*. John W. Kluge Center, Library of Congress. www.c-span.org/video/?184429-1/digital-future-meaning-digital (24/2/14).

Smith, David A., Jeffrey A. Rydberg-Cox and Gregory R. Crane. 2000. 'The Perseus Project: a Digital Library for the Humanities'. *LLC* 15.1: 15–25.

Smith, Mackenzie, Mick Bass, Greg McClellan, Robert Tansley, Mary Barton, Margret Branschofsky, Dave Stuve and Julie Harford Walker. 2003. 'DSpace: an Open Source Dynamic Digital Repository'. *D-Lib* 9.1.

Smith, Martha Nell. 2004. 'Electronic Scholarly Editing'. In Schreibman, Siemens and Unsworth 2004: 306–22.

Snow, C. P. 1998/1959. *The Two Cultures*. Cambridge: Cambridge University Press.

Solomon, Jon, ed. 1993. *Accessing Antiquity: the Computerization of Classical Studies*. Tucson: University of Arizona Press.

Somerville, Margaret A. and David J. Rapport, eds. 2003. *Transdisciplinarity: Recreating Integrated Knowledge*. Montreal, Quebec: McGill-Queen's University Press.

Sowa, John F. 2000. *Knowledge Representation: Logical, Philosophical, and Computational Foundations*. Pacific Grove CA: Brooks/Cole.

Spangenberg, Lisa. 2002. 'The Rhetoric of Web Logs'. *Digitalmedievalist.Com*. www.digitalmedievalist.com/it/archive/000075.html.

Spender, Dale. 1998/1980. *Man-made Language*. 4th edn. London: Pandora.

Sperberg-McQueen, C. M. 2002. 'What Matters?' Montreal, Quebec: Extreme Markup Languages. www.w3.org/People/cmsmcq/2002/whatmatters.html.

Stanford Digital Libraries Group. 1995. 'The Stanford Digital Library Project'. *CACM* 38.4: 59–60.

Stehr, Nico. 1996. 'The Salt of Social Science'. *Sociological Research Online* 1.1. www.socresonline.org.uk/1/1/stehr.html.

Steiner, George. 1978. *Heidegger*. Fontana Modern Masters. Glasgow: Fontana / Collins.

Stillinger, Jack. 1991. *Multiple Authorship and the Myth of Solitary Genius*. Oxford: Oxford University Press.

Suchman, Lucy A. 1987. *Plans and Situated Actions: the Problem of Human-Machine Communication*. Learning in Doing: Social, Cognitive, and Computational Perspectives. Cambridge: Cambridge University Press.

_____ 1995. 'Making Work Visible'. *CACM* 38.9: 56–64.

_____ Jeanette Blomberg, Julian E. Orr and Randall Trigg. 1999. 'Reconstructing Technologies as Social Practice'. *American Behavioral Scientist* 43.3: 392–408.

Sutherland, Kathryn, ed. 1997. *Electronic Text: Investigations in Method and Theory.* Oxford: Clarendon Press.

Taylor, Charles. 1985. *Philosophy and the Human Sciences*. Vol. 2 of *Philosophical Papers*. 2 vols. Cambridge: Cambridge University Press.

Teich, Mikuláš and Dorothy M. Needham. 1992. *A Documentary History of Biochemistry 1770–1940*. Leicester: Leicester University Press.

Thaller, Manfred. 2001. 'Bridging the Gap; Splitting the Bridge? Studying Humanities Computer Science in Cologne'. Duisburg: Computers – Literature – Philosophy (CLiP) 2001. www.uni-duisburg.de/FB3/CLiP2001/abstracts/Thaller_en.htm.

_____ 2004. 'Texts, Databases, Κλειω: a Note on the Architecture of Computer Systems for the Humanities'. In *Augmenting Comprehension: Digital Tools and the History of Ideas. Proceedings of a Conference at Bologna, 22–23 September 2002.* Ed. Dino Buzzetti, Giuliano Pancaldi and Harold Short. 49–76. London: Office for Humanities Communication, King's College London.

Thieme, Horst R. and Jinling Yang. 2000. 'On the Complex Formation Approach in Modeling Predator Prey Relations, Mating, and Sexual Disease Transmission'. *Electronic Journal of Differential Equations*. Conference 05: 255–83. www.ma.hw.ac.uk/EJDE/.

Thompson, Gordon B. 1979. *Memo from Mercury: Information Technology IS Different*. Montreal, Quebec: Institute for Research on Public Policy.

Tichy, Walter F. 1998. 'Should Computer Scientists Experiment More?' *IEEE Computer* 31.5: 32–40. wwwipd.ira.uka.de/~tichy/publications/moreexperiments/moreexperiments.html.

Tieszen, Richard. 1992. 'Kurt Gödel and Phenomenology'. *Philosophy of Science* 59: 176–94.

Tiles, Mary. 2000. 'Technology, Philosophy of'. In Newton-Smith 2000: 483–91.

Tomayko, James E. 2002. 'Software as Engineering'. In *History of Computing: Software Issues*. Ed. Ulf Hashagen, Reinhard Keil-Slawik and Arthur Norberg. 65–76. International Conference on the History of Computing, ICHC2000. Berlin: Springer Verlag.

Tosca, Susana Pajares. 1999. 'The Lyrical Quality of Links'. In *Proceedings of the Tenth ACM Conference on Hypertext and Hypermedia: Returning to Our Diverse Roots. Darmstadt.* 217–18. New York: ACM Press.

_____ 2000. 'A Pragmatics of Links'. *JoDI* 1.6.

Toulmin, Stephen. 1958. *The Uses of Argument*. Cambridge: Cambridge University Press.

_____ 1967/1953. *The Philosophy of Science: an Introduction*. London: Hutchinson University Library.

Traub, J. F., ed. 1981. 'Quo Vadimus: Computer Science in a Decade'. *CACM* 24.6: 351–69.

Tufte, Edward. 1990. *Envisioning Information*. Cheshire CN: Graphics Press.

Turing, Alan. 1936. 'On Computable Numbers, with an Application to the Entscheidungsproblem'. *Proceedings of the London Mathematical Society* 42: 230–65. Reprinted in Davis 1993/1965: 115–54. www.abelard.org/turpap2/tp2-ie.asp.

Turnbull, David. 1994/1989. *Maps are Territories. Science is an Atlas.* Chicago: University of Chicago Press.

———— 2000. *Masons, Tricksters and Cartographers: Makers of Knowledge and Space.* Studies in the History of Science, Technology and Medicine. London: Routledge.

Turner, Mark. 1995. 'As Imagination Bodies Forth the Forms of Things Unknown'. Review of *The Poetics of Mind: Figurative Thought, Language, and Understanding,* by Raymond W. Gibbs, *Pragmatics and Cognition* 3.1: 179–85.

———— 1996. *The Literary Mind: the Origins of Thought and Language.* New York: Oxford University Press.

Ulam, Stanislaw M. 1980. 'Von Neumann: the Interaction of Mathematics and Computing'. In Metropolis, Howlett and Rota 1980: 93–9.

Ullman, Jeffrey D. 1995. 'The Role of Theory Today'. *ACM Computing Surveys* 27.1: 43–4.

Unsworth, John. [For online versions of the following see www3.isrl.uiuc.edu/ ~unsworth/; exceptions noted as *.]

———— 1997. 'Documenting the Reinvention of Text: the Importance of Failure'. *Journal of Electronic Publishing* 3.2.*

———— 2000. 'Scholarly Primitives: What Methods do Humanities Researchers Have in Common, and How Might our Tools Reflect This?' Invited lecture, 'Humanities Computing: Formal Methods, Experimental Practice', King's College London, 13 May.

———— 2001. 'Knowledge Representation in Humanities Computing'. Lecture I in the *eHumanities* NEH Lecture Series on Technology & the Humanities, Washington DC, April 3.

———— 2002. 'What Is Humanities Computing and What Is Not?' *Jahrbuch für Computerphilologie* 4: 71–83.*

———— 2003a. 'The Humanist: "Dances with Wolves" or "Bowls Alone"?' Washington DC: Scholarly Tribes and Tribulations: How Tradition and Technology are Driving Disciplinary Change. Association of Research Libraries. www.arl.org/scomm/disciplines/Unsworth.doc.

———— 2003b. 'Tool-Time, or "Haven't We Been Here Already?"' Washington DC: Transforming Disciplines: The Humanities and Computer Science.

———— Katherine O'Brien O'Keeffe and Lou Burnard, eds. 2005 (forthcoming). *Electronic Textual Editing.* New York: Modern Language Association of America.

Vaihinger, Hans. 1924/1911. *The Philosophy of 'As If': a System of the Theoretical, Practical and Religious Fictions of Mankind.* Trans. C. K. Ogden. International Library of Psychology, Philosophy and Scientific Method. London: Kegan Paul, Trench, Trubner & Co., Ltd.

Valeton, J. M. and Dirk van Norren. 1983. 'Light Adaptation in Primate Cones: an Analysis Based on Extracellular Data'. *Vision Research* 23.12: 1539–47.

Vallance, John T. 1999. 'Galen, Proclus and the Non-Submissive Commentary'. In Most, ed. 1999: 223–44.

van Atten, Mark and Juliette Kennedy. 2003. 'On the Philosophical Development of Kurt Gödel'. *Bulletin of Symbolic Logic* 9.4: 425–76. www.math.ucla.edu/~asl/bsl/0904-toc.htm.

van Dam, Andries. 1988. 'Hypertext '87 Keynote Address'. *CACM* 31.7: 887–95. www.cs.brown.edu/memex/HT_87_Keynote_Address.html.

Veblen, Thorstein. 1906. 'The Place of Science in Modern Civilization'. *American Journal of Sociology* 11.5: 585–609.

Vera, Alonzo H. and Herbert A. Simon. 1993. 'Situated Action: a Symbolic Interpretation'. *Cognitive Science* 17: 7–48.

Vessey, Mark. 2004 (forthcoming). 'Erasmus' Lucubrations and the Renaissance Life of Texts'. *Erasmus of Rotterdam Society Yearbook* 23.

Vincenti, Walter G. 1990. *What Engineers Know and How They Know It: Analytical Studies from Aeronautical History*. Johns Hopkins Studies in the History of Technology. Baltimore: Johns Hopkins University Press.

von Staden, Heinrich. 2002. '"A Woman Does Not Become Ambidextrous": Galen and the Culture of Scientific Commentary'. In Gibson and Kraus 2002: 109–39.

Walker, Jill. 2005 (forthcoming). 'Weblog'. In *The Routledge Encyclopedia of Narrative Theory*. Ed. David Herman, Manfred Jahn and Marie-Laure Ryan. London: Routledge. huminf.uib.no/~jill/archives/blog_theorising/final_version_of_weblog_definition.html.

Wallerstein, Immanuel. 1998. 'The Heritage of Sociology, the Promise of Social Science'. Presidential Address, XIV World Congress of Sociology, Montreal, Quebec. fbc.binghamton.edu/iwpradfp.htm.

Warner, Marina. 2002. *Fantastic Metamorphoses, Other Worlds: Ways of Telling the Self*. The Clarendon Lectures in English 2001. Oxford: Oxford University Press.

Wartofsky, Marx W. 1979. 'Telos and Technique: Models as Modes of Action'. In *Models: Representation and the Scientific Understanding*. Ed. Robert S. Cohen and Marx W. Wartofsky. 140–53. Boston Studies in the Philosophy of Science XLVIII. Dordrecht: D. Reidel.

Watson, James D. 2001/1968. *The Double Helix: a Personal Account of the Discovery of the Structure of DNA*. New York: Simon and Schuster.

Wegner, Peter. 1997. 'Why Interaction is More Powerful than Algorithms'. *CACM* 40.5: 80–91.

———— and Dina Goldin. 1999. 'Interaction as a Framework for Modeling'. In *Conceptual Modeling: Current Issues and Future Directions*. Ed. Peter P. Chen, Jacky Akoka, Hannu Kangassalo and Bernard Thalheim. 243–57. Lecture Notes in Computer Science 1565. Berlin: Springer Verlag.

Weil, Simone. 1978/1959. *Lectures on Philosophy*. Trans. Hugh Price. Intro. Peter Winch. Cambridge: Cambridge University Press.

Weiser, Mark. 1996. 'Ubiquitous Computing'. www.ubiq.com/hypertext/weiser/UbiHome.html.

Weisstein, Eric W. 'Theory'. *MathWorld – A Wolfram Web Resource*. mathworld.wolfram.com/Theory.html.

West, Dave. 1997. 'Hermeneutic Computer Science'. *CACM* 40.4: 115–16.

White, Hayden. 1987. *The Content of the Form: Narrative Discourse and Historical Representation*. Baltimore: Johns Hopkins University Press.

Whitehead, Alfred North. 1925. *Science and the Modern World*. Lowell Lectures 1925. New York: Macmillan.

Wierzbicka, Anna. 1996. *Semantics: Primes and Universals*. Oxford: Oxford University Press.

Wigner, Eugene P. 1960. 'The Unreasonable Effectiveness of Mathematics in the Natural Sciences'. *Communications on Pure and Applied Mathematics* 13: 1–14.

Wiil, Uffe K., Peter J. Nürnberg and John J. Leggett. 1999. 'Hypermedia Research Directions: an Infrastructure Perspective'. *ACM Computing Surveys* 31.4es: 1–9.

Williams, Michael. 2001. *Problems of Knowledge: a Critical Introduction to Epistemology*. Oxford: Oxford University Press.

Willmott, Chris. 2001. 'Enzyme Kinetics and the Michaelis–Menten Equation'. Tutorial, Biochemistry Department, University of Leicester. www.le.ac.uk/by/teach/biochemweb/tutorials/michment1.html.

Wimsatt, William C. 1987. 'False Models as Means to Truer Theories'. In *Neutral Models in Biology*. Ed. Matthew H. Nitecki and Antoni Hoffman. 23–55. Oxford: Oxford University Press.

Winch, Peter. 1990/1958. *The Idea of a Social Science and its Relation to Philosophy*. 2nd edn. London: Routledge.

Winograd, Terry. 1979. 'Beyond Programming Languages'. *CACM* 22.7.

―――― 1991. 'Thinking Machines: Can There Be? Are We?' In *The Boundaries of Humanity: Humans, Animals, Machines*. Ed. James J. Sheehan and Martin Sosna. 198–223. Berkeley: University of California Press.

―――― 1995a. 'From Programming Environments to Environments for Designing'. *CACM* 38.6: 65–74.

―――― 1995b. 'Heidegger and the Design of Computing Systems'. In *Technology and the Politics of Knowledge*. Ed. Andrew Feenberg and Alastair Hannay. 108–27. The Indiana Series in the Philosophy of Technology. Bloomington IN: Indiana University Press.

―――― 1997. 'The Design of Interaction'. In *Beyond Calculation: the Next Fifty Years of Computing*. Ed. Peter J. Denning and Robert M. Metcalf. 149–61. New York: Copernicus. hci.stanford.edu/winograd/acm97.html.

―――― 2000. 'Foreword'. In *Heidegger, Coping, and Cognitive Science*. Ed. Mark Wrathall and Jeff Malpas. Vol. 2 of Essays in Honor of Hubert L. Dreyfus. vii–x. 2 vols. Cambridge MA: MIT Press.

―――― 2002. 'Convergence, Ambient Technology, and Success in Innovation: Talking with Terry Winograd'. *Ubiquity* 3.23.

―――― and Fernando Flores. 1986. *Understanding Computers and Cognition: a New Foundation for Design*. Boston: Addison-Wesley.

Winsberg, Eric. 2001. 'Simulations, Models, and Theories: Complex Physical Systems and Their Representations'. *Philosophy of Science (Proceedings)* 68.3: S442–S454.

Winton, Tim. 1998/1993. *Land's Edge*. Sydney: Picador.

Wirth, Niklaus. 2002. 'Computing Science Education: the Road Not Taken'. In *Proceedings of the ITiCSE Conference. Aarhus, Denmark*. New York: ACM Press.

Wirth, Uwe. 1998. 'Abductive Reasoning'. In *Encyclopedia of Semiotics*, ed. Paul Bouissac. 1–3. Oxford: Oxford University Press. www.rz.uni-frankfurt.de/~wirth/, articles.

Wittgenstein, Ludwig. 1967/1953. *Philosophical Investigations*. 3rd edn. Trans. G. E. M. Anscombe. Oxford: Blackwell.

Wood, Denis. 1992. *The Power of Maps*. Mappings: Society / Theory / Space. London: Guilford Press.

Wu, Hongjung, Eric de Kort and Paul De Bra. 2001. 'Design Issues for General-Purpose Adaptive Hypermedia Systems'. In *Proceedings of the Twelfth ACM Conference on Hypertext and Hypermedia. Aarhus, Denmark*. 141–50. New York: ACM Press.

Wulf, William A. 1995. 'Are We Scientists or Engineers?' *ACM Computing Surveys* 27.1: 55–7.

_____ 2000. 'The Nature of Engineering, the Science of the Humanities, and Gödel's Theorem (Interview)'. *Ubiquity* 1.28.

Wunsch, Guillaume. 1995. 'God has chosen to give the easy problems to the physicists, or why demographers need theory'. Milano: European Population Conference, 4–8 September. Louvain-la-Neuve, Belgium: Working Paper 179, Institut de Démographie, Université, Catholique de Louvain. www.un.org/popin/confcon/milan/plen6.html.

Yeandle, David N. 1998. 'A Line-by-line Bibliographical Database of Wolfram von Eschenbach's *Parzival*'. *Bulletin of International Medieval Research* 4: 1–22.

_____ 2002. *Stellenbibliographie Zum 'Parzival' Wolframs von Eschenbach, für die Jahrgänge 1984–1996*. Ed. unter Mitarbeit von Michael Beddow bearbeitet von Carol Magner, John Bradley, David Powell, Harold Short und Roy Wisbey. Tübingen: Max Niemeyer Verlag.

Yu, Pauline. 1997. 'The Course of the Particulars: Humanities in the University of the Twenty-First Century'. In *Transformation of Humanistic Studies in the Twenty-First Century*. 21–9. ACLS Occasional Paper 40. New York: ACLS.

Zeitlin, David, Matthew David and Jane Bex, eds. 1999. *Knowledge Lost in Information: Patterns of Use and Non-Use of Networked Bibliographic Resources*. British Library Research and Innovation Centre Research Report no. RIC/G/313. London: Office for Humanities Communication.

Zelkowitz, Marvin V. and Dolores R. Wallace. 1998. 'Experimental Models for Validating Technology'. *IEEE Computer* 31.5: 23–31.

Ziman, John. 1991/1978. *Reliable Knowledge: an Exploration of the Grounds for Belief in Science*. Cambridge: Canto.

_____ 2000. *Real Science: What It Is, and What It Means*. Cambridge: Cambridge University Press.

Zorich, Diane M. 2003. *A Survey of Digital Cultural Heritage Initiatives and their Sustainability Concerns*. Washington DC: Council on Library and Information Resources. www.clir.org/pubs/abstract/pub118abst.html.

Index

'An Index is the *bag* and *baggage* of a book, of more use then honour, even such who seemingly slight it, secretly using it, if not for *need*, for *speed* of what they desire to finde. '

(Thomas Fuller, *A Pisgah Sight of Palestine* (London, 1650): 337)

In this index ♦ denotes second-level, ❖ third and ♦ fourth. In cross-references an asterisk denotes the nearest headword, thus 'abduction, *see* reasoning, by *' corresponds to the entry 'reasoning ... ♦ by abduction (hypothesis)', 'algorithm, *see* computer science, *' to the entry 'computer science... ♦ algorithm in'.

CPSIA information can be obtained at www.ICGtesting.com
Printed in the USA
LVOW04s1800260814

401026LV00012B/327/P